Agrarianism in
American History

*STUDIES IN HISTORY AND POLITICS*

Under the editorial direction of Gerald E. Stearn

RUSSIA AND THE WEST FROM PETER TO KHRUSHCHEV

Edited by L. Jay Oliva, New York University

CHURCH AND STATE IN AMERICAN HISTORY

John F. Wilson, Princeton University

THE AMERICAN IMAGE

PAST AND PRESENT

Edited by G. D. Lillibridge, Chico State College

SOLDIERS AND STATES

CIVIL-MILITARY RELATIONS IN MODERN EUROPE

Edited by David B. Ralston, Massachusetts Institute of Technology

THE DEVELOPMENT OF THE COMMUNIST BLOC

Edited by Roger Pethybridge, University College, Swansea

BRITISH POLITICS

PEOPLE, PARTIES AND PARLIAMENTS

Edited by Anthony King, University of Essex

FRENCH POLITICS

Edited by Martin Harrison, University of Keele

THE POLITICS OF AMERICAN FEDERALISM

Edited by Daniel J. Elazar, Temple University

MODERN IMPERIALISM

WESTERN OVERSEAS EXPANSION AND ITS AFTERMATH, 1776-1965

Edited by Ralph A. Austen, University of Chicago

AGRARIANISM IN AMERICAN HISTORY

Edited by Louis H. Douglas, Kansas State University

Other volumes in preparation

STUDIES IN HISTORY AND POLITICS

# Agrarianism in American History

Edited with an introduction by

*Louis H. Douglas*
Kansas State University

D. C. HEATH AND COMPANY

A Division of Raytheon Education Company
Lexington, Massachusetts

# Table of Contents

20912

*Table of Contents*

# Introduction

Agriculture has loomed large in American history ever since the establishment of the Republic. From earliest times, land was eagerly sought, and, at least for the first century following the American revolution, the existence of a frontier offered cheap or even free land for those who would settle upon it. This long period of seeking to occupy and exploit the land went far to implant a set of social values that gave a lofty place to the American agrarian. But this was not the only factor contributing to the peculiarly important role of agriculture in American society. A system of land ownership which effectually minimized the likelihood of a peasant-based agriculture being established was given an enthusiastic testimonial by Thomas Jefferson. His defense of rural virtues made a durable impression.

Even more of an "extreme agrarian" than Jefferson was John Taylor of Caroline, the "Philosopher of Jeffersonian Democracy." Taylor never deviated from his faith in the singular virtues of agrarianism. His argument rested on the premise that only "farmers and mechanics" contributed to the nation's wealth and therefore all secondary forms of economic activity were parasitic and a threat to the health of the society.

Both Jefferson and Taylor envisaged an American society based upon a yeoman class of cultivators, numerically superior and politically dominant in a system of democratic decision-making. A large measure of economic self-sufficiency was implicit in this arrangement, and the diversity of activities and development of individual versatility contributed to a high quality of rural citizenry.

Admittedly, Jeffersonian agrarianism was a utopian rather than an ideological expression. The expressed values became a continuing theme in political literature and a basis of the voice given to agriculture by voluntary rural organizations. The advocacy of these values in altered physical settings has been called agricultural fundamentalism. The term "altered physical settings" refers to empirical changes in American agriculture in the nineteenth and twentieth centuries — changes which have consistently taken American society away from the conditions necessary for Jeffersonian agrarianism.

In broad terms, these changes constituted a transformation from self-sufficient to commercial farms and were, of course, a function of increasing urban populations, developing transportation systems, and industrialization — a total evolution of society from atomistic to interdependent forms. While the changes diminished the percentage of the American population living on farms, the concept that agriculture was fundamental to the well-being of the total society was successfully perpetuated. Thus "agricultural fundamentalism" came to be an important part of the value system of American society.

Agricultural fundamentalism must, therefore, be understood in two set-tings—the pre-industrial or agrarian setting, which we term classical funda-mentalist, and the post-industrial setting, described as commercial funda-mentalist. The classical period, ending about 1850, was given a utopian cast by the Jeffersonian vision of an agrarian commonwealth in which free-holding families would constitute the main citizenry of the Republic.

## CLASSICAL AGRARIANISM

It was noted above that early American agrarian thought was utopian in nature. Conditions among the small farmers were very unlike those postulated by Jefferson as the proper environment for "the chosen people of God, . . . whose breasts he has made his peculiar deposit for substantial and genuine virtue." However, by comparing American with European society, it was possible to see both the need and the opportunity for developing agriculture in the U.S. so that vastly improved conditions would result. Undoubtedly, an easily observed difference lay in the land situation. In Europe, Jefferson noted, "the lands are either cultivated, or locked up against the cultivator." It was thus necessity, not choice, that drove surplus populations into cities. In America, no limit to the availability of small farms could be foreseen, the land of America could be de-veloped by freeholders, and the conditions of rural life would provide the best environment for the regeneration of freedom and happiness among the people.

A theory and plan of government accompanied that of agricultural develop-ment. The theory was representative democracy and the plan was based on developing the local units of government. Representative democracy was not a new concept, but the emphasis in this case was relocated and strengthened. The distribution of population in small rural landholdings made the township, or town, a logical and potentially useful unit and one most suitable for popular control. Selection of a representative of the township, or *ward*, to supervise the affairs of the larger county marked the beginning of the process of selecting the "natural aristocracy," a process closely interrelated with the system of education.

A free system of elementary education was offered to all by each of the local units. The talented, moreover, should be given secondary education, and state universities ought to be established and maintained to provide higher educa-tion in science and philosophy for those few who proved to be the most gifted. Thus a natural elite would continuously rise through the educational system, displacing the older, traditional process of hereditary aristocracy.

The utopian plan for nation-building based on small, largely self-sufficient farms was, of course, not realized. It has never, however, been completely abandoned. Later on, the westward settlement was encouraged by a succession of "homestead acts," designed to achieve an evenly distributed land settlement. With the disappearance of public lands for private acquisition, the agrarian dream was perpetuated in the phrase "the family farm." Preservation of the family farm remained an avowed objective of public policy even in the twentieth century, a symbol above partisan politics.

## Westward Movement or Western Frontier

The existence of an area of western territory open to settlement was one of the facts of life throughout nineteenth-century America. Interpretations of this fact vary but its pervasive importance cannot be doubted, particularly with regard to agriculture. From 1820 on, domestic observers of and commentators on the American scene were fascinated by the presence of the great frontier—its problems, excitement, and prospects. This is no less true of foreign observers, who frequently contributed keen insights into the sociology of the American West.

The intellectual interest generated by the frontier gave rise to what is called the "frontier thesis of American history," sometimes called the "Turner thesis." One of the most influential writings ever produced in American history was an essay written in 1893 by Frederick Jackson Turner entitled "The Significance of the Frontier in American History." This piece provided the clearest exposition and defense of the proposition that American democracy—essentially the American way of life—came from the frontier. American democracy "came out of the American forest, and it gained new strength each time it touched a new frontier."

That American democracy or, more broadly, the American way of life was primarily a product of the frontier is a doubtful proposition for the nineteenth as well as for the twentieth century. Undeniably, however, the frontier was one of the many elements that influenced American values, attitudes, and institutions. The West and land settlement were of special importance to agriculture and its development.

The frontier did much to preserve the agrarian tradition. While older areas soon began to substitute urban and commercial development to some degree for agriculture, the frontier went through a period of strong reliance upon farming. For a transitory period, the frontiersmen experienced dependence upon the products of the soil wherever the frontier was located.

## Land Settlement Policy

In the nineteenth century there was a vast domain of federal land which could be transferred to large or small private owners or retained in government ownership. Therefore, hand in hand with the frontier concept as a historic force in American development was land settlement policy. It, too, was shaped by the values associated with a free and independent citizenry of small farmers.

Although exceptions can be found, the general tenor of federal land legislation had the objective of transferring the public domain into an area of widely distributed private ownership. Land ownership, though soon discarded as a legal requirement for voting, was valued as a symbol of full citizenship, and an ambition to acquire land was characteristic of the people. At the beginning of the nineteenth century, ninety percent of the gainfully employed were occupied in agriculture. This proportion declined only gradually and agrarian concepts and values were strengthened throughout the century. The occupation of farming remained firmly linked with concepts of public and private morality, with achievement, and with equality.

Typically, the initial unit considered best for transfer to private ownership was a quarter-section or 160 acres. Multiples and divisions of this unit were common. Whether this is a large or small land holding is purely relative; in the context of agricultural development in the United States the basic 160 acre unit served to maintain the myth of small private farm enterprise that lasted into the twentieth century.

Nevertheless, some very large land acquisitions also occurred. Speculators were attracted to land purchases easily made from small owners, some large grants were made outright to corporations, and under slipshod administration fraudulent land claims were sometimes successfully completed for large acreages. A trend toward larger ownership accompanied trans-Missouri settlement and the twentieth-century technological revolution.

The Homestead Act of 1862 reaffirmed the unit of 160 acres as the "family-farm," and by 1890 most of the arable land, including much that was marginal, had been transferred into private hands. In the Plains States, however, difficulties soon arose over the inadequacy of the size of that unit. Larger-scale farming was necessary in view of semi-arid climatic conditions and a tendency toward limited diversification.

All in all, the land and land policies remained powerful supports for American social and political ideals. The democratic and agrarian philosophy of Jefferson endured the frontier, western settlement, and agricultural development. Unoccupied lands became part of the federal domain and were opened to settlers on terms that were thought to be inviting enough. When difficulties arose over terms of the transfer from government to private holders, the latter were heard from through Western representatives to Congress or through pressure groups organized for the purpose of obtaining relief. The tendency to recognize and to respond to such pressure is indicative of the strength of agrarian values in our society. The "family farm" continues to be a symbol of the good American life.

Viewed purely from the standpoint of land policy, the new problems that have arisen in the mid-twentieth century have to do with policy for non-agricultural uses of land. These include metropolitan annexations and subdivisions, highways and transportation facilities, and other alternative uses to farming. Employing land for such purposes tends to generate conflicts which involve the compromising of some basic values.

## Some Summary Observations

Accordingly, great changes occurred in the proportionate dimensions of rural life as compared to the total society. In 1800, 90% was agricultural, 10% non-agricultural. By 1960, these proportions had been approximately reversed. The overwhelming rural majority had been transformed into a diminutive minority. Yet much could still be said for the importance of the agricultural sector to the national well-being. Although small, this sector has developed a prodigious capacity to produce food and fiber, so much so, in fact, that by 1930 farm "surpluses" appeared in the market and became a national concern.

To add another complication to the situation, only a portion of the nation's farmers acquired the role of commercial producers. A large portion were unwilling or unable to keep abreast of the continual flow of technological changes and the demands for capital, expanded acreage, and some specialized skills. The resulting deeply-stratified rural society, with big commercial producers pushing for expansion at one extreme and the outmoded old-fashioned small farmer at the other, violated the equalitarian theme central to the earlier agrarian philosophy.

Agriculture had moved from the independent and self-sufficient to the inter-dependent and specialized. The process, in the earlier years, had been a gradual one that could be assimilated into the existing structure of institutions and values. Many of the changes, probably the total effect of change, seemed to strengthen the position of agriculture as a component of American society.

In public affairs, agriculture had an important role. By tradition, farmers were expected to be participants at all levels of government and government was responsive to their needs. Representative arrangements gave extra weight to rural representatives, though the substance of policy frequently failed to make a real contribution to agricultural interests.

## AGRICULTURE AND THE REVOLUTION IN TECHNOLOGY

The hundred years from 1840 to 1940 comprised a century in which the application of new agricultural techniques was gradually accelerated. The generation since 1940 has witnessed such a rapid acceleration of this process that the changes induced are of quite a different order. By 1890 the signs of significant change were apparent—production for national and export markets, dependence upon price and business cycles, implication with agriculture-related business, and emergence of a rural society differentiated both by sections and by stratified economic structure. These were some of the developments indicating that the virtues earlier associated with the rural ways of life would be under stress. Formerly, their survival has been accomplished by the perpetuation of agrarian symbols, by political organization and communication, and by the realization of significant agricultural payoffs.

Leaders in agriculture were always sensitive to the importance of applied science to the farming enterprise. Material improvements were the subject of many speeches and articles, in public and private publications. Apprehension about declining production and deteriorating physical conditions were perennial expressions. Several practical inventions appeared before 1860 and the need for rural education was expressed.

Production of agricultural products more than doubled between 1870 and 1900 (100:269). Population growth became an urban phenomenon and the productive capacity of agriculture was challenged by the need to support an increasingly urban-industrial culture. Productivity kept pace with population growth and market demands by bringing new lands into production and, concurrently, by improving production techniques.

The western emphasis—the frontier fixation—gave great importance to western lands and western farmers. The western push took agriculture well into semi-arid longitudes where production fluctuated but cereal-crop and livestock remained significant. The trans-Mississippi West contributed a distinctive type of agriculture and agricultural politics; a deviant but recognizable agrarian theme was perpetuated.

As the natural conditions in the arid west posed a barrier to further agricultural development, the government explored the possibility of reclamation policies by which additional areas might be brought under production. The Reclamation Act of 1902 provided federal funds for this type of development. This and related measures reflect the value which the American polity continuously placed upon supporting agriculture.

One of the results of the development of commercial agriculture was an increasing involvement with institutions of finance, transportation, marketing, and industry — the total American economy. The results of this interdependence were complicated and somewhat ambivalent. On the one hand, the agricultural producer saw himself as caught within a market system in which prices were set by the buyers of what he offered to sell and by the sellers of what he needed to buy. He sought, by cooperatives and by influencing government policy, to intervene in a process which he believed made him a victim. On the other hand, the farmer was becoming a business man, by necessity and by virtue of the role of commercial agriculture in which he found himself making business decisions and dealing with the business community. In doing so, he naturally tended to acquire the values and outlook of business. The alliance of the commercial sector of agriculture with the business world is one of the most significant modern characteristics of the American economy. Many values were mutually shared and many current policies are explained only in terms of an agro-business relationship.

## GOVERNMENT INTERVENTION IN AGRICULTURE

Although throughout the history of American agriculture a strong emphasis was placed on the freedom and self-reliance of the individual, this emphasis did not interfere with the uninterrupted flow of public policies designed to develop agriculture and to enhance the lot of the cultivator. The earliest of such policies were concerned with western settlement and contributed to the ownership of small farms. The first settlers frequently encountered unexpected hardships and looked to the government for help. As the line of settlement moved westward both the difficulties faced and the level of government intervention increased. Numerous agrarian and Populist-type movements that accompanied the rapid settlement of the Plains States after 1880 indicated a natural reaction to the economic distress in which the settlers found themselves. The government pursued the policy of transferring the public domain to private ownership, making huge grants to railroads that served to accelerate agricultural development. The railroad land grants complicated the picture by establishing a powerful private beneficiary in competition with the farmer for political favors and economic shares.

## Education, Research, Extension

Although the beginnings were small indeed, research and education in agriculture steadily gained general approval, and in the twentieth century agriculture became one of the most strongly supported areas of education. A college of agriculture was established in Michigan in 1857 and the Morrill Act was passed five years later providing land grants to the states for the support of agricultural colleges. From this beginning, a steady stream of federal laws followed which supported education and research in agriculture by greatly strengthening the "land-grant colleges and universities," giving cabinet status to the Department of Agriculture in 1889, providing increasingly large grants for research beginning in 1887, and providing support for agricultural extension education beginning in 1914. The states made additional appropriations with the result that organized research, higher education, and county extension services developed a strong network of institutions which could give technical services accompanied by political support to American agriculture. The total system was able to exert a telling influence on agricultural policy.

Education was naturally linked to improvements in the quality of rural living. In a report in 1907, President Roosevelt's Rural Life Commission indicated some of the hardships confronting the rural population. Practical vocational courses for farm youth and the organization of rural clubs and social opportunities were among the steps recommended to reduce these disadvantages. Federal aid for vocational education in agriculture at the high school level was approved in the Smith-Hughes Act in 1917. Programs for rural youth were developed as a part of the extension services and by agricultural societies and organizations.

## Expanded Government Policies

As commercial agriculture developed, government policies designed to assist with credit and marketing problems were formulated. Pressure arose to make available better long-term mortgage arrangements for buying farms, intermediate credit for purchasing machinery and providing capital outlay, and short-term crop loans. A Federal Farm Loan Board was established in 1917 and a system of federal land banks. These underwent several delays until the depression began in 1929 and precipitated a drastic expansion of diverse federal farm credit programs. The Farm Credit Act of 1933 provided a cooperative plan for making mortgage loans through twelve federal land banks, twelve intermediate credit banks to serve production credit associations, and a system of banks for extending credit to cooperatives. Additional legislation was passed to provide credit for farmers in marginal situations, loans for rural electrification cooperatives, and other types of farm credit legislation.

Federal policy toward agriculture in the twentieth century reflected the close involvement of farming with the commercial economy. Some of this interdependence had been recognized in the earlier Granger movement in the 1870's, though most of its effects had been felt in state legislation. The "Granger laws," a term applying to state laws regulating transportation and marketing of farm products during the 70's and 80's, sought to regulate rates and eliminate abuses in freight and warehouse rates. Midwestern states, such as Minnesota, Iowa, Missouri, and Illinois, led in the output of regulatory legislation in this period.

Particularly acute problems of marketing farm products arose in the decade of the 1920's. The federal government took up the program of regulation, enacting such legislation as the Parkers and Stockyards Act of 1921, the Grain Futures Act of 1922, the Cotton Standards Act of 1923, the Produce Agency Act of 1927, and the Perishable Agricultural Commodities Act of 1930. In addition, solicitude for agricultural marketing was shown by the encouragement of cooperatives (the Capper-Volstead Act of 1922) and by the Cooperative Marketing Act of 1926.

The Commitment to commercial agriculture rather than agriculture "as a way of life" became virtually complete by the close of the decade. The Herbert Hoover administration (1928-1932) saw enactment of the Agricultural Marketing Act, a far-reaching federally-funded plan designed to support farm prices by establishing a Federal Farm Board empowered to buy and sell farm commodities. This agency proved to be inadequate for the purposes for which it was created, especially when total depression immediately engulfed the land.

It is significant that the dominant policies and politics of agriculture became those designed for commercial farming. Production for the market, economic rationality, technological changes, factor advantage—these became the central concepts at the heart of government policy. Perpetuation of the values of agrarianism assured generosity toward the emerging agricultural industry and also encouraged a spillover of public policy bounties for related agro-businesses which grew up in abundance as a result of the increasingly complex interdependencies and specializations.

## The New Deal and Agriculture

The agricultural policies of the New Deal can be seen in the light of historic continuity, but the urgency of the depression required a vastly increased scope of legislation and more far-reaching and swifter-acting programs. The major emphasis was given to achieving "parity in the marketplace," a price relationship in which a farmer's sales and his purchases would correspond to similar sales and purchases averaged over the years 1909-1914 (a period of favorable farm prices). To attain this objective, the government limited production by restrictions on acreage, direct payments, government purchase (and storage) of surplus grain, and marketing agreements and price-fixing in perishable commodities. These basic approaches generated related activities, such as federal crop insurance, distribution of commodities for school lunch and welfare programs, "ever normal granary" and "soil-bank" concepts, and many others.

In 1935, the Supreme Court invalidated the basic New Deal farm legislation, the Agricultural Adjustment Act of 1933. This invalidation caused a temporary slowdown in federal programs, but had no permanent effects. It may, in fact, have encouraged the more ingenious and diversified approaches that immediately followed as the New Deal Congress and the "Brain Trust" assembled by President Roosevelt sought public policies that would support and develop the complex pattern of economic activities making up American agriculture.

A survey of federal government policies dealing with agriculture inescapably leads to the conclusion that this sector of the American economy is accorded a very important place on the scale of social values. Farming is associated with the good—it adds strength to the nation's moral fibre as well as being an economic activity of fundamental importance. Agriculture "supports" urban society—a feat that becomes more and more heroic as the number of farmers declines in proportion to the nonfarming population. Productivity has been a goal of land policy, experimental research, agricultural education, and the agricultural extension services. Even as surpluses accumulated, policies for greater and more efficient production continued. The ruthless curtailment of production under the first AAA was considered sinful; later programs toward this end utilized acreage reductions, the least effective means of diminishing productivity.

### Postwar Problems

Surplus continued to mount after World War II, and the government had an investment of almost nine billion dollars in stored grain by 1959.

The existence of federally-owned surpluses encouraged efforts to find ways to transport some of these commodities into food-deficient areas of the world. The fact that American surpluses were as an island surrounded by hunger and malnourishment was quite obvious. This situation bore on problems of international politics; agricultural production was a potential instrument of foreign policy.

Legislation passed in 1954, Public Law 480, provided that under specified arrangements farm commodities could be exchanged for credit in the currency of the receiving country. These credits were then expended by the United States government in the conduct of its embassies and consular services, projects for educational and cultural exchanges, and similar activities. In addition, in countries of great need, such as India, long-term credits were extended for purchase of American wheat. Finally, the search for foreign markets was intensified, particularly in Europe. Efforts were made to work out reciprocal tariff concessions so that artificial barriers to the movement of farm products would be scaled down. These efforts were particularly characteristic of the Kennedy administration, and the 1960's have seen a marked reduction in surplus stocks in government storage.

The continuing decline in the number of farm units in the United States and the percentage of the population classified as "rural" brought about significant political and governmental results. It was quite generally accepted that agriculture was losing its "political" power. This belief was strengthened by a series of Supreme Court decisions during the 1960's that required state governments to apportion their legislative bodies, as well as their House of Representative districts, according to population. The bitter reaction to these requirements from conservative quarters was a clue to the vitality of agrarian norms even in an urbanized society.

There has been no indication of a diminishing interest in agriculture on the part of public policy makers. The major focus of attention continues to be on commercial agriculture. Farm units are measured in terms of efficiency of market production, and public policies plus technological advances encourage increasing size and capital outlay. Public investment in research, education, and subsidies for agriculture go hand in hand with private investment in machinery, scientific equipment, and chemical fertilizers and pest-controllers.

Commercial agriculture has developed a very substantial community of interests. The agri-business complex in the private sphere interrelates with the public agencies that have been established. The Department of Agriculture has within it partially autonomous systems or services—the Agricultural Stabilization and Conservation Service, the Agricultural Extension Service, the Commodity Credit Corporation, the Soil Conservation Service, the Farm Credit Administration, among others. The Department of Agriculture has not declined as the number of farms has decreased. It has maintained a steadily increasing annual budget, reaching seven billion dollars at the time of this writing.

## Non-Commercial Agriculture

During the first half of the nineteenth century, the most obvious development in agriculture was in the growth of commercial agriculture. As a consequence, differences became acute in the degree to which farm operators matched the emerging image. Not all farmers could qualify under the new standards, and those that could pushed to expand acreage at the expense of the others. Thus, great inequalities in production developed. By mid-century, 50% of the farms produced 90% of the marketed farm commodities and the top 10% produced about half of all that was placed on the market.

We have noted that the principal governmental policies were oriented so as to serve the interests of the upper portion of commercial producers. Such policies were of little or no benefit to the rural dweller whose farm operations were capable of producing only a small quantity for market and who sought to be to some extent self-sufficient. This "other agriculture" contained most of the rural poverty of the United States, some of which was non-agricultural but all of which, while incompletely documented, was known to contain some of the most deprived and exploited people in the country.

While, as has been pointed out, government policy was for the most part designed to aid the large-scale commercial farmers, it must also be noted that a minor and less well supported effort was directed toward the small commercial farmer, the disadvantaged tenant, and the share-cropper. At the bottom of the economic scale, the subject of the migratory farm workers has occasioned congressional hearings, but, until some scattered efforts were made under the Economic Opportunities Act, or the "War on Poverty," almost nothing had been done by way of public policy to deal constructively with their problems.

The low-income farm groups began to receive attention during the Depression. For the first time, large numbers of farm families were compelled to seek public relief and many more could legitimately have done so. A Resettlement Administration was set up to try to move farmers away from lands that were submarginal and to establish them in better circumstances. Rehabilitation loans for livestock and equipment purchases were made. These programs were merged in 1937 into the Farm Security Administration which in 1946 became the Farmers Home Administration. Meagerly supported in proportion to the size of the task confronting them, these agencies were not able to make any significant progress in reducing poverty in rural areas.

Additional approaches to the problem were proposed after World War II as areas of poverty in the United States were exposed and the incongruities of "poverty amid affluence" were clarified. Several factors combined to make it possible to overcome conservative opposition in 1963-1964 and to obtain legislation at the federal level designed to deal with the problem. Two of the programs of particular importance to rural America provided an area approach to the problem. These were Rural Area Development in the Department of Agriculture and an Area Redevelopment Act encouraging community development funded in part through the Department of Commerce. Related to those was a specific measure, the Appalachian Development Act, focusing on a program of economic development in the poverty-infested Appalachia region. The area-type development projects were of course intended to provide support so that individual farmers could become more efficient participants in commercial agriculture, but, nonetheless, such programs were not given the same kind of strong support offered to programs directly related to commercial agriculture.

## Continuity and Change

These introductory comments may be concluded by indicating several points of continuity of agrarian values within a changing rural environment.

a. First of all, the power with which affirmative attitudes toward rural life were implanted in the beginning days of the Republic gave agriculture a distinctive and permanent social value. Farmers were thought to be entitled to public policies as beneficent as the situation would allow.

b. On each successive frontier, the virtues of the farmer were reestablished and reimplanted. Agricultural development continued for fully a century, each successive westward movement bringing a reenactment of the process. Land generosity to facilitate settlement became a fixed policy and provided a framework for making the "family farm" characteristic of American agriculture.

c. With the influence of the technological revolution on agriculture, the family farm became a commercial unit emphasizing production and marketing. The position of agriculture was such that this commercial role, under laissez-faire policies, would very likely have subordinated agriculture to a system of absentee landlordism and latifundia. The government made generous efforts to provide education and research facilities that would slow this trend.

d. The commercial-style agriculture was extremely productive. At the same time, however, rural poverty was intensified and spread.

e. A note of impending disaster is characteristic of the most thoughtful writings dealing with agriculture. John Taylor's dismal prophesies at the beginning of the last century have been and continue to be taken up by succeeding writers. Security and stability for the farmer have been elusive goals. The technology that has played a major role in shaping rural life has favored big commercial farm operations; effects on small farmers—the people left behind—have been correspondingly disastrous. In this respect, the Jeffersonian dream lacks fulfilment. But the value placed upon the agricultural sector is not gone and, if the American city fails society, it may reappear with the vitality of old.

The readings that follow seek to offer a continuing thread that traces the development of agricultural policy from 1800 to the present. Farming has been and continues to be an important component of American life. The size of the topic has made it necessary to present only a limited number of representative works that have appeared in the field. Those which, in the author's view, are most illustrative and authoritative have been selected.

# I.    *The Concept of Classical Agrarianism: 1760–1840*

The early American agrarians, led by Thomas Jefferson, created and projected an agricultural dream. Utopian in its envisioned harmony and contentment, America was destined to become a nation of independent, landowning small farmers. Admitting that, by necessity, there must be some manufacturing and commerce, they nevertheless expected the preponderant emphasis to be on the ever-improving art and science of farming. Enough trade and industry to serve as a "handmaiden" for agriculture would be tolerable; more should be avoided.

As agricultural development moved westward, the older sections of the country tended to undergo industrial development while agriculture leveled off and later declined. Thus agriculture came to be regarded as the "handmaiden" of industry, and out of this situation grew the concept that agriculture was fundamental (supportive) to the economy. The theory of agricultural fundamentalism is usually applied to the whole of nineteenth- and early twentieth-century agriculture.

The distinction that we prefer to make sets apart the Jeffersonian utopian vision from the later, more commercial period. In the latter era the concept of agricultural fundamentalism is appropriate, whether or not all of the implications drawn from it can be defended. The earlier view is referred to as "classical agrarianism." The differentiating characteristics lie first in the existent conditions, second in the promise of the future. In the early period, the basic fact is demographic: over 90 percent of the people were cultivators. Most of them were independent small farmers and, because of encouraging public policies, even more could attain that state. In the period of fundamentalism, it was expected that this rural predominance would continue and that the western lands would make it possible to extend the agrarian commonwealth indefinitely into the future.

Jefferson succeeded in implanting a philosophical attitude toward rural life that went far towards explaining American attitudes generations later. Agriculture was not just the basis of wealth and economic activity, it was the basis of human virtues—it was the way of life that enabled man to reach the nobility of character for which he was intended.

John Taylor spoke out even more strongly than Jefferson against the encroachment of commercialization and expanding government. He saw in even

1

the small federal bureaucracy of that day a menace to the liberties of the citizen and a nonproductive use of human energy.

After 1830, the frontier played a vital role in strengthening and shaping agrarian values. The concepts of individualism and equality were strengthened in the agricultural phase of development of the frontier. Accompanying these values, there also developed a pronounced affinity for cooperative and socializing activities. These took a variety of forms. Mutual assistance in harvesting, cattle driving, and building are just a few examples. At a more formal level, protective associations were often formed to cooperate in countering the activities of cattle thieves or other kinds of outlaws. All parts of the nation went through this frontier experience and were deeply impressed by it. The agricultural values that emerged were a combination of Jeffersonian idealism and frontier practicality.

*Vernon L. Parrington*

## 1. THE AGRARIAN DEMOCRACY UNDER FIRE

The constitutional convention, held in 1787, regarded as one of its objectives to "remedy the excesses of democracy." The difficulties experienced by the infant government of the United States added to the need for increasing and centralizing power, stabilizing the economy, and strengthening the public credit. To accomplish these aims, a new constitution was transmitted to the Congress and by the Congress to the states.

The government established under the Constitution was dominated by leaders who continued the spirit of the Constitutional Convention. Authority, order, and stability were given priority over freedom and democratic rights. It is this turn of events that Professor Vernon Parrington refers to as a "great defeat," one that was "disastrous to the party of agrarian democracy."

The disaster, as a matter of fact, was short lived and may have been a blessing in disguise. Economic development was given a strong sendoff. The Jeffersonian concepts were strengthened by being put in a defensive position that required a marshalling of arguments as well as forces.

In the selection below, Professor Parrington, a leading authority on the democratic tradition in America, reconstructs Jefferson's political philosophy as it was woven into the fabric of early American political thought.

The years following the great defeat were disastrous to the party of agrarian democracy. Under the brilliant leadership of Hamilton the Federalists went forward confidently, gaining daily a firmer grip on the machinery of government, and establishing their principles in far-reaching legislative enactments. Their appeal to the wealthy classes, to those who made themselves audible above the clamor, was electrical. Hamilton was the hero of the hour, and the effusive approval that augmented with every added profit to the money brokers, seemed to indicate that the country was enthusiastically behind the Federalist policy. To what despondency the democrats were reduced is revealed in Maclay's *Journal*, with its caustic comment on political measures and motives. But the tide was already at the turn. The ideas let loose by the French Revolution were running swiftly through America, awakening a militant spirit in the democracy. Antagonism to the aristocratic arrogance of Federalism, and disgust at its coercive measures, were mounting fast. If that inchoate discontent were organized and directed by a skillful leader, it might prove strong enough to thrust the Hamiltonian party from power. To that work Thomas Jefferson devoted himself with immense tact and untiring patience. A master of political strategy, he spun his webs far and wide, quietly awaiting the time when the bumbling Federalist bees should range too carelessly in search of their honey. Accepted at once as the leader of agrarian America, he was to prove in the course of a long life the most original and native of the political leaders of the time. . . .

From the distinguished group of contemporary political thinkers Jefferson emerges as the preeminent intellectual, widely read, familiar with ideas, at home in the field of speculation, a critical observer of men and manners. All his life he was a student, and his devotion to his books, running often to fifteen hours a day, recalls the heroic zeal of Puritan scholars. He was trained in the law, but he was too much the intellectual, too curious about all sorts of things, to remain a lawyer. For such a man the appeal of political speculation was irresistible, and early in life he began a wide reading in the political classics that far outweighed Coke and Blackstone in creative influence on his mind. He was equally at home with the English liberals of the seventeenth century and the French liberals of the eighteenth; and if he came eventually to set the French school above the English, it was because he found in the back-to-nature philosophy, with its corollary of an agrarian economics and its emphasis on social well-being, a philosophy more consonant with Virginian experience and his own temperament than Locke's philosophy of property. But he was very far from being a narrow French partisan, as has been often charged; rather he judged old-world theory in the light of its applicability to existing American conditions, and restrained his love of speculation by immediate practical considerations. The man of affairs kept a watchful eye on the philosopher in his study.

In the major doctrines of his political philosophy Jefferson was an amalgam of English and French liberalisms, supplemented by the conscious influence of the American frontier. That fusion early took place in his mind. The first bill that he introduced into the Virginia Assembly, at the age of twenty-six, was a bill to permit slave-owners to manumit their slaves; and his first published pamphlet, issued in 1774,[1] rejected the legal reasoning of John Dickinson and Daniel Dulaney — supporting the parliamentary right to impose external taxation — and took its stand on the doctrine of natural right to local self-government and freedom of trade. When two years later he drafted the Declaration of Independence the fusion was complete. The strong influence of French humanitarianism is revealed in the passage on slavery that was stricken out on the floor of Congress, and more significantly in the change in the familiar phrasing of the several natural rights. Samuel Adams and other followers of Locke had been content with the classical enumeration of life, liberty, and property; but in Jefferson's hands the English doctrine was given a revolutionary shift. The substitution of "pursuit of happiness" for "property" marks a complete break with the Whiggish doctrine of property rights that Locke had bequeathed to the English middle class, and the substitution of a broader sociological conception; and it was this substitution that gave to the docu-

---

[1] *A Summary View of the Rights of British America*, Williamsburg.

ment the note of idealism which was to make its appeal so perennially human and vital. The words were far more than a political gesture to draw popular support; they were an embodiment of Jefferson's deepest convictions, and his total life thenceforward was given over to the work of providing such political machinery for America as should guarantee for all the enjoyment of those inalienable rights. If the fact that he set the pursuit of happiness above abstract property rights is to be taken as proof that Jefferson was an impractical French theorist, the critic may take what comfort he can from his deduction. . . .

In the broad spaces of America the old-world coercive state had dwindled to a mere police arrangement for parochial duties; the free citizen refused to be regimented; the several communities insisted on managing their affairs by their own agents. Such was the natural consequence of free economics; but with the turning of the tide would not the drift towards centralization nullify the results of earlier American experience and repeat here the unhappy history of European peoples?

To the philosophic mind of Jefferson, such a question was not academic, but urgent and vital. He had been bred in that older world, he believed passionately in the excellence of its virtues, and his political and social philosophy was determined by that experience. He sprang from a society deep-rooted in an agrarian economy, and he wished to preserve that society. Born on the Virginia frontier, he had never seen a hamlet so large as twenty houses before his eighteenth year; his neighbors and associates were capable and vigorous frontier democrats, who managed the affairs of local government with the same homespun skill that went to their farming. "It is not difficult," remarks an acute critic, "to see how the great principle of Jefferson's life — absolute faith in democracy — came to him. He was the product of the first West in American history; he grew up with men who ruled their country well, who fought the Indians valiantly . . . . Jefferson loved his back-

woods neighbors, and he, in turn was loved by them."[2] This early conviction of the excellence of a freehold order was confirmed by later experience; wide observation and much travel convinced him that no other people was so favored by circumstance as the American, or so vigorously self-reliant. That such well-being resulted from a plastic economics, he regarded as self-evident; and from this economic freedom came political freedom. In his European travels he saw everywhere want and wretchedness dwelling in the shadow of the aristocratic state, and he could not dissociate the two. Political tyranny was the outward and visible sign of greater tyrannies that ran down to the very roots of society; the leviathan state was the convenient instrument through which those tyrannies took their heavy toll of the common well-being. America was a land of free men; it was exploited neither by an aristocracy nor a plutocracy. Surely there could be no greater or nobler ambition for an American than to assist in preserving his country from the misery that must attend a change from the present happy condition of democratic industry, to the serfdom of the European wage-taker and peasant.

To a mind imbued with such conceptions the appeal of the Physiocratic theory of social economics would be irresistible. The ground was prepared for the sowing of the seeds of the liberal French thought. With its emphasis laid upon agriculture, its doctrine of the *produit net,* its principle of *laissez faire,* and its social concern, the Physiocratic theory accorded exactly with his familiar experience, and it must have seemed to Jefferson that it was little other than a deduction from the open facts of American life. He had read much in the works of the Physiocratic group, and was intimately acquainted with DuPont de Nemours; and the major principles of the school sank deep into his mind and creatively determined his thinking, with the result that Jeffersonian democracy as it spread through Virginia and west along the frontier assumed a pro-

[2]Dodd, *Statesmen of the Old South,* p. 23.

4

nounced Physiocratic bias. The sharp struggle between Jefferson and Hamilton must be reckoned, in part at least, a conflict between the rival principles of Quesnay and Adam Smith, between an agrarian and a capitalistic economy. Much as Jefferson feared the ambitions of an aristocracy, he feared quite as much the creation of a proletariat. As he looked into the future he saw great cities rising to breed their Roman mobs, duped and exploited by demagogues, the convenient tools of autocracy; and counting the cost in social well-being, he set his face like flint against the rising capitalism. A free yeomanry he regarded as the backbone of every great people, the producers of the real wealth, the guardians of manly independence; and the number of factory workers measured for him the extent of social disease. It is this Physiocratic conception that explains his bitter hostility to protective tariffs, national banks, funding manipulations, the machinery of credit, and all the agencies of capitalism which Hamilton was skillfully erecting in America. Not to have hated such things Jefferson must first have emptied his mind of the teachings of experience and the lessons of the social philosophers.

In the *Notes on Virginia* there is a well-known passage that amplifies his favorite thesis that a sound American economy was an agrarian economy:

The political economists of Europe have established it as a principle, that every State should endeavor to manufacture for itself; and this principle, like many others, we transfer to America. . . . But we have an immensity of land courting the industry of the husbandman. Is it best then that all our citizens should be employed in its improvement, or that one half should be called off from that to exercise manufactures and handicraft arts for the other? Those who labor in the earth are the chosen people of God, if ever he had a chosen people, whose breasts he has made his peculiar deposit for substantial and genuine virtue. It is the focus in which he keeps alive that sacred fire, which otherwise might escape from the face of the earth. Corruption of morals in the mass of cultivators is a phenomenon of which no age nor nation has furnished an example. It is the mark set on those, who not looking up to heaven,

to their own soil and industry, as does the husbandman, for their subsistence, depend for it on casualties and caprice of customers. Dependence begets subservience and venality, suffocates the germ of virtue, and prepares fit tools for the designs of ambition. . . . Generally speaking the proportion which the aggregate of the other classes of citizens bears in any state to that of its husbandmen, is the proportion of its unsound to its healthy parts, and is a good enough barometer whereby to measure its degree of corruption. While we have land to labor then, let us never wish to see our citizens occupied at a work-bench, or twirling a distaff . . . for the general operations of manufacture, let our work-shops remain in Europe. It is better to carry provisions and materials to work-men there, than bring them to the provisions and materials, and with them their manners and principles. . . . The mobs of great cities add just so much to the support of pure government, as sores do to the strength of the human body. It is the manners and spirit of a people which preserve a republic in vigor. A degeneracy in these is a canker which soon eats to the heart of its laws and constitution.[3]

*   *   *

The practice of local home rule had grown up in America in response to native conditions; it had resulted from democratic needs; and Jefferson was too thoroughly American, too instinctively democratic, to overlook the significance of local sovereignties in a democratic philosophy. From the sharp contrast between American and European practice he deduced a cardinal principle, namely, that good government springs from a common interest in public affairs, and that such common interest is possible only when the field of activities is circumscribed. Set government apart from the people, or above them, and public interest is lost in a sense of futility. The danger of an encroaching tyranny by a superimposed sovereignty, is made easy by the public lethargy in respect to distant and unfamiliar things, and establishes itself through the psychology of custom. Jefferson was never greatly concerned about stable government; he was very much more concerned about responsive government—that it should faithfully serve the majority will. He made no god of the political state. He had no conventional reverence for established law and

[3]*Writings*, Vol. III, pp. 268-296.

order; he inquired rather what sort of law and order he was asked to accept, was it just or unjust. Changing conditions make ancient good uncouth, and established institutions tend to fall into dry-rot, or to become tyrannical. Men are more important than constitutions, and the public well-being is more sacred than statutes. An occasional revolution, he commented grimly apropos of the hue and cry over Shays' Rebellion, is salutary; if it does not come of itself it might well be brought about. Progress in government results from experiment; and it is easier and safer to experiment on a small scale than on a great. Inertia increases with size, and the more consolidated the government, the more unyielding it becomes. The longest delayed revolutions are the gravest. . . .

Granted the truth of Jefferson's premises that power tends to contract to the hands of a few, and that all government of the few is vicious, then democracy is the only form of government under which an approximation to justice can be realized. A class will serve class interests. Government by an aristocracy is government in the interest of the aristocracy. For the staple argument of the Federalists, that gentlemen of principle and property alone may be intrusted with affairs of state, Jefferson had a quiet contempt. "I have never observed men's honesty to increase with their riches," he remarked. On the contrary, he regarded the "better sort of people" as a chief hindrance to the spread of social justice. The past had been evil because the past had been exploited by gentlemen of principle and property. They had kept government away from the people, and with their secret councils and secret diplomacy they had plundered the taxpayers and drenched nations in blood. Their selfish rivalries everywhere exacted a heavy toll of society and left behind a trail of poverty and wretchedness. The future would be better in the degree that mastery passed into common hands.

From the conclusions of his democratic premise he did not shrink. If it were indeed true that the people were beasts, then the democratic government of the future would be a bestial government—and even that might be better than the old arrangement of masters and slaves. But the American people whom Jefferson trusted were very far from beasts; he was convinced that they were honest and well-meaning; and if government were brought close to them, kept responsive to their will, a new and beneficent chapter in human history would open. The populistic laws passed by the legislatures of Rhode Island and New Hampshire, about which such an uproar was raised by fearful creditors, and which were urged as an argument against popular government, gave him no concern. He understood the ways of propaganda, and he never accepted judgment of the American people from the mouths of their enemies. The cure for the evils of democracy, he believed, was more democracy. The whole are far less likely to be unjust than the few; and if sovereignty does not rest in the majority will, where shall it lodge?

Hume, the great apostle of toryism, says "the Commons established a principle, which is noble in itself, and seems specious [i.e. pleasing], but is belied by all history and experience, *that the people are the origin of all just power.*" And where else will this degenerate son of science, this traitor to his fellow men, find the origin of *just* power, if not in the majority of the society? Will it be in the minority? Or in the individual of the minority?[4]

The America of Jefferson's day was a simple world, with a simple domestic economy. More than ninety percent were plain country folk, farmers and villagers, largely freeholders, who managed their local affairs in the traditional way. There were no great extremes of poverty and wealth, no closely organized class groups. With its sharp restrictions on suffrage and the prestige accorded the gentry, it was still far from a political democracy; but it was hastening towards a more democratic order. Remote from the cesspools of European diplomacy, and not yet acquainted with imperialism, it had no need for a leviathan state. Economic conditions sanctioned a *laissez-faire* government,

[4]Ibid., Vol. VII, p. 356.

simple and unambitious. In such a world the well-known words of Jefferson's first inaugural address, justified themselves to all who did not seek to use the state for personal advantage.

A wise and frugal government, which shall restrain men from injuring one another, which shall leave them otherwise free to regulate their own pursuits of industry and improvement, and shall not take from the mouth of labor the bread it has earned. This is the sum of good government, and this is necessary to close the circle of our felicities.

In one significant direction he would extend the scope of government—the encouragement of education. An intelligent people is necessary to a democracy; free schools are a sign of a free society. Tyranny thrives on ignorance and superstition, and every exploiting group fears popular education. Free himself in thought and action, believing in the unshackled commerce of ideas, hating all censorships, Jefferson accounted the founding of the University of Virginia his largest contribution to the well-being of his native commonwealth.

To all who profess faith in the democratic ideal Jefferson is a perennial inspiration. A free soul, he loved freedom enough to deny it to none; an idealist, he believed that the welfare of the whole, and not the prosperity of any group, is the single end of government. He was our first great leader to erect a political philosophy native to the economics and experience of America, as he was the first to break consciously with the past. His life was dedicated to the service of freedom, and later generations may well recall his words, "I have sworn upon the altar of God eternal hostility against every form of tyranny over the mind of man." Europe made Jefferson wholly American. From his studies in France he came to see that where men enjoy free access to the sources of subsistence, government is likely to be simple and honest, and society free and content; but where a policy of preemption has run its course, the function of government is seduced from its social purpose to perpetuate the inequalities which spring from the progressive monopolization of natural resources, with augmenting corruption and injustice. To preserve government in America from such degradation, to keep the natural resources open to all, were the prime desire and object of his life. That such an effort was foredoomed to failure, in presence of imperious forces that shape society beyond the capacity of political means to change or prevent, cannot detract from the nobility of his ideal, or the inspiration of his life. Among the greater thinkers of the constitutional period Jefferson remains by far the most vital and suggestive, the one to whom later generations may return most hopefully.

*John Taylor of Caroline*

## 2. AGRICULTURE IMPERILLED AND AGRARIANISM TRIUMPHANT

Jefferson lived to see his party prosper by adopting the economic policies of its rival, and he accepted commercial development as inevitable and beneficent. The burden of defending a pure agrarian ideology was then assumed by John Taylor of Caroline, a substantial planter with a flair for public service and also for philosophical composition. Numerous essays and at least two major books on agriculture and political philosophy were authored by Taylor. He defended agriculture, described improvements in animal and plant husbandry, and articulated the values of agrarian democracy as he saw them.

### NUMBER 1:
#### THE PRESENT STATE OF AGRICULTURE

I shall consider in a succession of short essays, the present state of agriculture in the United States, its oppressions and defects, and the remedies, political and domestick, which it needs. It is confessed, however, that the chief knowledge of the author, as to modes of agriculture, is confined to the states of Maryland, Virginia and North Carolina. And therefore, whilst his remarks in relation to its political state, will generally apply to the whole union, those in relation to these modes, will particularly apply to all states using slaves, or to the three enumerated states.

Mr. Strickland, an Englishman, reputed to be sensible and honest, published at London in the year 1801, a pamphlet upon the agriculture of the United States, being the result of his own observation, during a considerable period spent in travelling through the country, for the special purpose of investigating it. — The judgment of this impartial stranger appears in the following quotations — Page 26: "Land in America affords little pleasure or profit, and appears in a progress of continually affording less." — P. 31: "Virginia is in a rapid decline." — P. 38: "Land in New York, formerly producing twenty bushels to the acre, now produces only ten." — P. 41: "Little profit can be found in the present mode of agriculture of this country, and I apprehend it to be a fact that it affords *a bare subsistence.*" — P. 45: "Virginia is the southern limit of my inquiries, because agriculture had there already arrived to its lowest state of degradation." — P. 49: "The land owners in this state are, with a few exceptions, in low circumstances; the inferiour rank of them wretched in the extreme." — P. 52: "Decline has pervaded all the states."

These conclusions, if true, are awfully threatening to the liberty and prosperity of a country, whose hostage for both is agriculture. An order of men, *earning a bare subsistence, in low circumstances, and whose inferiour rank is wretched in the extreme*, cannot possibly constitute a moral force, adequate to either object. It is therefore highly important to the agricultural class, to ascertain whether it is true, that agriculture is in a decline. — A decline terminates like every other progress, at the end of its tendency.

Essays Nos. 1-5 from *Arator: Being a Series of Agricultural Essays, Practical and Political* in sixty-one numbers, Third Edition, Revised and Enlarged, Baltimore: John M. Carter, 1817, pp. 5-8.

Upon reading the opinion of this disinterested foreigner, my impressions were, indignation, alarm, conviction; inspired successively, by a love for my country, a fear for its welfare, and a recollection of facts.

The terrible facts, that the strongest chord which vibrates on the heart of man, cannot tie our people to the natal spot, that they view it with horrour, and flee from it to new climes with joy, determine our agricultural progress, to be a progress of emigration, and not of improvement; and lead to an ultimate recoil from this exhausted resource, to an exhausted country.

### NUMBER 2:
#### THE PRESENT STATE OF AGRICULTURE, CONTINUED

A patient must know that he is sick, before he will take physick. A collection of a few facts, to ascertain the ill health of agriculture, is necessary to invigorate our efforts towards a cure. One, apparent to the most superficial observer, is, that our land has diminished in fertility. — Arts improve the work of nature — when they injure it, they are not arts, but barbarous customs. It is the office of agriculture, as an art, not to impoverish, but to fertilize the soil and make it more useful than in its natural state. Such is the effect of every species of agriculture, which can aspire to the character of an art. — Its object being to furnish man with articles of the first necessity, whatever defeats that object, is a crime of the first magnitude. Had men a power to obscure or brighten the light of the sun, by obscuring it, they would imitate the morality of diminishing the fertility of the earth. Is not one as criminal as the other? Yet it is a fact, that lands in their natural state, are more valuable, than those which have undergone our habit of agriculture, of which emigrations are complete proofs.

The decay of a multitude of small towns, so situated as to depend for support on unalterable districts, is another proof of the impoverishment of the soil. It is true, that a few large towns have grown up, but this is owing, not to an increased product, but to an increased pasture; whereas, in every case, where the pasture is limited, or isolated by local circumstances, small towns have sprung up, whilst the lands were fresh, and decayed, as they were worn out. I have no facts to ascertain certainly the products of agriculture at different periods relatively to the number of people; such would furnish a demonstration of its state. But I have understood, that sixty-thousand hogsheads of tobacco were exported from Virginia, when it contained about one-fourth of its present population. If so, had the fertility of the country remained undiminished, Virginia ought now to export two hundred and forty thousand hogsheads, or an equivalent. In this estimate, every species of export except tobacco, is excluded at one epoch, and exports of every kind included at the other; yet the latter would fall far short of exhibiting the equivalent necessary to bring itself on a footing, as to agriculture, with the former. Two hundred and forty thousand hogsheads of tobacco, which, or an equivalent, Virginia would now export, if the state of agriculture had been as flourishing as it was sixty or seventy years past, at the present value, by which all our exports are rated, would be worth above seventeen millions of dollars; and supposing Virginia to furnish one seventh part of the native agricultural exports of the United States, these ought now to amount to one hundred and twenty millions of dollars, had the products of agriculture kept pace with the increase of population. If this statement is not exactly correct, enough of it certainly is so, to demonstrate a rapid impoverishment of the soil of the United States.

The decay of the culture of tobacco is testimony to this unwelcome fact. It is deserted because the lands are exhausted. To conceal from ourselves a disagreeable truth, we resort to the delusion, that tobacco requires new or fresh land; whereas every one acquainted with the plan knows, that its quantity and quality, as is the case with most or all plants, are both greatly improved

9

by manured land, or land, the fertility of which has been artificially increased. Whole counties, comprising large districts of country, which once grew tobacco in great quantities, are now too sterile to grow any of moment; and the wheat crops substituted for tobacco, have already sunk to an average below profit.

From the mass of facts, to prove that the fertility of our country has been long declining, and that our agriculture is in a miserable state, I shall only select one more. The average of our native exports, is about forty millions of dollars annually. Some portion of this amount consists of manufactures, the materials for which are not furnished by agriculture; another, as is extensively the fact in the case of flour, has passed through the hands of the manufacturer. Of the first portion he receives the whole price, of the second a proportion. And a third portion of our products is obtained from the sea. Of the forty millions exported, agriculture, therefore, receives about thirty-five. The taxes of every kind, state and federal, may be estimated at twenty millions of dollars, of which agriculture pays at least fifteen, leaving twenty millions of her exports for her own use. Counting all the slaves, who ought to be counted both as sources of product and expense, in estimating the state of agriculture, the people of the United States may probably amount to about seven millions, and it may be fairly assumed, that the interest or occupation of six millions of these seven, is agricultural. Of the whole surplus product of agriculture exported, after deducting the taxes it pays, there remains for each individual a few cents above three dollars. Out of this mass of profit, he is to pay for the manufactures, luxuries and necessaries he consumes, not raised by himself; and the only remaining article to be carried to the credit of agriculture, is the small gain it derives from its domestick sales, not to itself, or from sales by one of its members to another, for that does not enrich it, but to other classes, such as manufacturers and soldiers. Against the former, agriculture is to be debited with the bounties she is made by law to pay them; against the latter, she has been already debited by deducting her taxes from her exports. Neither can be a source of much wealth or profit to her, because in one case she furnishes the money by taxation, and in the other by bounties, with which her products are purchased. It is, therefore, nearly true, that the income of agriculture is only three dollars per poll, and that this income is her whole fund for supplying her wants and extending her improvements. This estimate is infinitely more correct, than one drawn from individual wealth or poverty. To infer from the first, that every body might become rich, as a defence of our agricultural regimen, would be a conclusion as fallacious, as to infer from the second, that every body must become poor, as a proof of its badness. Extraordinary talents or industry will produce extraordinary effects. Instances of happiness or wealth under a despotism, do not prove that its regimen is calculated for general wealth or happiness. A system, commercial, political or agricultural, so wretched as not to exhibit cases of individual prosperity, has never appeared, because an universal scourge would be universally abhorred. It is not from partial, but general facts, that we can draw a correct knowledge of our agriculture. Even a personal view of the country, might deceive the thoughtless, because neither the shortness of life, nor the gradual impoverishment of land, are calculated to establish a visible standard of comparison. A man must be old and possess a turn for observation from his youth, to be able to judge correctly from this source. I have known many farms for above forty years, and though I think that all of them have been greatly impoverished, yet I rely more upon the general facts I have stated, for agreeing with Strickland in opinion, "That the agriculture of the United States affords only a bare subsistence—that the fertility of our lands is gradually declining—and that the agriculture of Virginia has arrived to the lowest state of degradation."

\* \* \*

NUMBER 5:
## THE POLITICAL STATE OF AGRICULTURE, CONTINUED

English agriculture has completely tried the project of enriching itself, by buying markets with bounties. It has provided more of these markets, than the agriculture of any other nation. Yet it is unable to feed its own people, many of whom are indebted to foreign agriculture for daily bread. No profession in England is deficient in hands, but the agricultural, and none other a cypher in government. They have lords, bishops, officers civil and military, soldiers, sailors, bankers, loaners and capitalists in abundance, and all of them have an influence in the government. These are the markets in which the English agriculturists have successively laid out their money, in order to get good prices, and the more of these markets they buy, the less liberty and wealth they retain.

If the agriculture of the United States would only consider how it happens, that it can yet live upon six shillings sterling a bushel for wheat, when the English agriculture is perishing with sixteen, the film drawn over its eyes by the avarice with which those charge it, who design to cheat it, would fall off. The solution of the apparent wonder, lies in the delusion of buying price by bounties. The bounties are partly, but never completely reimbursed by the price. Though the payer of the bounties gets more price, he gains less profit than from the lower price, when he paid no bounties. Therefore the receivers of the bounties become rich and idle, and the receivers of the price, poor and laborious. And this effect is inevitable, because the bounties must for ever out-run the prices they create, or nobody could subsist on them. If the bounty paid was equal to one shilling a bushel on wheat, and should raise the price nine pence, the receivers of the bounty would gain three pence a bushel on all the wheat of the nation, and agriculture would lose it, though it got a higher price. And this obvious fraud is precisely the result of every promise in every form made by charter and privilege to enrich or encourage agriculture.

The agriculture of the United States, found itself in the happiest situation for prosperity imaginable, at the end of the revolutionary war. It had not yet become such an egregious gudgeon as to believe, that by giving ten millions of dollars every year to the tribe of undertakers, to make it rich, they would return it twenty; and it could avail itself of all the markets in the world, where this ridiculous notion prevailed. These were so many mines of wealth to the agriculture of the United States. The idle, clerical, military, banking, loaning, and ennobled classes, as has been stated, do certainly have the effect of raising agricultural prices very considerably; but the agriculturists who pay and maintain these classes, still lose more by them than they gain. Now the United States, as a section of the commercial world, might have shared in the enhancement of agricultural price, produced by such unproductive orders in other countries; and paid none of the ruinous expense of wealth or liberty, which they cost. They might have reaped the good, and avoided the evil. And agriculture, for once in its life, might have done itself justice. But the wiseacre chose to reap the evil, and avoid the good; and if its situation has been occasionally tolerable, it was sorely against its will, or by accident.—In the first eight years after the revolution, being the first period in the latter ages of the world, that agriculture could make laws, it legislated sundry items of the British system for buying markets or raising prices. In the next twelve, it nurtured their growth, so as to raise up some to a large, and one to a monstrous size; and also most sagaciously prohibited itself, first from sharing in the benefit of the high prices produced by aristocratical institutions in France, and secondly from sharing in those produced in the same way in England. European agriculture is gulled or oppressed by others; American, gulls or oppresses itself. The first is no longer weak enough to think, that its battalion of aristocratical items, does it any good; but it is now unable to follow its judgment; the second, though able to follow its own judgment, has adopted the exploded errours heartily repented of by the first, and far outstrips it in the celerity of its progress towards a state of absolute submission to other interests, by shutting out itself from markets enhanced at the expense of other nations; and at the same time by creating the English items of capitalists, or masters for manufacturers, bankers, lenders, armies, and navies. Our true interest was to pay nothing for markets, spurious and swindling to those who buy them, and yet to share in their enhancement of prices. We have pursued a different course, and I do not recollect a single law, state or continental, passed in favour of agriculture, nor a single good house built by it since the revolution; but I know many built before, which have fallen into decay. Our agriculture is complimented by presidents, governours, legislators and individuals; and the Turks reverence a particular order of people as being also favoured by heaven.

A. *Whitney Griswold*

## 3. THE AGRARIAN DEMOCRACY OF THOMAS JEFFERSON

A late president of Yale University, A. Whitney Griswold was a devoted scholar of Jeffersonian political philosophy and the author of *Farming and Democracy*, in which he challenges the theme that the two endeavors are interdependent.

If the past determines or in any way influences the present, the present invariably reverses the process. One of the more striking instances of this rule has been the recent apotheosis of Thomas Jefferson as a national hero equal in stature to Washington and Lincoln. In an atmosphere of industrialism, urban living, and strong, impersonal national government that tradition might lead us to suppose would kill it, the Jefferson legend has blossomed and put forth new shoots. As Mr. Douglass Adair has pointed out, the pioneer democrat and agrarian liberal "discovered" by Frederick Jackson Turner and Charles A. Beard and celebrated by Parrington, Nock, and Bowers, has lately found more complicated, more interesting, and incidentally more timely, portrayal at the hands of Carl Becker, Gilbert Chinard, and Adrienne Koch. These writers, whose company is now joined by Mr. Joseph Dorf-

man, have been at pains to show the range and diversity of Jefferson's thought, and above all how he moved with his times to espouse the cause of commerce, industry, and national power. Mr. Dorfman crowds all these qualities together under the label, "Thomas Jefferson: Commercial Agrarian Democrat" which, if the trend continues, may have to be stretched to "Commercial Industrial Agrarian Democratic Federalist."

Does the label fit? The legendary Jefferson was an agrarian; and even as modern scholars were finding in his writings political precepts for an industrial age, the farmers of the United States were recognizing him as the founder of American agriculture and adopting him as their patron saint. Jefferson was not an agrarian fundamentalist; he did move with his times. No doubt the highly moral nature of his interest in public affairs and his pragmatic attitude would have led

Reprinted from *The American Political Science Review*, Vol. XL (August, 1946), pp. 657-667, by permission of The American Political Science Association.

him, in the modern setting, to seek his end by modern means. Yet he started and ended life an agrarian at heart, and it was against an agrarian background that he saw his ideal of American democracy most clearly. So congenial was this background to him, and so vividly does it continue to display itself behind his legend, that it cannot be painted out of the portrait of Jefferson in modern dress.

The agrarian tradition has thrived on the legend and *vice versa*; witness the ceremonies attending the two hundredth anniversary of Jefferson's birth, in 1943. In that critical war year, with the democracy he helped to found engaged in a struggle for its life, the whole American agricultural community paid tribute to him "as a man of abiding passion for human liberty and the sacred rights of the common people, and as one who, throughout his entire career, remained preeminently and above all a farmer." So runs the preamble to a joint resolution of Congress establishing the National Agricultural Jefferson Bicentenary Committee, representing the Department of Agriculture, the land-grant colleges, the national farm organizations, the agricultural press, scientific and learned societies dealing with agriculture, and the Office of Education. In this preamble, as in the nationwide ceremonies held under the auspices of the Bicentenary Committee, the two dominant and interrelated themes are agrarianism and democracy:

Whereas throughout his whole social philosophy runs a theme which recognizes the dignity of the agricultural way of life and a deep appreciation of the satisfactions which accrue, through science, education, and faith, to the farm family and the rural community; and
Whereas he recognized the importance of the perpetuation of a sound agriculture as a paramount factor in the development of the economy and the permanence of our national institutions.

Jefferson was not the only founding father to practice farming or to hold these views; yet it was he above all who bequeathed them to the country. George Washington, like George III, ran a model farm and corresponded with the British agricultural writer Arthur Young concerning its management. "Agriculture has ever been amongst the most favourite amusements of my life," he wrote Young in 1786, modestly deprecating his skill in the art. James Madison served as president of the Albemarle Agricultural Society, founded at Charlottesville in 1817. John Taylor, one of Jefferson's strongest and most articulate political supporters and a fellow-planter from Caroline county, Virginia, has been called "the philosopher and statesman of agrarianism," and "the philosopher of Jeffersonian democracy." But in his numerous polemics and two principal works, *Arator* (1803) and *An Inquiry into the Principles and Policy of the United States* (1841), as, indeed, in his career in state and national politics, he displayed a dominant motive that set him apart from Jefferson in spirit, however identical their written opinions may seem. This motive was to defend his own particular interest as a large-scale planter and a country gentleman, whether in terms of an agrarian as opposed to an industrial economy or of states' rights versus federalism. Democracy, to him, meant the opportunity to maintain a commanding position in government and in society for a class of enlightened—and prosperous—planter aristocrats. For this reason, rather than because of the dullness and prolixity of his works, Taylor must be disqualified as official interpreter of Jefferson's agrarian and democratic ideals. We must read Jefferson in his own words, for no one combined those ideals in a working philosophy so deliberately as he, and with such lasting effect.

The ideals stand out most clearly in his social pattern of American agriculture. This, he believed, should consist of a community of small farmers, freemen unencumbered either by feudal obligations to a distant sovereign or by archaic practices of primogeniture or entail among themselves. One of his earliest political acts was to abolish these practices in Virginia. His draft of a constitution for the state, drawn up in June, 1776,

13

contained, under the title of "Rights, Private and Public," the following provisions:

Unappropriated or Forfeited lands shall be appropriated by the Administrator with the consent of the Privy council.

Every person of full age neither owning nor having owned (50) acres of land, shall be entitled to an appropriation of (50) acres or to so much as shall make up what he owns or has owned (50) acres in full and absolute dominion. And no other person shall be capable of taking an appropriation.

Lands heretofore holden of the crown in fee simple, and those hereafter to be appropriated shall be holden in full and absolute dominion, of no superior whatever.

Later in the same year (October, 1776), he drafted and saw through the Virginia legislature bills abolishing primogeniture and entail, thus preventing the creation and perpetuation of a landed aristocracy.

The two measures—the constitutional provisions governing the acquisition of land and the law prohibiting its entailment—were conceived in the interest of the rank and file of frontier farmers, the constituency to which Jefferson entrusted his political fortunes. "The earth is given as a common stock for man to labour and live on," he wrote from Paris in 1785.

If for the encouragement of industry we allow it to be appropriated, we must take care that other employment be provided to those excluded from the appropriation. If we do not the fundamental right to labour the earth returns to the unemployed. It is too soon yet in our country to say that every man who cannot find employment but who can find uncultivated land shall be at liberty to cultivate it, paying a moderate rent. But it is not too soon to provide by every possible means that as few as possible shall be without a little portion of land. The small landholders are the most precious part of a state.

Looking back at his efforts on behalf of small landholders from the vantage point of 1944, Secretary of Agriculture Wickard acclaimed Jefferson as "father of the idea of the family-size farm." Only four years earlier, a committee appointed by Wickard, representing all federal agencies concerned with agriculture had reported:

The U.S. Department of Agriculture believes that the welfare of agriculture and of the Nation will be promoted by an agricultural land tenure pattern characterized by efficient family-size owner-operated farms, and one of the continuing major objectives of the Department will be the establishment and maintenance of such farms as the predominating operating farm unit in the United States.

Jefferson's pattern had survived a century and a half of trial and stress to become "a continuing major objective" of modern policy.

How did Jefferson come by these ideas, so germinal to our democracy and so influential in its history? In a sense, it is not necessary to seek the answer beyond his own temperament and times. He was born to farming, as were most of his countrymen. He loved the land, trying again and again to escape to it from "the hated occupations of politics." His years at Monticello were unquestionably his happiest. "I return to farming with an ardor which I scarcely knew in my youth," he wrote Adams in 1794; and in later years:

I have often thought that if heaven had given me choice of my position and calling, it should have been on a rich spot of earth, well watered, and near a good market for the productions of the garden. No occupation is so delightful to me as the culture of the earth. . . .

These were no idle sentiments. As his correspondence and notebooks show, his interest in farming was sincere and consistent throughout his life. They also reveal him as an experimental agriculturist of distinction. His observations and adaptations of European crops, livestock, and methods of farming put him in the vanguard of his contemporaries. He introduced the threshing machine in America and was one of the first importers of Merino sheep from Spain. His improved mold-board plow won him international awards. The agricultural societies he founded and encouraged and his plan to include scientific agriculture in the curriculum of the University of Virginia foreshadowed our whole national system of agricultural education. Instead of patenting his innovations and improvements, moreover, he gave them freely to the public, and instead of profiting from them, he ended his years in virtual bankruptcy. This he attributed to the "disgusting dish of politics" which had lured him from his chosen vocation and cost him his proficiency in it. But his personal loss was the farmers' gain. It justifies his fame in agricultural circles, and it vividly bespeaks his personal interest in farming.

His political concern for agriculture was equally obvious. He had espoused the cause of the common man. At that time in our history, the common man was a farmer. Ninety per cent of all Americans, common or uncommon, were farmers. To champion the people, therefore, was to champion agriculture, a political theorem no politician could deny, however lofty or disinterested his purposes. The character of these people and their geographical surroundings might have determined their economic life without benefit of political theory. Lack of capital and a wilderness that yielded only to hard, slow, manual labor made small-scale family farming the rule before Jefferson became its advocate. The tobacco, rice, and cotton plantations of his Southern compatriots were exceptions to the rule. It would be possible to ascribe his solicitude for the small landholders to an astute rationalization of things as they were among the largest and, to him, most sympathetic group of voters.

But Jefferson was more than a farmer and a politician. He was a serious student of philosophy. The diligence with which he applied himself to his philosophical studies, to a search for moral guidance and for counsels of law and government, is collateral for the sincerity of his political and economic ideas. We know from his letters and commonplace books the time and thought he devoted to the Greek and Latin classics, to Locke, Bolingbroke, Hume, Montesquieu, Adam Smith, Destutt de Tracy, and many another English and French writer represented on the shelves of his library. We know from the Declaration of Independence, his principal state paper, the degree to which he had steeped himself in the natural rights philosophy of John Locke. During his residence in Paris (1784-1789), he made the acquaintance of the Physiocrat Du Pont de Nemours, and the economist Destutt de Tracy. Du Pont, who took up residence in America, and whose son founded the "gunpowder manufactory" that was eventually to gain un-Physiocratic fame as the eighth largest industrial corporation in the United States, became one of Jefferson's closest intellectual friends. Their correspondence over a period of seventeen years (1800-1817) weighed and appraised not only the principles of Physiocracy but most of the leading ideas of government and political economy current at the time. Jefferson's admiration for Destutt de Tracy was extravagant. He translated and edited De Tracy's *Commentary and Review of Montesquieu's Spirit of Laws* and his *Treatise on Political Economy*, which he considered the leading works in "civil government" and political economy. He persuaded the president of his alma mater, William and Mary, to adopt the *Commentary* as a text and appealed so enthusiastically about it to his friends that Du Pont, for one, accused him of having written it.

What is of interest to us in all this intellectual trafficking is not the genealogy of Jefferson's ideas, at best a speculative theme, but their substance, the elements of which they were composed, the process of composition. Many of his ideas he translated into policy and handed down as tradition, among them that "continuing major objective" of agricultural policy for which he was acclaimed by Secretary Wickard in 1944. A tradition is best explained by its origin. It is not often that a founder of tradition lets us look so deeply into his first principles and purposes as does Jefferson in his scholarly notes and correspondence.

How, then, did he relate agrarianism to democracy in the meaning of our present inquiry? As to his democratic convictions

15

and labors, his record, beginning with his enumeration of "inalienable rights" in the Declaration of Independence and concluding with the philosophical reflections of his old age, speaks for itself. In all his works he was the champion of those basic civil liberties and methods of popular government by which democracy enabled people to rule themselves and express themselves as individuals. There is scarcely an item in our national bill of rights, the first ten amendments to the Constitution, that is not directly traceable to his precept or example. "More than any other man," says Carl Becker, "we think of Jefferson as having formulated the fundamental principles of American democracy, of what we now like to call the American way of life." The tribute is specific: Jefferson did not originate the fundamental principles, he "formulated" them. Jefferson was not an original thinker, but a representative one. His sensitive mind was a conductor for all the intellectual currents of his age. In a theoretical sense, he must share the credit for founding our democratic institutions with the philosophers whose ideas he borrowed and adapted. In a political sense, he must share it with Franklin, Adams, Washington, Hamilton, Madison, Marshall, and the other founders, some of whom history may judge more effective and practical than he. But for his definition of those institutions, his expression of them in letter and spirit in the critical period of their infancy, history judges him to have represented them more completely than any of his colleagues.

His general views on agriculture may require no more complicated explanation than, as already suggested, that they were perfectly logical deductions from his own tastes and environment. Undoubtedly he found moral support for them in his reading, especially in the classics. But the character of the views, their obviousness, generality, and fundamental simplicity, discourages a search for more specific doctrinal influences. The Physiocratic influence that is sometimes inferred in this connection has been discounted not only by historical scholars but by Jefferson himself. The inference derived largely from their common emphasis upon agriculture, the similarity of the moral philosophy which both drew independently of each other from Locke, and from Jefferson's friendship with Du Pont. But Jefferson's homespun agrarianism stopped a long way short of the elaborate "arithmetical formularies," as Adam Smith called them, by which the Physiocrats proved agriculture the sole source of wealth and a single tax upon its net product the sole method of public finance. As Chinard has pointed out, Jefferson was never an economist in the formal sense of the word. There is no trace of Physiocratic or any other systematic economic analysis in his writings. He did not make Du Pont's acquaintance until some time during his tour of duty in Paris, nearly a decade after he had formulated and published his political philosophy, and at least two years after he had done the same for his views on agriculture. These he had set forth in his *Notes on Virginia*, which he had written in 1781 and revised in the winter of 1782–1783. His exposure to the revolutionary intellectual ferment of Paris, far from revising his political opinions, strengthened them. . . .

Jefferson from the outset cast his lot with poor, frontier farmers and never, even in their interest, conceived of economic measure so complex in detail or specific in purpose as those of the Physiocrats. To him, agriculture was not primarily a source of wealth, but of human virtues and traits most congenial to popular self-government. It had a sociological rather than an economic value. This is the dominant note in all his writings on the subject. . . .

*Bray Hammond*

## 4. BANKING, FREE ENTERPRISE, AND AGRICULTURE

One of the exciting struggles of the spokesmen for agrarian interests in the Jacksonian era was waged for the principle of "hard money," against the note-issuing authority of chartered banks. The hard money position appears at first to have been later contradicted by the Populist agitation for easier credit and bimetallism. However, the basic congruence of the two positions is shown by Bray Hammond in tracing the evolution of banking policy in the states on the frontier. In the selection below, the tension between agricultural and commercial interests over appropriate banking policies is clarified.

In 1852 the Secretary of the Treasury reported that there were "no incorporated banks in regular and active operation" in Arkansas, California, Florida, Illinois, Iowa, Texas, and Wisconsin—seven of the thirty-one states then in existence—in the District of Columbia, nor in the two organized territories, Minnesota and Oregon. In most of these jurisdictions corporate banking was constitutionally prohibited; in others it was kept out by current opposition. At the same time it was a state-controlled monopoly in Indiana and Missouri, as it was a little later in Iowa. Going to the opposite extreme, Michigan in 1838 made banking free. Her experiment was eventually repeated by Illinois, by Wisconsin, and by Indiana. Meanwhile, there were unincorporated banks throughout the region, though their creation of credit was probably small compared with that of incorporated banks.

Thus, in three or four decades before the Civil War, in the states of the upper Mississippi Valley, public policy ranged from absolute prohibition of bank credit, through state monopoly, to laissez faire. On balance, policy tended to be restrictive; for while the

craving for bank credit increased, the aversion to it increased still more. The craving and the aversion are both significant, but the aversion now seems much the more curious of the two. It is out of accord with the idea that as a regular thing farmers and settlers in new regions are eager borrowers, and it has little in common with the habits and convictions of a posterity for whom credit is the lifeblood of economic activity. Yet the aversion for credit used to be stronger than the craving for it and comes closer to tradition. Easy money is not early American.

I

Prohibition and laissez faire—the extreme positions taken with respect to banking in the West—were the products respectively of agrarianism and of enterprise. The agrarians' position is easy to identify, for they had an intellectually respectable doctrine to which Thomas Jefferson and John Taylor of Caroline had ably contributed in its earlier years and which in its later more radical and belligerent form was champi-

From Bray Hammond, "Banking in the Early West: Monopoly, Prohibition, and Laissez-Faire," in *The Journal of Economic History*, Vol. VIII (May, 1948), pp. 1-4, 18-20. Reprinted by permission of The Economic History Association, and Mrs. Melitta de Kern Hammond.

oned by William Gouge, its most literary apologist, by Andrew Jackson, Thomas Hart Benton, and Roger Taney and by the Loco-focos. The two characteristics of banking that roiled the agrarians were incorporation and note issue. As corporations, banks had artificial, monopolistic privileges, with "neither bodies to be kicked nor souls to be damned." As sources of circulating notes, they had the obvious power to create money. With these twin evils, banking was an unconstitutional, aristocratic device by which private groups acquired undemocratic powers. It was "the *principal* cause of social evil in the United States." The agrarians believed in gold and silver, the money of the Constitution. This, they held, was the only honest money, the only money suitable to a simple, individualistic economy; paper money made prices rise, enticed men into debt, and then cast all but a favored few into ruin. Their ideals were those of Jackson, for whom, according to Benton, "abhorrence of debt, public and private, dislike of banks and love of hard money — love of justice and love of country were ruling passions . . . ."

For all agrarians and for most of their contemporaries, the essential function of banking was note issue; accordingly, when they discussed banking, note issue was what they had in mind. From 1830 to 1860 notes and deposits seem to have been about equal in amount, for the country as a whole, but deposits were inconspicuous, their nature was not understood, and they were characteristic principally of banks in the eastern centers. Where the agrarians lived, circulation was not only more conspicuous but actually larger in volume.

According to Gouge, the harmful effects of banking were evident everywhere; banks were the agents of a vicious cycle of expansion and contraction. "Anything that excites the spirit of enterprise," he said, "has a tendency to increase the amount of bank issues. Whatever damps the spirit of enterprise or of speculation has a tendency to reduce the amount of bank issues. As the wild spirit of speculation has in most cases its origin, and in all its aliment, in banking transactions, these various causes operate in a circle. The banks, by expanding their issues, give aliment to the wild spirit of speculation when it begins; and by their contractions they aggravate the evils of the natural reactions." Gouge attacked Nicholas Biddle's idea that "the value of bank medium consists in its elasticity — in its power of alternate expansion and contraction to suit the wants of the community." The flexibility or elasticity of bank credit, he averred, "is not an excellence but a defect." For, "if banks at any time make money more plentiful than it would be if only gold and silver circulated, they diminish its value in increasing its quantity."

Having so deep a conviction of the evils of banking, the agrarians hoped they could abolish it entirely. The governor of Kentucky in 1819 recommended that the legislature propose an amendment to the federal Constitution providing that "no incorporated bank should exist in the United States . . ."; and a resolution was introduced declaring it to be "the duty of the general government and of every individual state composing it (gradually if necessary but ultimately and certainly) to abolish all banks and moneyed monopolies. . . ." Such a reform, it was realized, could not be accomplished readily. Years of effort would be required. "Though strong in the confidence of the people," Benton said in discussing Jackson's policy, "the President was not deemed strong enough to encounter all the banks of all the states at once. Temporizing was indispensable — and even the conciliation of a part of them." So the tactics were to attack the Bank of the United States first, using the help of the private banks, and then to dispose of the latter.

The position contrary to that of the agrarians is much harder to identify, for it was not literary or doctrinaire. It dominated more than enterprise proper; its left wing reached beyond the speculators to cheats pure and simple, and its right wing comprised men of substance and integrity. It dominated the heterogeneous host of Americans who were intent on making money. Gallatin, who was Jeffersonian but not agrarian, wrote of it as follows: "The energy of this nation is not to be controlled; it is at present exclusively applied to the acquisition of wealth and to improvements of stupendous magnitude. Whatever has that tendency, and of course an immoderate expansion of credit, receives favor. The apparent prosperity and the progress of cultivation, population, commerce, and improvement are beyond expectation. But it seems to me as if general demoralization was the consequence; I doubt whether general happiness is increased; and I would have preferred a gradual, slower, and more secure progress."

The relative political strength of these two opposed forces was influenced, of course, by the vicissitudes of economic life. The agrarians gained ground against banking when business was bad and lost it when business was good. They were strongest in the forties while fits of prostration were prolonging the depression begun with the panic of 1837; but the stalwarts among them kept their quivers full of Jeffersonian convictions and furnished leadership in a cause whose successes were partly opportunistic and partly doctrinaire. Eventually, after a struggle that occupied the four decades from 1820 to 1860, they succumbed to the money-makers. Their austere and simple ideals were ecologically impossible in a land of wealth and individualism. Through legislation, partly state and partly federal, the money-makers made banking free and insured the mounting supply of bank credit employed in the great expansion of the economy in the latter part of the century. The struggle then ended had been between two concepts: one of these could not be realized without enormously expansible bank credit, the other could not be realized with it.

*　*　*

VIII

. . . That the agrarians had no objection to deposit banking seems to me of little or no significance as to their general purpose. They found it obnoxious that banks created money. It happened that they recognized that creation only in the issue of notes; had they recognized it in the deposit function, had they seen that "every bank is a bank of issue," had they understood that deposit liabilities are created money as much as bank notes are, then they must have opposed banks of deposit as heartily as banks of circulation. They deliberately intended, to the limit of their understanding, to curb the extension of bank credit. And their prohibitions and monopolies expressed the will of vigorous majorities, over a wide region, whose people were mostly agricultural and on conventional, materialistic grounds should have wanted abundant credit as much as anyone.

Consistently with their reasons for seeking to interdict banking, the agrarians sought no alternative to bank credit. They asked for no easy money of any sort. They looked for no social benefits from low interest rates — they saw no fostering influence in them nor any other blessing than the negative one derived from avoiding usury. Andrew Jackson was himself a chronic debtor, and debt was for him a misfortune into which men were inveigled or forced. He and his agrarians might acknowledge the need or advisability of debt on occasion for the purchase of land and equipment, but such tolerance did not imply a demand for the provision of credit by the government or by any other agency. "The business of lending money is no part of the duty of any government either state or federal." The conviction was that relatively little credit was needed on the whole and that banks generated a spurious demand for it. Their operations led to the distress whence arose the clamor from impoverished debtors for relief laws. When funds are plentiful, a Virginia congressman had argued in 1811, there arises competition among banks to lend; and this "fictitious credit . . . will expose the farmers and planters to the most serious injury." He said that in Baltimore available bank funds had always exceeded the de-

19

mand by solvent customers, and hence had gone to the accommodation of "mere speculators." A Pennsylvania legislative committee in 1821 observed that before the establishment of banks "in the interior" farmers "who possessed credit and character" had no difficulty in borrowing on their simple bond. "Embarrassments and failures, in those days, were scarcely known among our husbandmen, and society moved on by a regular, sure, and happy march." In the cities, on the contrary, "where loans have been made chiefly by incorporated banks," bankruptcies occurred regularly. Were credit confined to legitimate demand, "banking long since would have been abandoned as an unprofitable trade." These views were supported by a belief held by others than agrarians that agricultural yields were scarcely adequate to meet interest charges and to retire principal. "The profits of agriculture are so moderate," Gallatin wrote in 1831, "at least in the Middle States, and the returns so slow, that even loans on mortgages are rarely useful." And he indicated that in the West the ability to discharge agricultural indebtedness would be still less.

Bank issues were the direct object of attack because paper money was issued in no other form; in principle the agrarian repugnance to government issues was quite as great. According to Gouge, such issues would encourage "extravagance in public expenditures in even the best of times, would prevent the placing of the fiscal concerns of the country on a proper basis, and would cause various evils." In 1837 when the Treasury found itself absolutely strapped as the result of a unique combination of circumstances—the federal debt having been paid off in full, the federal surplus being in process of distribution to the states, payment for public lands being required in specie, and specie payments being universally suspended—the Jacksonians were galled by the ineluctable necessity of issuing Treasury notes. These notes bore interest, they were not legal tender, and they were redeemable in a year; yet it hurt the agrarian conscience to use them. Over half the amount authorized was redeemed before the full amount was issued, and Secretary Woodbury, of the Treasury, emphasized the fact that the amount used was less than the amount due the Treasury from suspended banks. Half a century later, when the Supreme Court announced that the Constitution empowered Congress to issue paper money and make it legal tender, the venerable George Bancroft, who had been one of the numerous intellectuals among the Jacksonians, was shocked. "Our federal Constitution," he declared, "was designed to end forever the emission of bills of credit as legal tender in payment of debts, alike by the individual states and the United States."

*John M. Brewster*

## 5. PERPETUATING THE AGRARIAN DREAM

I take the Jeffersonian Dream to mean Jefferson's affection for and desire to establish and preserve an agriculture of freeholders— full-owner operators, debt-free, unrestricted by any contractual obligations to anyone— all in all, pretty much the monarchs of all they survey.

The freehold concept of the family farm was an unusually effective policy directive throughout most of the settlement era. Then

Reprinted from "The Relevance of the Jeffersonian Dream Today," by John M. Brewster in Howard W. Ottoson, ed., *Land Use Policy and Problems*, pp. 86-92, by permission of University of Nebraska Press. Copyright 1963 by the University of Nebraska Press.

the worm turned. An appreciable transformation of freeholders into debtors and tenants was noticeable by 1880. But since that date, the relevance of the Jeffersonian Ideal to present problems has continued to decline in the sense that it has failed to generate the kinds of policies and programs required to maintain a high approximation of a freeholder agriculture.

But we know that a predominantly family-farm agriculture has not disappeared; that the fostering of this institution remains an important objective of farm policy. In my judgement this will be the case for many years because the family farm is not on the way out, although some dangers confront it now as in the past. Naturally in taking this position I have in mind a definition, a concept, of the family farm. It is my gauge for what facts are relevant and what facts are not relevant to the issue.

As used here, a family farm is an agricultural business in which the operating family does most of the work and is a *manager* of ongoing operations of the business as well as a *risk-taker* in the outcome (financial returns) of the business venture. In this definition, *operatorship is equated with varying degrees of managerial power and with risk-taking involving management and production inputs, including labor.* As used here, managerial power is equated with the operator's prerogative to negotiate contracts and to make decisions concerning the combination of resources.

This definition applies to the Jeffersonian freeholder and the modern family farmer alike. In both cases, most of the farm work is done by the operating family who is a risk-taking manager in the outcome of the business. However, in the usual case, they differ substantially in their degree of risk-taking managerial power. The Jeffersonian freehold was a very high approximation of the self-sufficient firm. By this we mean a firm from which the will and interest of all conceivable participants in the business, except those of the operator, are totally excluded. In the self-sufficient firm, the operator alone is the sole risk-taker in the outcome of production activities he is guiding and coordinating. Thus the managerial power of the Jeffersonian freeholder was absolute, since he was totally independent of all commitments to outside parties concerning the way he used the resources of the firm and the kind of products it produced. In his managerial decisions, it was unnecessary to take account of the will or interest of another living soul. The Ages had always equated managers of self-sufficient firms as lords, the monarchs of all they surveyed.

But in industry, this self-sufficient firm disappeared as a representative institution with the close of the handicraft era, and agriculture has been making departures from it since about 1870. And each step in its progressive extinction has aroused new anxieties concerning the future of the family farm.

Yet farms on which operating families are risk-taking managers and do most of the work are not losing their relative position in American agriculture. I regard these as family farms. But usually the managerial power of their operators is not absolute; it is limited in varying degrees by contractual commitments of the operators with outside participants in the farm business, such as the landlord, the banker, the contractor seeking products of specified qualities, and even the government. Committing certain of their services to the operator, these outsiders seek legally binding commitments of the operator to follow certain lines of behavior as means of protecting them against loss of their stakes in the operator's business. The operator enters into these commitments because he believes the services of the outsiders will enable him to achieve a more profitable business than otherwise. Whether this proves to be the case turns on his abilities to guide and coordinate the operations of his business to a successful issue. No one would assume a modern road-builder not to be an independent operator simply because he agrees to produce a product that meets the specifications of his customers who send out inspectors to see if he is complying with the specifications he agreed to meet. We do not do so because his contract specifications do not negate the fact that he remains to some degree a risk-taking manager in the outcome of a business. The same principle applies to farming.

It may be that much of the confusion about what is meant by the family farm stems from the lack of a clear image of the operator's degree of risk-taking managerial power under the contractual foundations of modern farming. We know it lies somewhere between two extremes. It lies to the left of that absolute lordship which belonged to the self-sufficient firm that excludes all participants in the business except the operator, as did the Jeffersonian freeholder. It also lies to the right of the "directed worker" with whom the farm operator is sometimes equated in literature on "vertical integration." In line with this fact, I equate farm operators with managers and risk-takers in the outcome of their business undertakings, and then equate a family farm with a business in which the operating family does most of the farm work. By a larger-than-family farm, I mean any agricultural business whose total labor requirement is too great for the usual farm operating family to supply most of it.

One further definitional matter. In this paper I commonly use the term "proficient family farm." By this I mean a family business in agriculture with sufficient resources and productivity to yield income to meet expenses for (a) family living (b) farm expenses including depreciation, maintenance of the livestock herd, equipment, land, buildings, and interest on borrowed capital (c) enough capital growth for new farm investments required to keep in step with technological advance and rising levels of living. Farms without this level of resources and productivity are inadequate farms, and they are either disappearing or being supplemented by income from nonfarm sources, usually off-farm employment.

Proficient family farms may come into being through the reorganization of inadequate units or through hitherto larger-than-family farms falling into the category of family farms as a result of substituting capital for labor to the point where the operating family is able to do most of the farm work.

In using these concepts, I do not mean that they are *the* true ones—their status in this respect will turn on how useful they may prove to be as guides in measuring and interpreting the kinds and directions of changes now occurring among the business units of American agriculture. I expect to modify the concepts I am here using whenever further research investigations warrant it.

In these terms, we will have a family-farm agriculture so long as most of our farm production is done by business units in which operating families are risk-taking managers who do most of the work. In keeping with his times, Jefferson thought of the family farm in terms of the restricted freeholder meaning of the term. However, I believe it is in keeping with his larger spirit to expand his Dream to include contractual as well as highly self-sufficient firms like the freehold. In Jefferson's time, there was no conflict between an agriculture of proficient family farms and the need of opportunities for farm people. There is a severe conflict today, since only around one million such farms would be needed to supply all the foods and fibers which society wants at reasonable prices.

With these preliminary remarks in mind, these five major themes will be elaborated:

*First*: Since Colonial times, two distinct personal and policy-guiding beliefs have been indigenous to the farm and nonfarm sectors of our society. First is a deeply moving commitment to proficient work as the hallmark of praiseworthy character; the second is an equally firm belief in the natural or moral right of men to acquire all the property they can from the earnings of their work. The first of these commitments stemmed from the revolutionary interpretation of the ethical significance of proficient work by the religious reformers of the late sixteenth and seventeenth centuries, and was a complete reversal of ancient and medieval attitudes toward economic work. In line with this new sense of obligation, people soon found themselves producing beyond the limit required to support their customary needs. But in doing so, they ran into head-on conflict with the age-old belief that the natural or moral right of men to acquire property, as a fair reward for work, is limited to the amount required to produce their customary needs. John Locke, the greatest of the natural rights philosophers, resolved this conflict by demonstrating that the older belief was true only in very primitive, savage societies in which a money economy was totally absent.

*Second*: From early Colonial times, American settlers carried the radical belief in proficient work, as the badge of superior merit, alongside the equally radical Lockean belief in the natural or moral right of individuals to acquire as much property as they can from the earnings of their work. These directives have been stable motivations throughout both the settlement and postsettlement phases of our history.

Throughout the era of cheap land and relatively inexpensive farm technologies, these directives were a powerful generator of the Freeholder ideal to which the name of Jefferson is attached. For, if land is free or very cheap, obviously farm families can achieve a greater reward for their proficient work as debt-free, full-owner operators, than as renters, or as owners with varying degrees of credit obligations. This is not necessarily the case, however, if land is increasingly scarce and capital requirements of proficient farms are growing larger. As these conditions came to pass with the close of the settlement era, the same directives called for departures from the freeholds to contractual relationships with creditors, landlords, and others as means of achieving proficient farms. This separation between the farmer's actual status of limited managerial power and his hitherto absolute power was made sufferable by the new idea of an "agricultural ladder" that enabled farm people to envision their departures from the Freeholder Ideal as actual stepping stones to its fulfillment.

*Third*: Working hand in hand with the foregoing directives to a freeholder agriculture in the settlement era, was the carryover of the feudal aversion to tenantry and wage status as a badge of inferior character. More specifically, farmers demanded freeholds as the best means of enabling them to earn as much as they could as a fair reward for working as proficiently as they could, and they also demanded freeholds as the best possible means of escaping the ancient onus of tenantry and wage status as a badge of inferior character. But this "marriage of convenience" began disintegrating with the disappearance of cheap land and the increasing capital requirements of proficient farms. These conditions generated increasing conflict between the ancient devotion to the Freeholder Ideal with the more modern devotions to proficient work as a badge of personal excellence and to acquisition of as much earnings and property as one can get as fair reward for his proficiency. In this conflict, the age-old devotion to a freehold agriculture, as a citadel of superior virtue, proved an increasingly weak competitor.

*Fourth*: In developing the foregoing themes, emphasis is placed on the economic or materialistic implications of the ethical directive to proficient work at the expense of its larger humanitarian or idealistic implications. To correct this imbalance, we shall point out that the operation of this directive in American life not only has led the whole nation along remarkable paths of material progress, but has also enkindled a "practical idealism" which has long distinguished our people, and has infused the higher reaches of the spirit with the promise of the American Dream of what lies in store for men devoted to proficient use of their creative power. Furthermore, our historic commitment to proficient work, as tangible evidence of personal excellencies, includes commitments to distributive as well as commutative justice, both of which the plain man calls the "justice of equal opportunity." If we fail to counterbalance the economic import of our historic commitment to proficient work with its equally idealistic import, then with our own voice we convict ourselves of the common but false charge that America is the most materialistic civilization on earth. We shall seek to avoid this error.

*Fifth*: Our fifth theme concerns the current status and prospects of the family farm, considered as a business in which the operating (management and risk-taking) family does most of the work of the business they operate. . . .

### C. C. Hazewell

## 6. AGRARIANISM AS A TERM OF REPROACH

Over a long period of time the cultural divergencies of rural and urban life resulted in intercultural conflicts in which each developed to some extent a negative and suspicious view of the other. These negative aspects of the rural culture tended to become attached to the concept of agrarianism. As Alvin Johnson wrote in the *Encyclopaedia of the Social Sciences*, ". . . an agrarian movement under way is almost always characterized by violence of thought, and often violence of action." The rural view of the "city slicker" categorized him as a nonproductive idler and trickster. The cities were seats of vice. At this level of activity, the farmers sometimes sought affiliation with workingmen's protest movements which also took violent forms.

In the selection below, a conservative writer of the mid-nineteenth century attempts to picture American agrarianism as free from ideas and techniques of violence.

If we can believe an eminent authority, in which we are disposed to place great trust, the oldest contest that has divided society is that which has so long been waged between the House of HAVE and the House of WANT. It began before the bramble was chosen king of the trees, and it has outlasted the cedars of Lebanon. We find it going on when Herodotus wrote his History, and historians of the nineteenth century will have to continue writing of the actions of the parties to it. There seems never to have been a time when it was not old, or a race that was not engaged in it, from the Tartars, who cook their meat by making saddle-cloths of it, to the Sybarites, impatient of crumpled rose-leaves. Spartan oligarchs and Athenian democrats, Roman patricians and Roman plebeians, Venetian senators and Florentine *ciompi*, Norman nobles and Saxon serfs, Russian boyars and Turkish spahis, Spanish hidalgos and Aztec soldiers, Carolina slaveholders and New England farmers,—these and a hundred other races or orders have all been parties to the great, the universal struggle which has for its object the acquisition of property, the providing of a shield against the ever-threatening fiend which we call WANT. Property once obtained, the possessor's next aim is to keep it. The very fact, that the mode of acquisition may have been wrong, and subversive of property-

From "Agrarianism," in *The Atlantic Monthly*, vol. 3, no. 18 (April, 1859), pp. 393-397.

rights, if suffered to be imitated, naturally makes its possessor suspicious and cruel. He fears that the measure he has meted to others may be meted to him again. Hence severe laws, the monopoly of political power and of political offices by property-holders, the domination of conquering races, and the practice of attributing to all reformers designs against property and its owners, though the changes they recommend may really be of a nature calculated to make the tenure of property more secure than ever. Even the charge of irreligion has not been found more effective against the advocates of improvement or change than that of Agrarianism,—by which is meant hostility to existing property-institutions, and a determination, if possible, to subvert them. Of the two, the charge of Agrarianism is the more serious, as it implies the other. A man may be irreligious, and yet a great stickler for property, because a great owner of it,—or because he is by nature stanchly conservative, and his infidelity merely a matter of logic. But if there be any reason for charging a man with Agrarianism, though it be never so unreasonable a reason, his infidelity is taken for granted, and it would be labor lost to attempt to show the contrary. Nor is this conclusion so altogether irrational as it appears at the first sight. Religion is an ordinance of God, and so is property; and if a man be suspected of hostility to the latter, why should he not be held positively guilty towards the former? Every man is religious, though but few men govern their lives according to religious precepts; but every man not only loves property and desires to possess it, but allows considerations growing out of its rights to have a weight on his mind far more grave, far more productive of positive results, than religion has on the common person. If there be such a thing as an Agrarian on earth, he would fight bravely for his land, though it should be of no greater extent than would suffice him for a grave, according to the strictest measurement of the potter's field. Would every honest believer do as much for his religion?

But what is Agrarianism, and who are Agrarians? Though the words are used as glibly as the luring party-terms of the passing year, it is no very easy matter to define them. Indeed, it is by no means an easy thing to affix a precise and definite meaning to any political terms, living or dead. Let the reader endeavor to give a clear and intelligible definition of Whig and Tory, Democrat and Republican, Guelph and Ghibelline, Cordelier and Jacobin, and he will soon find that he has a task before him calculated to test his powers very severely. How much more difficult, then, must it be to give the meaning of words that are never used save in a reproachful sense, and which originated in political battles that were fought nearly two thousand years ago, and in a state of society having small resemblance to anything that has ever been known to Christendom! With some few exceptions, party-names continue to have their champions long after the parties they belonged to are as dead as the Jacobites. Many Americans would not hesitate to defend the Federalists, or to eulogize the Federal party, though Federalism long ago ceased even to cast a shadow. The prostitution of the Democratic name has lessened in but a slight degree the charm that has attached to it ever since Jefferson's sweeping re-election had the effect of coupling with it the charming idea of success. But who can be expected to say a word for Agrarian? One might as well look to find a sane man ready to do battle for the Jacobin, which is all but a convertible term for Agrarian, though in its proper sense the latter word is of exactly the opposite meaning to the former. Under the term Agrarians is included, in common usage, all that class of men who exhibit a desire to remove social ills by a resort to means which are considered irregular and dangerous by the great majority of mankind. Of late years we have heard much of Socialists, Communists, Fourierites, and so forth; but the word Agrarians comprehends all these, and is often made to include men who have no more idea of engaging in social reforms than they have of pilgrimizing to the Fountains of the Nile. It is a not uncommon thing for our political parties to charge one another with Agrarianism; and if they used the term in its proper sense, it would be found that they had both been occasionally right, for Agrarian laws have been supported by all American parties, and will continue to be so supported, we presume, so long as we shall have a public domain; but in its reproachful sense Agrarianism can never be charged against any one of the party organizations which have been known in the United States. A quarter of a century ago, one of the cleverest of those English tourists who then used to contrive to go through — or, rather, over — the Republic, seeing but little, and not understanding that little, proclaimed to his countrymen, who had not then recovered from the agitation consequent on the Reform contest, that there existed here a regular Agrarian party, forming "the *extreme gauche* of the Worky Parliament," and which "boldly advocated the introduction of an AGRARIAN LAW, and a periodical division of property." He represented these men as only following out the principles of their less violent neighbors, and as eloquently dilating "on the justice and propriety of every individual being equally supplied with food and clothing, — on the monstrous iniquity of one man riding in his carriage while another walks on foot, (there would have been more reason in the complaint, had the gigless individual objected to walking on his head,) and after his drive discussing a bottle of Champagne, while many of his neighbors are shamefully compelled to be content with the pure element. Only equalize property, they say, and neither would drink Champagne or water, but both would have brandy, a consummation worthy of centuries of struggle to attain." He had the sense to declare that all this was nonsense, but added, that the Agrarians, though not so numerous or so widely diffused as to create immediate alarm, were numerous in New York, where their influence was strongly felt in the civic elections. Elsewhere he predicted the coming of a "panic" time, when workingmen would be thrown out of employment, while possessed of the whole political power of the state, with no military force to maintain civil order and protect property; "and to what quarter," he mournfully asked, "I shall be glad to know, is the rich man to look for security, either of person or fortune?"

Twenty-five years have elapsed since Mr. Hamilton put forth this alarming question, and some recent events have brought it to men's minds, who had laughed at it in the year of grace 1833. We have seen Agrarian movements in New York, demonstrations of "Workies," but nothing was said by those engaged in them of that great leveller, brandy, though its properties are probably better known to them than those of water. They have been dignified with the name of "bread riots," and the great English journal that exercises a sort of censorship over governments and nations has gravely complimented us on the national progress we have made, as evidenced in the existence here of a starving population! One hardly knows whether to fret or to smile over so provoking a specimen of congratulation. Certainly, if a nation cannot grow old without bringing the producing classes to beggary, the best thing that could happen to it would be to die young, like men loved of the gods, according to the ancient idea. Whether such is the inevitable course of national life or not, we are confident that what took place a few months ago in New York had nothing to do with Agrarianism in reality, — using the word after the manner of the alarmists. It belonged to the ordinary bald humbug of American politics. It so happened that one of those "crises" which come to pass occasionally in all business communities occurred at precisely the time when a desperate political adventurer was making desperate efforts to save himself from that destruction to which he had been doomed by all good men in the city that he had misgoverned. What more natural than that he should seek to avail himself of the distress of the people? The trick is an old one, — as old as political contention itself. Was it not Napoleon who attributed revolutions to the belly? — and he knew something of the matter. The "bread riots" were neither more nor less than "political demonstrations," got up for the purpose of aiding Mr. Wood, and did not originate in any hostility to property on the part of the people. It is not improbable that some of those who were engaged in them were really anxious to obtain work,— were moved by fear of starvation; but such was not the case with the leaders, who were "well-dressed, gentlemanly men," according to an eye-witness, with excellent cigars in their mouths to create a thirst that Champagne alone could cure. The *justemilieu* of brandy, so favored in 1832, if we can believe Mr. Hamilton, was not thought of in 1857. A quarter of a century had made a change in the popular taste. Perhaps the temperance reformation had had something to do with it. The whole thing was as complete a farce as ever was seen at an American or an English election, and those who were engaged in it are now sincerely ashamed—of their failure. If foreigners will have it that it was an outbreak of Agrarianism, the first in a series of outrages against property, so be it. Let them live in the enjoyment of the delusion. Nations, like individuals, seem to find pleasure in the belief that others are as miserable as themselves.

Of that feeling which is known as Agrarianism we believe that there is far less in the United States now than there was at the time when Mr. Hamilton was here, and for a few years after that time. From about the year 1829 to 1841, there was in our politics a large infusion of Socialism. We then had parties, or factions, based on the distinctions that exist in the social state, and those organizations had considerable influence in our elections. The Workingmen's party was a powerful body in several Northern States, and, to an observer who was not familiar with our condition, it well might wear the appearance of an Agrarian body. No intelligent American, however, fell into such an error. It was evident to the native observer, that the Workingmen's party, while aiming at certain reforms which it deemed necessary for the welfare of the laboring classes, had no felonious purposes in view to the prejudice of property,—and this for the plain reason, that most workingmen were property-owners themselves. Few of them had much, but still fewer had nothing, and the aggregate of their possessions was immense. They would have been the greatest losers, had there been a social convulsion, for they would have lost everything. Then they were intelligent men in the ordinary affairs of life, and knew that the occurrence of any such convulsion would, first of all, cut off, not only their means of acquisition, but the very sources of their livelihood. Industry wilts under revolutionary movements, as vegetation under the sirocco, and they bring to the multitude anything but a realization of Utopian dreams. In the long run, there has rarely been a revolution which has not worked beneficially for the mass of mankind; but the earliest effects of every revolution are to them bad, and eminently so. It is to this fact that we must look for an explanation of the slowness with which the masses move against any existing order of things, even when they are well aware that it treats them with singular injustice. For nothing can be better established than that no revolution was ever the work of the body of the people,—of the majority. Revolutions are made by minorities, by orders, by classes, by individuals, but never by the people. The people may be dragged into them, but they never take the initiative even in those movements which are called popular, and which are supposed to have only popular ends in view. That very portion of mankind who are most feared by timid men of property are those who are the last to act in any of the great games which mark the onward course of the world. Complain they do, and often bitterly, of the inequalities of society, but action is not their strong point.

The American observer of 1829–41 would have seen, too, in the Workingmen's party, and in other similar organizations, only sections of the Democratic party. They were the light troops of the grand army of Democracy, the *velites* who skirmished in front of the legions. They never controlled the Democratic party; but it is undeniable that they did color its policy, and give a certain tone to its sentiment, at a very important period of American history. The success of President Jackson, in that political contest which is known as the "Bank War," was entirely owing to the support which he received from the workingmen of some two or three States; and it is quite probable that the shrewd men who then managed the Democratic party were induced to enter upon that war by their knowledge of the exalted condition of political opinion in those States. For their own purposes, they turned to account sentiments that might have worked dangerously, if they had not been directed against the Bank. One effect of this was, that the Democratic party was compelled to make use of more popular language, which caused it to lose some of its influential members, who were easily alarmed by words, though they had borne philosophically with violent things. For five years after the veto of the Bank Bill, in 1832, the Democratic party was essentially radical in its tone, without doing much of a radical character. In 1837, the monetary troubles came to

a head, and then it was seen how little reliance could be placed on men who were supposed to be attached to extreme popular opinions. It was in the very States which were thought to abound with radicals that the Democracy lost ground, and the way was prepared for their entire overthrow in the memorable year 1840. That year saw American politics debauched, and from that time we find no radical element in any of our parties. The contest was so intense, that the two parties swallowed and digested all lesser factions. Since then, a variety of causes have combined to prevent the development of what is termed Agrarianism. The struggle of the Democracy to regain power; the Mexican war, and the extension of our dominion, consequent on that war, bringing up again, in full force, the slavery question; and the discovery of gold in California, which led myriads of energetic men to a remote quarter of the nation;—these are the principal causes of the freedom of our later party-struggles from radical theories. From radical practices we have always been free, and it is improbable that our country will know them for generations. . . .

# II. *The American Frontier and Land Policy: 1840–1860*

The concept of agricultural fundamentalism was well expressed by Jesse Buel in 1838, when he wrote that ". . . agriculture . . . constitutes the base which supports the whole superstructure of civilized society." The economic and social development of a nation, according to this argument, was dependent upon the improvement of her agricultural system. Improvement in agriculture was, therefore, a public responsibility; government policies should encourage improvement by education and other appropriate means.

Throughout the nineteenth-century, the western frontier played a major role in shaping agrarian values. The notion that agriculture was the support of all other human endeavors was not lost in the westward movement; on the contrary, it was strengthened. As development proceeded behind the frontier, moreover, agrarian values gave evidence of their durability. Land policy was clearly one of the most important factors in these areas. Unquestionably affected by classical and fundamentalist agrarianism, government policies made its values operable even as commerce, industry, and new cities sprang up.

The basic land policy of the federal government was that the federal lands should be transferred to private ownership. The conditions controlling the transfer were guided by the tenets of Jefferson and the continuing doctrine of agricultural fundamentalism. These guidelines suggested that ownership of a farm of a size suitable for supporting a family should be readily attainable and that the acquisition of great estates should not be encouraged.

The public land domain of the United States was a vast natural resource, a treasure which the government sought to distribute among its citizens. The process was complicated and very difficult, although it was easier distributing the land than determining to what extent and by what means subsequent land development should be promoted. The distribution of so much wealth naturally attracted a great amount of speculation and the "one-man, one-farm" formula was consistently breached. Veterans of the War of 1812 were granted land without requiring proof of occupancy, hence these tracts were frequently sold to speculators. The policy was perpetuated by similar statutes granting veterans warrants entitling them to certain amounts of land in unspecified locations. By purchasing the warrants, speculators obtained much of the land granted originally to veterans.

To the extent that land passed into the hands of intermediaries with objectives other than the development of family farms, the program of land distribution miscarried. Speculators, large and small, converged on the public lands, diluting the interest in agricultural development with that of making a quick resale profit.

Besides those who bought land, either for speculation or settlement, were many who migrated west and settled or "squatted" on land, asserting preemptive rights to ownership. Forbidden by Congress in 1807, the prior right of the squatter to buy 160 acres of the land upon which he had settled at the minimum price set by the government was by 1841 recognized in law. The squatters themselves, of course, were not always free from the speculative urge. Oftentimes they found ways of purchasing more than 160 acres, frequently going into debt to do so. Imperfect as the functioning of the system was, the myth of Jeffersonian agrarianism was perpetuated.

The historical literature on United States public land policy is extensive, and no effort is made here to do more than relate it to its background. Reference may be made to Benjamin F. Hibbard, *History of the Public Land Policies* (New York: The Macmillan Company, 1924); Roy M. Robbins, *Our Landed Heritage: The Public Domain 1776-1936.* (Princeton: Princeton University Press, 1924); George M. Stephenson, *Political History of the Public Lands from 1840-1862* (Boston: R. G. Badger, 1917); and Thomas Donaldson, *The Public Domain*, House Miscellaneous Documents, 47th Congress, 2nd Session, No. 45, Part 4, 1884.

*Harry J. Carman*

## 7. ON THE NECESSITY AND MEANS OF IMPROVING OUR HUSBANDRY

In his paper delivered before the New York State Agricultural Convention in 1838, Jesse Buel emphasized the need for aricultural education. His argument is that the "whole superstructure of civilized society" rests upon agriculture, therefore the government must take steps to keep it strong and improving.

This statement is revealing because it reveals the continuing sense of fear that agriculture was beginning to deteriorate and would carry downward with it our free institutions.

Jesse Buel was one of the leading spokesmen of his day for agricultural development. The selection below is from his paper read before the New York State Agricultural Convention, February 1, 1838, and reprinted in *The Cultivator*, Vol. V (March, 1838), pages 28-29.

We cannot be too often reminded of the contrast which exists between good and bad husbandry, nor too often admonished to search into the causes of this difference and to apply the needful remedies. The difference does not consist alone in a single crop, or a single season: the soil in one case is becoming more and more exhausted of fer-

From Harry J. Carman, *Jesse Buel: Agricultural Reformer* (New York: Columbia University Press, 1947), pp. 8-12, 15-21. Reprinted by permission of Columbia University Press.

tility, and losing its intrinsic value, while in the other its relative worth is on the increase, and the difference in product is consequently annually increasing. . . .

Now, what has been our progress during the last sixty years? Has it not been retrograde in agriculture? We have, to be sure, obtained abundant crops from our rich virgin soils, and when these have become exhausted under bad management we have occupied and exhausted others in their turn. But what is the condition *now* of the lands that were cultivated by our fathers half a century ago? Do *they* produce the average crops which are given above as the products of Scotch husbandry under all our favorable circumstances of climate and civil liberty? Are our crops *half* as large? Nay, are they more than a *third* as large? Do we get from our old districts an average of more than 10 to 13 bushels of wheat, or 14 to 17 of barley, or of 17 to 21 bushels of oats per acre? At the close of the last and in the beginning of the present century, the surplus products of northern agriculture were *exported*, to an immense amount. Now we *import* the agricultural products of Europe to avert the evils of famine! The cause of this remarkable difference in the surplus products of the soil may be partially owing to unpropitious seasons, but is mainly to be sought for in the neglect of our agriculture — both by the people and the governments. In Europe, the governments and influential individuals have bestowed spirited attention upon the improvement of agriculture, as constituting the basis of national prosperity and independence; while with us improvement in husbandry has been considered a minor concern — it at least has not received the consideration of the statesman or the political economist. Party politics and local or personal schemes of aggrandizement have so much engrossed the attention of the men who *ought* to lead in these matters, and who *do* lead in every other public improvement, that the humble claims of agriculture have failed to attract their notice or engage their attention, although it constitutes the base which supports the whole superstructure of

civilized society. If we would preserve the superstructure with its embellishments, we must take care to make strong and permanent this foundation. Our farmers, too, seem generally indifferent or spiritless in regard to the general improvement of our agriculture, either because they mistake their duty and true interest or that, under the influence of a strange fatuity, they fear they shall sink as others rise.

We should consider our soil as we do our free institutions, *a patrimonial trust to be handed down,* UNIMPAIRED, *to posterity;* to be *used,* but not *abused.* Both are more easily impaired than they are restored; both belong, in their pristine vigor and purity, as much to our children as they do to us. In some of the once populous and fertile districts of the old continent, the fertility of the soil has been recklessly wasted by men whose descendants have, consequently, become poor and wretched, and their country almost virtually a desert. In other portions, where the fertility of the soil has been sedulously preserved for ages, or centuries, the population has continued prosperous, wealthy, and happy.

It is undeniably true that our general system of farming is bad; that in most parts of our country the natural fertility of the soil has been gradually diminishing and its products becoming less; that the evil is increasing; and, that without a radical reform we shall, in the north, not only cease to have surplus products to pay for the foreign commodities which long habit has rendered necessary to our convenience, but lack a supply of bread stuffs for our own population. To what degrading dependence will this course of things in a few years reduce us, unless prompt and efficient means are adopted to check our down-hill course in the products of agricultural labor! With the finest country in the world, a population almost entirely agricultural — exempt from the enormous burthens, as tithes, rents and poor rates, which press like an incubus upon the agricultural labor of Europe — and dependent on foreign supplies for the means of subsistence!! The idea is humiliating, is alarming, to all who look to the ultimate prosperity and happiness of our country. Our maritime commerce depends upon contingencies which we can neither foresee nor control. Venice and Genoa, and Portugal and Spain, have each in turn had their "days of commercial prosperity"; they successively rose to opulence, to power, and successively sunk, the victims of corruption, into effeminacy, vice, and despotism. Manufactures too, as we have had abundant cause to know, are but a precarious dependence for national greatness. Commerce and manufactures are the shaft and capital of the social column, of which agriculture constitutes the base; and without this base, they can no more withstand the shocks and revolutions of time than could the short-lived glory of the nations we have named. Great Britain now wields the trident, and the world is made tributary to her workshops. But great as she is in commerce and in manufactures, these are considered secondary and auxiliary to her agricultural greatness. Land is the basis of her national wealth; it is the surplus marketable produce of her soil, says Sir John Sinclair, that is the source of all her political power and of the personal enjoyment of her citizens; and there is no source of domestic industry, or of foreign commerce, he adds, that can in any respect be put in competition with the improved cultivation of her soil. The agriculture of Great Britain employs but two thirds of her population; and yet the surplus products of her soil suffice to feed and support the other third and to assist in supplying our deficiencies. Our population is at least five sixths agricultural; yet during the two last years we have had to import about ten millions' worth of bread stuffs to supply our deficiency in this first element of life; and even in the most favorable seasons, the exports of the surplus products of our northern soil have been merely nominal.

We will state one fact, derived from official documents, which will demonstrate beyond the power of refutation our downhill course in this great branch of national industry. It is this: the average increase of bread stuffs, passing from our canals to tide waters, from the great grain district of the west—from the Flanders of America—has amounted to three and three quarters per cent; while our population has increased in the ratio of six per cent per annum! If such has been the deficiency in our grain-growing, new and fertile districts, to meet the wants of our increasing population, how much greater must that deficiency have been in the exhausted soils of old, settled districts? Many portions of our country which once exported grain have, by bad husbandry, become dependent upon the comparatively new settlements, or upon foreign supplies, for this indispensable necessary of life. This remark will apply to almost our entire Atlantic border. Will any mathematician tell us how long it will require, according to the disproportionate ratio of increase between our population and our means of subsistence, to reduce us to a state of absolute dependence? or, to a state of national want and famine? . . .

We may almost lay it down as a maxim, that THE MENTAL AND MORAL CONDITION OF AN AGRICULTURAL DISTRICT IS IN THE RATIO OF ITS IMPROVEMENT IN HUSBANDRY. To borrow the spirit of a political saying, *as goes agriculture, so goes the state.* There is certainly much truth in the remark that where the farming is slovenly and bad, ignorance, indolence, and vice most generally abound; and that where agricultural improvement is most advanced, the population are most industrious, most intelligent, and most moral. Knowledge begets a love of knowledge; and when a man has acquired enough of it to convince him of its utility in his business he considers it a part of his farming capital, and he is anxious to increase his stock of it, as the readiest means of improving his condition in life, independent of the mental pleasures which it imparts. But not having acquired the requisite degree to enable him to appreciate its value, or to show him the defects of his system of management, he plods on, with listless indifference, in the ways of his fathers; and as great success nowadays seldom rewards such labors, he too often becomes spiritless and dissatisfied, and relaxes into indolence, of which vice is too frequently the concomitant.

Under the existing state of things, how does it become us to act? What are we to do? Shall we fold our arms, leave agriculture to decline further or to shift for itself, and depend upon more propitious seasons and other Providential interpositions to supply our wants? Shall we depend upon the cotton, rice, and tobacco of the south, which constitute our almost entire exports, to pay for the foreign commodities which we consume in the north? Or shall we, animated by the enterprise and love of independence which were wont to animate our fathers, take in hand resolutely to provide abundantly for ourselves by encouraging and enlightening agriculture, elevating its character, and stimulating it to new efforts, by suitable honors and rewards?

As regards the means of improvement, much has been done, and much is doing, by the agricultural periodicals of the day. The first of these was established at Baltimore by John S. Skinner[1] in 1819; and we can now enumerate nearly twenty that are diffusing light, awakening enterprise, and inciting to industry, in every section of our country. Probably one hundred thousand farmers are now deriving instruction and improving their practice by the perusal of these journals; and it is not extravagant to say that the benefits they are dispensing to the nation are equivalent to millions of dollars every year. But what is one hundred thousand compared to the gross agricultural population of the union? and how much greater

would be their benefits if these journals had access to every farmhouse, or even to every schoolhouse, in the state? Besides giving much that is useful in the science or the first principles of husbandry, they are continually advertising their readers of every improvement which is being made in the practical operations of the farm—of new seeds, and plants, and the mode of cultivating them, and of every improvement in labor-saving machines. In twelve numbers of *The Cultivator* may be noticed more than a hundred and twenty communications, mostly from practical farmers residing in the different states, detailing their practice in different departments of husbandry, thus making their improvements known, in a short time, to its twenty thousand patrons.

By thus concentrating, as it were in a focus, the practical knowledge of the country and then scattering it like the solar rays into every corner of the land, to fructify the earth, and by thus rendering it subservient to the benefit of all, some individuals have been enabled to obtain a clear profit of fifty, one hundred, and even one hundred and fifty dollars on an acre of corn, or an acre of Swedish turnips, who had never before obtained a profit of thirty dollars an acre from either. And the benefits of these splendid results are not confined to the individuals who effected them; they are heralded in the agricultural journals; become known all over the country; and every new and successful effort at improvement soon has its fifty, its hundred, and its thousand imitators. Suppose, for instance, what we hope will yet prove true, that an individual should discover an effectual preventive of the ravages of the Hessian fly, or grain worm; instead of benefitting him and a few neighbors, or becoming gradually known as in olden times, the knowledge of it would now be spread in a few days, by the agricultural periodicals, into every corner of the land, and the advantages of the discovery would thus amount to millions in a single year. So with every other improvement in husbandry. It is not the province nor is it the study of news journals and literary edi-

[1] *The American Farmer*, pioneer American farm journal, was established on April 2, 1819 in Baltimore, Maryland, by John Stuart Skinner, lawyer and government official. Not only did it deal with almost every conceivable agricultural subject but with all sorts of extraneous subjects which Skinner thought would have appeal to farm families. Internal improvements were especially stressed. From the beginning, *The American Farmer* had the enthusiastic cooperation of agricultural societies throughout the country. Among its more able contributors were John Taylor of Caroline, Thomas Jefferson, James Madison, John C. Calhoun, Timothy Pickering, Henry Clay, James M. Garnett, General H. A. S. Dearborn, Sir John Sinclair, Thomas W. Coke, and General Lafayette. *The American Farmer* ceased publication in 1834, four years after Skinner deemed it advisable to dispose of his interest in it. See A. L. Demaree, *The American Agricultural Press, 1819-1860* (New York, 1941), pp. 23-38.

tors to deal extensively in agricultural concerns. They seldom publish even the incidental notices which are designed to subserve the interests of husbandry, without a special request, and a fee in the bargain, as though *they* had no personal interest in the progress of agricultural improvement. We would infer from these premises that every man will promote his interest, and benefit the public, by patronising and endeavoring to extend the circulation of our agricultural papers. They tend to no possible evil, while they are certainly calculated to do much public good.

Another means of facilitating agricultural improvement is to introduce class books into our common schools, for the senior boys, which shall teach those elementary principles of science which are indispensable to the successful practice of agriculture. A boy may be almost as easily taught to analyze soils and to comprehend the leading principles of animal and vegetable physiology as he can commit to memory pages of matter the knowledge of which seldom serves him any useful purpose in manhood. We must begin in youth, if we would bring about any material improvement in the habits of society. The good seed that is sown in the springtime of life is never lost; it will ultimately sprout and grow, and give its increase, as surely as the grain which we deposit in a fertile soil. The tree *will* grow as the twig is bent. Youth is the season to get instruction in the principles of the business which is to constitute the employment of life; and the more the knowledge which boys acquire in these principles before they start life for themselves, the more likely they are to prosper and become useful to society. The time that the senior boys in school devote to the business of the farm, will give to studies which are connected with their present and future business an interest and an influence which will be as abiding as life.

But we would go farther in the business of agricultural instruction; we would establish schools to teach, simultaneously, both the theory and practice of agriculture. We would carry something of the theory into

the primary schools, and much of the practice into the schools of science. Veterinary schools, to instruct in the anatomy and management of domestic animals, have long been established in Europe; their usefulness has been highly extolled and their numbers are increasing. Switzerland, Prussia, and France have also their schools in which the science and practice of agriculture are taught to hundreds of young men, who are thereby enabled to manage their estates, with greater benefit to themselves and the public, or to obtain honorable and lucrative situations as managers for others. We give bounties on our fisheries to make them a nursery of seamen; but we give none upon agriculture, which is the best nursery of freemen. We spend millions annually to protect our commerce; but we give nothing to improve agriculture, which is the basis and support of that commerce. We protect our manufactures by a heavy tariff; yet agriculture, which furnishes the raw materials and buys the fabrics which the manufacturer consumes and vends, is left to protect itself. We have expended nearly three millions in this state to aid in educating almost exclusively professional and other gentlemen; and yet we have given nothing exclusively to educate our agriculturists, who constitute the great mass of our population. And yet there is probably no employment in life capable of being more benefited by a professional education — none in which a professional education would conduce more to the public prosperity — than that of managing our farms. A proper knowledge of soils, manures, vegetables and animals, of the agency of caloric, of moisture, of the atmosphere, and of light, in the economy of vegetable and animal growth, are all of great use to the farmer, and yet in what existing school can he acquire this knowledge during the period of life which he ought to obtain his practical knowledge? . . .

It has been stated as an objection to the establishment of agricultural schools that they would be only accessible to the rich. This objection, even if well founded, would not go to lessen their value to the state. For if we could convert a few hundred drones, as the sons of rich men may generally be termed, into working bees, the public, as well as the young men themselves, would certainly be gainers by the transformation. The complaint is that we have too many consumers and too few producers. This would tend to restore an equilibrium. For the example of the rich, be they good or bad, have an imposing influence on the middling and lower classes; and thus to improve the habits and morals of the rich would be the surest way to improve the condition of society. Hence, therefore, if agricultural schools can be instrumental in annually converting a few hundred of the idle and dissipated sons of wealth — or rather in preserving them from these habits — into wholesome industrious farmers, agricultural pursuits will be more respectable and more followed; and we venture to predict that then we shall not long continue to do what we have done, import potatoes from Ireland and Germany, hay and oats from Scotland, eggs from France, and bread stuffs from all the countries of Europe, including the dominions of the autocrat of Russia and of the Grand Turk.

But it is not exactly true that the rich alone would find access into agricultural schools, were such established. The rich rely upon their paternal wealth and have not often the ambition to become useful, at least by the habits of manual labor, which would be rigidly required in such schools. The schools would be filled with the youth, from all classes of society, who aspired to fortune and independence by a manly exercise of their mental and physical powers; the young men of this description, even from the poorer classes, do obtain admission into literary institutions, and they would into agricultural ones with greater facility (because the terms of admission here would be more reasonable) and with equal prospect of distinction and usefulness in after life. But whether these schools should be filled from the rich or poorer classes, or, as we have supposed, from all classes indiscriminately, a certain and great public good would result from their establishment: the pupils would go to swell the producing classes of society, with habits of application and usefulness, minds imbued with scientific knowledge, bodies hale and robust, and hands practiced in all the manual operations of the farm.

It verily seems to us certain that, if the importance of the subjects which we have discussed could be justly appreciated by the community at large, every class of our citizens would concur in the propriety of a united effort to improve the condition of our husbandry and of speedily adopting the measures we have suggested, or others equally availing, to produce the desired result.

*Frederick L. Paxson*

## 8. THE AMERICAN FRONTIER

For more than a century the American western frontier was one of the most significant facts in American history. Its immediate relevance to agricultural development is obvious, although the "farmers' frontier" is only one of several that marked the growth of the United States.

The American frontier was a line, a region, or a process, according to the context in which the word is used. As a *process*, its most significant meaning is found. A universal common task was impressing its standardizing influence upon all the people who came within its reach. Everywhere on the frontier civilization was being manufactured out of raw material and personnel. Few persons came to the frontier except to make homes for themselves, and to stake their hardihood and fortune against the chances of isolation and hardship. Most of them had little to hope for in their older homes, and made the emigration to advance their chances and their children's. For the interval between two generations, in any frontier region, the typical life was that of the frontier farmer clearing his field and building his cabins. The immediate family needs came first, then came the group—the school and the church, local government and statehood—and the crafts of industrial supply followed the more primitive ones of agriculture. After the lapse of twenty or twenty-five years these needs had ordinarily been met in any typical frontier region, and the first-born children of the early household had grown to maturity and gone off in couples to a newer frontier to repeat their parents' experience. In the multiple experience of this, at every crossroads in America, through nearly three centuries,

each generation has in turn been able to challenge the social values of the common heritage, and to modify its institutions to fit the shifting need. History has here more nearly repeated itself than in the other experiences of the past. This was a social laboratory for the mixed races that thronged the continent. The frontier process and its consequences give the special meaning to American life.

\* \* \*

In analyzing the psychology of the West, it must never be lost sight of that the persistent fight with nature made of the pioneer an individual with sharply developed peculiarities. It is a nice question whether the equalitarian or the individualizing forces were the weightier. The one condition that the pioneer could not get away from was the oppressive similarity of his life with that of his neighbors. He had a tendency to suffer from whatever affected them; and when by chance he escaped the epidemics of thought or condition that swept the West, his instinct of imitation made him often assume the condition he lacked. He resented the equality, but shrank from standing out as different. He was keenly resentful of anything that seemed like coercion, but saw nothing inconsistent in being intolerant of the habits or opinions

From Frederick L. Paxson, *History of the American Frontier, 1763-1893* (New York: Houghton Mifflin Co., 1924), pp. 43-44, 251-252. Reprinted by permission of the publishers.

of others. The uniformity of frontier life did not make for toleration.

His intense individuation made him likely to admire those who seemed to have the traits that he admired in himself. The dueling code survived longest in the parts of the United States in which frontier roughness lasted longest. In part this may have been due to a real need for self-help and to the fact that the man who was quickest on the trigger finished the fight. But it was equally due to the intense sensitiveness bred by loneliness and equality. He could not bear the thought that another might look down upon him. He could see the extra loneliness that peculiarities brought to certain individuals and was quick to resent any slur or fancied slight. The frontier rather admired Burr for his duel with Hamilton. It never thought less of Jackson because he carried in his body for a quarter of a century a bullet he had stopped in an altercation with the Bentons in 1813. Popularity was easily built up upon hero worship, and the best hero was he who had no traits that the frontier could not understand.

The equalitarian conditions thus bred a dislike of superiority; and the individuation produced a high regard for those in whom it was most pronounced. There was also in the western character, and quite as firmly grounded in experience as either of these, an expansive trait that the word idealism only roughly describes.

The successful pioneer lived a life of progress. He began with untouched nature, and each year saw a larger area of cleared lands, a better group of buildings, a more selected herd of stock, and greater freedom due to increase in financial resources. The young and poor bore their lot the better because of the firm conviction that they were some day to be established and rich. There was no class of permanent farm labor-ers, and almost no certain domestic help. There were no barriers of caste to prevent a man from rising in the esteem of his community; and in spite of the language of democratic equality, influence was largely based upon attainment. The habit of believing in personal progress and growth had a parallel in the certitude of social progress and development. The first scattered farmers of a region knew that they were to become leaders in local and county government; that improvements would surely come; that statehood was inevitable. The mature men were entitled to believe that the senatorial toga might descend upon them; and they brought up their boys in the belief that any of them might be President. The American worship of the self-made man has been founded in this general knowledge that most Americans were in the beginning self-made. The frontier citizens saw the forest and prairie melting before the attack of the advancing farms. They saw the Indians recede towards further western homes. They heard that the United States was moving its empire west. Only the conviction that the country beyond the Missouri was worthless kept them at the beginning of the nineteenth century, from visualizing the United States as a continental power. But they took for granted the idea that progress and expansion would come as needed. And none of them shied at a new idea merely because it had not yet come to pass. The life of change and growth they lived made them natural expansionists and idealists. And when they came together on their local feast days, the Fourth of July, or Washington's Birthday, or the anniversary of New Orleans, their orators let their fancy play around that future greatness of themselves which all conceded. The stabler communities, with less mobility for the individual, kept their fancies closer to the ground.

*Henry Nash Smith*

## 9. THE MIXED ECONOMY

To the extent that the agrarian idea has persisted, it has done so in a society that turned boldly to urbanism and industrialism. Had its continuance depended upon a western section characterized by primitive agriculture the myth could not have endured. Its survival was conditioned by the growth of cities and industrial life. The way in which these factors impressed agricultural development as early as the 1830's is the subject of the piece that follows.

The system of political economy that developed was one of unquestionable strength and vigor. The maintenance of an agricultural system commensurate with the burgeoning commerce and industry of the Mississippi valley and the Great Lakes area was due in large measure to the implanted agrarian values and the belief in the fundamental support given to civilized life by agriculture.

The very fertility of the Northwest posed a dilemma with respect to the agrarian ideal. The hardy yeoman came out into the wilderness seeking land, and his search was rewarded: he acquired title to his farm and reared his numerous children amid the benign influences of forest and meadow. But the land was so fertile and the area under cultivation increased so rapidly that a surplus of grain and livestock quickly appeared, and the Western farmer was no longer content within the primitive pattern of subsistence agriculture.

Timothy Flint noted this problem as early as 1827: everyone who was willing to work had an abundance of the articles which the soil produced, far beyond the needs of the country, and it was a prevalent complaint in the Ohio Valley that this abundance greatly exceeded the chances of profitable sale. A farmer who wants access to markets becomes interested in internal improvements. He agitates for highways and canals, for improved navigation of the rivers, and later for railways. Developing commerce creates depots like Cincinnati and Louisville— cities in the wilderness. The cities have banks and at least rudimentary manufactures such as the packing industry, and eventually it is they rather than the farming communities that set the tone of the West.

The rapid growth of cities and the development of an elaborate transportation system presaged a time when the West—at least the older West of the Ohio Valley and the Great Lakes—would no longer be predominantly agricultural. This process led to a greater and greater disparity between the agrarian ideal cherished by the society and the changing facts of its economic organization. The agrarian ideal had supplanted mercantilist theory in the latter part of the eighteenth century because at that time it had corresponded more closely to the actual state of affairs in the North American interior and had provided a much more reliable basis for charting the course of Western history in the immediate future. One index to its adequacy was the vigor and persuasive power of the symbol of the yeoman that had been developed from its premises. But by the 1830's a new calculus and new symbols were required to interpret the new West that was being created by force wholly foreign to the agrarian assumptions. The greatest of the new forces was the technological revolution which set loose the power of steam — in boats on the western waters, somewhat later in railways, and eventually in factories. Steam power hastened the transition from subsistence to commercial agriculture, caused the accumulation of capital in units of unprecedented size, transformed the older western cities, and created new cities on a metropolitan scale like Cleveland and Chicago. These changes spelled the end of the simple economy which in the first stages of settlement had corresponded at least approximately to the agrarian ideal. In the long run the virtuous yeoman could no more stand his ground against the developing capitalism of merchant and banker and manufacturer in the Northwest than he could against the plantation system in the Southwest.

But the disparity between the static agrarian ideal and the drive of economic change was by no means clear to contemporary observers. Amos Stoddard, for example, the Massachusetts lawyer and veteran of the Revolution whom Jefferson appointed first governor of Louisiana, was equally enthusiastic over the future agricultural development of the vast regions on the Mississippi and the splendid tokens of industry and commerce which they would exhibit. The prophetic picture of the West drawn in 1815 by Daniel Drake, a Cincinnati physician with an interest in social science, has much in common with Stoddard's:

... the opinion that these states cannot support even a denser population than any in the East, is altogether groundless; the associations of wildness and ferocity — ignorance and vice, which the mention of this distant land has hitherto excited, must ere long be dissolved; and our Atlantic brethren will behold with astonishment, in the green and untutored states of the West, an equipoise for their own. Debarred, by their locality, from an inordinate participation in foreign luxuries, and consequently secured from the greatest

corruption introduced by commerce — secluded from foreign intercourse, and thereby rendered patriotic — compelled to engage in manufactures, which must render them independent — secure from conquest, or even invasion, and therefore without the apprehensions which prevent the expenditure of money in solid improvements — possessed of a greater proportion of freehold estates than any people on earth, and of course made industrious, independent and proud; — the inhabitants of this region are obviously destined to an unrivalled excellence in agriculture, manufactures and internal commerce; in literature and the arts; in public virtue, and in national strength.

[The West, in other words, can have everything; it does not need to choose among good ends.]

The contemporary attitude toward the introduction of steam transportation upon the western waters illustrates the general failure to comprehend the magnitude of the new forces. Timothy Flint, for example, saw in the internal commerce of the valley merely a means of extending the society of virtuous yeomen over a wider area. He depended on the old agrarian calculus, for which the technological novelties of canals and steamboats and railways had no real meaning. Few of his contemporaries were able to see into the future more clearly than he did. It is true that John Filson in the 1780's and Gilbert Imlay in the 1790's had understood that the experimental steamboat of James Rumsey of Virginia might be highly valuable for Kentucky. And beneath the dazzled awe with which backwoodsmen greeted the first snorting river monsters there was a dim intimation of what these machines might do to the shape of society in the West. Morgan Neville of Pittsburgh and Cincinnati wrote in James Hall's *Western Souvenir* in 1829:

The rudest inhabitant of our forest ... is struck with the sublime power and self-moving majesty of a steamboat; — lingers on the shore where it passes — and follows its rapid, and almost magic course with silent admiration. The steam-engine in five years has enabled us to anticipate a state of things, which, in the ordinary course of events, it would have required a century to have produced. The art of printing scarcely surpassed it in its beneficial consequences.

39

[Yet it was natural to be impressed most of all, as Flint was, by the sheer picturesqueness of the steamboat.] In 1827 he wrote:

An Atlantic cit, who talks of us under the name of backwoodsmen, would not believe, that such fairy structures of oriental gorgeousness and splendor, as the Washington, the Florida, the Walk in the Water, the Lady of the Lake, etc. etc., had ever existed in the imaginative brain of a romancer, much less, that they were actually in existence, rushing down the Mississippi, as on the wings of the wind, or plowing up between the forests and walking against the mighty current "as things of life," bearing speculators, merchants, dandies, fine ladies, everything real, and everything affected, in the form of humanity, with pianos, and stocks of novels, and cards, and dice, and flirting, and love-making, and drinking, and champaigne, and on the deck, perhaps, three hundred fellows who have seen alligators, and neither fear whiskey, nor gunpowder.

Flint had a literary interest in the way such an apparition brought a little of Paris, a section of Broadway, a slice of Philadelphia to the backwoods, troubling the minds of the young, and no doubt of their elders as well.

Other observers, however, were beginning to perceive that the steamboat had more important functions than these. As Henry S. Tanner remarked in his clear-headed *View of the Valley of the Mississippi*, "No other country on earth will be benefitted to an equal extent by this wonderful invention." For one thing, the steamboat would tend to weld the nation into unity. Caleb Atwater of Ohio had pointed out as early as 1829 that the river system seemed designed by God to make the Americans one people. James Hall declared that

. . . the name of Fulton should be cherished here with that of Washington: if the one conducted us to liberty, the other has given us prosperity — the one broke the chains which bound us to a foreign country, the other has extended the channels of intercourse, and multiplied the ties which bind us to each other.

Hardly to be distinguished from the function of the steamboat in fostering unity was its impetus to commercial prosperity, for trade was the force that was expected to bind the parts of the nation together. The genius of man was never more nobly employed, wrote the Mississippi historian John W. Monette in the middle of the 1840's, than when Fulton applied the force of steam to the navigation of the western waters. This was all that the West required to make it the noblest and richest country on earth. Nature and a great man had collaborated in the Mississippi Valley to exhibit the triumph of steam in the exaltation of the American Republic. Monette declared that the revolution wrought in the West by this magical power was equal to any recorded in the annals of history.

Yet even when such men called the advent of steam a revolutionary force, they hardly seem to have realized what drastic changes it was destined to work. The steam engine was not only to subordinate the yeoman farmer to the banker and merchant of the new Western cities; eventually it transformed him into a producer of staple crops for distant markets and thus placed him at the mercy of freight rates and of fluctuations in international commodity prices. One of the most significant facts of American intellectual history is the slow and inadequate fashion in which the momentum of the new forces was appreciated, or, to put the matter another way, the astonishing longevity of the agrarian ideal as the accepted view of Western society. In 1846 an Illinois newspaper editor declared, "The West is agricultural; it has no manufactures and it never will have any of any importance." This opinion persisted long after it ceased to correspond to the facts. Writers reporting on the World's Columbian Exposition at Chicago in 1893 for Eastern magazines note with naïve surprise that the West had grown up into urbanism and industrialism while the world's back was turned. An observer as shrewd as Henry Adams found it difficult to assimilate what had happened in the interior. "That the Exposition should be a natural growth and product of the Northwest," he wrote, "offered a step in evolution to startle Darwin. . . ."

Despite the educational impact of the

Exposition, most Americans long continued to think of the West as a primitive agricultural region. The persistence of this idea throws into bold relief the prescience of a solitary Western analyst who had begun fifty years earlier to assess the industrial revolution in the Mississippi Valley. This man was Jessup W. Scott, Whig editor of the Toledo (Ohio) *Blade*. Between 1843 and the outbreak of the Civil War, Scott contributed almost a score of articles to *Hunt's Merchants' Magazine* of New York and *DeBow's Review* of New Orleans, discussing the probable future development of the West. In Scott's analysis agriculture had all but sunk out of sight. He fixed his attention on the forces of trade and industry that were rapidly becoming dominant, and protested against the prevalent notion that the destiny of the Mississippi Valley had "fixed it down to the almost exclusive pursuit of agriculture, ignorant that, as a general rule in all ages of the world, and in all countries, the mouths go to the food, and not the food to the mouths." Scott likewise pointed out how outmoded was the doctrine of the primacy of maritime commerce.

Old ideas (he remarks), whether hereditary, or the fruit of early education, are hard to eradicate or supplant. The salt sea, and commerce, and great cities, are naturally associated together in the minds of Western Europeans, and their descendants in America. As naturally is the interior of a broad continent associated, in their minds, with gloomy forests, desert prairies, and slow movements in all the channels of business.

Both these old beliefs ceased to be valid when steam transportation came to the Mississippi Valley. Although the fact had been slow to register itself on the public mind, internal commerce had developed to such a point that it now rivaled foreign trade in importance. Future changes resulting from the use of steamboats, locomotives, and Macadam highways would be even greater, for

. . . these machines are but just being brought into use; and he is a bold man who, casting his eye 100 years into the future, shall undertake to tell the present generation what will be their effect on our North American valley, when their energies shall be brought to bear over all its broad surface.

Scott used his new calculus to predict the course of Western society. He saw first of all that it would be urbanized. The use of machines in transportation and industry fostered "the increasing tendency to reside in towns and cities, which is manifested by the inhabitants of all countries, as they make progress in the arts and refinements of civilization. Vast cities would grow up at points determined by transportation routes and the availability of raw materials and fuel for factories. In 1843 Scott declared that the dominant Western city would be near the Great Lakes, although he was not certain just where: it might be Cleveland, or Maumee, Ohio (where he had once lived), or Detroit, or Chicago. But regardless of the exact location, "No logical induction, no mathematical demonstration can be clearer to our mind, than that here will come together the greatest aggregation of men in cities,—outrivalling in splendor as in magnitude, all which past ages have produced."

The growth of huge cities would hasten the inevitable shift of dominance from the Atlantic seaboard to the interior: the central power of the continent was certain to move to the border of the Great Lakes and remain there permanently. For industrial developments sooner or later control the political element, so that the economic analyst need not concern himself with political forms. Economic forces unrecognized a generation earlier gave new meaning to the old theme of the westward course of empire. The climactic moment in universal history which Gilpin had prophesied as a consequence of American access to the trade of Asia, Scott foresaw as the outcome of the economic development of the Mississippi Valley.

The westward movement of the Caucasian branch of the human family [he declared] from the high plains of Asia, first over Europe, and thence, with swelling tide, pouring its multitudes into the New World, is the grandest phenomenon in history.

The entrance of this tide into America was its climax: the whole process began to find its true meaning when population streamed into the great valley of the west.

While . . . we contemplate with patriotic pride

(Scott asked in conclusion) the position which, as a nation, we hold in the world's affairs, may we not indulge in pleasant anticipations of the near approach of the time when the commercial and social heart of our Empire will occupy its natural place as the heart of the continent, near the centre of its natural capabilities.

George W. Julian

## 10. THE PUBLIC LANDS

By 1850, the disposition of the public lands had become one of Congress's major continuing problems. Conflicting interests had to be pressed into some sort of a workable policy. Long-run interests contributing to nation-building competed with short-run interests in speculative profits.

Sectional differences were discernible. Eastern shop and factory employers were reluctant to have potential workers, young people and newly arrived immigrants, tempted by free lands in the West. In the Old South, there was a fear that free homesteads would bring a rush of settlers from the non-slave-holding states, backed by emigrant aid societies. From the states of the New South as well as those of the Northwest Territory came strong demands for freer and more orderly opening of the public lands to settlement and development. The latter arguments ultimately prevailed and with them the democratic principle of "homestead" rights.

The speech below was made in favor of a bill granting to every head of a family in the United States the right to a 160-acre homestead on the public lands, provided he or she occupy and cultivate the land for an uninterrupted period of five years.

*Speech of Hon. George W. Julian of Indiana, in the House of Representatives, Wednesday, Jan. 29, 1851, On the Bill reported from the Committee on Agriculture . . . .*
*The motion to reconsider the vote by which the bill was referred to the Committee of the Whole being under consideration —*

*Mr. Julian said:*

Mr. Speaker: The anxiety I feel for the success of the measure now before us, and its

great importance, as I conceive, to the whole country, have induced me to beg the indulgence of the House in a brief statement of the reasons which urge me to give it my support. . . .

I advocate the freedom of our public domain, in the first place, on the broad ground of natural right. I go back to first principles; and holding it to be wrong for governments to make merchandise of the earth, I would have this fundamental truth recognized by Congress in devising measures for the settlement and improvement of

From *Congressional Globe and Appendix*, vol. 20 (1850-1851), 31st Congress, 2nd Session, pp. 135-138.

our vacant territory. I am no believer in the doctrines of agrarianism, or socialism, as these terms are generally understood. The friends of land reform claim no right to interfere with the laws of property of the several States, or the vested rights of their citizens. They advocate no *leveling* policy, designed to strip the rich of their possessions by any sudden act of legislation. They simply demand, that in laying the foundations of empire in the yet unpeopled regions of the great West, Congress shall give its sanction to the natural right of the landless citizen of the country to a home upon its soil. The earth was designed by its Maker for the nourishment and support of man. The free and unbought occupancy of it belonged, originally, to the people, and the cultivation of it was the legitimate price of its fruits. This is the doctrine of nature, confirmed by the teachings of the Bible. In the first peopling of the earth, it was as free to all its inhabitants as the sunlight and the air; and every man has, by nature, as perfect a right to a reasonable portion of it, upon which to subsist, as he has to inflate his lungs with the atmosphere which surrounds it, or to drink of the waters which pass over its surface. This right is as inalienable, as emphatically *God-given*, as the right to liberty or life; and Government, when it deprives him of it, independent of his own act, is guilty of a wanton usurpation of power, a flagrant abuse of its trust. In founding States, and rearing the social fabric, these principles should always have been recognized. Every man, indeed, on entering into a state of society, and partaking of its advantages, must necessarily submit the natural right of which I speak (as he must every other) to such regulations as may be established for the general good; yet it can never be understood that he has renounced it altogether, save by his own alienation or forfeiture. It attaches to him, and inheres in him, in virtue of his *humanity*, and should be sacredly guarded as one of those fundamental rights to secure which "governments are instituted among men."

The justness of this reasoning must be manifest to any one who will give the subject his attention. Man, we say, has a natural right to life. What are we to understand by this? Surely it will not be contended that it must be construed strictly, as a mere right to *breathe*, looking no farther, and keeping out of view the great purpose of existence. The right to life implies what the law books call a "right of way" to its enjoyment. It carries necessarily with it the right to the *means* of living, including not only the elements of light, air, fire, and water, but *land* also. Without this, man could have no habitation to shelter him from the elements, nor raiment to cover and protect his body, nor food to sustain life. These means of living are not only necessary, but absolutely indispensable. Without them life is impossible; and yet without land they are unattainable, except through the charity of others. They are at the mercy of the land holder. Does Government then fulfil its mission when it encourages or permits the monopoly of the soil, and thus puts millions in its power, shorn of every right except the right to beg? The right to life is an empty mockery if man is to be denied a place on the earth on which to establish a home for the shelter and nurture of his family, and employ his hands in obtaining the food and clothing necessary to his comfort. To say that God has given him the right to life, and at the same time that Government may rightfully withhold the means of its enjoyment, except by the permission of others, is not simply an absurdity, but a libel on his providence. It is true, there are multitudes of landless poor in this country, and in all countries, utterly without the power to acquire homes upon the soil, who, nevertheless, are not altogether destitute of the essential blessings I have named; but they are dependent for them upon the saving grace of the few who have the monopoly of the soil. They are helpless pensioners upon the calculating bounty of those by whom they have been disinherited of their birthright. Was it ever designed that men should become vagrants and beggars by reason of unjust legislation, stripped of their right to the soil, robbed of the joys of home, and of those virtues and affections which ripen only in the family circle? Reason and justice revolt at such a conclusion. The gift of life, I repeat, is inseparable from the resources by which alone it can be made a blessing, and fulfill its great end. And this truth is beginning to dawn upon the world. The sentiment is becoming rooted in the great heart of Humanity, that the right to a *home* attaches of necessity to the right to live, inasmuch as the physical, moral, and intellectual well-being of each individual cannot be secured without it; and that government is bound to guaranty it to the fullest practicable extent. This is one of the most cheering signs of the times. "The grand doctrine, that every human being should have the means of self-culture, of progress in knowledge and virtue, of health, comfort, and happiness, of exercising the powers and affections of a man—this is slowly taking its place as the highest social truth."

But quitting the ground of right, I proceed to some considerations of a different character. I take it to be the clear interest of this Government to render every acre of its soil as productive as labor can make it. More than one half the land already sold at the different land offices, if I am not mistaken, has fallen into the cold grasp of the speculator, who has held it in large quantities for years without improvement, thus excluding actual settlers who would have made it a source of wealth to themselves and to the public revenue. This is not only a legalized robbery of the landless, but an exceedingly short-sighted policy. It does not, as I shall presently show, give employment to labor, nor productiveness to the soil, nor add to the Treasury by increased returns in the shape of taxation. It is legislative profligacy. The true interest of agriculture is to widen the field of its operations as far as practicable, and then, by a judicious tillage, to make it yield the very largest resources compatible with the population of the country. The measure now before us will secure this object by giving independent homesteads to the greatest number of cultivators, thus imparting dignity to labor, and stimulating its activity. It may be taken for granted as a general truth, that a nation will be powerful, prosperous and happy, in proportion to the number of independent cultivators of its soil. All experience demonstrates that it is most favorable to agriculture to have every plantation cultivated by its proprietor; nor is it less conducive to the same object, or less important to the general welfare, that every citizen who desires it should be the owner of a plantation, and engaged in its cultivation. The disregard of these simple and just principles in the actual policy of nations, has been one of the great scourges of the world. We now have it in our power, without revolution or violence, to carry them into practice, and reap their beneficent fruits; and a nobler work cannot engage the thoughts, or enlist the sympathies of the statesman. No governmental policy is so wise as that which keeps constantly before the mind of the citizen the promotion of the public good, by a scrupulous regard for his private interest. This principle should be stamped upon all our legislation, since it will establish the strongest of all ties between him and the State. A philosophic writer of the last century, in sketching a perfectly-organized commonwealth, has the following:

As every man ploughed his own field, cultivation was more active, provisions more abundant, and individual opulence constituted the public wealth.

As the earth was free, and its possession easy and secure, every man was a proprietor, and the division of property, by rendering luxury impossible, preserved the purity of manners.

Every man finding his own well-being in the constitution of his country, took a lively interest in its preservation: if a stranger attacked it, having his field, his house, to defend, he carried into the combat all the animosity of a personal quarrel, and devoted to his own interests he was devoted to his country.

Here, sir, are principles worthy to guide our rulers in the disposition of the public lands. Give homes to the landless multitudes in the country, and you snatch them from crime and starvation, from the prison and the alms-house, and place them in a situation at once the most conducive to virtue, to the prosperity of the country, and to loyalty to its Government and laws. Instead of paupers and outcasts, they will become independent citizens and freeholders, pledged by their gratitude to the Government, by self-interest, and by the affections of our nature, to consecrate to honest toil the spot on which the family altar is to be erected and the family circle kept unbroken. They will feel, as never before, the value of free institutions, and the obligations resting upon them as citizens. Should a foreign foe invade our shores, having their homes and their firesides to defend, they would rush to the field of deadly strife, carrying with them "all the animosity of a personal quarrel." "Independent farmers," said President Jackson, "are everywhere the basis of society, and true friends of liberty"; and an army of such men, however unpractised in the art of war, would be invincible. Carry out this reform of multiplying independent cultivators, and thus rendering labor at once honorable and gainful, and I verily believe more will be done than could be accomplished by any other means to break down our military establishments, and divert the vast sums annually expended in maintaining them, to the arts of peace. It is emphatically a peace movement, since it will curb the war spirit by subsidizing to the public interest the "raw material," of which our armies are generally composed. By giving homes to the poor, the idle, the vicious, it will attach them to the soil, and cause them to feel, as the producers of the country ought to feel, that upon *them* rest the burdens of war. The policy of increasing the number and independence of those who till the ground, in whatever light considered, commends itself to the Government. England, and the countries of western Europe, have risen in prosperity, just in proportion as freedom has been communicated to the occupiers of the soil. The work of tillage was at first carried on by slaves, then by villains, then by metayers, and finally by farmers; the improvement of those countries keeping peace with these progressive changes in the condition of the cultivator. The same observations would doubtless apply to other countries and to different ages of the world. But I need not go abroad for illustrations of this principle. Look, for example, at slave labor in this country. Compare Virginia with Ohio. In the former, the soil is tilled by the slave. He feels no interest in the Government, because it allows him the exercise of no civil rights. It does not even give him the right to himself. He has of course no interest in the soil upon which he toils. His arm is not nerved, nor his labor lightened by the thought of home, for to him it has no value or sacredness. It is no defence against outrage. His own offspring are the property of another. He does not toil for his family, but for a stranger. His wife and children may be torn from him at any moment, sold like cattle to the trader, and separated from him forever. Labor brings no new comforts to himself or his family. The motive from which he toils is the lash. He is robbed of his humanity by the system which has made him its victim. Can the cultivation of the soil by such a population add wealth or prosperity to the Commonwealth? The question answers itself. I need not point to Virginia, with her great natural advantages, her ample resources in all the elements of wealth and power, yet dwindling and dying under the curse of slave labor. But cross the river Ohio, and how changed the scene! Agriculture is in the most thriving condition. The whole land teems with abundance. The owners of the soil are in general its cultivators, and these constitute the best portion of the population. Labor, instead of being looked upon as degrading, is thus rendered honorable and independent. The ties of interest, as well as the stronger ties of affection, animate the toils of the husbandman, and strengthen his attachment to the Government; for the man who loves his home will love his country. His own private emolument and the public good are linked together in his thoughts, and whilst he is rearing a virtuous family on his own homestead, he is contributing wealth and strength to the State. Population is rapidly on the increase, whilst new towns are springing up almost as by magic. Manufactures and the mechanic arts, in general, are in a flourishing condition, whilst the country is dotted over with churches, schoolhouses, and smiling habitations. The secret of all this is the distribution of landed property, and its cultivation by freemen. But even in the virgin state of Ohio, the curse of land monopoly, or *white* slavery is beginning to exhibit its bitter fruits, as it will everywhere, if unchecked by wise legislation. Let Congress, therefore, see to it, *in the beginning*, by an organic law for the public domain yet remaining unsold, that this curse shall be excluded from it. The enactment of such a law should not be delayed a single hour. Now is the "golden moment" for action. The rapidity with which our public lands have been melting away for the past few years under the prodigal policy of the Government, renders all-important the speedy interposition of Congress. . . .

The complaint is sometimes made, that if the public lands are *given* to actual settlers, it will in effect be taxing the remainder of the people to pay for their farms, since the public revenue will be diminished in proportion to those gifts, and would of course have to be supplied from other sources. But is not one class of the people taxed for the benefit of another, in the money raised from the agriculturist in the cases I have mentioned? The cultivator has always been taxed for the support of other interests. I deny, however, that the public revenue would be diminished by making the public lands free. According to the report of the Secretary of the Treasury, these lands can no longer be looked to as a source of revenue, at least for many years to come, under our present system. He shows that our late bounty land acts will yet require about seventy-nine millions of acres, and that when they have finally exhausted themselves they will have diverted from the Treasury the sum of more than $113,000,000. The warrants issued under these acts are made assignable, and will be bought at greatly-re-

duced prices by speculators, who will pick and cull all the choice lands, hoard them up for their own selfish advantage, and thus exclude the settler from them, and at the same time drive the Government from the market which it has thus glutted by its own improvident policy. Besides, if the present system should be persisted in, Congress will continue, and probably multiply, its grants of land for internal improvements, and for other purposes, thus making large additional drains upon the revenue otherwise derivable from this source. The old-fashioned project, therefore, of raising a *revenue* from the public domain is perfectly chimerical, and must be abandoned. This is now very generally admitted. If adhered to, the Government would realize from it but little, if anything, for the next quarter of a century, beyond the six or seven hundred thousand dollars annually required to defray the expense it occasions, as must be manifest, I think, from the calculations of the Secretary. It follows, therefore, that the sums heretofore raised from the sales of the public lands must be made up from other sources, whether we continue or abandon our present policy. The question of revenue is excluded.

But admitting that the passage of this bill would divert some two or three millions annually from the public Treasury, for the direct benefit of actual settlers, it still would not follow that a tax of this amount would be imposed upon the rest of the community. Whilst the freedom of the public domain to actual settlers, would be a measure emphatically for the benefit of the poor, all classes would share in the advantages resulting from it. It would decrease poverty, and the vices and crimes to which it gives birth, by withdrawing its victims from our crowded cities and the slavery of capital, and giving them homes upon the fertile acres of the West. It would drain pauperism from the old States, and thus relieve them from the burden of a population of superabundant laborers, whilst enterprise, industry, and wealth, would abound in the new. Instead of diminishing, it would increase the public revenue. This, chiefly, is derived from duties on foreign imports. The amount of revenue thus obtained depends upon the number of consumers of imported articles. Increase the number of agricultural producers, therefore, and you increase the number of those who consume foreign imports, thus increasing the revenue derived from this source; because, by giving a man a home upon the soil, you add to his ability to produce, and thereby increase his ability to buy articles of necessity or luxury which pay duty. If we export annually one hundred millions worth of agricultural products, we shall import at least an equal amount of foreign goods subject to duty. If our vacant lands are made free to actual settlers, and we are thus enabled by their products to export one hundred and *fifty* millions, our imports will of course increase in proportion, and so will the receipts at the custom-house. If *revenue* be the object, here is its true source; and Congress, instead of madly endeavoring to raise money from the *sale* of the public lands, should adopt the policy that will promote their greatest productiveness. Their *settlement*, and *improvement*, should be the paramount object. By this policy we shall thus accomplish the double object of giving homes and employment to the landless laborers of the country, and, at the same time, replenishing the national Treasury. Humanity and the dollar will go together. The public lands in their wild state are yielding nothing. It is the obvious interest of the Government, as I have before stated, that they should be rendered as productive as possible. Under our present system, selling as we do from two to three millions worth of land annually, it will require hundreds of years to dispose of the whole of our public domain; and as there is no law prohibiting land traffic, the sales that are made as often prevent as promote the settlement of the country. The millions of acres which this policy would continue in unproductive idleness, slowly diminishing in quantity for centuries, should all the time be sustaining a hardy yeomanry, and filling the coffers of

the nation; and the Government robs itself of wealth, to whatever extent its policy fails to secure these objects. It acts like the miser, who buries his treasure so that it can yield nothing. On the other hand, make the public lands free on condition of occupancy and improvement, and the labor of our landless and homeless population, who have no capital but their muscles, will be united to the soil in the production of wealth. The public domain will thus be improved and the Government enriched by giving homes and employment to the poor; for it is as difficult to raise a revenue by taxing its paupers, as by preventing the settlement of its lands. The Treasury will be filled by rescuing starving thousands from the jaws of land monopoly, and imparting to them happiness and independénce. The degraded vassal of the rich, who is now confined to exhausting labor for a mere pittance upon which to subsist, or

"Who begs a brother of the earth
To give him leave to toil,"

will find a home in the West; and, stimulated by the favor of the Government, the desire for independence, and the ties of the family, the wilderness will be converted into smiling landscapes, and wealth poured into the nation's lap. Humanity to the poor thus unites with the interest of the nation in making the public domain free to those who so much need it; taking gaunt poverty into the fatherly keeping of the Government, and giving it the home of which land monopoly has deprived it; administering to it the blessings of existence, and at the same time using it as an instrumentality for building up the prosperity and wealth of the Republic. Sir, I ask gentlemen if these things are not so? I ask those who mean to oppose this policy if any wiser or better one can be proposed with respect to our public lands? Some disposition of them must be made. By some method or other they should be rendered a source of agricultural and financial wealth. The administration of them is costing us annually nearly three quarters of a million of dollars under our present system. The Government, as I have shown by reference to the late Treasury report, has already practically repudiated the pledge which it made of these lands in 1847 for the payment of our public debt. The management of them, I repeat, presses upon us as a serious, practical question; and I call upon those who denounce this measure to meet the views I have advanced fairly, and, if they are untenable, to bring forward some plan for disposing of our public domain more conducive to the interest of the whole country, and more likely to command the favor of a majority of Congress.

## 11. REPRESENTATIVE W. R. W. COBB ON THE PUBLIC LANDS

The following are remarks made in the House of Representative by Hon. W. R. W. Cobb of Alabama, August 2, 1852, on the bill proposing to graduate and reduce the price of the public lands.

*Mr. Cobb said*:

Mr. Chairman: In availing myself of the present opportunity to address this committee, I hope I will be pardoned for more particularly alluding to a bill reported by me, now upon your calendar, proposing to graduate and reduce the price of the public lands, as well as briefly to allude to the homestead bill, which has passed this House, and is now in the Senate. My principal purpose is to call the attention of the House, and of the country, to the importance of the question of graduating and reducing the price of the public lands, as proposed in the bill, which is to be subject to entry by the occupant and cultivator, or to those that have public lands adjoining their farms who may desire to enter for the use of their farms, all land that has been in market for ten years at one dollar per acre; that which has been in market for fifteen years, seventy-five cents; twenty years, fifty cents; twenty-five years, twenty-five cents; and thirty years, twelve and a half cents; and in discussing the question, I shall assume that land being the true basis of all individual and national prosperity, its disposition, and the tenure by which it is held, has in every age of the world and in every civilized nation, engaged the most ardent attention of the statesman and the philanthropist. There is no subject in the whole range of political science, that so readily and directly interests the great body of the people as that of the right of soil. Therefore, its disposition is not only a question of utility, but one of expediency, and one, too, involving great and important principles, upon which may hang the destiny of man and Government. So intimately identified is it with the form and system of government, and the principal rights and privileges of man, that we are frequently enabled to read the history of a nation, either for weal or woe, for glory or shame, in the mere regulation of her land system. That system, no matter by what name it may be called, that scatters the land among the great body of the people, who will become agriculturists, and be left unfettered to pass from generation to generation, thereby preserving and perpetuating an independent yeomanry, must forever enjoy a high state of political freedom. Further, the Government which adopts a system and pursues a policy tending to concentrate its soil into the hands of a few to the detriment of the many, its ultimate destiny is the destruction of every vestige of equality and liberty. If

From *Congressional Globe and Appendix*, vol. 21 (1850-1851), 32nd Congress, 1st Session, pp. 1180-1181.

you wish to preserve a good form of government, you must pursue a policy tending to distribute the lands among the largest possible number of the people; hence the necessity of a system that will so reduce the lands according to their value, as to enable all classes to possess them, both by graduation and reduction, as well as by all other equitable and proper means, should it even favor the granting of lands to those who will occupy and cultivate them for a term of years. In my remarks it would hardly be admissible to go back and trace the land system from the origin of society, when it was free to the common enjoyment of all, without stint or diminution, up to the time it was found to be capable of individual appropriation and proprietorship, at first temporary, but subsequently permanent. From that day to this the land systems of every country have stamped their impress upon their institutions for good or evil. History is filled with examples in illustration of this fact . . . .

Having endeavored to show the principles involved in this question, and the effects of a liberal system upon the moral, physical, and political world, let us now turn our attention to our own system, and see what is likely to be its effects if rigidly adhered to. I can tell gentlemen in advance, who fancy a kind of veneration for the present land system, that this bill does not contemplate either its radical change or destruction, but merely to give such a direction to its operations as will ultimately destroy the relation of landlord and tenant between this Government and the States, and place the new States upon the elevated platform of equality guaranteed by the Constitution. That any policy we may see proper to adopt, ought to look to a period when that relation should cease to exist, I presume no gentleman will deny. And yet it requires but little foresight to perceive that the present system, rigidly adhered to, will necessarily render it perpetual.

Are there no evils in this relation, which, as statesmen, we are bound to ferret out and remedy? I think there are. What are its effects upon this Government — upon the free, sovereign, and independent people? Yes, and even upon the legislation of this Hall. Sir, it is a familiar spectacle here to see the States, through their Representatives, like sturdy beggars at the foot-stool of power, asking appropriations of a pittance of land (I was going to say their own land) for some public purpose. Are gentlemen prepared to adhere to the workings of a system which is destined to give perpetuity to this condition of things? If not, the remedy is at hand; not by a radical and sudden change of the system. The people of the land States seek not to take the lands which is the joint product of all; they ask not to deprive you of your interest in it, but only that it shall not be held up in masses at a price beyond its value, blighting their prosperity and their hopes of future aggrandizement. Another evil of the system upon the new States, for which this bill is an ultimate remedy, is the constant and eternal drain of money from these States in payment for their lands. This is a drain which nothing but the indomitable and unconquerable energies of the pioneer could withstand. I am well aware that the bill affords no immediate remedy for this, but rather aggravates it for the time, as I will show when I come to examine it as a revenue measure; but it does look to a termination of it at a period when it will cease, and the new States can husband their resources, and employ them in advancing their own prosperity. They preferred a sudden attack and return to health, to a lingering and interminable disease. Though the drain upon their resources would be greater, it would be of shorter duration. Were the lands in the hands of individual proprietors, it would contribute to the resources of the State, and the general wealth of the nation. This course of reasoning is intended to apply as well to the homestead bill, as to the one now under consideration.

Having briefly reviewed the evils of the present system, I shall now proceed to the investigation of the general character of the bill, and test it by the soundest principles of justice. It is but justice to sell those lands for their intrinsic worth,—justice to the purchaser, who pays his money; justice to the State in which they lie, as she is deeply interested in their occupation and cultivation. Sir, to fix a standard price upon all the land of the country, regardless of the character of the soil, rich or poor, is unjust to the purchaser, and grossly unjust to the States interested in their settlement. Such a doctrine is absurd, if it is intended for any other purpose than retarding the growth and prosperity of the country. There is nothing in which a greater variety exists than in the qualities of the soil of any large extent of country. And to put the poor at the standard price of the rich, is, in effect, to reserve them from market. But suppose, against any reasonable hypothesis, they could be sold, is it just in this Government, like a monopolizing speculator, to prey upon the necessities of its citizens, and force from them more than the land is worth? In the next place, it is the tendency of this bill, as well as the homestead bill, to foster and encourage emigration and settlement in the new States, and consequently, their growing

wealth and prosperity. Is it the policy of this Government to keep obstacles in the way of that advancement? Is it just to retard them in their onward march to greatness and to glory? We ask no special favors; we ask to be exempt from no general burdens; we ask no special favors to aid us in our march to greatness and to empire. We only ask you not to place obstacles in our way; that you leave our action free, and the enterprise, energy, and industry of the same people who subdued forests in their march, and made the wilderness to yield abundant harvests, will make the country prosper. The rich soil, the magnificent rivers, the mild and genial climate of the West and Southwest, all contribute to invite emigration amongst us, and that policy would be suicidal that would obstruct or retard it. The West and Southwest need population to develop its great resources, and it will be one of the blessings of these great measures that they will contribute to its increase without impairing the best interests of other portions of the confederacy.

## 12. DEBATE ON THE HOMESTEAD BILL

The Senate, as in Committee of the Whole, resumed the consideration of the bill (H. R. No. 280) to secure homesteads to actual settlers on the public domain, the pending question being on the amendment of Mr. Brown to the amendment of the Committee on Public Lands.

*Mr. Johnson, of Tennessee.* I have been authorized by the Committee on Public Lands to withdraw the amendment heretofore reported, in lieu of the House bill referred to that committee, and to offer the amendment that I hold in my hand, instead of it. There is an amendment offered by the Senator from Mississippi (Mr. Brown) to

take the place of the amendment reported by the Committee on Public Lands. I understand the Senator has no objection to withdrawing that until this can be introduced, and then it comes regularly in its place.

*Mr. Brown.* None at all. I withdraw my amendment for the time being, to allow the amendment of the Senator from Tennessee to be presented.

*Mr. Johnson, of Tennessee.* Then I withdraw the amendment heretofore reported by the Committee on Public Lands, for the original House bill, and offer in its place the

From *Congressional Globe*, Vol. 29, Part 2 (1859–1860), Thirty-sixth Congress, 1st Session, pp. 1651, 1655-6.

following amendment, which I hope may be read.

The Secretary read the amendment; which is, to strike out all after the enacting clause of the bill, and insert:

That any person who is the head of a family, and a citizen of the United States, shall, from and after the passage of this act, be entitled to enter one quarter section of vacant and unappropriated public lands, or a quantity equal thereto, to be located in a body, in conformity with the legal subdivisions of the public lands, and after the same shall have been surveyed.

*   *   *

But when we come to examine the homestead proposition, where do we start with it? I want the Senator's attention. We start with it in 1791, under the administration of General Washington, and I think he was from the Old Dominion. In 1791, the first homestead proposition was introduced, and, in the language of the law, it was enacted:

"That four hundred acres of land be given to each of those persons who in the year 1783, were heads of families at Vincennes, or the Illinois country, or the Mississippi, and who, since that time, have removed from one of the said places to the other; but the Governor of the Territory northwest of the Ohio is hereby directed to cause the same to be laid out for them at their own expense, &c.

That law makes use of the word "give," and it received the approval of General Washington. I think that is tolerably good company. Tennessee is willing to be associated with Washington, and especially upon homestead propositions. That law was approved by the immortal Washington. I think he was about as great a man as any of the modern lights; and so far as I am concerned, I prefer following in the lead of the larger, instead of what I consider the lesser, lights. What next do we find on this subject? Mr. Jefferson recommended, in one of his messages to the Congress of the United States, the homestead policy. In the administrations of Washington and Jefferson, this policy was inaugurated by this Govern-

ment. I prefer to follow the lead and to be associated with Washington and Jefferson, than the lights that now shine from the Old Dominion. There are forty-four precedents of law approved and sanctioned by various Presidents, running through every Administration, from Thomas Jefferson down to the present time, carrying out the same principle. Where did this policy have its origin? Where did it start? Its very germ commenced with Virginia and it has been followed up and brought down to the present time. But, without dwelling on all the cases, I will refer to what was done in 1850. The fourth section of "An act to create the office of surveyor general of public lands in Oregon, and to provide for the survey, and to make donations to settlers on the said public lands," approved in 1850, is in these words:

Sec. 4. And be it further enacted, That there shall be, and hereby is, granted to every white settler or occupant of the public lands, American half-breed Indians included, above the age of eighteen years, being a citizen of the United States, or having made a declaration according to law of his intention to become a citizen, or who shall become a resident thereof on or before the 1st day of December, 1850, and who shall have resided upon and cultivated the same for four consecutive years, and who shall otherwise conform to the provisions of this act, the quantity of one half section, or three hundred and twenty acres of land, if a single man, and if a married man, or if he shall become married within one year from the 1st day of December, 1850, the quantity of one section, or six hundred and forty acres, one half to himself, and the other half to his wife, to be held by her in her own right. — Statutes at Large, vol. 9, p. 497.

There is a homestead bill. There is a grant of six hundred and forty acres to a married man, and three hundred and twenty acres to a single man, not being the head of a family, but twenty-one years of age. That was passed in 1850. I should like to know where the vigilant and watchful Senator from Virginia was when that law passed. I presume that this flood of light had not then been shed. He did not see its bearings and tendencies as he seems to understand them now. How did the Senator vote upon that question? I suppose the Senator knows, for surely a measure so important, and embracing principles so sacred and vital, could not have passed through this body without the Senator knowing how he recorded his vote. Where was this faithful sentinel that should have been standing upon the watch-tower, and should have sounded the alarm and aroused the people of the United States to the dangerous inroads that were being made on their rights and institutions? Where was he? Did he speak? Did he say "yea" or "nay," either by speech or vote? No; but he sat with his arms folded, and allowed this "infamous measure," this "agrarian measure," that was to work such dangerous influences upon certain institutions of the country, to pass without saying either yea or nay.

There was one homestead proposition passed in 1850. Yesterday I quoted a law passed in 1854, and it seemed to be a little difficult for Senators to understand it. One Senator understood it one way, and another understood it another. Sometimes it is a good plan to examine, and see how a thing is. One said that the law of 1854 was to give homesteads in New Mexico; and if they were given in New Mexico, and not in Kansas, that would change the principle! Now, I should like to know the difference in principle. But let us see how the thing stands. I read one section from the act of 1850; and, before I could get to read another section, the Senator from Missouri (Mr. Green) took the floor, and made an issue with me; and then the Senator from Virginia resumed the floor, and did not permit me to read another section, and make it understood. The act of 1854 is entitled "An act to establish the offices of surveyor general of New Mexico, Kansas, and Nebraska, to grant donations to actual settlers therein, and for other purposes." Well, what do we find in the second section of that act?

*Sec. 2. And be it further enacted,* That, to every white male citizen of the United States, or every white male above the age of twenty-one years, who has declared his intention to become a citizen, and who was residing in said Territory prior

to the *1st* day of January, 1853, and who may be still residing there, there shall be, and hereby is, donated one quarter section, or one hundred and sixty acres of land. And to every white male citizen of the United States, or every white male above the age of twenty-one years, who has declared his intention to become a citizen, and who shall have removed, or shall remove to and settle in said Territory between the *1st* day of January, 1853, and the *1st* day of January, 1858, there shall, in like manner, be donated one quarter section, or one hundred and sixty acres, on condition of actual settlement and cultivation for not less than four years. — *Statutes at Large*, vol. 10, p. 308.

There is a clear and distinct grant; but the answer was that it was not a homestead, because the grant was made in New Mexico. Would there be any difference, in principle, between holding out inducements to go into New Mexico to free homes, and holding out inducements to go anywhere else? What is the difference? Even in regard to New Mexico, where there was a prospect of slavery, here was a bill passed inviting settlers to go into the Territory and take the land free; and to carry out this very disastrous idea in reference to slavery that the Senator from Virginia speaks of. And where was he? Yesterday, when we referred to it, the Journal was produced to show that there was no vote taken on it; and the answer to the principle and the inconsistency I was exhibiting was, that "donated" was bad English, as if thereby to escape from the inconsistency in which the Senator was involved. . . .

*Mr. Johnson, of Tennessee.* But let us travel on a little further. That was in New Mexico. Next we come right over into Kansas, now in the midst of the Emigrant Aid Society, and see how it operates when we get over into Kansas. We find this is the law now providing for preemptions there—I read from the same law which I have just quoted:

*Sec. 12. And be it further enacted,* That all the lands to which the Indian title has been, or shall be, extinguished within said Territories of Nebraska and Kansas, shall be subject to the operations of the preemption act of *4th* September, 1841, and under the conditions, restrictions, and stipulations therein mentioned: *Provided, however,* That where unsurveyed lands are claimed by preemption, notice of the specific tracts shall be filed within three months after the survey has been made in the field, &c. — *Statutes at Large*, vol. 10, p. 310.

These acts were referred to by the Senator from Ohio (Mr. Pugh) the other day. He was referring to them in the range of precedents, in the speech that he made on this subject vindicating the measure against the objections that were made both as to its expediency and constitutionality. He referred to this as one of the precedents, and made an argument (permit me to say here in parenthesis) that cannot be answered. Some may attempt, as some have attempted, to answer it; but it cannot be answered. Why try to associate the measure with prejudices that may exist North or South? If it is unconstitutional, come up and meet it on constitutional grounds. If it is inexpedient and dangerous, show it to be so. But here is a preemption granted, in Kansas, and when? In 1854, at the time of all the alarm in reference to emigrant aid societies. Where was the vigilant, sleepless sentinel then? Where was he who came forth with such power and eloquence yesterday, after receiving that new flood of light — from a Republican source, too?

In 1850 a homestead was granted. In 1854, in the midst of the excitement about emigrant aid societies, an act was passed granting homesteads and preemptions to young men who were not heads of families. Anybody could go into Kansas, and squat down upon land. Inducements were held out for them to run in. Where was this sentinel that has now become so alarmed, and who wants to know how Tennessee can stand up by such a proposition? Was he here, and did not understand the measure? Was he here understanding it, and standing upon the watch-tower as the faithful sentinel, and did not sound the alarm? Was he here, and did not say to those inside the citadel that the enemy was at the gate? If he was, and knew it to be so, I ask why a sentinel of that kind, entertaining the views he does in reference to this subject, when he saw such a dangerous encroachment upon the institu-

tion peculiar to the South, did not sound the alarm? Failing to do so, knowing how the facts stand, he is no longer entitled to the confidence of those who placed him here. If he was here, and had not sagacity or acumen enough to see it, or if his mind was not so constructed as to go from cause to effect, and look a little into the distance, and see the operation of this preemption law; and if he has not been enlightened until he has received light from Republicans, his mind is dark, and not to be trusted. A sentinel, standing on the watch-tower, to have eyes and not see, ears and not hear, a tongue and not speak, deserves to be taken down, and another put in his place. Sir, think of the mariner who is placed on deck, when he descries in the distance the approaching storm, or the man who is familiar with the forest, and hears the roaring of the trees — an indication of the whirlwind — and will be so listless, so indifferent, as not to sound the alarm that danger is approaching. I say he is an unworthy and unfaithful sentinel.

When the Senator talks about the representatives of Tennessee, or Kentucky, or any other States, I desire to know where he was when these things were being done? Did he vote? It seems some gentlemen thought yesterday that they got him out of the dilemma, because he did not vote. When a bill is before the Senate, and it passes and no objection is made, it is understood that it receives the sanction of the body — it has at least the tacit consent of all — and every member here is committed to the passage of the bill. If there was all this danger, would it not have been the duty of the Senator to rise in his place, sound the alarm, call for the yeas and nays, and let the country know where all parties stood?

\* \* \*

*Mr. Mason* . . . The honorable Senator has said that this homestead policy, as he calls it, takes its date from the foundation of this Government, the days of Washington. He has pursued through the statute-book the recommendation of various Presidents, until he comes down to the legislation of 1850, when he taunts me with having voted for a policy which I now repudiate, and thinks that I attempted yesterday, to use his language, to escape the consequences of that by sitting silent and refraining from a vote on those bills. Sir, I told that honorable Senator yesterday, in reference to the law that he cited — and I thought he understood me — and I tell him now again, that so far as I recollect, I voted for those laws — I mean so far as the policy was of bringing settlers on the unsettled lands in unoccupied Territories. I doubt not that if we were now thrown back to 1850 with these unsettled lands then to be organized into Territories, I should vote for it; and the Senator thinks he has caught me now in a great departure from what that honorable Senator calls a principle. The honorable Senator says it has been his policy in life, and he ascribes it to his State, to ascertain what is the true principle, and then follow it out to its consequences; and thus he has found the principle of the homestead bill in this legislation of 1850. Mr. President, with those who are not accustomed to think for themselves alone, it is usual first to be satisfied that they understand the principle before they expound it to others. It is very important, I should think; but, with great deference to the opinions of better thinkers, before you pursue a principle to its consequences, that you should understand what the principle is. The Senator says, because this policy of bringing settlers on unoccupied lands was adopted in the early stages of this Government, and was carried out in the laws of 1850, it follows, as a consequence, that the homestead bill is the result of the same principle. I deny it absolutely. The two things are as wide apart as great measures of policy can be. What was the policy recommended by the earlier Presidents, and carried into the legislation of 1850 and since? In the first instance, according to my recollection, it was in the case of the Territory of Oregon, a law to which the Senator has adverted, and for which doubtless I voted, although I do not remember it; and an honorable Senator has been good enough to

call to my notice the fact, that before the Oregon question was settled; before it was determined where the boundaries of Oregon were, and while it was a matter of dispute between Great Britain and the United States, a bill was introduced into the Senate in 1842, by a very learned and able Senator at that day, from Missouri, the intention of which was, while the question remained unsettled, to invite American citizens into that country for the purpose of occupying it; for the purpose of having a nucleus of American citizenship there when the right of property should be ultimately ascertained and the boundary distinctly traced out between the two Governments. That bill shadowed out the policy. It was introduced by Mr. Linn, in 1842, and contained this clause in the second section:

> That six hundred and forty acres, or one section of land, shall be granted to every white male inhabitant of said Territory, of the age of eighteen years and upwards, who shall cultivate and use the same for five years, or to his heir or heirs at law, if such there be.

There was the commencement of this policy on the part of the Government. What was it? To give away the public lands to actual settlers in the Territories and in the States wherever public lands were to be found? No; but the wise policy of inviting American citizens into the unoccupied Territories of the country, or those which the country was about to acquire, for the purpose of forming a nucleus of population for different uses, and amongst others, doubtless, the great one was to be prepared, by an armed population, against an Indian occupation of the country. That was afterwards carried into the Oregon bill, to which the honorable Senator has referred, as the institution of the principle which he says he is now carrying out. The bill creating the office of surveyor general of public lands in Oregon, in 1850, provided in its fourth section that all white persons or half-breed Indians then actually resident in the Territory should have a certain amount of land granted to them. How came they there before the title was adjusted? Invited there by this bill of 1842, and found there when the law passed; invited there by the bill of 1842, as I have been told by the honorable Senator who now so ably represents the State of Oregon, and who is familiar with all the legislation and the results of the legislation in that Territory. The next section was an invitation to others to go there, to whom should be given like amounts of lands. The fifth section provided that all white male citizens, or persons who had made a declaration of intention to become such, and who would go into the Territory between the 1st of December, 1851, and the 1st of December, 1853—limiting the period—should be entitled to a certain quantity of the public lands, provided they would actually settle on them. What was that policy? It was that which any wise and prudent Government would institute in relation to an immense and unoccupied Territory, such as Oregon was at that day—an invitation to citizens of the country and to those foreigners, also, who would become citizens, to go there and occupy lands that were unoccupied; in other words, to take possession of a wilderness, giving to the Government strength and power within the wilderness when it should be necessary to use it.

So in the case of Nebraska and Kansas. That was an Indian country, set apart exclusively for them, not open to settlement. There were no white people there, or but very few. According to my recollection at that time, there were none there unless by the authority of law, for purposes specified in the law, who were not trespassers; but the trespassers were very few. In the law passed in 1854, organizing these two Territories, the policy of the Oregon law was pursued in part. It was unoccupied, except by Indians; and an invitation was given to white settlements there, not by giving away the public land, but giving a right of preemption, for the purpose of placing the wilderness in the hands of civilization. That was the policy, that was the principle which the honorable Senator from Tennessee says he is now working out. How? By giving away the public lands; not in the wilderness, not in territory unoccupied, but giving the public lands in the States and Territories to the first comer who will take possession of them as a gratuity. Why, sir, if it could be brought in connection with this original purpose, with the policy of bringing settlements into Territories unsettled and unoccupied, it would be brought into connection with it in contrast; not in furtherance of the principle, but in defeat of it, and in contrast with it.

Then, again, the honorable Senator from Tennessee thinks that I have been guilty of a very great inconsistency, at least, in voting for the graduation bill, introduced by my colleague some five or six years since, which made the minimum price of the public lands twelve and a half cents an acre. He looks upon that as a carrying into execution of the great principle that he relies upon for the sanction of his homestead bill. He would seem to consider that the policy of the graduation bill and the policy of the homestead bill were the same; and if I voted for the graduation bill, and refuse now to vote for the homestead bill, I am inconsistent! Well, Mr. President, if the Senator were right, I should not be afraid of the inconsistency. I should be concerned, if it could properly be ascribed to me that, from a desire to shrink responsibilities that devolved on me, or from a desire to promote any sinister ends, I had voted in departure from the faith of a previous vote that I had given; but I should never be apprehensive of its being charged on me as an inconsistency that I had changed my mind, and changed my policy with it.

But, sir, here again is the interpretation that the Senator puts on his principle. What was the graduation bill? It was an effort on the part of those who represented the older States, where there were no public lands, to save from the wreck of the public domain, as far as they could, something from the general and apparent purpose of the legislation of the country to appropriate those public lands to the States where they were found without paying for them at all. It was said constantly by honorable Senators here from the new States, where there are public lands—and they said it with truth, and I felt the force of the appeal—that it was a matter of great moment to those States to have their land settled; and they were held at such high prices, or upon such rigorous terms, as represented by them, as prevented their settlement; and that measure of graduating the price of the public lands was one introduced with their assent and with their vote, for the purpose of doing—what? Of carrying out any policy in the Government to give homesteads or lands to those who were either unable or too worthless to buy them? No; the furthest thing from it; but it was in response to that demand of the landholding States that the price of land should be graduated in proportion to their actual value and to their fertility; and that when the Government had offered the lands for sale for a certain period, and they had not been entered at the minimum price of $1.25, then that they should be open to entry at lower rates; and the lands were graduated according to the times they had been in market—that being adopted as the best standard, and a very proximate one it was (at least it was the best standard) of the comparative fertility of the lands. The highest price, I think, in that bill, was one dollar, and the lowest twelve and a half cents. There was no homestead in that—I mean to say no policy of the homestead bill. It was a graduation measure which I understood would be acceptable to the landholding States and which was mod-

eled by a concurrence of opinion between them and carried into effect. Its practical operation has been, according to my recollection, that although it seemed to be well devised in theory, it has had little effect in practice.

Mr. President, I did not design anything further yesterday than to bring to the notice of the Senate the necessary operation of this bill brought from the other House, and which is now the subject of our deliberations. The necessary effect will be to transplant, by the allurement of land gratuities at the public expense, people from the non-slaveholding States to preoccupy these lands in the Territory, to the exclusion of those from the slaveholding States; and I said, and still believe, that if the policy should be adopted, it would be followed up on the part of the people of the free States by bringing to the aid of the law, emigrant aid societies to force out that sort of population. I cannot vote for it in any form or shape, not only because it seems to have that policy, but because I should be opposed to the whole system of making gratuities of the public lands. In reference to the honorable Senator from Tennessee, I certainly did not mean to provoke any quarrel on this side of the Chamber; I meant to call his attention only to the necessary effect of his policy in the hands in which it now was; and my suggestion to him, certainly not an admonition, was, that he should neither touch nor handle the unclean thing.

# III. *Agricultural Fundamentalism and Science: 1860—1890*

Agricultural development in the generation following the Civil War was indicative of the complexities that were to characterize this branch of endeavor a century later. Geographical expansion into the Great Plains brought a new set of challenges. Trans-Missouri conditions required new and larger-scale technology and revised more positive public policies toward farming. Economic differentiations among farmers became discernible as a function of the new technology, which created a "subsistence" class at one pole and a moderately affluent class of successful commercial farmers at the other.

The percentage of the population living in rural areas declined at an increasing rate throughout the period. By 1870, the percentage of the population engaged in farming had dropped below 50 percent of the total of gainfully employed workers. The first warning of agriculture's loss of numerical preeminence had been sounded. The displacement of rural America by an urban society was beginning.

The decline in the proportional numerical strength of farmers did not, however, mean a comparable decline in the importance or the recognition of the agricultural industry; rather it tended to put in motion a variety of responses intended to improve or to encourage improvement in agriculture. Public policies helpful to agriculture appeared with undiminished frequency. Assistance to agriculture was accepted as a desirable and legitimate governmental activity. It became essential, however, to view farming in the context of a growing industrial technology. The family farm was to become a commercial unit, with price levels, markets, and credit matters of prime concern.

Foreign markets became an important consideration for the American economy as a whole and farm products, being about 75 percent of the total United States exports, were significant in this respect. The gearing of agricultural production to the export markets, with resulting dependence upon world prices, became and remained a factor of prime importance to commercial agriculture.

Organized efforts to obtain better economic conditions in farming revealed that not all of agriculture was adapting satisfactorily to the new commercial status. Individual farmers clung to the established socio-economic patterns, or changed very slowly. Others sought, with varying degrees of success, to adapt to the technological changes that were enveloping American culture.

Farm organizations during the period 1860–1890 reflect the undifferentiated image of the agricultural community at the same time that their activities furnish a clue to the diffused pattern that was to come. The leading post-Civil War farm organization was the Grange, formed in 1867. This group prospered during the hard times of the 1870's, reaching a high point of 858,000 members by 1875. Its activities in obtaining state laws regulating the railroads (a model for the Interstate Commerce Commission Act of 1887) are well known and the Illinois statute of 1871 (regulating many aspects of interstate rail transportation) set the pattern for the so-called Granger laws. The objectives of the Grange were quite broadly conceived and extended into many aspects of rural educational improvement and community development, electoral reform, and elimination of corruption in public administration.

As the Grange began to decline after 1875, it was overshadowed for a time by the Farmers Alliance movement, made up of relatively autonomous groups functioning in a local or regional context. These groups continued the struggle against economic inequities and injustices, by both their political and economic activities. They served to strengthen the agrarian identity and to prepare for the more trying struggles that lay ahead.

*Gilbert C. Fite*

## 13. LAND POLICIES IN THE TRANS-MISSOURI WEST

Between 1860 and 1890 the western frontier with its free arable land reached the vanishing point. Agriculture and American society in general were greatly influenced by this transformation. At the same time that the physical problems of agricultural settlement were greatly changed by the climatic conditions of the trans-Missouri West, agricultural policy also underwent an important maturation. The products of agricultural fundamentalism took shape in legislation of direct and great significance to the New West. The selection below continues and completes the material on land policy in the United States presented in the last chapter.

Land was the greatest undeveloped resource on the upper midwest prairie frontier. It was land which most pioneers hoped to exploit, either by actual farming or by holding it for speculative gain. The three main ways of acquiring land were by purchase, preemption, or under the Homestead Act of 1862. Known as "an act to secure homesteads to actual settlers on the public domain," the homestead law was cast in a democratic mold and was a victory for those who believed that it was socially and economically important to people the land with small proprietors. President Andrew Johnson said in 1865 that, "the lands in the hands of industrious settlers, whose labor creates wealth and contributes to the public resources, are worth more to the United States than if they had been reserved as a solitude for future purchasers." Alvin Saun-

From Gilbert C. Fite, *The Farmers' Frontier 1865-1900* (New York: Holt, Rinehart, and Winston, Inc., 1966), pp. 15-21. Reprinted by permission of the publisher.

ders, territorial Governor of Nebraska, declared: "What a blessing this wise and humane legislation will bring to many a poor, but honest and industrious family. Its benefits can never be estimated in dollars and cents." Although this early exuberance over the Homestead Act later proved to be somewhat unjustified, it did represent a great democratic principle of trying to give more people a propertied stake in society.

Under the Homestead Law, a male or female citizen over 21 years old, the head of a family, or a person who had declared his intention to become a citizen, was permitted to file on 160 acres of the public domain. The only cost was a filing fee of $10, plus some other small miscellaneous charges. After making improvements and residing on the tract for 5 years, the applicant could apply for the final patent, or title. If a homesteader did not want to fulfill the 5-year residence requirement, he could, after 6 months, gain title to his land by paying the government $1.25 an acre in cash ($2.50 in designated railroad land grant areas). This was known as commutation of a homestead. Although the commutation provision opened up a way to violate the democratic intent of the Homestead Act and made it possible to monopolize land, the law specifically sought to promote actual farm settlement. Section 2 provided that every person applying for a homestead had to swear that it was "for his or her exclusive use and benefit, and that said entry is made for the purpose of actual settlement and cultivation, and not, either directly or indirectly, for the use or benefit of any other person or persons whomsoever. . . ."

Settlers could also obtain land under the preemption law of 1841. This measure permitted a qualified person to acquire 160 acres of government land for the minimum price of $1.25 an acre. The preemptor also had to make some improvements and live on the land about 14 months before he could gain final title. As was true under the Homestead Act, the preemptor had to swear that the land was for his own exclusive use

and that it was not being acquired for sale or speculation. The laws permitted a settler to file for both a homestead and preemption claim, making it possible to acquire a total of 320 acres directly from the federal government.

The third principal method of getting land was by purchase. This had always been the main way of acquiring land on the American frontier and it continued to be the most usual means to obtain a farm after 1865. Despite what appeared to be liberal land laws, which were aimed at helping actual settlers acquire a farm for little or no cash, there was much less land open to public entry than was generally assumed. This was because the federal government gave away millions of acres to the states for educational and other purposes, and to the railroads in order to stimulate the rapid building of transportation facilities in the West. Moreover, additional millions of acres acquired when Indian titles were extinguished were put up for sale and specifically barred from homestead and preemption entries.

For example, when Kansas entered the Union, the state was given 3,495,494 acres for education and internal improvements, and additional land was turned over to the state later. Land grants and land controlled by railroads in Kansas amounted to 10,340,512 acres, or about one fifth of the entire state. In Nebraska the Union Pacific was granted 4,846,108 acres and the Burlington approximately 2,400,000. Thus while 1,471,761 acres were acquired in Nebraska between 1863 and 1872 under the Homestead and Preemption acts, land granted to railroads, and that bought with agricultural college scrip and with soldiers' bounty land warrants amounted to 9,435,796 acres. About 40 percent of the land in Kansas was withdrawn from the public domain, removing it from homestead and preemption entry. These millions of acres owned by the railroads, the states, and those held for sale by the federal government were sold at the most favorable figure obtainable. Moreover, those who had land for sale often owned the most desirable tracts. In Nebraska, for example, much of the best land in the Platte River Valley was owned by the Union Pacific.

Consequently, when the settler arrived in southwestern Minnesota, southeastern Dakota, northwestern Iowa, or eastern Nebraska and Kansas in the late 1860s and early 1870s, he frequently found that much of the best land was already owned by the state, corporations, or land speculators and was unavailable for homesteading or preemption. Therefore, he had to buy land. Much of the advertising to attract settlers to the Western states and territories in this period emphasized that good lands were for *sale.* Even where land was available for homesteading, many farmers continued to purchase their farms from the federal government, state, railroads, or large holders because much of the land subject to homestead entry was likely to be far from transportation facilities and distant from markets. It was thought good business to pay $2.50 to $10 an acre for choice land near the railroad, rather than obtain free land or pay the government price of $1.25 an acre and be forced to locate 20 to 50 miles from transportation.

There were harsh complaints against those who moved in ahead of the actual settlers and through grants or purchases acquired and held large quantities of the best land for speculative gain. The Saint Paul *Weekly Pioneer* bitterly declared on January 4, 1867, that "almost two whole counties have been entered with college scrip and land warrants by speculators. . . . These two counties had far better have been visited by the locusts of Egypt or the grasshoppers of the Red River than by these speculators." Because of the practice of holding land for speculation, the editor continued: "Whole townships have been *doomed* as the homes of whippoorwills and owls—and 'No Admittance' written over them with 'agricultural college scrip,' to the hardy pioneers in search of homes." Evidences of extensive land holdings were reported by other fron-

tier newspapers. The Nebraska City *News* for example, declared in September 1867 that "seven thousand acres of land lying west of Lincoln (Nebraska) were entered by a gentleman from Pennsylvania last week." The editor of the *Kansas Farmer* complained that "the settlement of the state is retarded by land monopolists, corporate and individual." The worst offenders, he said, were the owners of college scrip. He argued that Kansas would have been much better off if the state contained "but two classes of land owners—the government and the actual settler. The public lands should have been kept for homesteads and pre-emption." This Kansan believed that the government should have given money or credit to the railroads and agricultural colleges, rather than land.

By the late 1860s and early 1870s, criticisms of land monopoly, along with a growing concern about the disappearance of good public lands upon which settlers could establish a farm under the homestead or preemption laws, prompted Congress to review its land policies. In March 1870, William S. Holman of Indiana offered a resolution in the House of Representatives stating that "the policy of granting subsidies in public lands to railroads and other corporations ought to be discontinued . . .," and that public lands should be held for "the exclusive purpose of securing homesteads to actual settlers under the homestead and preemption laws. . . . The next year Congress discontinued granting land to railroads. Moreover, both major political parties became concerned with the land question by 1872. The Liberal Republicans, with Democratic support, and Republicans stated in their respective platforms that the national domain should be "held sacred to actual settlers," and "for free homes for the people."

Part of the resentment against those who held large acreages for speculation was due to the fact that farmers themselves were a breed of land speculator who objected to seeing their opportunity for speculative profits reduced. Many pioneer farmers had no intention of developing their homestead or preemption claim. Like the big speculator, thousands of small farmers were convinced that they could make more money by getting land cheap, or for nothing, and holding it for increased prices, than by the slow, hard work of farming.

Commenting on small-scale speculation in 1879, the editor of the *Kansas Farmer* complained that a large number of settlers "have no other purpose than to go on the outskirts of the settlements, preempt the best lands," build a cabin, and stay only long enough to secure a patent so the land could be mortgaged or sold. "This is averse to the intention and spirit of the law," the editor continued, "and no such scheme of small speculation should be permitted. The restless spirit which consumes his day in squatting, does not add to the wealth of the nation or contribute to the welfare of society. . . ." This writer suggested that the time of residence should be extended to 10 or even 15 years. Thus, he said, "the mania for frontier wandering would be sensibly checked," and "the frontiers would be much better improved if they were not advanced so rapidly. . . ."

Despite the fact that millions of acres fell into the hands of corporations and speculators who held them for profitable prices, there was no real lack of good land on the Minnesota, Dakota, Nebraska, and Kansas frontier in the late 1860s and early 1870s that could be obtained free or at very cheap prices. Between the western edge of settlement in 1865 and a line roughly from Valley City, North Dakota, to Hutchinson, Kansas, there were millions of unoccupied acres of productive land that farmers could obtain by homesteading or preemption. There would have been millions of additional acres if the federal government had not given land to railroads and if former Indian lands had been opened for public entry rather than placed on the market for sale. But until at least the middle of the 1870s there was enough good land for homesteading and preemption within areas of fairly dependable rainfall for about all of the farmers who actually wanted to farm. It was not

until the late 1870s when settlers had to push farther west into areas where the soil was poorer and rainfall scarcer that the problem of getting a good quarter section became acute and the question of reserving land for actual settlers became a national issue. By that time, however, it was too late to do much about reserving land for farmers because most of the area susceptible to farming under conditions of natural rainfall and the then known agricultural technology was already in private hands. It should be emphasized again, too, that many of the "actual settlers" about whom so much was said in and out of Congress never intended to farm their homesteads. They were nothing but small-time speculators.

After 1873 land could also be obtained from the federal government under the Timber Culture Act. The purpose of this law was to promote the planting and growth of timber on the western prairies. It was argued that groves of trees would reduce the winds, attract increased rainfall, and provide lumber for building and fuel. Under this measure, a person could obtain 160 acres of government land in return for planting and cultivating 40 acres of trees. At the end of 10 years, later reduced to 8, final title would be granted if the settler could prove that the specified number of trees per acre were healthy and growing. Since it was not feasible for most farmers to plant and care for 40 acres of trees, an amendment in 1878 reduced the acres to 10. Between 1873 and 1880 some 64,535 original entries were made for 9,346,660 acres, mostly in Kansas, Nebraska, and Dakota. Even though a farmer might have already filed on a homestead and preempted land, he could also enter what was known as a tree claim. Consequently, many of the entries under this law were by farmers who wanted to get more land and expand their operations. A relatively small amount of land was obtained under the Timber Culture Act, and up to 1904, final patents had been issued on some 9,745,000 acres.

Although the westward movement of settlers continued during the Civil War, not many homesteads were filed in the states and territories of this north central frontier until the late 1860s. The first homestead was filed by Daniel Freeman a few miles west of Beatrice, Nebraska, on January 1, 1863. Up to 1868 more homesteads were entered in Minnesota than in any other state. During the 6 years from 1863 to 1868, inclusive, 19,251 persons filed on approximately 2,500,000 acres there. This was more than the combined total of Kansas, Dakota, and Nebraska, which had 6244, 1205, and 7858 entries, respectively, during that period. In 1869 Nebraska drew the most homesteaders, and the next year Kansas took the lead with 5024, or 2000 more than Minnesota.

The first real boom in homesteading on the Minnesota-Dakota-Nebraska-Kansas frontier, however, took place in the early 1870s. In 1871 entries in these states and territories totaled 20,237 and covered 2,571,209 acres. When a new land office was opened in Concordia, Kansas, on January 16, 1871, there was a mad scramble to file claims. A receiver at the office recalled: "The door was opened—a shout—a rush—a scramble over each other—a confused shouting of the number of the range and township, as a half-dozen or more simultaneously presented their papers to the officers. . . ." Kansas alone had more than 9000 entries in both 1871 and 1872. Not until the hard times of the middle 1870s was there a marked decline in filings, and this was only temporary. Thousands of homesteaders on this frontier received final patent through the regular homestead procedure before 1880 after living on their land for 5 years. Others took advantage of the commutation feature so they could gain full title more quickly.

Despite this record of homestead settlement in the 1860s and 1870s, the Homestead Act has been severely criticized on the basis that it really did not help a great many farmers get established on the land. It has been charged that the law was superimposed on a land system that continued extensive sales of public lands, that the commutation privilege permitted the act to be abused, that it encouraged monopoly and speculation, and that it perverted the law's democratic aims. Moreover, critics have held that 160 acres was not enough land on which to make a living in much of the West still available for settlement after 1862. To put it another way, the law was not suited to the geography of the Great West.

Although the Homestead Act had many weaknesses in both form and administration, most of the critics have misjudged its value as a farm-making measure, at least on the upper midwest prairie frontier. Moreover, much of the complaint completely ignores the time and circumstances under which the law was passed and placed in operation. While it is true that the Homestead Act was not suitable for much of the area west of the 100th meridian, no one in 1862 was thinking of applying the law to the arid and semiarid portions of the West. Indeed, most Americans who thought anything about it were convinced that much of the Far West could never be settled by crop farmers under any circumstances. When the measure was enacted, settlement was still well within the humid region of the Mississippi Valley, where 160 acres was sufficient for the average family.

# 14. THE FIRST MORRILL ACT OF 1862

*An act donating public lands to the several States and territories which may provide colleges for the benefit of agriculture and mechanic arts.*

*Be it enacted by the Senate and House of Representatives of the United States of America in Congress assembled,* That there be granted to the several States, for the purposes hereinafter mentioned, an amount of public land, to be apportioned to each State a quantity equal to thirty thousand acres for each Senator and Representative in Congress to which the States are respectively entitled by the apportionment under the census of eighteen hundred and sixty: *Provided,* That no mineral lands shall be selected or purchased under the provisions of this act.

*Sec. 2. And be it further enacted,* That the land aforesaid, after being surveyed, shall be apportioned to the several States in sections or subdivisions of sections, not less than one-quarter of a section; and whenever there are public lands in a State subject to sale at private entry at one dollar and twenty-five cents per acre, the quantity to which said State shall be entitled shall be selected from such lands within the limits of such State, and the Secretary of the Interior is hereby directed to issue to each of the States in which there is not the quantity of public lands subject to sale at private entry at one dollar and twenty-five cents per acre to which said State may be entitled under the provisions of this act land scrip to the amount in acres for the deficiency of its distributive share; said scrip to be sold by said States and the proceeds thereof applied to the uses and purposes prescribed in this act and for no other use or purpose whatsoever: *Provided,* That in no case shall any State to

which land scrip may thus be issued be allowed to locate the same within the limits of any other State or of any Territory of the United States, but their assignees may thus locate said land scrip upon any of the unappropriated lands of the United States subject to sale at private entry at one dollar and twenty-five cents, or less per acre: *And provided further,* That not more than one million acres shall be located by such assignees in any one of the States: *And provided further,* That no such location shall be made before one year from the passage of this act.

*Sec. 3. And be it further enacted,* That all the expenses of management, superintendence, and taxes from date of selection of said lands, previous to their sales, and all expenses incurred in the management and disbursement of the moneys which may be received therefrom, shall be paid by the States to which they may belong, out of the treasury of said States, so that the entire proceeds of the sale of said lands shall be applied without any diminution whatever to the purposes hereinafter mentioned.

*Sec. 4. (original). And be it further enacted,* That all moneys derived from the sale of the lands aforesaid by the States to which the lands are apportioned, and from the sales of land scrip hereinbefore provided for, shall be invested in stocks of the United States or of the States, or some other sale stocks, yielding not less than five per centum upon the par value of said stocks; and that the moneys so invested shall constitute a perpetual fund, the capital of which shall remain forever undiminished (except so far as may be provided in section five of this act), and the interest of which shall be inviolably appropriated by each State which may take and claim the benefit of this act, to the endowment, support, and maintenance of at

From 12 *Statutes-at-Large* (1862), p. 503.

least one college where the leading object shall be, without excluding other scientific and classical studies, and including military tactics, to teach such branches of learning as are related to agriculture and the mechanic arts, in such manner as the legislatures of the States may respectively prescribe, in order to promote the liberal and practical education of the industrial classes in the several pursuits and professions in life.

*Sec. 4* (as amended Mar. 3, 1883). That all moneys derived from the sale of lands aforesaid by the States to which lands are apportioned, and from the sales of land scrip hereinbefore provided for, shall be invested in stocks of the United States or of the States, or some other safe stocks; or the same may be invested by the States having no State stocks in any other manner after the legislatures of such States shall have assented thereto, and engaged that such funds shall yield not less than five per centum upon the amount so invested and that the principal thereof shall forever remain unimpaired: *Provided,* That the moneys so invested or loaned shall constitute a perpetual fund, the capital of which shall remain forever undiminished (except so far as may be provided in section five of this act), and the interest of which shall be inviolably appropriated, by each State which may take and claim the benefit of this act, to the endowment, support, and maintenance of at least one college where the leading object shall be, without excluding other scientific and classical studies, and including military tactics, to teach such branches of learning as are related to agriculture and the mechanic arts, in such manner as the legislatures of the States may respectively prescribe, in order to promote the liberal and practical education of the industrial classes in the several pursuits and professions in life.

*Sec. 5. And be it further enacted,* That the grant of land and land scrip hereby authorized shall be made on the following conditions, to which, as well as to the provisions hereinbefore contained, the previous assent of the several States shall be signified by legislative acts:

*First.* If any portion of the fund invested, as provided by the foregoing section, or any portion of the interest thereon, shall, by any action or contingency, be diminished or lost, it shall be replaced by the State to which it belongs, so that the capital of the fund shall remain forever undiminished; and the annual interest shall be regularly applied without diminution to the purposes mentioned in the fourth section of this act, except that a sum, not exceeding ten per centum upon the amount received by any State under the provisions of this act, may be expended for the purchase of lands for sites or experimental farms whenever authorized by the respective legislatures of said States.

*Second.* No portion of said fund, nor the interest thereon, shall be applied, directly or indirectly, under any pretense whatever, to the purchase, erection, preservation, or repair of any building or buildings.

*Third.* Any State which may take and claim the benefit of the provisions of this act shall provide, within five years, at least not less than one college, as described in the fourth section of this act, or the grant to such State shall cease; and said State shall be bound to pay the United States the amount received of any lands previously sold and that the title to purchasers under the State shall be valid.

*Fourth.* An annual report shall be made regarding the progress of each college, recording any improvements and experiments made, with their cost and results, and such other matters, including State industrial and economical statistics, as may be supposed useful, one copy of which shall be transmitted by mail free, by each, to all the other colleges which may be endowed under the provisions of this act, and also one copy to the Secretary of the Interior.

*Fifth.* When lands shall be selected from those which have been raised to double the minimum price, in consequence of railroad grants, they shall be computed to the States at the maximum price and the number of acres proportionately diminished.

*Sixth.* No State while in a condition of

rebellion or insurrection against the Government of the United States shall be entitled to the benefit of this act.

*Seventh.* No State shall be entitled to the benefits of this act unless it shall express its acceptance thereof by its legislature within two years from the date of its approval by the President.

*Sec. 6. And be it further enacted,* That land scrip issued under the provisions of this act shall not be subject to location until after the first day of January, one thousand eight hundred and sixty-three.

*Sec. 7. And be it further enacted,* That the land officers shall receive the same fees for locating land scrip issued under the provisions of this act as is now allowed for the location of military bounty land warrants under existing laws: *Provided,* That their maximum compensation shall not be thereby increased.

*Sec. 8. And be it further enacted,* That the governors of the several States to which scrip shall be issued under this act shall be required to report annually to Congress all sales made of such scrip until the whole shall be disposed of, the amount received for the same, and what appropriation has been made of the proceeds.

*Leonard D. White*

## 15. **THE DEPARTMENT OF AGRICULTURE**

The establishment of the U.S. Department of Agriculture was a significant development in the administration of the federal government. Professor Leonard D. White, professor of public administration at the University of Chicago until his death in 1958, has placed this department in the context of administrative history in the selection below, a part of a well-known series of studies in the historical development of federal administration.

This newcomer to the administrative scene was unique in more than one respect. It was the first client-oriented Department; it was firmly based on science; it had a strong sense of mission; and it represented a new set of relations between the federal and the state governments. Beyond these outstanding characteristics the Department, after it acquired Cabinet status in 1889, enjoyed superior leadership in the succession of able Secretaries and famous scientists who were in charge of its fortunes.

The Department was organized in 1862, a year of agricultural developments whose significance has hardly been surpassed. In addition to establishing the Department (headed only by a Commissioner as a token of less than Cabinet status), Congress also passed the Morrill Act granting land to the states to found and support agricultural colleges, and the Homestead Act, opening up the public domain to home-owner farmer settlers. These were three major statutory foundations of federal agricultural policy for nearly a century.

The charter of the Department of Agriculture was comprehensive. Its "general designs and duties" were to acquire and to diffuse among the people useful information on subjects connected with agriculture "in the most general and comprehensive sense of that word," and to procure and dis-

Reprinted with permission of the Macmillan Company from *The Republican Era: A Study in Administrative Management* by Leonard D. White, pp. 232–248. Copyright 1958 by The Macmillan Company.

tribute new and valuable seeds and plants. The Commissioner of Agriculture was authorized to conduct practical and scientific experiments and to appoint persons skilled in the natural sciences pertaining to agriculture. Congress thus formally committed itself to science on a scale far beyond the slender enterprises of earlier years.

The new Department began its life with less than superior leadership. Isaac Newton, its first Commissioner, was a Pennsylvania Quaker, a friend of President Lincoln, who may perhaps not unfairly be described as an agricultural politician. Dr. Warner W. Stockberger, a later distinguished scientist-executive in the Department, observed that "he acquired a large circle of warm friends and became skilled in the art of practical politics." His appointment was severely criticized by the agricultural press, and the removal of a respected chief clerk to make room for his nephew forfeited confidence. To Newton's credit, it must be acknowledged that he also appointed some outstanding scientists: Charles M. Wetherill, educated in chemistry at the University of Pennsylvania and with a Ph.D. degree from the German University of Giessen; Dr. Thomas Antisell, trained in chemistry and medicine at Trinity College, Dublin, and the Dublin School of Medicine; William Saunders, horticulturist from the University of Edinburgh; and others.

Newton died in office in 1867. General Horace Capron, his successor, brought able executive talent to the new Department. Grant's Commissioner, Frederick Watts, was an elderly lawyer and judge with a passion for economy. He is said on occasion to have personally supervised employees tying up seed packets to guarantee no twine was wasted. He was lax in administration, testy and easily ruffled, but he, too, maintained high standards in his scientific appointments. Hayes' Commissioner, William G. LeDuc, another general, fought off the politicians vigorously and made no congressional friends.

His successor, George B. Loring, a noted Massachusetts physician and surgeon

turned farmer and politician, served on the State Board of Agriculture from 1860 to 1877 and was president of the New England Agricultural Society from 1864 to 1889. He was elected to Congress for two terms (1887-91) and was chairman of the state Republican committee from 1869 to 1877. He thus had good credentials, political, professional, and agricultural.

Despite vicissitudes of leadership and some congressional criticism, the functions of the Department steadily expanded during its early years. Small beginnings were made in the control of plant and animal diseases, in the search for new forage plants and grass suitable for arid regions, in agricultural chemistry, in forestry, and in two areas having a primarily economic significance: the collection of crop statistics as an aid to marketing, and the culture of cotton, silk, and especially sugar. Two functions of notable importance were added in the 1880's: the inspection of meat in interstate and foreign commerce, and guidance and leadership to the state agricultural experiment stations established in 1887 by the Hatch Act. The administrative significance of these activities is discussed at a later point.

In 1889, at the close of Cleveland's first administration, the Department was raised to Cabinet status. "For years," declared Secretary Jeremiah M. Rusk in his first annual report, "there had been a demand on the part of a large majority of the farmers of the country that that Department at the seat of government which was organized to represent their interests should be clothed with the same dignity and power that other Executive Departments had, and that it should have its influence in national affairs and be recognized in the councils of the nation." Thus culminated a movement that in its early days had been resisted as a dangerous piece of class legislation, opening the door to demands of other great economic groups for departments protective of their interests.

Elevation to Cabinet status sustained the triple foundation on which the Department had come to rest during its early years: scientific research, production, and marketing. Succeeding years were to strengthen and deepen these three basic functions. The first Secretary was the last and ablest Commissioner, Norman J. Colman. He served only a few weeks as Secretary, awaiting the inauguration of Benjamin Harrison.

### DEPARTMENTAL LEADERSHIP

Agriculture was exceptionally fortunate in its Secretaries, three of whom occupied this post from 1889 to 1913; Jeremiah M. Rusk of Wisconsin, Julius Sterling Morton of Nebraska, and James Wilson of Iowa. Their views concerning the function of government in agriculture were markedly different: Rusk was an expansionist, Morton held to laissez faire, Wilson, a former professor, was particularly concerned with agricultural education. All were men thoroughly familiar with agricultural problems; all were men of integrity; and all were dedicated to the improvement of the farmers' lot.

Jeremiah M. Rusk, known familiarly as "Uncle Jerry," came from a poor farm family, settled in Wisconsin, and almost immediately became a political success: county sheriff, coroner, and member of the state assembly. A brigadier general in the Civil War, he returned to political life as state bank comptroller and a member of Congress from 1871 to 1877. He was governor of Wisconsin from 1882 to 1889 and evidenced a lively and intelligent interest in farm life and movements. Harrison appointed him Secretary of Agriculture in 1889, desiring, he said, "a man who, primarily, had a good practical knowledge of agriculture—not of fancy farming, but of farming as a business, as a means of getting a livelihood; that he ought to come from one of the great agricultural states; that he ought to be a man in close touch with the class described by Mr. Lincoln as the 'plain people'; and that . . . he ought to be a man experienced in public affairs and public administration."

Rusk was impatient with small plans and determined to build a great department. In his first annual report he remarked that in establishing Agriculture as an executive department, "The intention of our lawmakers was not simply to add the luster of official dignity to an industry already dignified by the labor of its votaries, but to give it added influence and power for good in their behalf." After commenting on the broad scale of European departments he continued, "It is my desire to organize the Department upon even a broader plane than these and other countries have established." Disappointed because Congress had not already increased appropriations before he took office, he told the legislative branch that former resources "must not be regarded as a correct basis for the consideration of its present needs, and I, for my part, must absolutely refuse to recognize any such standard of comparison." To emphasize the point he declared, "I beg you to bear in mind that I speak in the name of the agricultural interests of the United States, and I opine that no member of either House will for a moment depreciate the extent, importance and influence of these interests in this country."

Rusk looked far beyond the present to a distant future when the population of the country would exceed 100,000,000 and the value of agricultural products would be double the three or four billion of his time. "It is rarely given to any single man," he wrote, "to superintend the completion of a great work which it has required a wide and mature experience to successfully plan, but the wise builder knows well that without a well-determined plan the building, when completed, will surely be found deficient in some respects. What this Department must eventually be . . . is the consideration which now deeply concerns me." He returned to this theme in his annual report for 1892: ". . . in the affairs of the nation true prescience is an essential attribute to the wise administrator. I must not, therefore, be deemed extravagant if I present designs for the future development of the Department which I conceive to be necessary to meet the demands not only of the near future but those of a score of years hence."

# III. Agricultural Fundamentalism and Science: 1860-1890

The vision of this man of the people was remarkable. He was equally concerned with pure and applied research, with the education of farmers in improved methods, with aid to marketing at home and abroad, and with the inspection of food products on a large scale. He it was, educated in the common schools alone, who sent experts abroad to establish contacts with agricultural institutions in other countries and who indignantly repelled his critics. "The suggestion of sending a well-qualified representative abroad purely in the interest of agriculture is cavilled at as a means of affording a pleasure trip to some broken-down professor. It is time that we rose superior to such humiliating and unworthy puerility."

Cleveland's Secretary of Agriculture, J. Sterling Morton, the originator of Arbor Day, was a Nebraska farmer and agricultural journalist. He was a man of strong opinions and had no reluctance in expressing them, let the consequences be what they might. Rusk had been an expansionist in government programs for farmers; Morton was his opposite—opposed to paternalism, devoted to *laissez faire*, insistent upon economy, but nevertheless a defender of the scientific work of the Department. In his first annual report in 1893 he declared that "the Department of Agriculture offers opulent opportunities for the exercise of the most pronounced paternalism." Within a few months he had reduced the departmental payroll by over 500 employees. In 1895 he was reported to have said that "if the department of agriculture is to be conducted in the spirit of paternalism the sooner it is abolished the better for the United States."

Morton's biographer, James C. Olson, recorded that he looked with suspicion upon every bill to appropriate money for special purposes, or that would extend the functions of government. Invited to comment on a proposed appropriation to exterminate the Russian thistle, Morton asked whether it was "the business of the Government of the United States to make appropriations out of which men, women, and boys are to be hired, at wages fixed by law, to exterminate weeds, called Russian thistles, any more than it is the business of that Government to prescribe the manner of plowing, planting, and cultivating cereals, cotton, and tobacco, and to limit the wages to be paid cultivators?"

Morton thus started with a social philosophy the antithesis of that held by Rusk. It naturally predisposed him to economy. He probed every division in search of opportunities to economize, and personally investigated individual accounts. Olson quoted from Morton's Letterbook a communication to an unfortunate director of an experiment station: "I notice that the feed-bill for your horses during the past ten months has averaged $178.77 per month. That I consider extravagant beyond all reason. . . . I wish it distinctly understood that wherever there is an opportunity to economize, it should be embraced with alacrity, and that if you do not economize some one will be put in your place who will."

*Laissez faire* doctrine and a passion for economy brought Morton into a head-on collision with Congress over the free distribution of seeds. This ancient function, in high favor with Congressmen, had grown to major proportions. Morton criticized the program in 1893, and in 1894 declared in his second annual report, "it is difficult to see how any practical statesman can advocate an annual disbursement of $160,000 for such a purpose. . . . If, in a sort of paternal way, it is the duty of this Government to distribute anything gratuitously, are not new ideas of more permanent value than old seeds? Is it a function of government to make gratuitous distribution of any material thing?" The special agent for the purchase of seeds, Enos S. Harnden, was equally candid. In the same annual report he wrote:

In the light of my experience as a former seedsman, however, I consider the free distribution of seeds by this Department as an infringement upon and interference with a legitimate business, and I believe it should be abolished.

The seed business, whether wholesale or retail, is to-day as much an established legitimate business as manufacturing or trading in any product or merchandise. I hold that this Department has no moral right to interfere with this or any other legitimate business interest by a free political distribution of garden seeds, spades, shovels, or plows, or of new styles of dress goods, or of any other commodity the subject of legitimate trade.

In 1895 Morton exercised his official discretion by rejecting all bids for the purchase of seeds, in effect impounding the appropriation and terminating the function. Congress loved its seed perquisites, however, and promptly passed a joint resolution directing Morton to proceed. He had no alternative.

Whatever the Secretary's views on such activities, they did not affect his support for those functions he considered appropriate. He was as strong an advocate of the Department (in its more restricted role) as had been Rusk. Morton believed that the central purpose of the Department was scientific investigation, and he was gratified to report in 1894 that his economies had not impaired capacity for research. For the fiscal year 1893, 45.6 per cent of the Department's expenditures went toward science; in 1894, the percentage was 51.8. During his four-year term Morton added three new lines of work—development of agrostology, the study of agricultural soils and crop production, and investigation of methods of road improvement. He was an able, courageous Secretary, but not one to expand the Department's functions to trench on the private economy.

Morton retired with Cleveland to be replaced by a professor of agriculture and director of the experiment station at Iowa State College, James Wilson. He was destined to hold the Secretary's office from 1897 to 1913, under McKinley, Roosevelt, and Taft. Wilson had been active in public affairs as well as in practical farming, teaching, and research. From 1867 to 1871 he was a member of the Iowa State house of representatives and sat in Congress from 1873 to 1877, and again from 1883 to 1885. He served on the House Committee on Agriculture. In the interim between his two terms he was a member of the Iowa Railway Commission,

and after his retirement from Congress he engaged in farming and in writing for farm journals until his association with Iowa State College in 1891. Wilson was eminently qualified by experience to head the Department of Agriculture. He had a commanding figure, was a tireless worker, and a Presbyterian of high moral principles. Under his administration the Department expanded in all directions. In his final report he summarized the work over which he had presided.

. . . Bureaus have been created and expanded. Lines of research, investigation, and demonstration have been multiplied. Congress has piled duty on duty from year to year. The corps of experts needed in the increasing amount and variety of service has grown greatly. The department has become a great agricultural university for postgraduate work. Discoveries for the benefit of farm practices and improvements of old ones have been countless. The department has both promoted and begun a revolution in the art and science of agriculture. Its influences for agricultural betterment have penetrated all regions of the national domain. . . .

Agriculture was thus fortunate in its leadership. Each of three successive Secretaries (like others in later years) were men who knew much about agriculture from personal experience and/or from professional activities. Each, moreover, had been active in public affairs and was quickly at home in the official world of Washington. On some policy matters they differed, but they were united in their devotion to agriculture, and above all to the application of science and research to agricultural practice. These men were more than politicians. They possessed a sense of mission, an attribute that permeated the whole Department.

## AGRICULTURE: A CLIENT-ORIENTED DEPARTMENT

The Department of Agriculture was concerned exclusively with the affairs of farmers. Secretary Rusk recognized that he was regarded in a special manner as the representative of the agricultural interest in government. In his first annual report he referred to "the class the Department was primarily designed to serve, i.e., the farmers." In his last annual report he noted "that agriculture is the only industry in this country having an individual representation in the National Government, possessing, as it does, an executive department devoted exclusively to its service. . . ." Throughout subsequent reports by Secretaries and division heads runs this undercurrent of devotion to the betterment of farm life.

The orientation of the Department toward its public was in full evidence in the publication program. In pursuance of farmers' interests, scientists worked out discoveries, but to translate science into terms usable by plain farmers was a separate art to which the Department bent much effort. "The very essence of the duties devolving on this Department of the Government," Rusk declared, "is that its results shall be promptly made available to the public by a comprehensive scheme of publication." Science was of little value to farmers unless and until it had been digested, and its findings stated in language that they could understand. Science, had, nevertheless, its own intrinsic value and deserved dissemination in scientific circles. There consequently developed a varied series of departmental publications. The annual report early fell into two parts: one concerned with administrative matters, the other—the *Yearbook*—with the science and art of agriculture. The *Yearbook*, with annual editions of 500,000, was the largest single government publication.

A publications division was established in 1890 to ensure oversight and vigor in the Department's program. Special bulletins emanating from the scientific laboratories were encouraged in language suitable for the average layman; and also, in briefer form and plain terms, the practical conclusions of the scientific investigations "on a scale so extensive as to practically reach all the farmers of this country." Rusk reported in 1889 that in nine months the number of publications circulated by the Department

was 469,100. The folding room, as the mailing division was called, was hard put to it to keep abreast of the flood.

Rusk also cultivated the rural press. He always prepared the releases covering important transactions of the Department. As Ex-President Harrison noted: "The favor and aid of the agricultural press he regarded as essential, and sought by every means to make it a channel of communication between the Department and the farmers." In his press relations, Rusk was a pioneer.

The Department knew how to use its clientele for mutual advantage, notably in crop reporting. In 1893 the departmental statistician was supported by two corps of field correspondents, each numbering 10,000. One reported crop and other statistics directly to the Department, the other reported similar data to state agents of the Department. Beyond these correspondents the Department maintained a list of over 150,000 selected farmers who from time to time assisted in checking the accuracy of crop reports. Such a complex of client-relations was unknown in other governmental agencies.

Rusk sent his men directly to the farmers, attending agricultural institutes, state and county fairs, and meetings of specialized rural organizations—an activity that he had pressed with good results while governor of Wisconsin. In his first report Rusk included a special section on farmers' institutes. "I regard this institute work as one of the most beneficent movements the agricultural history of this country has ever witnessed." In his second report he was emphatic in his recommendations: "Not only do I deem it to be the utmost importance, indeed a solemn duty devolving upon this Department, that these meetings and gatherings should be encouraged in every possible way by this representative Department in the National Government, but I conceive it to be absolutely necessary for the intelligent conduct of the work of this Department that it should be frequently represented at such meetings. . . ." "Everything," he declared, "that leads to a more intimate acquaintance between the Department and the farmers throughout the country must be mutually advantageous."

None of the older Departments had an opportunity such as fell naturally to the lot of Agriculture. The interests of the Treasury and the taxpayer did not always seem identical, particularly to the latter; the Post Office served the whole people, not one group; the Pension Office was, by bitter experience, suspicious of its "customers" and had to renounce service for policing; neither War nor Navy had a definite clientele whom it served or upon whom it could rely for support in time of need. Agriculture had a special position, and it capitalized on its resources.

### AGRICULTURE AND SCIENCE

Another of the unique qualities of the Department of Agriculture was its solid foundation in science. The Organic Act of 1862 directed the Department to conduct practical and scientific experiments and authorized the appointment of chemists, botanists, entomologists, and other natural scientists. Despite the dominant interest of many Congressmen in the free distribution of seeds to their constituents, the departmental personnel was predominantly concerned with science, not seeds; with experimentation, not partisanship; with long-run, not merely immediate gains.

Scientific research and experimentation came into its own during the administration of Commissioner Norman J. Colman. He was one of the principal authors of the Hatch Act of 1887, authorizing funds for the establishment and partial support of the state agricultural experiment stations. A farm journalist professionally, Colman had deep convictions about the value of scientific research in crop production. "The path to success in this experiment-station enterprise," he wrote in 1888, "passes by the fountains of abstract science and by the farms and firesides of the American people." He declared that the Department should bring the best science of the world to the stations and help carry their findings home to the farmer.

Assistant Secretary Edwin Willits, in charge of the scientific bureaus and divisions, declared two years later: "Agriculture to be permanently successful must be founded on, and conducted according to scientific principle. . . . Nature can not be cheated, and her implacable laws will surely find out their transgressors . . . there are arts that promote and arts that prevent injury. Science is at the bottom of each." The halls of the Department, he wrote, "are instinct with science. The chiefs of their divisions and many of their subordinates are eminent in their special lines, and are recognized for their work and their ability the world over as the peers of any like body of investigators, seek where you may."

Willits was not idly boasting in his praise of the scientific corps of the Department. It had always possessed a group of men who stood high in their respective circles. A glimpse at the heads of the scientific divisions in 1891 suggests their eminence. Thirteen were recorded in the *Official Register* for that year; forty years later eight of them had earned a place in the *Dictionary of American Biography*.

The first chief of the Office of Experiment Stations, Wilbur O. Atwater, was a pioneer in agricultural chemistry, holding a Ph.D. from Yale and having two further years of advanced work in Leipzig and Berlin. He had been a professor of chemistry at Connecticut Wesleyan University and director of the first state agricultural experiment station at Middletown, Connecticut. He demonstrated that leguminous plants absorb free atmospheric nitrogen, and with a colleague invented the Atwater-Rosa calorimeter, an instrument that opened new vistas of research. He wrote several hundred scientific papers and translations.

The first chief of the Bureau of Animal Industry, Daniel E. Salmon, held the degree of doctor of veterinary medicine and had studied this specialty in Paris after doing basic work at Cornell University. During his long tenure as bureau chief (1884-1905), he demonstrated both high scientific attainment and great administrative ability. He wrote nearly one hundred papers on veterinary research, and was president of the American Public Health Association and of the American Veterinary Medical Association. After leaving the Bureau he organized the veterinary department of the University of Montevideo, Uruguay.

Bernard E. Fernow, chief of the Division of Forestry (1886-1898), received his professional training at the German University of Konigsberg and the Hanover-Munden Forest Academy. He quickly became a leader of the embryonic forestry conservation movement in this country, and after leaving the Department became dean of the Cornell University Forestry School. He also wrote prolifically, having a list of over two hundred articles and addresses on forestry.

The list need not be lengthened to confirm the high quality of the responsible scientists in the new Department. It was indeed instinct with science: astronomer Mark W. Harrington in the Weather Bureau; Dr. Harvey W. Wiley, chief chemist and protagonist of pure food; George Vasey, departmental botanist and distinguished specialist on grasses; Jacob R. Dodge, eminent statistician in charge of crop reporting; Charles V. Riley, noted entomologist; and others. Looking back over the years, Secretary James Wilson wrote: "A choice corps of scholarly experts in their special lines of endeavor has been growing in membership, in breadth of view, and in the practical application of their efforts. They have been and are men both good and true, men with high ideals, often sacrificing greater remuneration in private employment for love of the great results of their public service. No great work can be begun, nor sustained, by this department without such men."

These were years in which scientists had already begun the exchange of ideas and experimental findings through their professional organizations. In many of them departmental scientists participated, and in some of them they played a leading part. Notable among the latter group was the Association of Official Agricultural Chemists, whose annual conventions were held in Washington under departmental auspices, whose secretary was the chief chemist of the Department of Agriculture, and whose proceedings were published as a bulletin of the Chemical Division.

In 1891 Secretary Rusk had occasion to note summer conventions in Washington of ten scientific associations in whose work the Department had a lively interest, including by way of illustration the American Microscopical Society, the Conference of American Chemists, and the Association of Economic Entomologists. Rusk spoke with appreciation of the opportunity for the Department's scientific force to participate in these deliberations.

Rusk did not hesitate, either, to send his scientists abroad to attend professional and scientific meetings, despite the carping criticism against favors to broken-down professors. In 1891 he sent Daniel E. Salmon to the International Congress of Hygiene and Demography in London, and the International Congress of Agriculture at The Hague. Salmon was promptly elected first vice president of the International Congress of Agriculture. Rusk also sent Mark W. Harrington and one of his assistants in the Weather Bureau, Professor Cleveland Abbe, to the International Congress of Meteorologists at Munich.

Other departments, notably War and Navy, had pioneered in special areas of science, such as meteorology, oceanography, geology, and exploration. Agriculture was the first department for which science was the central fact of existence. The quality of departmental life in Agriculture was consequently markedly different from that of Treasury, the Post Office, or Interior, where science played almost no part and mass routine required the employment of clerks rather than the service of men trained in science. There were few, if any, doctors of philosophy elsewhere than in Agriculture. Here they dominated the official scene.

## THE BUREAU OF ANIMAL INDUSTRY

The quarantine and destruction of diseased animals was the first major regulatory function of the Department of Agriculture, the forerunner of an immense development in later years. The exportation of livestock to Great Britain began in the 1870's. It soon encountered restrictions intended to prevent the introduction of diseased cattle, especially those afflicted with pleuropneumonia. This disease had been prevalent among American herds for many years; state-wide attempts to eliminate it were inept and unsuccessful. Agitation for federal action began by 1880 but Congress was dilatory. A German embargo on American meat imports in 1883 and renewed agitation in the cattle trade finally induced Congress in 1884 to establish the Bureau of Animal Industry. Its duties were primarily to suppress communicable diseases among livestock. The Secretary of the Treasury was empowered to make regulations concerning their export and transportation, a duty soon transferred to Agriculture. The authority of the Bureau was increased in 1886 by permitting the purchase and destruction of diseased animals. The Bureau now made a determined effort in conjunction with the states. Pleuropneumonia was completely eradicated by 1892.

The European market was not fully restored. Meat inspection so far as it existed was carried on by state and local authorities and was far from adequate. A Senate select committee reported in 1890 that inspection was "in a singularly loose and unsatisfactory condition, without system, and in many localities entirely neglected . . . we have no hesitation in declaring that the failure of State and municipal authorities, within whose exclusive jurisdiction the matter rests, to provide stringent and efficient inspection of all animals intended for slaughter is in the highest degree criminal." Congress responded to this call for aid to foreign markets by authorizing the inspection of livestock destined for the export trade. Rusk had already made the strongest representations in favor of national inspection of cattle in the interest of both foreign trade and domestic health. Administrative authority over the slaughter and transportation of infected livestock was gradually but steadily enlarged on the basis of this original legislation.

The Bureau of Animal Industry thus became the earliest regulatory arm of the Department of Agriculture. It also engaged in scientific research, formally recognized by Congress in 1896 by appropriations for a pathological division and a biochemic division, but the bulk of its effort went into the eradication of animal disease by inspection and quarantine.

## THE EXPERIMENT STATIONS: FEDERAL-STATE RELATIONS

The first agricultural experiment station was established in Connecticut in 1875. By 1886 there were seventeen. They were usually associated with the land grant colleges, and there was some interchange of faculty and research personnel between them. They were exclusively state institutions, financed by state funds, and had no connection with the Department of Agriculture.

In 1887 Congress passed the Hatch Act setting up cooperative relations between the stations and the Department. By this legislation Congress authorized the establishment of agricultural experiment stations in the land grant colleges and appropriated $15,000 to the support of each one of them subject to the consent of the respective state legislatures. The stations were directed to conduct original research or to verify experiments on the physiology and diseases of plants and animals, on the analysis of soils and water, and to carry on such other research as might be deemed advisable. This was a generous charter of authority. Legislative assent by the states and territories was quickly forthcoming, and the number of stations rapidly increased.

The Hatch Act made no provision for federal control over the state experiment stations or the expenditure of the federal grant. The Commissioner was merely directed "to furnish forms . . . for the tabulation of results of investigation or experiment . . . to indicate, from time to time, such lines of inquiry as to him shall seem most important; and, in general, furnish such advice and assistance as will best promote the purposes of this act." Each station, furthermore, was required to make a full and detailed report of its operations, including receipts and expenditures, to the governor of the state. A copy was sent to the Department of Agriculture and to the Treasury for information. Congress obviously intended no federal control over the research projects, organization, or expenditures of the state experiment stations. It did encourage all the states to establish stations, and it did foresee some vague effort toward coordination of research results, all on a voluntary basis.

## 16. ACT OF 1887 ESTABLISHING SCIENTIFIC RESEARCH IN AGRICULTURE

The further development of a potent system of federal support for commercial agriculture was indicated by the provision of federal subsidies for research and experimentation in the application of science to agriculture. These provisions were embodied in federal legislation enacted in 1887, known as the Hatch Act, which is reprinted below.

*An act to establish agricultural experiment stations in connection with the colleges established in the several States under the provisions of an act approved July second, eighteen hundred and sixty-two, and of the acts supplementary thereto.*

*Be it enacted by the Senate and House of Representatives of the United States of America in Congress assembled,* That in order to aid in acquiring and diffusing among the people of the United States useful and practical information on subjects connected with agriculture, and to promote scientific investigation and experiment respecting the principles and applications of agricultural science, there shall be established under direction of the college or colleges or agricultural department of colleges in each State or Territory established, or which may hereafter be established, in accordance with the provisions of an act approved July second, eighteen hundred and sixty-two, entitled "An act donating public lands to the several States and Territories which may provide colleges for the benefit of agriculture and the mechanic arts," or any of the supplements to said act, a department to be known and designated as an "agricultural experiment station": *Provided,* That in any State or Territory in which two such colleges have been or may be so established the appropriation hereinafter made to such State or Territory shall be equally divided between such colleges, unless the legislature of such State or Territory shall otherwise direct.

*Sec. 2.* That it shall be the object and duty of said experiment stations to conduct original researches or verify experiments on the physiology of plants and animals; the diseases to which they are severally subject, with the remedies of the same; the chemical

From 24 *Statutes-at-Large* (1887), p.440.

composition of useful plants at their different stages of growth; the comparative advantages of rotative cropping as pursued under the varying series of crops; the capacity of new plants or trees for acclimation; the analysis of soils and water; the chemical composition of manures, natural or artificial, with experiments designed to test the comparative effects on crops of different kinds; the adaptation and value of grasses and forage plants; the composition and digestibility of the different kinds of food for domestic animals; the scientific and economic questions involved in the production of butter and cheese; and such other researches or experiments bearing directly on the agricultural industry of the United States as may in each case be deemed advisable, having due regard to the varying conditions and needs of the respective States or Territories.

Sec. 3. That in order to secure, as far as practicable, uniformity of methods and results in the work of said stations, it shall be the duty of the United States Commissioner (now Secretary) of Agriculture to furnish forms, as far as practicable, for the tabulation of results of investigation or experiments; to indicate from time to time such lines of inquiry as to him shall seem most important, and, in general, to furnish such advice and assistance as will best promote the purpose of this act. It shall be the duty of each of said stations annually, on or before the first of February, to make to the governor of the State or Territory in which it is located a full and detailed report of its operations, including a statement of receipts and expenditures, a copy of which report shall be sent to each of said stations, to the said Commissioner (now Secretary) of Agriculture, and to the Secretary of the Treasury of the United States.

Sec. 4. That bulletins or reports of progress shall be published at said stations at least once in three months, one copy of which shall be sent to each newspaper in the States or Territories in which they are respectively located, and to such individuals actually engaged in farming as may request the same and as far as the means of the station will permit. Such bulletins or reports and the annual reports of said stations shall be transmitted in the mails of the United States free of charge for postage, under such regulations as the Postmaster General may from time to time prescribe.

Sec. 5. That for the purpose of paying the necessary expenses of conducting investigations and experiments and printing and distributing the results as hereinbefore prescribed, the sum of fifteen thousand dollars per annum is hereby appropriated to each State, to be specially provided for by Congress in the appropriations from year to year, and to each Territory entitled under the provisions of section eight of this act, out of any money in the Treasury proceeding from the sales of public lands, to be paid in equal quarterly payments on the first day of January, April, July, and October in each year, to the treasurer or other officer duly appointed by the governing boards of said colleges to receive the same, the first payment to be made on the first day of October, eighteen hundred and eighty-seven: Provided, however, That out of the first annual appropriation so received by any station an amount not exceeding one-fifth may be expended in the erection, enlargement, or repair of a building or buildings necessary for carrying on the work of such station; and thereafter an amount not exceeding five per centum of such annual appropriation may be so expended.

Sec. 6. That whenever it shall appear to the Secretary of the Treasury from the annual statement of receipts and expenditures of any of said stations that a portion of the preceding annual appropriation remains unexpended, such amount shall be deducted from the next succeeding annual appropriation to such station, in order that the amount of money appropriated to any station shall not exceed the amount actually and necessarily required for its maintenance and support.

Sec. 7. That nothing in this act shall be construed to impair or modify the legal relation existing between any of the said colleges, and the government of the States or Territories in which they are respectively located.

*Sec. 8.* That in States having colleges entitled under this section to the benefits of this act and having also agricultural experiment stations established by law separate from said colleges, such States shall be authorized to apply such benefits to experiments at stations so established by such States; and in case any State shall have established, under the provisions of said act of July second aforesaid, an agricultural department or experimental station in connection with any university, college, or institution not distinctly an agricultural college or school, and such State shall have established or shall hereafter establish a separate agricultural college or school, which shall have connected therewith an experimental farm or station, the legislature of such State may apply in whole or in part the appropriation by this act made to such separate agricul-

tural college or school, and no legislature shall by contract, express or implied, disable itself from so doing.

*Sec. 9.* That the grants of moneys authorized by this act are made subject to the legislative assent of the several States and Territories to the purposes of said grants: *Provided,* That payment of such installments of the appropriation herein made as shall become due to any State before the adjournment of the regular session of its legislature meeting next after the passage of this act shall be made upon the assent of the governor thereof duly certified to the Secretary of the Treasury.

*Sec. 10.* Nothing in this act shall be held or construed as binding the United States to continue any payments from the Treasury to any or all the States or institutions mentioned in this act, but Congress may at any time amend, suspend, or repeal any or all the provisions of this act.

## 17. **THE SECOND MORRILL ACT OF 1890**

*An act to apply a portion of the proceeds of the public lands to the more complete endowment and support of the colleges for the benefit of agriculture and the mechanic arts established under the provisions of an act of Congress approved July second, eighteen hundred and sixty-two.*

*Be it enacted by the Senate and House of Representatives of the United States of America in Congress assembled,* That there shall be, and hereby is, annually appropriated, out of any money in the Treasury not otherwise appropriated, arising from the sales of public lands, to be paid as hereinafter provided, to each State and territory for the more complete endowment and maintenance of colleges for the benefit of agriculture and the mechanic arts now established, or which may be hereafter established, in ac-

cordance with an act of Congress approved July second, eighteen hundred and sixty-two, the sum of fifteen thousand dollars for the year ending June thirtieth, eighteen hundred and ninety, and an annual increase of the amount of such appropriation thereafter for ten years by an additional sum of one thousand dollars over the preceding year, and the annual amount to be paid thereafter to each State and Territory shall be twenty-five thousand dollars, to be applied only to instruction in agriculture, the mechanic arts, the English language, and the various branches of mathematical, physical, natural, and economic science, with special reference to their applications in the industries of life and to the facilities for such instruction: *Provided,* That no money shall be paid out under this act to any State or Territory for the support and mainte-

From 26 *Statutes-at-Large* (1890), p. 417.

nance of a college where a distinction of race or color is made in the admission of students, but the establishment and maintenance of such colleges separately for white and colored students shall be held to be a compliance with the provisions of this act if the funds received in such State or Territory be equitably divided as hereinafter set forth: *Provided,* That in any State in which there has been one college established in pursuance of the act of July second, eighteen hundred and sixty-two, and also in which an educational institution of like character has been established, or may be hereafter established, and is now aided by such State from its own revenue, for the education of colored students in agriculture and the mechanic arts, however named or styled, or whether or not it has received money heretofore under the act to which this act is an amendment, the legislature of such State may propose and report to the Secretary of the Interior a just and equitable division of the fund to be received under this act, between one college for white students and one institution for colored students, established aforesaid, which shall be divided into two parts, and paid accordingly, and thereupon such institution for colored students shall be entitled to the benefits of this act and subject to its provisions, as much as it would have been if it had been included under the act of eighteen hundred and sixty-two, and the fulfillment of the foregoing provisions shall be taken as a compliance with the provision in reference to separate colleges for white and colored students.

*Sec. 2.* That the sums hereby appropriated to the States and Territories for the further endowment and support of colleges shall be annually paid on or before the thirty-first day of July of each year, by the Secretary of the Treasury, upon the warrant of the Secretary of the Interior, out of the Treasury of the United States, to the State or Territorial treasurer, or to such officer as shall be designated by the laws of such State or Territory to receive the same, who shall, upon the order of the trustees of the college or the in-

stitution for colored students, immediately pay over said sums to the treasurers of the respective colleges or other institutions entitled to receive the same, and such treasurers shall be required to report to the Secretary of Agriculture and to the Secretary of the Interior on or before the first day of September of each year a detailed statement of the amount so received and of its disbursement. The grants of moneys authorized by this act are made subject to the legislative assent of the several States and Territories to the purpose of said grants: *Provided,* That payments of such installments of the appropriation herein made as shall become due to any State before the adjournment of the regular session of legislature meeting next after the passage of this act shall be made upon the assent of the governor thereof, duly certified to the Secretary of the Treasury.

*Sec. 3.* That if any portion of the moneys received by the designated officer of the State or Territory for the further and more complete endowment, support, and maintenance of colleges, or of institutions for colored students, as provided in this act, shall, by any action or contingency, be dismissed or lost, or be misapplied, it shall be replaced by the State or Territory to which it belongs, and until so replaced no subsequent appropriation shall be apportioned or paid to such State or Territory; and no portion of said moneys shall be applied, directly or indirectly, under any pretense whatever, to the purchase, erection, preservation, or repair of any building or buildings. An annual report by the president of each of said colleges shall be made to the Secretary of Agriculture, as well as to the Secretary of the Interior, regarding the condition and progress of each college, including statistical information in relation to its receipts and expenditures, its library, the number of its students and professors, and also as to any improvements and experiments made under the direction of any experiment stations attached to said colleges, with their cost and results and such other industrial and economical statistics as may be regarded as useful, one copy of which shall be transmitted by mail free to all other colleges further endowed under this act.

*Sec. 4.* That on or before the first day of July in each year, after the passage of this act, the Secretary of the Interior shall ascertain and certify to the Secretary of the Treasury as to each State and Territory, whether it is entitled to receive its share of the annual appropriation for colleges, or of institutions for colored students, under this act and the amount which thereupon each is entitled, respectively, to receive. If the Secretary of the Interior shall withhold a certificate from any State or Territory of its appropriation, the facts and reasons therefor shall be reported to the President, and the amount involved shall be kept separate in the Treasury until the close of the next Congress, in order that the State or Territory may, if it should so desire, appeal to Congress from the determination of the Secretary of the Interior. If the next Congress shall not direct such sum to be paid it shall be covered into the Treasury. And the Secretary of the Interior is hereby charged with the proper administration of this law.

*Sec. 5.* That the Secretary of the Interior shall annually report to Congress the disbursements which have been made in all the States and Territories, and also whether the appropriation of any State or Territory has been withheld, and, if so, the reasons therefor.

*Sec. 6.* Congress may at any time amend, suspend, or repeal any or all of the provisions of this act.

Frank M. Drew

## 18. FARMERS' SEARCH FOR IDENTITY

Farmers' movements became more prominent and more influential in the decades following the Civil War. Between 1860-1890 the groundwork was laid not only for the agrarian revolts of the 1890's but also for ongoing progressive and reform movements that took a variety of forms.

The following were the major farm organizations of the period:

1. *The Grange, or Patrons of Husbandry.* This organization, formed in 1867 principally for educational purposes, passed through an innovative stage to become a permanent, rather conservative and ritualistic interest organization, with national headquarters and State Granges throughout the Union.

2. *The National Farmers Alliance.* The Alliance was formed in 1880 as the Grange declined. It was oriented toward local action and was soon divided into "northern" and "southern" groups.

3. *The Agricultural Wheel* was an offshoot of the Alliance Movement during the 1880's.

4. *The National Farmers Alliance and Industrial Union* was formed in 1889, one of the early efforts to align farmers and laborers in reform efforts.

5. *The Colored Farmers Alliance and Cooperative Union* was formed in Texas in 1886 and prospered briefly.

6. *The National Farmers League* was incorporated in Albany, New York, in 1890.

From Frank M. Drew, "The Present Farmers' Movement." Reprinted with permission from the *Political Science Quarterly*, vol. VI (June, 1891), pp. 290-294, 297-306.

In addition, as Frank M. Drew points out "there are a host of state organizations, such as farmers' clubs, co-operative unions, alliances, agricultural wheels, and so on . . . . There is a Farmers National Congress, composed of one farmer from each congressional district, appointed by the governors of the respective states." In the selection below, Mr. Drew describes the objectives and the activities of farmer organizations in 1890.

### DEMANDS OF THE FARMERS

In considering the demands that are actually expressed in the platforms of the various organizations, two facts present themselves at the outset: first, that these demands are based often on precisely contradictory theories as to the source of the farmers' troubles; second, that the demands involve a very wide departure from the ideas contained in the original "purposes" of the different orders. As to the first point, compare the complaint of the Mutual Benefit Association, that the price of the farmers' grain is "below the cost of production," with the declaration of the Grange that if the farmers would but use as much sense as men in other lines of work, "there would be much less cause for complaint of our depressed condition." As to the second point, it is evident that the farmers have become infected with the restless and money-making spirit of the town and city life which is developing all around them, and are aggrieved that they cannot grow rich rapidly. They have come to believe that the lack of money is the root of all evil, and a most popular article of their faith attributes this lack in their case to the machinations of Old-World capitalists.

The most famous of their "demands," which has served as the model for both national and state organizations, is the St. Louis platform, adopted by the "Southern" Alliance, in conjunction with the Knights of Labor, on December 6, 1889. This platform, with the changes made by the annual meeting at Ocala, Florida, in December, 1890, is as follows:

1. We demand the abolition of national banks (and the substitution of legal tender treasury notes in lieu of national bank notes; issued in sufficient volume to do the business of the country on a cash system; regulating the amount needed on a per capita basis as the business interests of the country expand; and that all money issued by the government shall be legal tender in payment of all debts, both public and private).

2. We demand that Congress shall pass such laws as shall effectually prevent the dealing in futures of all agricultural and mechanical productions; preserving a stringent system of procedure in trials as shall secure the prompt conviction, and imposing such penalties as shall secure the most perfect compliance with the law.

3. We demand the free and unlimited coinage of silver.

4. We demand the passage of laws prohibiting the alien ownership of land, and that Congress take early steps to devise some plan to obtain all lands now owned by aliens and foreign syndicates; and that all lands now held by railroad and other corporations in excess of such as is actually used and needed by them, be reclaimed by the government and held for actual settlers only.

5. Believing in the doctrine of "equal rights to all and special privileges to none," we demand that taxation, national (or state), shall not be used to build up one interest or class at the expense of another. We believe that the money of the country should be kept as much as possible in the hands of the people, and hence we demand that all revenues, national, state (or country), shall be limited to the necessary expenses of the government economically and honestly administered.

(6. That Congress issue a sufficient amount of fractional paper currency to facilitate exchange through the medium of the United States mail.)

(7. That the means of communication and transportation should be owned by and operated in the interest of the people as is the United States postal system.)

The "Northern" Alliance adopted a platform at the same time that the preceding was prepared. I give this also, because on these two documents the leaders in the political campaign of 1890 relied for guidance:

WHEREAS, the farmers of the United States are most in number of any order of citizens, and with

79

the other productive classes have freely given of their blood to found and maintain the nation; therefore be it

RESOLVED, that the public land, the heritage of the people, be reserved for actual settlers only, and that measures be taken to prevent aliens from acquiring titles to lands in the United States and Territories, and that the law be rigidly enforced against all railroad corporations which have not complied with the terms of their contract, by which they have received large grants of land.

2. We demand the abolition of the national banking system and that the government issue full legal tender money direct to the people in sufficient volume for the requirements of business.

3. We favor the payment of the public debt as rapidly as possible, and we earnestly protest against maintaining any bonds in existence as the basis for the issue of money.

4. We favor a graded income tax, and we also favor a tax on real-estate mortgages.

5. We demand economy and retrenchment as far as is consistent with the interests of the people in every department of the government, and we will look with special disfavor upon any increase of the official salaries of our representatives or government employees.

6. We favor such a revision and reduction of the tariff that the taxes may rest as lightly as possible upon productive labor and that its burdens may be upon the luxuries and in a manner that will prevent the accumulation of a United States Treasury surplus.

7. The stability of our government depends upon the moral, manual and intellectual training of the young, and we believe in so amending our public school system that the education of our children may inculcate the essential dignity necessary to be a practical help to them in after life.

8. Our railroads should be owned and managed by the government, and be run in the interest of the people upon an actual cash basis.

9. That the government take steps to secure the payment of the debt of the Union and Central Pacific railroads and their branches by foreclosure and sale, and any attempt to extend the time again for the payment of the same beyond its present limit will meet with our most emphatic condemnation.

10. We are in favor of the early completion of a ship canal connecting the Great Lakes with the Gulf of Mexico, and a deep water harbor on the southern coast in view of opening trade relations with the Central and South American states, and we are in favor of national aid to a judicious system of experiments to determine the practicability of irrigation.

11. We sympathize with the just demands of labor of every grade and recognize that many of the evils from which the farming community suffers oppress universal labor, and that therefore producers should unite in a demand for the reform of unjust systems and the repeal of laws that bear unequally upon the people.

12. We favor the Australian system, or some similar system of voting, and ask the enactment of laws regulating the nomination of candidates for public office.

13. We are in favor of the diversification of our productive resources.

14. We [will] favor and assist to office such candidates only as are thoroughly identified with our principles and who will insist on such legislation as shall make them effective.

The various state orders of the "Northern" Alliance adopted platforms in substantial conformity to the foregoing. But in January, 1891, at a session of the national order in Omaha, all the resolutions but number 2, 7, 8, 11 and the second clause of 4 were dropped, and further demands were made as follows: the election of President, Vice-President and United States Senators by popular vote, restriction of the liquor traffic, women's suffrage, liberal pensions, passage of the Conger Lard bill, free and unlimited coinage of silver and the increase of the currency to $50 per capita. The convention pledged itself to demand "that the government allow us to borrow money from the United States at the same rate of interest as do banks." It was resolved not to affiliate with either the Republican or the Democratic party, and a declaration was made in favor of nominating a national ticket in 1892, but by a convention in which "representation shall be one delegate from each state in the Union."

\* \* \*

The money question is uppermost in the farmer's mind, and so, as is natural, he favors an income tax, "heavily graduated," in the words of the Mutual Benefit Association's memorial, and affecting "especially the income of rich corporations."

The idea that "the tariff is a tax" has only very lately made much headway among the farmers of the North and West. The California and Indiana State Alliances make no reference to the subject in their platforms of 1890. The Grange, in 1889, mumbled over the subject in phrases that would do credit to a professional politician; and the Mutual Benefit Association followed the same lead. Whether or not the "Southern" Alliances referred to the tariff in the St. Louis platform, is purely a matter of inference, and the Ocala plank is not very radical. But the Minnesota trump gives no uncertain sound:

We demand that the war-tariff, which has too long survived the object of its creation, shall be radically revised, giving very material reductions on the necessaries of life, and placing raw materials upon the free list, to the end that we may compete with the world for a market; and that such luxuries as whiskey and tobacco shall in no manner be relieved from internal taxation, till the high protection tariff has been wholly divested of its extortions.

Minnesota also asks for laws that "will make the hidden property pay equal taxes with the visible property." In a number of the legislatures, efforts are making now (the first quarter of 1891) to enact measures which shall secure the listing for taxation of notes and other evidences of debt, by requiring a tax-assessor's stamp on the same as a necessary preliminary to legal collection. Taxation of mortgages is emphatically demanded from all sides, and the Massachusetts plan for effecting this is in good repute.

General Superintendent Humphrey, of the Colored Alliance, in his annual address at Ocala, came out distinctly in favor of a single tax on land. The Grange, on the contrary, expressly condemned the land-tax in 1889. . . .

\* \* \*

The interest in food adulteration has of late centered around two measures, the Paddock Pure Food bill, and the Conger Pure Lard bill. The former is general in its nature, the latter is of a piece with the oleomargarine law. It is claimed by some that the two bills are only a part of a scheme designed by shrewd conspirators who hope,

by stirring up war between the two "monopolies" interested,—cotton-seed oil and lard,—to draw the attention of the people away from the real cause of the farmer's ills, *i.e.* vicious financial legislation. The liquor question arouses but little interest in the South, probably because there local option and practical prohibition are already well established.

The railroad problem is another matter that has aroused but little feeling in the South. The "Southern" Alliance, in 1887, made no mention of railway troubles, nor has it in later manifestos done more than formulate general demands. But the Mutual Benefit Association demands

. . . that they (the railways) should not be permitted to water their stock; . . . that they should not recklessly squander their earnings and thus necessitate exorbitant charges for services rendered the public; that they be requested to manage their business with reasonable economy, that they may serve the public effectively and cheaply. If these ends cannot be secured, through corporate control and management of railways and telegraphs, then we demand that the corporations be dissolved, their franchises resumed, and their tangible property taken and paid for by the government, and that they be operated by the government for the good of the people.

The Union and Central Pacific railways are chronic grievances with all the agricultural orders. The "Northern" Alliance, in 1887, believed

. . . that the ultimate solution of the transportation problem may be found in the ownership and operation by the government of one or more transcontinental lines, with their connections and feeders; [and further] that the present situation of the Union Pacific railroad offers a fair opportunity for such an experiment.

In 1891 this belief had become certainty, and the Alliance demanded that the Pacific railroads "be taken in charge by the government, and run in the interests of the people, with a view to extending both these lines to the eastern seaboard." In the summer of 1890, a movement began—so far as I can learn, in Missouri—against government ownership of transportation lines. Besides the great cost and increased taxation which such a step would necessarily entail, it was feared that the government "might take charge of something we did not want it to." Accordingly, at Ocala, the St. Louis platform was so modified as to ask first for a trial of "government control and supervision." The "Northern" Alliance, in 1889, after commending the Interstate Commerce law, continues:

We favor even more restrictive measures. The proposed plan of making the foreign corporations subject to the state courts, in the states where they do business, and depriving them of the power to remove these cases to the United States courts, meets our approval.

In April, 1890, while the executive committee of the Minnesota Alliance was in session, word came that the United States Supreme Court had decided that the state railroad commission (and inferentially the state legislature) had no power to prescribe rates on the railroads of the states. Thereupon the committee declared that this decision signified "the subjection of the people and the states to the unlimited control of the railroad corporations of this country." It was further resolved to "appeal from this second Dred Scott decision to the people of the nation . . . with a request that they unite with us in an effort to so amend the constitution as to abolish this new slavery."

No set of resolutions, whether township or national, is complete without a denunciation of alien ownership of land. An Iowa county goes farther, and demands national prohibition of alien ownership of any kind of property "for the purpose of gaining wealth." All orders demand that the public lands shall be held for actual settlers only. The "Northern" Alliance asked for governmental experiments in irrigation, but the Grange, in 1889, could not see any benefit to be derived by increasing the farming area so long as the present tariff policy was maintained. The Mutual Benefit Association holds "that private ownership in real estate should be limited to use and occupation of the owner." The Connecticut Farmers' League would have the constitution so amended as to enable Congress

. . . to make it easily possible for any one desiring to own and occupy sufficient land from which to gain a livelihood, by obliging the largest landholders, when necessary to this end, to sell enough of their land for this purpose on easy terms and at a price not exceeding its assessed value for taxation.

The influence of the Knights of Labor may be traced in various planks of state platforms. Thus, the Michigan Alliance demands an eight-hour day "in factories, mines and shops;" Nebraska favors eight hours "except on farms." But a Missouri union, "profoundly convinced that every interest of the farmer will be best secured by preventing over-production," accordingly resolved that the welfare of the class depended on reducing both their acreage and their hours of labor. Mississippi wants convict labor used in making cheap cotton-bagging; Minnesota would employ it in the manufacture of cheap binding-twine. In several states — Indiana, South Dakota and others — Pinkerton men are denounced. Louisiana and North Carolina promise to use the influence of their respective state orders to maintain law and order.

Besides the demands already mentioned, there is a large mass not susceptible of classification. The pension-crop is one of Indiana's most productive industries, and so the Alliance of that state favors it, though "opposed to private pensions." The Mutual Benefit Association favors liberal pensions to those disabled in service, but opposes "retaining a list of retired office-holders either civil or military, as pensioners. . . . It is unrepublican, and smacks strongly of aristocracy and royalty." Simple and democratic they mean to be, according to the resolutions, and they pledge themselves to rear their children to respect a farmer's life. Kentucky wishes to put this reform on a legal basis and so demands "that our legislature enact laws that will tend to make industrial and 'moral worth,' not wealth, the true standard of individual and national greatness." The merit system in the regulation of our civil service gets no recognition in any platform. The Mutual Benefit Association memorial reads:

We are opposed to all tenure of office either during life or good behavior. . . . If this is not the people's government, whose government is it? If it is the people's government, who should choose their officers?

And so they demand the election of United States judges for limited terms, by popular vote. The demand for election of President, Vice-President and United States Senators by popular vote is quite general, and some states wish to elect postmasters in the same way. The Illinois Mutual Benefit Association wishes to wipe out all appointive state offices. California demands an educational qualification for the exercise of the elective franchise, but no discrimination on account of sex. In the last demand the "Northern" Alliance and the North Dakota state organization concur. All the orders unite in demanding the adoption of the Australian ballot system, and to date (May 1, 1890) legislatures of eleven states have adopted it in sessions of 1891.

A Kansas Alliance refused to support for Congress any lawyer or national bank officer. Virginia voters ostracized the "representatives or paid attorneys of railroad transportation companies or other corporations." Minnesota refuses membership to all railroad employees and stockholders, provides for conventions to nominate state tickets and heads off bolters by prescribing: "No person shall be a member of any such nominating convention unless he . . . pledges himself publicly to abide by the action of such convention." Except in places where they believed themselves strong enough to sweep everything before them, the farmers did not nominate tickets, but presented to candidates already in the field copies of their demands with appended pledges, and asked for signatures. The following is a copy of the Missouri pledge, and the instructions to the canvasser, as they appeared in the "official organ":

I hereby pledge myself to work and vote for the above demands irrespective of party caucus or action.

Name of candidate _____
Politics _____
Office _____
Post-office _____
County _____
State _____

Cut the above out and have every candidate, irrespective of party, sign, and put these contracts into the hands of your county secretary under the supervision of your county executive board. If any candidate refuses to sign unqualifiedly, vote against him and use your influence to elect those who do sign, irrespective of party.

The use of this pledge was called "applying the yard-stick." Nor is the measuring process to end with election day. From many quarters lobbying is denounced roundly, and a Missouri union resolved to "demand that the state furnish any person requesting it, a printed account of how each senator and representative vote on all bills brought before the legislature."

What the red rag is to the traditional bull, a trust is to the modern agricultural reformer. Every set of resolutions contains some clauses that stigmatize these organizations. Various states ask "that gambling in products which are articles of food be made a criminal offence"; and yet the Minnesota Alliance, in the preamble to its constitution, says that one purpose of the order is "to obtain higher prices for all that the farmer produces, and cheapen prices for all that he consumes of others' products." To get the higher prices, an Illinois lodge of the Mutual Benefit Association, "believing that the farmers' products are far below the average cost of production, and believing that agriculturists can through their organizations control the market," resolved to request their general assembly, the Grange and the Alliance, "to fix the day and date for taking all the cattle, hogs and grain off the market in this month for twenty days." The Chicago Board of Trade is a sore grievance to Illinois farmers. The Mutual Benefit Association's assembly of that state declared it to be "a den of thieves," and denounced all such bodies "as whited sepulchres, full of dead men's bones—men ruined by these gambling institutions." These are hard words, and yet expressions in the great majority of "demands" are well summed up by the Pennsylvania Alliance:

RESOLVED, that notwithstanding nearly all classes of persons, excepting the farming and industrial classes, have had special legislation beneficial to themselves, yet as we regard class legislation (as) wholly wrong and inequitable, we shall not demand it for ourselves, but we shall demand from henceforth equal and exact justice to all.

On the question of education, the attitude of the farmers is altogether creditable. They endorse the public schools, and quite generally the cause of higher education. North Carolina's recommendation of "an increase of our present public-school tax of at least twenty-five per centum," shows no more than the common spirit. South Dakota has a large foreign population, yet, despite the agitation in the Northwest during the past two years for parochial schools, the state Alliance in 1890 demanded an English education for each child. An almost universal demand goes up for state manufacture of text-books. This, of course, means uniformity and long tenure,—features very likely to injure the work of the schools. Arkansas, however, has a purpose to accomplish in having the state control the texts. After stating that

. . . the very quintessence of democracy, the bed-rock of a republican form of government, and the perpetuity of the American Republic, rests upon the proper training and education of the youth of our land, and especially in the love of our land and country,

and that our land is overrun with trusts, among which is "a gigantic combine (of) publishers of school-books," the Alliance announces that

. . . there has been eliminated from the school-books nearly all matter calculated to instil in the minds of the youth a love of independence and liberty—for instance, extracts from the speeches of such patriots as Washington, Jefferson, the two Adamses, Clay, Webster, Calhoun and Lincoln, of our own land, and extracts from Burke, Pitt, Walpole and others, of the Old World. We believe the omission has been done with the deliberate intent and malice aforethought to destroy the last vestige of patriotism and dam up the fountain of independence in our youth.

The demand which follows this calls for a department of public printing, and the appointment of a committee to prepare a series of books fitted "to instil and beget within our children a deeper love of country and an abiding spirit of patriotism."

## WHAT HAS BEEN ACCOMPLISHED?

The great work which the Grange set before itself was to break down the farmers' isolation. This was conceived to be the first essential step in bettering their condition. This purpose has been kept steadily in view, and today all over the land are Grange halls, built by the local lodges, wherein are discussed matters ranging all the way from international law to athletics for boys. In Pennsylvania are "parks"—one of five thousand acres—in which are held annual encampments of the farmers' orders. Able speakers are secured, model buildings exhibited, and in many ways the meetings are made centres of educational force. The other orders do less educational work than the Grange, because they are convinced that their troubles are due not to ignorance, but to vicious legislation.

Co-operation has been attempted as a rule only in distributive operations. Missouri is dotted over with stores run on the Rochdale plan. The much-tried Texas co-operative agency is at last, I believe, dead. There are twenty-one (or more) state business agencies,—joint stock corporations,— the shares of which are held by local lodges. These do a purely distributive business. In

1888 the ubiquitous Macune called a meeting of state business agents then in being. These met in New Orleans in May of that year and partially organized an association. In 1890, at Ocala, the association asked to be constituted a committee of the "Southern" Alliance, and its request was granted. In Kentucky local enterprise takes the form of tobacco warehouses; elsewhere in the South are co-operative cotton-gins; in Nebraska and the Northwest, farmers' elevators form one of the means of saving. Farmers' insurance companies constitute another field worked in the Western states. Iowa is said to have 116 of them. In marked contrast to this spirit of self-help, the Connecticut farmers call for state insurance. In productive co-operation, dairying and milling seem to be the only lines at present worked to any extent. . . .

# IV.  *The Populist Movement: 1890–1900*

The tidal wave of protest that swept over the land in the form of agrarian revolt during the 1890's was unmatched in American history until, in a different context, the 1960's erupted in the revolt of the urban dispossessed. However, the propensity toward independent action based on a felt need for self-preservation was not lacking in the American tradition. Shays' Rebellion about a century before was an early model. Perhaps from that time until the Civil War the frontier served to release the pressures that might otherwise have been felt in organized political protest. Soon after the close of that war sporadic efforts at organized action were characteristic of agriculture, particularly in the trans-Mississippi West. There were numerous organizations and groupings of agriculturists but little real national unity. The most unified were the Greenback party, endorsed by many farm groups in 1872, and the Grange, a political force throughout the period from 1870–1890. The Granger movement was responsible for a series of legislative acts at the state level that sought to control rates of carriers and warehouses for farm products. This type of effort achieved national prominence in the Populist movement of the 1890's, a time when the frontier ceased to beckon for new settlers.

Probably more significant to this movement than the historical tradition of protest was the geographical factor. The "new" farming regions were in a West that was precariously situated in a semi-arid landlocked plain, singularly unsuited for independent, self-sufficient farming. In particular, farmers were forced into an uneasy dependence upon the railroads for transportation and on the East for capital and for markets for their unprocessed farm products. Frequently recurring drouths were devastating in their effects. These seemed to come in cycles, creating a series of crop failures that could be disastrous.

Fully as damaging as drouth to the debtor-farmers were falling prices. Since it was believed these could be controlled by monetary policy, the Populists gave themselves wholeheartedly to the cause of free silver as a means of increasing the supply of legal tender and raising prices.

From their home base in the plains states, the Populists, organized into the People's party, looked for national support to influence national elections, particularly the election of the President. In the states of the South, a generally depressed agriculture provided a source of considerable strength for Populism. In the North and East, the situation was different. The most exploitable discontent seemed to be in the urban laboring classes, whose economic condition resembled that of the western farmer. That these groups found it practically impossible to make common cause was a decisive factor in the future of American politics.

The Populist movement was an effort to use political means to gain economic ends. It appealed to the economically underprivileged, yet the base of the People's party remained too narrow to be effective, even though some support was obtained throughout the nation. The agrarian Populists wanted their distress alleviated and when after 1900 the money supply eased and prices worked upward, their motivation was hopelessly weakened. Long-range socialist goals were not theirs by any means. They were interested in the success of their own private enterprises; to accomplish this they were agreeable only to socializing the railroads and utilities—no comrades of the farmers.

An appraisal of the Populist movement as narrow and short-sighted would be misleading. The movement made a number of enduring contributions. It called attention to the problems and the needs of a growing interdependence, economic and cultural, across the nation. The nature of income variances and the processes by which these might be articulated by disadvantaged groups in a pluralistic society were clarified. Their action in behalf of impoverished farmers paved the way for similar efforts. Wary of political parties as vehicles for group betterment, farm leaders formed the Farmers Educational and Cooperative Union in 1902, appealing to the more marginal farmers in approximately the same area where the Populists had earlier thrived. Later the National Farmers Organization was formed to remedy market disadvantages of producers of certain farm commodities. Basing their program first upon economic efforts independent of politics, the N. F. O. later turned toward legislative interests. Whether using the economic means of withholding from the market or the political means of influencing public policy, the cooperative effort to achieve economic improvement along fairly specific lines is a common pattern of action—described by the late Professor Francis Coker as "empirical collectivism"—for which agrarian protests such as Populism, the Farmers Union, and the N. F. O. serve as excellent examples. The goals of the Populist movement were in many respects achieved, leaving an important substantive legacy. And further reforms, for which Populists had striven, were brought about with some modification by progressives operating within both the major parties.

C. S. Walker

## 19. " . . . THE FARMER FINDS HIMSELF AT A GREAT DISADVANTAGE"

Classifying the details of late nineteenth-century agrarian movements into the organizational, educational, cooperative, and political types of action, the author of this article describes the general trends toward group action for economic improvement among farmers.

The widespread movement among the farmers to-day is their effort to adapt themselves and their occupation to the ever-changing environment, so that they shall be once more masters of the situation, receiving their due share of the product of American industry and exerting their due influence in the formation and development of national character. As a result of his industry the farmer has made food and the raw material of our factories produced from the soil more and more plenty, of better quality and cheaper. Here we find an efficient cause of his pecuniary embarrassment; the supply of agricultural products has been increased beyond the demand, with the consequent fall of price. If the surplus of agricultural products was matched by a corresponding surplus of gold, of personal services, of means of transportation, and of the comforts, conveniences and luxuries of life, such universal plenty would enrich all, beggaring none. But with over-production in agriculture, and monopolies of coal, of telephones, of electric railroads and of other essentials of modern civilization, the farmer finds himself at a great disadvantage.

Farmers have been content in the past to confine their labors to the production of wealth, leaving to others the control of those conditions which determine the distribution of this wealth. At last, however, they have awakened to the fact that the problems of distribution have not been successfully solved. They believe that they get too little for the product of their labor and others too much, that they must bear heavy burdens of society while they are at the same time practically debarred from the enjoyment of the advantages of the progressive culture of modern life. When in this discussion we speak of the farmer, it must be born in mind that we refer to the average farmer, who tills on his own account his own or another's farm. We do not refer to those who derive a large share of their income from other sources than their farms, nor do we mean the farmer of exceptional ability or those whose opportunities have been remarkably fortunate. An investigation, carried on for a number of years, upon different lines, based upon statistics official and unofficial, as well as upon other reliable sources of information, shows that the average farmer, east and west, north and south, receives a lower remuneration for manual labor and for labor of superintendence than the average man in any other of the great classes of bread-winners, much less than those who have not carefully considered the matter will think possible.

Because of this comparative decadence the farmer has for years demanded equal taxation, in order that the farmer's thousand dollars invested in his farm shall bear no more burdens than the thousand dollars of

From C. S. Walker, "The Farmers' Movement," in *Annals of the American Academy of Political and Social Science*, Vol. 4 (March, 1894), pp. 790-798.

other men. But the statesman has confessed that he has not been able to remedy the evils of unjust taxation. He even acknowledges that they are growing worse.

The farmer has been content to refer questions of finance to the banker. Every autumn the farmers of America have hundreds of millions of dollars worth of crops which makes a demand for millions of currency. The supply of money at that season is inadequate to meet the demand. Hence, the price of crops falls relatively and the price of money advances. Year after year the farmer has been forced to sell in a glutted market and buy in times of scarcity. He demands a system of finance that shall make the supply of money at all times equal to the demand. He wants an elastic currency that shall do the money work of the nation with justice to both buyer and seller, to both creditor and debtor. But the bankers appear to confess that they cannot produce a medium of exchange and a standard of deferred payment that is capable of meeting the exigencies.

The farmer demands cheap transportation *between the farm and the market*; and he is met with the reply that the rates from the elevator of the middleman to the ship of the foreigner were never before so low as now, but this proves of little benefit to the farmer. When the farmer insists that modern masters of transportation might devise a system of cheap transportation from the country station to the city, he is told that the intricacies of the modern railroad system are too great and it cannot be done; to attempt it would bankrupt the roads. Moreover, when the farmers themselves, or their friends, organize an electric railroad to carry themselves and their freight at reasonable prices from the farm-house to the city, the great railroad corporations oppose them at every point, going even to the extent of waging open war against the selectmen of the country town who lawfully attempt to lay the rails of the electric road across the track of the steam railroad.

The farmer turns to the politician and asks of him that his party shall champion the cause of the farmer and see to it that the government guarantee to the agricultural classes their rights and promote their interests equally with those of other citizens. But the farmer finds the politician more abundant in promises than prolific in efficient action.

Finally, the farmer has, in his emergency, turned to the scholar and asked of him a fair statement of the problem and a clear solution, based upon historic and economic grounds. But the scholar has been too preoccupied and prejudiced to give the question that painstaking investigation and careful and impartial decision which alone can make his answer of much practical value to the hard-pressed agriculturist.

Thus has experience taught the farmer that the solution of the problem of the future of American agriculture and of the American agriculturist depends upon himself. The farmers' movement is simply the awakening of these sturdy citizens from engrossment in manual labor and the struggle after material wealth, to a sense of their duty first to themselves and then to society. Such a movement may have obstacles, it may be slow, it may do much apparent damage, but it is irresistible, and in the end its results will prove to be of value. It has reached the stage where guidance, rather than ridicule and denunciation, is needed.

The innumerable details of the movement may be classified under organization, education, co-operation, political action.

I. Organizations of farmers are now many and strong, constantly increasing in numbers, usefulness and power. The Massachusetts Board of Agriculture devotes fifteen pages of its report for 1892 to a directory of the agricultural organizations of the State. In other States organization is carried to as great, or to a greater extent. Besides these there are many national bodies. At the St. Louis Conference, year before last, twelve or more distinct national organizations of farmers were represented, whose aggregate membership numbered hundreds of thousands.

Of the many national bodies several are worthy of especial mention. The twelfth annual session of the National Farmers' Congress, composed of delegates from each State, appointed by the Governor thereof, was held November, 1892, at Lincoln, Neb. This body is non-partisan, deliberative and advisory in its action, and exerts its influence upon the formation and direction of public opinion. It has created a National Board of Agriculture with headquarters at Washington, whose duty shall be to study the general agricultural interests of the whole country and see to it that no conflicting legislation shall injure the industries of any State. Two hundred members, from the majority of the States, attend the annual sessions, paying their own expenses. They represent the more wealthy and better educated agriculturists.

The National Grange, the oldest and most conservative of the distinctively agrarian organizations, held its twenty-seventh annual session last year. Its membership numbers many thousands, its finances are sound, its organization is stable, its work is becoming more and more extended and valuable. Having experienced the flood and ebb of the tide which accompanies reform movements, it is content to advance with the even stream of national development, intent upon exerting its power at the opportune moment and place to secure the best effect.

Beginning in the South, but extending through the North, under the leadership of the late President L. L. Polk, the National Farmers' Alliance has been an aggressive power. This union of the farmers of the South with the farmers of the North, ignoring sectional lines and old causes of division, is one marked characteristic of this new phase of the agrarian movement. It illustrates and proves that the farmers of America have at last learned the value and the method of permanent organization. They have moreover shown a disposition to join forces with organizations of artisans and other citizens, whenever such union proves itself desirable.

Another organization of great value to the farmers' movement is the Association of American Agricultural Colleges and Experiment Stations. It has a full corps of officers and an executive committee. It is composed of delegates from each of the fifty-seven agricultural schools and colleges and of the fifty-three experiment stations of the United States. The association, therefore, represents the fifteen hundred members of the faculty and corps of workers connected with these institutions and also the many thousands of students and alumni of these colleges, a large number of whom are farmers or intimately connected with and dependent upon the agricultural classes. While this association is a scientific body, it is at the same time interested in the success of the farmer, and exerts a powerful influence upon Legislatures and Congress, so far as the educational or economic relations of agriculture and agriculturists are involved.

The farmers' movement is not then to be measured by the action of any one organization, but can only be properly understood when the resultant of many separate and varying forces is accurately determined.

II. In their endeavor to secure organization the farmers soon discovered the necessity of broadening their education, especially in the field of economics and politics. Hence, every farmers' organization has this object pre-eminently in view. These associations are themselves efficient schools, giving to their faithful members training in public speaking, in writing, in reading, in thinking and in administration. As a result of twenty-six years of this work the Grange has become a national university, employing hundreds of teachers, college educated as well as self-taught, who stimulate thought and lend inspiration to their fellows. Recently it was "resolved that the Worthy Lecturer of the National Grange be instructed to continue the distribution of subjects for discussion to Subordinate Granges, and that questions of political economy be given prominence, such as those relating to gold, silver, greenbacks, national banks, corporations, interstate and transcontinental transportation, and the tariff, as it relates to agriculture." A similar work is carried on in the Alliance, which has prepared for its local branches a system of weekly lessons in political science. Ballads and songs have been multiplied, as a method of propagating and fixing new ideas in the minds of the people. In all agricultural colleges the science of economics and of politics is receiving more and more attention.

A National Reform Press has been organized, including about a thousand newspapers, pledged to support the demands of the farmers' movement. There are a few dailies, but the most are weeklies. The circulation of many of these newspapers is 10,000, some reach 50,000, one perhaps 100,000. These are scattered over the whole country, and their influence cannot but be great. Besides these reform papers there is the agricultural press, an instrument of educational force not only in matters relating to agriculture, but also in subjects of political and economic science.

The town meeting, the district school, the public library, the Chautauqua movement, the country church, each and all, do much for the education of the farmer, far more than is commonly imagined. Upon one point the farmers of today are fully agreed. They are one in demanding for themselves and for their children the best education the times can afford. They have successfully insisted that the town, the State and the nation shall unite in providing every facility for educating the farmer in everything pertaining to the science and art of agriculture and to the knowledge and practice of manhood. As a consequence we find in America a system of agricultural education approaching the best the world affords. The great drawback is that only a few comparatively as yet are pecuniarily able to take advantage of the facilities thus offered by the State.

III. The farmers' movement has thrown a great deal of light upon co-operation, both distributive and productive. The educational results of the past twenty-five years of experiment have been of great value. The nature of the problem, the conditions of success, the dangers and difficulties in the way, have been made clear and the preparatory work accomplished which will make co-operation in the future more common and profitable.

So far as distributive co-operation is concerned the farmers have learned that the essential element of success lies in large orders for cash. As a result middlemen have not been driven out of business, but the farmers of the North have succeeded in escaping that thralldom to the storekeeper which has been so disastrous in the South.

There are throughout the country many successful co-operative stores, which benefit not only their patrons, but also indirectly all consumers. But the more common form of co-operative buying is through a business agent, who receives the orders of many farmers in the district or State, and so furnishes them goods at the lowest wholesale prices. In the business of insurance, co-operation among farmers has had good results; they report that hundreds of thousands of dollars have been saved in premiums on fire and life policies. Co-operation among milk-producers, fruit-growers and cattle-men, for the purpose of marketing their products, has proved very remunerative.

In productive co-operation many experiments have been made which have been only partially successful. Manufacturers who have charged exorbitant prices have been brought to terms, but the farmers have learned that they can rarely carry on the farm and the factory successfully at the same time. Nevertheless, in the production of butter and cheese, co-operation has proved eminently successful. As agricultural science introduces new methods and tends to make the farm a great factory, where raw material of the soil, properly treated with chemical fertilizers and manipulated by means of elaborate machinery, shall be transformed into the finished products for the market, the greater is the necessity and the profit of co-operation, and the more capable do farmers find themselves of working together.

IV. Organization, education, co-operation, have led the farmers' movement towards political action. For generations the farmer confined himself closely to agriculture and to participation in the affairs of the town meeting. In the meanwhile, the cities grew in number, in population, in wealth and in influence, until he found that the twenty to thirty per cent of the people who live in cities, largely recent importations from foreign countries, actually governed not only the municipalities, but also the States and the nation, leaving the votes of the other citizens scattering and devoid of power. In order to protect their interests the farmers made use of the right of petition. They elected lawyers and other professional men to represent them and their interests in Legislature and Congress. They appealed to their party leaders. They sought to interest the press in their behalf. They brought their case before the courts. They presented themselves before the bar of public opinion. But they were disappointed. It made little difference whether they sent a farmer or a politician to the Legislature. If the farmer went to the capital fresh from the plow, among a crowd of lobbyists, he was as clay in the hands of the potter. If his constituents kept him there year after year, until he learned the ways of legislation, then he ceased to be a farmer and became a member of some other class, perhaps a stockholder in a great railroad, or manufacturing corporation, with interests in common with the opponents of agricultural classes.

But from repeated failures and many disappointments the farmers are at length learning how to take care of themselves. They have become convinced that political action on their part is essential to their well being, that they must sustain their own interests, for others will not consider them. In their various subordinate organizations they discuss the situation. Their best representatives then bring the matter before their district, State and national bodies, where the whole subject is again debated. In this way they come to a decision as to what is practicable. They then formulate their demands, which they lay before the proper authorities in the town, the State or the nation, or in the caucus, or convention. They press and enforce their demands patiently and persistently, meeting all attacks bravely. They fight for their rights from their own point of view, believing that the free and fair contest of opposing interests will be the best for the whole people. If their interests are not presented as forcibly as those of other classes the result will be not only disastrous to them, but will also seriously endanger the public good. In the furtherance of these ends they have learned to trust no man implicitly, but to hold every man whom they choose to represent them responsible to them for his action.

The farmers have learned something of the methods of legislation. Hence when a hearing is given by a legislative committee, the farmers are on hand with their best speakers. When a bill is pending in which they are interested, letters, telegrams and petitions from all parts of the State come pouring in, urging legislators to do their duty. At State capitals, as well as at Washington, the farmers have their standing committees always on hand to watch legislation and see that their interests do not suffer. There are, however, so many ways of influencing legislation and the power of capital is so well-nigh irresistible, that the farmers have been beaten time and again and seen their cherished and just demands ignored. But their persistence has taught them and they are coming better to understand the science and practice of politics. Their organizations have been nominally and, to a large extent, really non-partisan, but from experience they have learned that votes in caucus and convention, as well as at the polls, are the real sources of power. Of these votes they still possess in many States a majority, and throughout the nation a large minority. United with other laboring men, their votes would constitute a clear majority over all others. They now realize that their votes are their own, to be used for the realization of their demands. During the last few years they have been experimenting with the ballot and some surprising results have followed. The movement within the old party lines has been strong, leading to notable results, but it has not been confined to these. The farmers have found that both of the leading parties have for so long a time been dependent upon other elements than the farmer's vote for success, that it is difficult to transform them at once into humble servants of the agriculturist.

During the year of the presidential election many of the farmers seemed inclined to support a distinctive People's party, not really expecting to elect a president, but hoping to learn something, attract national attention to their demands and cast a vote sufficiently large to give them a basis for future action, either as the People's party destined to supplant the old parties, or else as a body of producers allied with the artisans, whose real interests shall be made a serious object by one or the other of existing parties. The results show the measure of their success. Out of a total vote of 12,154,542, the People's party cast 1,122,045 ballots. Their candidates received votes in every State of the Union. They carried Colorado, Idaho, Kansas and Nevada by majorities, and North Dakota and Oregon by pluralities, which gave twenty-two votes in the electoral college, being the first time since 1856 that a third party has secured an electoral vote. Investigation shows that this vote was almost entirely from the rural districts of the South and West. The People's party succeeded in increasing their representatives in the House from three to twelve. In the Senate they have several senators. In four States they elected their candidate for governor. Considering the difficulties against which this new party was obliged to contend, the success gained was indeed remarkable.

The radical demands of the farmers, as set forth in the platform of the People's party, are socialistic and are not likely soon to be formally ratified by the public opinion of the nation. But the People's party and its platform are only an incident in the greater movement of the farmers of America. It is an experiment being tried by the radicals among the agrarian leaders, but which has not yet received the endorsement of the great mass of the farmers. A great political party is not the growth of a day. Whenever the farmers of the United States shall as a unit demand of either of the old parties a certain line of policy and prove it to be practicable and just, one or the other of these parties will surely submit to their will. Class legislation in behalf of the farmers may in some cases be secured, but the probabilities are that the final results will nevertheless be good. By pushing the system of class legislation to its logical outcome, the *reductio ad absurdum* will be apparent and a reaction must set in.

Farmers have suffered in the past because of their neglect to compete earnestly for their own interests, but now the signs of the times indicate that in all parts of our country they have at last aroused themselves and have begun a movement, the outcome of which will be to secure for them their full share of the products of the national industry and of the advantages of modern civilization.

*Paul W. Glad*

## 20. "PARTIES MUST MEET ISSUES AS THEY RISE . . ."

That the trans-Missouri West posed serious difficulties for the perpetuation of the agrarian tradition became starkly clear as the absence of conditions essential for a viable agriculture were revealed. The first reaction to the difficulties was to extract the necessary balances from the farmers themselves. As this process became more and more painful, the western farmers turned to politics for redress. An agrarian party was born, only to be eclipsed by the historically losing Democratic party. Problems of fusion, leadership, strategy, and issue selection beset the Populist party and ultimately it succumbed to the processes of absorption into the mainstream of American politics. The analysis of these processes is printed below.

Taking a page from Emerson, Professor Ralph Gabriel suggests that a *volksglaube* thrives best if it has a "fallacy to expose, a blunder to pillory." The acute distress that hovered darkly over the plains in the last years of the nineteenth century provided a setting well suited to the elaboration of a middle western faith. An agricultural revolution had gradually replaced diversified farming with a highly specialized, technologically complex, capitalistic form of business enterprise. Finding himself a part of the cash-market economy, dependent on railroads, middlemen, and other distributive facilities, in constant need of capital, and compelled to assume greater risks than ever before, many a prairie farmer failed to achieve the prosperity he had thought would be his in the Garden of the World. Whatever the causes of his suffering, real or imagined, he had his own way of looking at economic realities. He did not question the beliefs that were his inheritance; he sought instead the defect, the sin, in American life that thwarted his progress and suppressed his optimism. He seized upon a hero created in his own image and a devil created in the image of his oppressors, and he breathed into them the breath of that life which legendary figures enjoy. It was after contemplation of those mythical beings that the yeoman of the Middle Border found fallacies to expose and blunders to pillory. It was then too that he found a spokesman in William Jennings Bryan, prophet of the faith that made his reasoning plausible.

### AGRARIAN UNREST

Preachers and poets, essayists and editors, advertisers and orators, seers and statesmen had taught the farmer to regard himself as the "bone and sinew of the nation." He had been taught that the contented yeoman, garnering the products of the land God had given him, was a figure of noble proportions, the ideal man and the ideal citizen. Living in close and harmonious communion with a bountiful nature, he was led to believe that he had acquired an integrity and in mid-America enjoyed a salubrity incomprehensible to the depraved populations of urban centers. The Middle

Reprinted from *The Trumpet Soundeth* by Paul W. Glad, pp. 43-47, 48-57, by permission of University of Nebraska Press. Copyright 1960 by the University of Nebraska Press.

West had clearly justified even the high hopes of missionary planners; it had become "a land of churches, and schools, and charities, of pious homes, and great religious enterprises." . . .

In a famous editorial, written in 1896 at the height of rural unrest, William Allen White asked a rhetorical question: "What's the matter with Kansas?" The answer suggested by the staunchly Republican Emporia editor was not intended to please long-suffering farmers, but the question was crucial. What was the matter with Kansas? What, indeed, was the matter with agrarian sections of the entire West?

By the late nineteenth century farm mechanization had wrought agricultural wonders of deep significance. The invention of soil-working implements, seed planters, cultivators, and haymaking and harvesting machines resulted in fantastic savings in man-hours of labor. A one-acre crop of wheat which had required over sixty-one hours of hand labor could be harvested in less than three hours, twenty minutes by machine. Thirty-eight hours, forty-five minutes on one acre of corn was cut to fifteen hours, eight minutes. Farmers invested heavily in new farm implements, often going into debt on the assumption that they could pay for them later out of what they could earn. With the new implements the farmer could till more land, and he not infrequently mortgaged his holdings and made other sacrifices in order to expand his operations. Mechanization encouraged product specialization, and cash crop cultivation became commonplace. Urban industrialization also influenced the lives of farmers and their families; spinning and weaving were unprofitable when the real cost of store clothes was less than that of homemade garments. As Professor John D. Hicks has suggested, the independence of the farmer began to disappear when he, "like the manufacturer, came to produce a commodity for sale, and to live, not directly upon the fruits of the soil, but upon the profits of his factory farm."

Farm commodities, however, were not the only source of profit. The rapid expansion of the agricultural frontier in the nineteenth century led to phenomenal rises in land values, and this in turn created a boom psychology. Farmers often tended to rely on this process of appreciation for their margin of profit, and to capitalize more and more on it. When its real attachment was to land values and not to land itself, the agrarian society of the United States developed a peculiar mobility. The interplay among various forces at work on American agriculture thus become apparent: mechanization aided rapid expansion, expansion resulted in appreciation of land values, the appreciation of land values induced speculators to encourage further expansion, and increased expansion (particularly in the subhumid areas of the plains region) was a challenge to mechanical genius. The product of these influences was a rootless and harried farmer-businessman who gambled with his land when he was not competing with carrier, middlemen, and manufacturers for a share of the consumer's dollar.

Insecure as his position was, the prairie farmer was made sharply aware of other problems facing him. In marketing his cash crop he learned gloomy facts about railroads and railroad rates. From specializing in one kind of grain he discovered the middleman and was startled by the disparity between the prices of what he sold and the prices of what he bought. These difficulties were more in evidence in some sections of the West than in others. The eastern portions of the Middle West managed to remain relatively prosperous as compared with the trans-Missouri West (and with the South), and the reason for this prosperity lay in greater diversifications. The corn-livestock belt, which extended from Ohio westward through Iowa, experienced fewer economic pressures from railroads and middlemen than did wheat-growing areas. But out on the plains, far from his market and with little choice of carrier, the wheat farmer found that the costs of marketing his product often resulted in losses.

In spite of great expectations, then, and in part because of them, farmers of the Dakotas, Nebraska, and Kansas suffered reverses in the late eighties and throughout the nineties. And for somewhat different reasons hard times prevailed in the cotton South as well. Because of wide variation and inadequate data, farm prices have been an enigma. Nevertheless, it has been clearly established that markets for corn, wheat, and cotton were unfavorable and transactions frequently ruinous. The base-price index plummeted from 132 in 1865 to 46.5 in 1896, and agricultural prices were considerably below the average for all commodities. When the price of Kansas corn dropped to ten cents a bushel, it was apparently burned as fuel, a move hardly likely to warm the cockles of the rural heart whatever its effect on room temperature may have been. "Many a time," recalled Vernon L. Parrington, "have I warmed myself by the kitchen stove in which ears were burning briskly, popping and crackling in the jolliest fashion. And if while we sat around such a fire watching the year's crop go up the chimney, the talk sometimes became bitter . . . who will wonder?"

\*　\*　\*

What, then, was the matter with Kansas? In 1893, in response to a questionnaire sent out by the state bureau of labor and industry, farmers ticked off items: low prices, drought, money scarcity, high interest rates, high railroad rates, high taxes, middlemen. In analyzing the causes of their grievances, however, they found it difficult if not impossible to recognize harsh economic facts. The myth of the virtuous yeoman was too deeply ingrained. For generations the United States had been primarily a nation of farmers, and even after trade's unfeeling train had usurped the land, the farmer was identified with democracy and with the only kind of nobility possible in a democracy—nobility of character. He was a special creature, peculiarly blessed by God. If this was generally true of the American farmer, it was particularly true of those who braved

drought, prairie fires, grasshopper plagues, blizzards, and cinch bugs, and who survived the yet more terrible isolation of the wind-swept plains of the West. Lot had chosen the well-watered valley of the Jordan, but God made his covenant with Abraham, who had been left with the land of Canaan. The prairie farmer was therefore incapable of seeing himself as an organic part of the national economy. Special creature that he was, he nevertheless had to account for his plight. And so he adopted an explanation: he was the victim of a vast conspiracy emanating from urban financial centers. Eastern and foreign capitalists, reasoned the farmer, had deliberately brought about his misery. . . .

In this analysis, western and southern farmers were joined by residents of other sections. In Colorado, for example, there was widespread recognition that the development of the mineral empire was dependent upon outside capital. To many it seemed that eastern and foreign investors had made the Rocky Mountain West, with all its resources, a fief of Wall Street. With such support, the farmer refused to admit that improved communications had gone far toward making the world an economic unit, and that the low prices he received were indicative of an international price decline brought about, in part, by the extensive cultivation of hitherto untapped agricultural areas. He refused to admit that he had embarked on his current operations with insufficient capital, or that vast tracts of land in subhumid regions should never have been subjected to his plow. But he could readily believe the assertions of the Wichita *Courier:*

All this gigantic loaning on western real estate represents millions of English capital wrung from the poor of India by British brutality and shrewdness. Having invested their money they proceed to reduce the volume of our money by bribery and that masterly policy which they know well how to use. It is well known that the mortgage holder in most cases wants to get the property . . . and secure the owner as a tenant. When the foreclosures are finished up the proper measures will be taken to increase the volume of money . . . and hold our population as English tenants.

This and similar allegations made a significant impression on William Jennings Bryan and his supporters. For the prophet of midwestern moralism to agree with the farmer's conception of social sin was easy and natural. "You may go to New York or Boston and find financiers who doubt the greatness of this country and proclaim the necessity for foreign aid," he said in a typical observation during the campaign of 1896, "but the men who do that know more about Europe than they do about the United States." . . .

At the turn of the century, Flavius J. VanVorhis, chairman of the Indiana Silver Republican Committee, wrote a letter providing a link in the chain of recrimination against financial houses which was a dominant theme of Bryan's correspondence:

I do not see how any one can fail to realize that combinations beginning in New York of which the New York Association of Banks was the first organization, have been the foundation upon which has been builded all the subsequent combinations that now threaten the abandonment of the principles upon which our government was founded. For years the influences that organized and controlled this combination of banks, have controlled the organizations and machinery of both parties and kept them in a condition that it was a matter of no consequence to the financial interests which party succeeded in an election.

Long before VanVorhis penned this indictment, the farmers had attempted to secure redress of grievances and alleviation of suffering by political means. In trying politics, however, they had found political parties wanting. "The parties lie to us and political speakers mislead us," said Mary E. Lease bitterly. John Peter Altgeld was not a western farmer, but he agreed. "To be an eligible candidate now," he said in 1895, "often means to stand for nothing in particular and to represent no definite principle, but to be all things to all men and, in the end, be contemptible." Corruption resulting from the concentration of capital, he thought, had tainted everything it touched,

including politics, with "moral leprosy."

Political disillusionment born of economic disillusionment resulted in the launching of a full-scale attack upon the methods and forms of American politics. Pathetically aware of the indifference of major parties, and repelled by the activities of spoilsmen in both Republican and Democratic ranks, many farmers and agrarian sympathizers in the West and South saw a third party as the only way out of their distress. If both of the major parties refused to recognize agricultural problems or deal adequately with them, then dissatisfied farmers would have nothing to lose by forming a party of their own.

And so the People's party was born. For several years in the nineties Populist hopes ran high; it seemed to them not inconceivable that they could do what the Republican Party had done earlier—become one of the governing parties. During those years leaders of the new party patiently developed a program embracing a multitude of reforms designed to meet the fundamental problems of land, transportation, and finance. It was a program that included, among other things, the free coinage of silver at a ratio of sixteen to one; a circulating medium of at least $50 per capita as opposed to the $20 per capita then operative; a graduated income tax; postal savings banks; government ownership and operation of all railroads and telegraph and telephone systems; reclamation of all alien landholdings; the initiative and referendum; the direct election of senators; and one term only for the President and Vice President. Populists were not content merely to mouth the hackneyed phrases of old-line politicians, or to prop up dead political horses. They wished to hear discussions on "the living questions of financial and other reforms."

Populists, however, predicated their hopes for success upon an assumption that was delusive in its simplicity. They believed that there was a natural bond of interest among the producing class, among farmers, workers, small businessmen, and toilers everywhere. And they hoped for a working alliance among those groups that constituted the "producing masses." As one Populist manifesto proclaimed:

There are but two sides in the conflict that is being waged in this country today. On the one side are the allied hosts of monopolies, the money power, great trusts and railroad corporations who seek the enactment of laws to benefit them and impoverish the people. On the other are the farmers, laborers, merchants, and all other people who produce wealth and bear the burdens of taxation. . . . Between these two there is no middle group.

Concentrating on a kind of social dualism that pitted the common people against the hosts of wickedness, party leaders tended to ignore the heterogeneous character of American society. They had to learn from experience that small businessmen and farmers did not always agree, or that eastern laborers might have their own peculiar interests, or that southern farmers could be as concerned with racial as they were with economic questions.

There were other chinks in the Populist armor. There was, for example, the problem of leadership. Farmers had seldom elevated men of the soil to political office; they had depended, for the most part, upon country lawyers, small-town editors, and other professional men to serve as their spokesmen. Disappointed in the achievements of such persons, they had finally turned to their own ranks, only to be disappointed again. "If the farmer went to the capital fresh from the plow, among a crowd of lobbyists," observed one writer, "he was as clay in the hands of a potter. If his constituents kept him there year after year, until he learned the ways of legislation, then he ceased to be a farmer and became a member of some other class." It was this failure to secure adequate representation that had been a major impetus behind the formation of a third political party. Yet the new party still did not attract many leaders who could speak for agrarian interests and at the same time win elections. It is a matter of no small significance that while Populist leadership included men who had a genuine devotion

to agrarian principles, it also included men who had experienced the monotony of years of political failure and who had an overweening passion for success at the polls. The desire for victory left them open to temptation; they were willing to barter part of their program in exchange for public office. This willingness accounts, in part, for two developments that sounded the death knell of the Populist party; one was the rise of the free silver issue to monolithic proportions, and the other was fusion with the Democracy.

\*　\*　\*

While the silver issue had a certain utility, dangers were inherent in the sacrifices Populists made for its sake. Campaigning on free silver without reference to any of the other planks in the Populist platform (a policy advocated by General Weaver, Taubeneck, and others) meant tailoring the agrarian program to suit the tastes of those who had little sympathy with other reforms. A western silver mine owner or an eastern merchant could support silver vigorously but at the same time oppose the farmers' solution to problems of land and transportation. Organizational changes as well as compromises on principle could develop from emphasis on free silver. Republicans and Democrats both counted silverites among their number. Instead of joining the People's party as its leaders hoped, outsiders might effect a fusion in which Populists would lose their identity.

Yet if both major parties came out in opposition to silver inflation during the campaign of 1896, it was just possible that Populists would be able to establish their authority over dissident Republicans and Democrats. Taubeneck was less certain of a split in the Democratic party than he was of a Silver Republican bolt; yet he believed that "the Administration and the goldbugs" would control the Democratic convention. Bryan himself had urged Populist leaders to delay meeting until after the two major parties had committed themselves to platforms and candidates. The Populist convention could then "take advantage of the errors of the old parties" and with greater ease "bring about a consolidation of all the silver forces." But at Chicago, Democrats repudiated the only President they had elected in forty years, nailed a silver plank securely to the platform, and nominated the Nebraskan who told administration men that they could not "crucify mankind upon a cross of gold."

The Populists, who had staked everything on the possibility that the party of Grover Cleveland would never deny him, were thrown into confusion. Ignatius Donnelly posed for himself the vital question: "Shall we or shall we not endorse Bryan himself for president?" He clearly saw what such endorsement might mean. "I like Bryan," he wrote, "but I do not feel that we can safely adopt the Dem. candidates. I fear it will be the end of our party." The middle-of-the-road or orthodox element was inclined to ignore the action of the Democrats. As one loyal member of that faction put it, "Let the old Rotten Democrat machine with its camp followers, gold bugs, place hunters, straddle bugs, humbugs, demagogues etc. etc. go to the devil." On the other hand there were proponents of compromise, particularly in the West, who favored acceptance of the Democratic slate. William V. Allen, Senator from Nebraska, was a strong Bryan man, and Governor Davis H. "Bloody Bridles" Waite of Colorado wrote that "the silver crowd *must* support him."

In the end Populists saw no alternative to Bryan, and he was duly nominated at their St. Louis convention. They did, however, see an alternative to Arthur Sewell, the Democracy's nominee for vice president. Over strenuous objections from Democrats, Tom Watson, self-styled Jeffersonian radical from Georgia, became vice-presidential candidate of the People's party. The compromise at St. Louis complicated matters, for it gave Bryan two running mates and completely satisfied no one. (The Democratic idea of fusion, said Watson, was "that we play Jonah while they play whale.") Most Populists nevertheless displayed a marked willingness to cooperate with Democrats in the common cause. Even middle-of-the-road Ignatius Donnelly campaigned for Bryan and entertained the hope that he would receive a cabinet appointment for his efforts. As the campaign wore on, he persuaded himself that his candidate had been "raised up by Providence to save the country from sinking into old world conditions."

Bryan undoubtedly had a remarkable capacity to engender devotion and confidence. "I do not believe he can be beaten," James Manahan wrote his wife from Lincoln where he was in the thick of the fight. "I firmly believe that God is on his side and helping him for the sake of the poor all over the world. He is right and right must win over evil and injustice." Whether or not Bryan was on the side of the angels is beside the point: his campaign was far more attractive to western farmers than to the urban poor. Mark Hanna, Republican campaign manager, shrewdly observed, "He's talking Silver all the time, and that's where we've got him." The G.O.P., with a campaign fund at least ten times that of the Democracy, hired 1400 speakers to counter Bryan's thrusts. The burden of their message was essentially the theme of McKinley's letter of acceptance:

It is not an increase in the volume of money which is the need of the time, but an increase in the volume of business. Not an increase of coin, but an increase of confidence. Not more coinage, but a more active use of the money coined. Not open mints for the unlimited coinage of the silver of the world, but open mills for the full and unrestricted labor of American workingmen.

That coercion was used by employers had been clearly established. Yet a significant segment of the labor vote went to McKinley because it was believed that labor had nothing to gain from the free coinage of silver. After listening to Republican orators, urban workmen were not sure that they wanted the world's silver poured into United States mints. And many were certain that they did not want to be paid in fifty-three-cent dollars.

Election day came and went. Bryan polled

more votes than any candidate had ever received before — and lost. He had carried on a strenuous campaign in the Middle West and the Northeast, but every state east of the Mississippi and north of the Ohio went to McKinley. The Nebraskan's strength in urban areas was remarkable (fully two-thirds of his popular vote came from Mc-Kinley states), yet it was not enough. Up at

Nininger, Minnesota, Ignatius Donnelly read with mounting dismay the telegraphic reports that brought the news of Bryan's defeat. He opened his diary and poured out his feelings: "Will the long lane never have a turning? Will the sun of triumph never rise? I fear not." If his fears were for the People's party, they were justified.

*Kirk H. Porter and Donald B. Johnson*

## 21. ". . . THE FUNDAMENTAL PRINCIPLES OF JUST GOVERNMENT"

PEOPLE'S PARTY PLATFORM OF 1896

The People's Party, assembled in National Convention, reaffirms its allegiance to the principles declared by the founders of the Republic, and also to the fundamental principles of just government as enunciated in the platform of the party in 1892.

We recognize that through the connivance of the present and preceding Administrations the country has reached a crisis in its National life, as predicted in our declaration four years ago, and that prompt and patriotic action is the supreme duty of the hour.

We realize that, while we have political independence, our financial and industrial independence is yet to be attained by restoring to our country the Constitutional control and exercise of the functions necessary to a people's government, which functions have been basely surrendered by our public servants to corporate monopolies. The influence of European moneychangers has been more potent in shaping legislation than the voice of the American people. Executive power and patronage have been used to corrupt our legislatures and defeat the will of the people, and plutocracy has thereby been enthroned upon the ruins of

democracy. To restore the Government intended by the fathers, and for the welfare and prosperity of this and future generations, we demand the establishment of an economic and financial system which shall make us masters of our own affairs and independent of European control, by the adoption of the following declaration of principles:

THE FINANCES

1. We demand a National money, safe and sound, issued by the General Government only, without the intervention of banks of issue, to be a full legal tender for all debts, public and private; a just, equitable, and efficient means of distribution, direct to the people, and through the lawful disbursements of the Government.

2. We demand the free and unrestricted coinage of silver and gold at the present legal ratio of 16 to 1, without waiting for the consent of foreign nations.

3. We demand that the volume of circulating medium be speedily increased to an amount sufficient to meet the demand of the business and population, and to restore the just level of prices of labor and production.

4. We denounce the sale of bonds and the

From Kirk H. Porter and Donald B. Johnson, *National Party Platforms 1840-1960*, 2nd ed. (Urbana: University of Illinois Press, 1961), pp. 104-106. Reprinted by permission of The University of Illinois.

increase of the public interest-bearing debt made by the present Administration as unnecessary and without authority of law, and demand that no more bonds be issued, except by specific act of Congress.

5. We demand such legislation as will prevent the demonetization of the lawful money of the United States by private contract.

6. We demand that the Government, in payment of its obligation, shall use its option as to the kind of lawful money in which they are to be paid, and we denounce the present and preceding Administrations for surrendering this option to the holders of Government obligations.

7. We demand a graduated income tax, to the end that aggregated wealth shall bear its just proportion of taxation, and we regard the recent decision of the Supreme Court relative to the income-tax law as a misinterpretation of the Constitution and an invasion of the rightful powers of Congress over the subject of taxation.

8. We demand that postal savings-banks be established by the Government for the safe deposit of the savings of the people and to facilitate exchange.

### RAILROADS AND TELEGRAPHS

1. Transportation being a means of exchange and a public necessity, the Government should own and operate the railroads in the interest of the people and on a nonpartisan basis, to the end that all may be accorded the same treatment in transportation, and that the tyranny and political power now exercised by the great railroad corporations, which result in the impairment, if not the destruction of the political rights and personal liberties of the citizens, may be destroyed. Such ownership is to be accomplished gradually, in a manner consistent with sound public policy.

2. The interest of the United States in the public highways built with public moneys, and the proceeds of grants of land to the Pacific railroads, should never be alienated,

mortgaged, or sold, but guarded and protected for the general welfare, as provided by the laws organizing such railroads. The foreclosure of existing liens of the United States on these roads should at once follow default in the payment thereof by the debtor companies; and at the foreclosure sales of said roads the Government shall purchase the same, if it becomes necessary to protect its interests therein, or if they can be purchased at a reasonable price; and the Government shall operate said railroads as public highways for the benefit of the whole people, and not in the interest of the few, under suitable provisions for protection of life and property, giving to all transportation interests equal privileges and equal rates for fares and freight.

3. We denounce the present infamous schemes for refunding these debts, and demand that the laws now applicable thereto be executed and administered according to their intent and spirit.

4. The telegraph, like the Post Office system, being a necessity for the transmission of news, should be owned and operated by the Government in the interest of the people.

### THE PUBLIC LANDS

1. True policy demands that the National and State legislation shall be such as will ultimately enable every prudent and industrious citizen to secure a home, and therefore the land should not be monopolized for speculative purposes. All lands now held by railroads and other corporations in excess of their actual needs should by lawful means be reclaimed by the Government and held for actual settlers only, and private land monopoly, as well as alien ownership, should be prohibited.

2. We condemn the land grant frauds by which the Pacific railroad companies have, through the connivance of the Interior Department, robbed multitudes of *bona-fide* settlers of their homes and miners of their claims, and we demand legislation by Con-

gress which will enforce the exemption of mineral land from such grants after as well as before the patent.

3. We demand that *bona-fide* settlers on all public lands be granted free homes, as provided in the National Homestead Law, and that no exception be made in the case of Indian reservations when opened for settlement, and that all lands not now patented come under this demand.

### THE REFERENDUM

We favor a system of direct legislation through the initiative and referendum, under proper Constitutional safeguards.

### DIRECT ELECTION OF PRESIDENT AND SENATORS BY THE PEOPLE

We demand the election of President, Vice-President, and United States Senators by a direct vote of the people.

### SYMPATHY FOR CUBA

We tender to the patriotic people of Cuba our deepest sympathy for their heroic struggle for political freedom and independence, and we believe the time has come when the United States, the great Republic of the world, should recognize that Cuba is, and of right ought to be, a free and independent state.

### THE TERRITORIES

We favor home rule in the Territories and the District of Columbia, and the early admission of the Territories as States.

### PUBLIC SALARIES

All public salaries should be made to correspond to the price of labor and its products.

### EMPLOYMENT TO BE FURNISHED BY GOVERNMENT

In times of great industrial depression, idle labor should be employed on public works as far as practicable.

### ARBITRARY JUDICIAL ACTION

The arbitrary course of the courts in assuming to imprison citizens for indirect contempt and ruling by injunction should be prevented by proper legislation.

### PENSIONS

We favor just pensions for our disabled Union soldiers.

### A FAIR BALLOT

Believing that the elective franchise and an untrammeled ballot are essential to a government of, for, and by the people, the People's party condemns the wholesale system of disfranchisement adopted in some States as unrepublican and undemocratic, and we declare it to be the duty of the several State legislatures to take such action as will secure a full, free, and fair ballot and an honest count.

### THE FINANCIAL QUESTION "THE PRESSING ISSUE"

While the foregoing propositions constitute the platform upon which our party stands, and for the vindication of which its organization will be maintained, we recognize that the great and pressing issue of the pending campaign, upon which the present election will turn, is the financial question, and upon this great and specific issue between the parties we cordially invite the aid and co-operation of all organizations and citizens agreeing with us upon this vital question.

John D. Hicks

# 22. ". . . THE PEOPLE, NOT THE PLUTOCRATS, MUST CONTROL THE GOVERNMENT"

How many of the reforms advocated by the Populists were ultimately triumphant and how the Populist course of action may be justified by the circumstances of the 1890's is set forth in the concluding chapter of Professor Hicks's classic work on this subject.

Early in 1890, when the People's party was yet in the embryo stage, a farmer editor from the West set forth the doctrine that "the cranks always win." As he saw it,

The cranks are those who do not accept the existing order of things, and propose to change them. The existing order of things is always accepted by the majority, therefore the cranks are always in the minority. They are always progressive thinkers and always in advance of their time, and they always win. Called fanatics and fools at first, they are sometimes persecuted and abused. But their reforms are generally righteous, and time, reason and argument bring men to their side. Abused and ridiculed, then tolerated, then respectfully given a hearing, then supported. This has been the gauntlet that all great reforms and reformers have run, from Galileo to John Brown.

The writer of this editorial may have overstated his case, but a backward glance at the history of Populism shows that many of the reforms that the Populists demanded, while despised and rejected for a season, won triumphantly in the end. The party itself did not survive, nor did many of its leaders, although the number of contemporary politicians whose escutcheons should bear the bend sinister of Populism is larger than might be supposed; but Populistic doctrines showed an amazing vitality.

In formulating their principles the Populists reasoned that the ordinary, honest, will-ing American worker, be he farmer, or be he laborer, might expect in this land of opportunity not only the chance to work but also, as the rightful reward of his labor, a fair degree of prosperity. When, in the later eighties and in the "heart-breaking nineties," hundreds of thousands—perhaps millions—of men found themselves either without work to do or, having work, unable to pay their just debts and make a living, the Populists held that there must be "wrong and crime and fraud somewhere." What was more natural than to fix the blame for this situation upon the manufacturers, the railroads, the money-lenders, the middlemen—plutocrats all, whose "colossal fortunes, unprecedented in the history of mankind," grew ever greater while the multitudes came to know the meaning of want. Work was denied when work might well have been given, and "the fruits of the toil of millions were boldly stolen."

And the remedy? In an earlier age the hard-pressed farmers and laborers might have fled to free farms in the seemingly limitless lands of the West, but now the era of free lands had passed. Where, then, might they look for help? Where, if not to the government, which alone had the power to bring the mighty oppressors of the people to bay? So to the government the Populists

From John D. Hicks, *The Populist Revolt: A History of the Farmers' Alliance and the People's Party*, University of Minnesota Press, Minneapolis, pp. 404-410, 412-423. (c) Copyright 1931, University of Minnesota. Renewed 1959 by John D. Hicks.

turned. From it they asked laws to insure a full redress of grievances. As Dr. Turner puts it, "the defences of the pioneer democrat began to shift from free land to legislation, from the ideal of individualism to the ideal of social control through regulation by law." Unfortunately, however, the agencies of government had been permitted to fall into the hands of the plutocrats. Hence, if the necessary corrective legislation were to be obtained, the people must first win control of their government. The Populist philosophy thus boiled down finally to two fundamental propositions; one, that the government must restrain the selfish tendencies of those who profited at the expense of the poor and needy; the other, that the people, not the plutocrats, must control the government.

In their efforts to remove all restrictions on the power of the people to rule, the Populists accepted as their own a wide range of reforms. They believed, and on this they had frequently enough the evidence of their own eyes, that corruption existed at the ballot box and that a fair count was often denied. They fell in line, therefore, with great enthusiasm when agitators, who were not necessarily Populists, sought to popularize the Australian ballot and such other measures as were calculated to insure a true expression of the will of the people. Believing as they did that the voice of the people was the voice of God, they sought to eliminate indirect elections, especially the election of United States senators by state legislatures and of the president and the vice president by an electoral college. Fully aware of the habits of party bosses in manipulating nominating conventions, the Populists veered more and more in the direction of direct primary elections, urging in some of their later platforms that nominations even for president and vice president should be made by direct vote. Woman suffrage was a delicate question, for it was closely identified with the politically hazardous matter of temperance legislation, but, after all, the idea of votes for women was so clearly in

harmony with the Populist doctrine of popular rule that it could not logically be denied a place among genuinely Populistic reforms. Direct legislation through the initiative and referendum and through the easy amendment of state constitutions naturally appealed strongly to the Populists—the more so as they saw legislatures fail repeatedly to enact reform laws to which a majority of their members had been definitely pledged. "A majority of the people," said the Sioux Falls convention, "can never be corruptly influenced." The recall of faithless officials, even judges, also attracted favorable attention from the makers of later Populist platforms.

To list these demands is to cite the chief political innovations made in the United States during recent times. The Australian system of voting, improved registration laws, and other devices for insuring "a free ballot and a fair count" have long since swept the country. Woman suffrage has won an unqualified victory. The election of United States senators by direct vote of the people received the approval of far more than two-thirds of the national House of Representatives as early as 1898; it was further foreshadowed by the adoption, beginning in 1904, of senatorial primaries in a number of states, the results of which were to be regarded as morally binding upon the legislatures concerned; and it became a fact in 1913 with the ratification of the seventeenth amendment to the constitution.

The direct election of president and vice president was a reform hard to reconcile with state control of election machinery and state definition of the right to vote. Hence this reform never made headway; but the danger of one presidential candidate receiving a majority of the popular vote and another a majority of the electoral vote, as was the case in the Cleveland-Harrison contest of 1888, seems definitely to have passed. Recent elections may not prove that the popular voice always speaks intelligently; but they do seem to show that it speaks decisively.

In the widespread use of the primary election for the making of party nominations, the Populist principle of popular rule has scored perhaps its most telling victory. Tillman urged this reform in South Carolina at a very early date, but on obtaining control of the Democratic political machine of his state, he hesitated to give up the power that the convention system placed in his hands. At length, however, in 1896 he allowed the reform to go through. Wisconsin, spurred on by the La Follette forces, adopted the direct primary plan of nomination in 1903, and thereafter the other states of the Union, with remarkably few exceptions, fell into line. Presidential preference primaries, through which it was hoped that the direct voice of the people could be heard in the making of nominations for president and vice president, were also adopted by a number of states, beginning with Oregon in 1910.

Direct legislation by the people became almost an obsession with the Populists, especially the middle-of-the-road faction, in whose platforms it tended to overshadow nearly every other issue; and it is perhaps significant that the initiative and referendum were first adopted by South Dakota, a state in which the Populist party had shown great strength, as close on the heels of the Populist movement as 1898. Other states soon followed the South Dakota lead, and particularly in Oregon the experiment of popular legislation was given a thorough trial. New constitutions and numerous amendments to old constitutions tended also to introduce much popularly made law, the idea that legislation in a constitution is improper and unwise receiving perhaps its most shattering blow when an Oklahoma convention wrote for that state a constitution of fifty thousand words. The recall of elected officials has been applied chiefly in municipal affairs, but some states also permit its use for state officers and a few allow even judges, traditionally held to be immune from popular reactions, to be subjected to recall. Thus many of the favorite

ideas of the Populists, ideas that had once been "abused and ridiculed," were presently "respectfully given a hearing, then supported."

Quite apart from these changes in the American form of government, the Populist propaganda in favor of independent voting did much to undermine the intense party loyalties that had followed in the wake of the Civil War. The time had been when for the Republican voter "to doubt Grant was as bad as to doubt Christ," when the man who scratched his party ticket was regarded as little, if any, better than the traitor to his country. The Alliance in its day had sought earnestly to wean the partisan voter over to independence. It had urged its members to "favor and assist to office such candidates only as are thoroughly identified with our principles and who will insist on such legislation as shall make them effective," and in this regard the Alliance, as some of its leaders boasted, had been a "great educator of the people." The Populist party had to go even further, for its growth depended almost wholly upon its ability to bring voters to a complete renunciation of old party loyalties. Since at one time or another well over a million men cast their ballots for Populist tickets, the loosening of party ties that thus set in was of formidable proportions.

Indeed, the man who became a Populist learned his lesson almost too well. When confronted, as many Populist voters thought themselves to be in 1896, with a choice between loyalty to party and loyalty to principle, the third-party adherent generally tended to stand on principle. Thereafter, as Populism faded out, the men who once had sworn undying devotion to the Omaha platform, were compelled again to transfer their allegiance. Many Republicans became Democrats via the Populist route; many Democrats became Republicans. Most of the Populists probably returned to the parties from which they had withdrawn, but party ties, once broken, were not so strong as they had been before. The rapid passing of voters from one party to another and the wholesale scratching of ballots, so characteristic of voting today, are distinctly reminiscent of Populism; as are also the nonpartisan ballots by which judges, city commissioners, and other officers are now frequently chosen, wholly without regard to their party affiliations.

In the South the Populist demands for popular government produced a peculiar situation. To a very great extent the southern Populists were recruited from the rural classes that had hitherto been politically inarticulate. Through the Populist party the "wool hat boys" from the country sought to obtain the weight in southern politics that their numbers warranted but that the Bourbon dynasties had ever denied them. In the struggle that ensued, both sides made every possible use of the Negro vote, and the bugaboo of Negro domination was once again raised. Indeed, the experience of North Carolina under a combination government of Populists and Republicans furnished concrete evidence of what might happen should the political power of the Negro be restored. Under the circumstances, therefore, there seemed to be nothing else for the white Populists to do but to return to their former allegiance until the menace of the Negro voter could be removed.

* * *

The control of the government by the people was to the thoughtful Populist merely a means to an end. The next step was to use the power of the government to check the iniquities of the plutocrats. When the Populists at Omaha were baffled by the insistence of the temperance forces, they pointed out that before this or any other such reform could be accomplished they must "ask all men to first help us to determine whether we are to have a republic to administer." The inference is clear. Once permit the people really to rule, once insure that the men in office would not or could not betray the popular will, and such regulative measures as would right the wrongs from which the people suffered would quickly follow. The Populist believed im-

plicitly in the ability of the people to frame and enforce the measures necessary to redeem themselves from the various sorts of oppression that were being visited upon them. They catalogued in their platform the evils from which society suffered and suggested the specific remedies by which these evils were to be overcome.

Much unfair criticism has been leveled at the Populists because of the attitude they took towards the allied subjects of banking and currency. To judge from the contemporary anti-Populist diatribes and from many subsequent criticisms of the Populist financial program, one would think that in such matters the third-party economists were little better than raving maniacs. As a matter of fact, the old-school Populists could think about as straight as their opponents. Their newspapers were well edited, and the arguments therein presented usually held together. Populist literature, moreover, was widely and carefully read by the ordinary third-party voters, particularly by the western farmers, whose periods of enforced leisure gave them ample opportunity for reading and reflection. Old-party debaters did not tackle their Populist antagonists lightly, for as frequently as not the bewhiskered rustic, turned orator, could present in support of his arguments an array of carefully sorted information that left his better-groomed opponent in a daze. The appearance of the somewhat irrelevant silver issue considerably confused Populist thinking, but even so many of the old-timers kept their heads and put silver in its proper place.

The Populists observed with entire accuracy that the currency of the United States was both inadequate and inelastic. They criticized correctly the part played by the national banking system in currency matters as irresponsible and susceptible of manipulation in the interest of the creditor class. They demanded a stabilized dollar, and they believed that it could be obtained if a national currency "safe, sound, and flexible" should be issued direct to the people by the government itself in such quantities as the reasonable demands of business should dictate. Silver and gold might be issued as well as paper, but the value of the dollar should come from the fiat of government and not from the "intrinsic worth" of the metal.

It is interesting to note that since the time when Populists were condemned as lunatics for holding such views legislation has been adopted that, while by no means going the full length of an irredeemable paper currency, does seek to accomplish precisely the ends that the Populists had in mind. Populist and free-silver agitation forced economists to study the money question as they had never studied it before and ultimately led them to propose remedies that could run the gauntlet of public opinion and of Congress. The Aldrich-Vreeland Act of 1908 authorized an emergency currency of several hundred million dollars, to be lent to banks on approved securities in times of financial disturbance. A National Monetary Commission, created at the same time, reported after four years' intensive study in favor of a return to the Hamiltonian system of a central Bank of the United States. Instead Congress in 1914, under Wilson's leadership, adopted the federal reserve system. The Federal Reserve Act did not, indeed, destroy the national banks and avoid the intervention of bankers in all monetary matters, but it did make possible an adequate and elastic national currency, varying in accordance with the needs of the country, and it placed supreme control of the nation's banking and credit resources in the hands of a federal reserve board, appointed not by the bankers but by the president of the United States with the consent of the Senate. The Populist diagnosis was accepted, and the Populist prescription was not wholly ignored.

Probably no item in the Populist creed received more thorough castigation at the hands of contemporaries than the demand for subtreasuries, or government warehouses for the private storage of grain; but the subtreasury idea was not all bad, and perhaps the Populists would have done well

had they pursued it further than they did. The need that the subtreasury was designed to meet was very real. Lack of credit forced the farmer to sell his produce at the time of harvest, when the price was lowest. A cash loan on his crop that would enable him to hold it until prices should rise was all that he asked. Prices might thus be stabilized; profits honestly earned by the farmers would no longer fall to the speculators. That the men who brought forward the subtreasury as a plan for obtaining short-term rural credits also loaded it with an unworkable plan for obtaining a flexible currency was unfortunate; but the fundamental principle of the bill has by no means been discredited. Indeed, the Warehouse Act of 1916 went far towards accomplishing the very thing the Populists demanded. Under it the United States Department of Agriculture was permitted to license warehousemen and authorize them to receive, weigh, and grade farm products, for which they might issue warehouse receipts as collateral. Thus the owner might borrow the money he needed — not, however, from the government of the United States.

In addition to the credits that the subtreasury would provide, Populist platforms usually urged also that the national government lend money on farm lands directly at a low rate of interest. This demand, which received an infinite amount of condemnation and derision at the time, has since been treated with much deference. If the government does not now print paper money to lend the farmer, with his land as security, it nevertheless does stand back of an elaborate system of banks through which he may obtain the credit he needs. Under the terms of the Federal Reserve Act national banks may lend money on farm mortgages — a privilege they did not enjoy in Populist times — and agricultural paper running as long as six months may be rediscounted by the federal reserve banks. From the farm loan banks, created by an act of 1916, the farmers may borrow for long periods sums not exceeding fifty per cent of the value of their land and twenty per cent of the value of their perma-

107

nent improvements. Finally, through still another series of banks, the federal intermediate credit banks, established by an act of 1923, loans are made available to carry the farmer from one season to the next or a little longer, should occasion demand; the intermediate banks were authorized to rediscount agricultural and live-stock paper for periods of from six months to three years. Thus the government has created a comprehensive system of rural credits through which the farmer may obtain either short-term loans, loans of intermediate duration, or long-term loans, as his needs require, with a minimum of difficulty and at minimum interest rates.

It would be idle to indulge in a *post hoc* argument in an attempt to prove that all these developments were due to Populism; but the intensive study of agricultural problems that led ultimately to these measures did begin with the efforts of sound economists to answer the arguments of the Populists. And it is evident that in the end the economists conceded nearly every point for which the Populists had contended.

More recent attempts to solve the agricultural problem, while assuming, as readily as even a Populist could have asked, the responsibility of the government in the matter, have progressed beyond the old Populist panacea of easy credit. Agricultural economists now have their attention fixed upon the surplus as the root of the difficulty. In industry, production can be curtailed to meet the demands of any given time, and a glutted market with the attendant decline in prices can be in a measure forestalled. But in agriculture, where each farmer is a law unto himself and where crop yields must inevitably vary greatly from year to year, control of production is well-nigh impossible and a surplus may easily become chronic. Suggestions for relief therefore looked increasingly towards the disposal of this surplus to the greatest advantage.

The various McNary-Haugen bills that have come before Congress in recent years proposed to create a federal board through which the margin above domestic needs in years of plenty should be purchased and held, or disposed of abroad at whatever price it would bring. Through an "equalization fee" the losses sustained by "dumping" the surplus in this fashion were to be charged back upon the producers benefited. Although this proposition was agreeable to a majority of both houses of Congress, it met opposition from two successive presidents, Coolidge and Hoover, and was finally set aside for another scheme, less "socialistic." In 1929 Congress passed and the president signed a law for the creation of an appointive federal farm board, one of whose duties it is, among others, to encourage the organization of cooperative societies through which the farmers may themselves deal with the problem of the surplus. In case of necessity, however, the board may take the lead in the formation of stabilization corporations, which under its strict supervision may buy up such seasonal or temporary surpluses as threaten to break the market and hold them for higher prices. A huge revolving fund, appropriated by Congress, is made available for this purpose, loans from this fund being obtainable by the stabilization corporations at low interest rates. There is much about this thoroughly respectable and conservative law that recalls the agrarian demands of the nineties. Indeed, the measure goes further in the direction of government recognition of and aid to the principle of agricultural cooperation than even the most erratic Alliancemen could have dared to hope. Perhaps it will prove to be the "better plan" that the farmers called for in vain when the subtreasury was the best idea they could present.

To the middle western Populist the railway problem was as important as any other—perhaps the most important of all. Early Alliance platforms favored drastic governmental control of the various means of communication as the best possible remedy for the ills from which the people suffered, and the first Populist platform to be written called for government ownership and operation only in case "the most rigid, honest, and just national control and supervision" should fail to "remove the abuses now existing." Thereafter the Populists usually demanded government ownership, although it is clear enough from their state and local platforms and from the votes and actions of Populist office-holders that, pending the day when ownership should become a fact, regulation by state and nation must be made ever more effective.

Possibly government ownership is no nearer today than in Populist times, but the first objective of the Populists, "the most rigid, honest, and just national control," is as nearly an accomplished fact as carefully drawn legislation and highly efficient administration can make it. Populist misgivings about governmental control arose from the knowledge that the Interstate Commerce Act of 1887, as well as most regulatory state legislation, was wholly ineffectual during the nineties; but beginning with the Elkins Act of 1903, which struck at the practice of granting rebates, a long series of really workable laws found their way into the statute books. The Hepburn Act of 1906, the Mann-Elkins Act of 1910, and the Transportation Act of 1920, not to mention lesser laws, placed the Interstate Commerce Commission upon a high pinnacle of power. State laws, keeping abreast of the national program, supplemented national control with state control; and through one or the other agency most of the specific grievances of which the Populists had complained were removed. The arbitrary fixing of rates by the carriers, a commonplace in Populist times, is virtually unknown today. If discriminations still exist between persons or places, the Interstate Commerce Commission is apt to be as much to blame as the railroads. Free passes, so numerous in Populist times as to occasion the remark that the only people who did not have passes were those who could not afford to pay their own fare, have virtually ceased to be issued except to railway employees. Railway control of state governments, even in the old Granger states, where in earlier days party bosses took their orders directly from railway officials, has long since become a thing of the past. The railroads still may have an influence in politics, but the railroads do not rule. Governmental control of telephones, telegraphs, and pipelines, together with such later developments as the radio and the transmission of electric power, is accepted today as a matter of course, the issues being merely to what extent control should go and through what agencies it should be accomplished.

For the trust problem, as distinguished from the railroad problem, the Populists had no very definite solution. They agreed, however, that the power of government, state and national, should be used in such a way as to prevent "individuals or corporations fastening themselves, like vampires, on the people and sucking their substance." Antitrust laws received the earnest approval of Alliancemen and Populists and were often initiated by them. The failure of such laws to secure results was laid mainly at the door of the courts, and when Theodore Roosevelt in 1904 succeeded in securing an order from the United States Supreme Court dissolving the Northern Securities Company, it was hailed as a great victory for Populist principles. Many other incidental victories were won. Postal savings banks "for the safe deposit of the earnings of the people" encroached upon the special privileges of the bankers. An amendment to the national constitution in 1913, authorizing income taxes, recalled a contrary decision of the Supreme Court, which the Populists in their day had cited as the best evidence of the control of the government by the trusts; and income and inheritance taxes have ever since been levied. The reform of state and local taxation so as to exact a greater proportion of the taxes from the trusts and those who profit from them has also been freely undertaken. Labor demands, such as the right of labor to organize, the eight-hour day, limitation of injunctions in labor disputes, and restrictions on immigration were strongly championed by the Populists as fit measures for curbing the power of the trusts and were presently treated with great con-

109

sideration. The Clayton Antitrust Act and the Federal Trade Commission Act, passed during the Wilson regime, were the products of long experience with the trust problem. The manner in which these laws have been enforced, however, would seem to indicate that the destruction of the trusts, a common demand in Populist times, is no longer regarded as feasible and that by government control the interests of the people can best be conserved.

On the land question the Populist demands distinctly foreshadowed conservation. "The land," according to the Omaha declaration, "including all the natural resources of wealth, is the heritage of all the people and should not be monopolized for speculative purposes." Land and resources already given away were of course difficult to get back, and the passing of the era of free lands could not be repealed by law, but President Roosevelt soon began to secure results in the way of the reclamation and irrigation of arid western lands, the enlargement and protection of the national forests, the improvement of internal waterways, and the withdrawal from entry of lands bearing mineral wealth such as coal, oil, and phosphates. At regular intervals, since 1908, the governors of the states have met together in conference to discuss the conservation problem and this once dangerous Populist doctrine has now won all but universal acceptance.

It would thus appear that much of the Populist program has found favor in the eyes of later generations. Populist plans for altering the machinery of government have, with but few exceptions, been carried into effect. Referring to these belated victories of the Populists, William Allen White, the man who had once asked, "What's the matter with Kansas?" wrote recently, "They abolished the established order completely and ushered in a new order." Mrs. Mary E. Lease looked back proudly in 1914 on her political career:

In these later years I have seen, with gratification, that my work in the good old Populist days was not in vain. The Progressive party has adopted our platform, clause by clause, plank by plank. Note the list of reforms which we advocated which are coming into reality. Direct election of senators is assured. Public utilities are gradually being removed from the hands of the few and placed under the control of the people who use them. Woman's suffrage is now almost a national issue. . . . The seed we sowed out in Kansas did not fall on barren ground.

Thanks to this triumph of Populist principles, one may almost say that, in so far as political devices can insure it, the people now rule. Political dishonesty has not altogether disappeared and the people may yet be betrayed by the men they elect to office, but on the whole the acts of government have come to reflect fairly clearly the will of the people. Efforts to assert this newly won power in such a way as to crush the economic supremacy of the predatory few have also been numerous and not wholly unsuccessful. The gigantic corporations of today, dwarfing into insignificance the trusts of yesterday, are, in spite of their size, far more circumspect in their conduct than their predecessors. If in the last analysis "big business" controls, it is because it has public opinion on its side and not merely the party bosses.

To radicals of today, however, the Populist panaceas, based as they were upon an essentially individualistic philosophy and designed merely to insure for every man his right to "get ahead" in the world, seem totally inadequate. These latter-day extremists point to the perennial reappearance of such problems as farm relief, unemployment, unfair taxation, and law evasion as evidence that the Populist type of reform is futile, that something more drastic is required. Nor is their contention without point. It is reasonable to suppose that progressivism itself must progress; that the programs that would provide solutions for the problems of one generation might fall far short of meeting the needs of a succeeding generation. Perhaps one may not agree with the view of some present-day radicals that only a revolution will suffice and that the very attempt to make existing institutions more tolerable is treason to any real progress, since by so doing the day of revolution is postponed; but one must recognize that when the old Populist panaceas can receive the enthusiastic support of Hooverian Republicans and Alsmithian Democrats these once startling demands are no longer radical at all. One is reminded of the dilemma that Alice of Wonderland encountered when she went through the looking-glass into the garden of live flowers. On and on she ran with the Red Queen, but however fast they went they never seemed to pass anything.

"Well, in our country," said Alice, still panting a little, "you'd generally get to somewhere else — if you ran very fast for a long time as we've been doing."

"A slow sort of country!" said the Queen, "Now here, you see, it takes all the running you can do to keep in the same place. If you want to get somewhere else, you must run twice as fast as that!"

# V. The Progressives and Agriculture: 1901–1920

The first two decades of the twentieth century saw the flowering of the Progressive movement in the United States. Coming as it did directly after the Populist revolt, the Progressive movement is often thought of as an extension of Populism—its continuation under more respectable auspices. It has been described as the urban counterpart of Populism. Because the impetus of Progressivism came from the middle class, it was attractive to editorial writers, clergymen, and many others who felt menaced by more radical movements emanating from lower echelons of society, as the Populists were regarded. Thus it was possible for the Progressives to adopt many of the issue-positions held by Populists, secure their approval, and yet escape the blanket condemnation that had befallen the earlier reformers.

In agriculture, the distinction between the values of Populists and Progressives is quite clear. The differences illustrate the deep cultural cleavage that has become increasingly noticeable within agriculture after the turn of the century.

The Progressive view of agricultural improvement was related to the development of science and its application through education and technology. The use of government agencies to modernize and improve agriculture was approved, thus departing still further from the earlier "least-government" and laissez-faire notions. The production function and its improvement were given the first priority and government action in this direction was strongly upheld by Progressives. It was accepted by the Progressives generally that a vigorous and healthy agriculture was necessary to the national welfare. Agriculture was viewed as a business and the farmer as a businessman. The objective of policy then was to provide a situation in which the cards were not stacked against the farmer in the risks he had to take as a normal part of his business operation.

It happened that during most of the Progressive period farm prices were generally favorable to agriculture; it was a period of rising prices and agricultural expansion. In retrospect, during the years 1909-1914 prices for farm products seem fair in relation to the prices of things the farmer needed to purchase. Between World Wars I and II, years of severe agricultural distress, the objective of restoring the 1909-1914 price relationship became a major target of federal farm policy.

While the years of the Progressive period became known as the "golden age of agriculture," there were indications that, by comparative standards, there were some unsatisfactory conditions and trends. Compared with the cities, rural institutions, both public and private, were in a backward state. Farm tenancy was increasing and the harmful effects of "absentee landlordism" were apparent.

The poverty of the tenant cotton farmers in Texas motivated the organization of the Farmers Educational and Cooperative Union in 1902, which continued to be a voice for the less wealthy farmers, often tenants, throughout the South and the Plains States. A similar organization, the American Society of Equity, grew up in the North Central States, eventually merging with the Farmers Union. These movements more nearly represented the continuation of Populism than did the Progressives.

The gains that were made during the period were a reflection of the Progressive value orientation. Agricultural research and education, strongly promoted by the U. S. Department of Agriculture, made great strides. Scientific conservation and reclamation under plans to aid and encourage private ownership made considerable headway. The Progressive farm program provided some valuable assistance for improving the better farm enterprises. But basic and deep-rooted maladjustments in rural areas were untouched.

## CONSERVATION AND RECLAMATION

As the process of settling and developing land for agriculture moved westward, the problem of cultivation in arid and semi-arid regions was encountered. The basic homestead standard of 160-acre farms had been developed for settlement in regions of fairly abundant rainfall and the resulting pattern of agricultural technology was ill-adapted for use west of the 100th meridian of longitude. In more than half the areas of the Dakotas, Nebraska, Kansas, Oklahoma, and Texas climatic and geographical conditions limited the value of the homestead policy. These were, of course, the very states where the Homestead Act of 1862 was most pertinent.

Various adaptations of public policy were made in recognition of the physical problems attached to farming in arid regions. In addition to the fact that farmers soon began to find ways of expanding their acreage to a more suitable size, usually by purchase or rental, federal law made several accommodations to the situation. The Timber Culture Act of 1873, for example, made it possible for a homesteader to take a second 160 acres of land provided he would plant 40 acres of it in trees. Likewise, the Desert Land Act of 1877 allowed for the purchase of 640 acres of the public domain on conditions of "reclaiming" the land, and this policy was pursued further in 1888 by legislation providing for surveys of irrigation feasibility in the arid regions.

The Kincaid Act of 1904, Forest Homestead Act of 1906, Enlarged Homestead Act of 1909, and the Stock-Raising Homestead Act of 1916, all pursued the policy of extending farming into the West by expanding the acreage available for homesteading. By the time of this legislation, almost all of the area capable of being tilled by the then dominant techniques had been taken up. Expanding acreage through private purchase or rental from individual owners was soon to supersede the governmental arrangements for transfer of the public domain.

Another approach to the problems of agricultural development west of the 100th meridian was reclamation. Reclamation meant, given the nature of the land problem at the turn of the century, putting water on arid lands. The Desert Land Acts, mentioned above, and the Carey Act of 1894, which sought to encourage states to develop reclamation projects, were early efforts, though not very successful ones, in this direction.

With the conservation-minded Theodore Roosevelt as president, support for an ambitious policy of reclamation was obtained, not only from the executive but also from a Congress whose Senate contained by 1900 powerful representation of the western states. The passage of the Newlands Act of 1902 by the 57th Congress marked this change of policy.

## 23. **THE RECLAMATION ACT OF 1902**

*An Act Appropriating the receipts from the sale and disposal of public lands in certain States and Territories to the construction of irrigation works for the reclamation of arid lands.*

*Be it enacted by the Senate and House of Representatives of the United States of America in Congress assembled,* That all moneys received from the sale and disposal of public lands in Arizona, California, Colorado, Idaho, Kansas, Montana, Nebraska, Nevada, New Mexico, North Dakota, Oklahoma, Oregon, South Dakota, Utah, Washington, and Wyoming, beginning with the fiscal year ending June thirtieth, nineteen hundred and one, including the surplus of fees and commissions in excess of allowances to registers and receivers, and excepting the five per centum of the proceeds of the sales of public lands in the above States set aside by law for educational and other purposes, shall be, and the same are hereby, reserved, set aside, and appropriated as a special fund in the Treasury to be known as the "reclamation fund," to be used in the examination and survey for and the construction and maintenance of irrigation works for the storage, diversion, and development of waters for the reclamation of arid and semi-arid lands in the said States and Territories, and for the payment of all other expenditures provided for in this Act: *Provided,* That in case the receipts from the sale and disposal of public lands other than those realized from the sale and disposal of lands referred to in this section are insufficient to meet the requirements for the support of agricultural colleges in the several States and Territories, under the Act of August thirtieth, eighteen hundred and ninety, entitled "An Act to apply a portion of the proceeds of the public lands to the more complete endowment and support of the colleges for the benefit of agriculture and the mechanic arts, established under the provisions of an Act of Congress approved July second, eighteen hundred and sixty-two," the deficiency, if any, in the sum necessary for the support of the said colleges shall be provided for from any moneys in the Treasury not otherwise appropriated.

*Sec. 2.* That the Secretary of the Interior is hereby authorized and directed to make examinations and surveys for, and to locate

From 32 *Statutes-at-Large*, part 1 (1902), p. 388.

and construct, as herein provided, irrigation works for the storage, diversion, and development of waters, including artesian wells, and to report to Congress at the beginning of each regular session as to the results of such examinations and surveys, giving estimates of cost of all contemplated works, the quantity and location of the lands which can be irrigated therefrom, and all facts relative to the practicability of each irrigation project; also the cost of works in process of construction as well as of those which have been completed.

*Sec. 3.* That the Secretary of the Interior shall, before giving the public notice provided for in section four of this Act, withdraw from public entry the lands required for any irrigation works contemplated under the provisions of this Act, and shall restore to public entry any of the lands so withdrawn when, in his judgment, such lands are not required for the purposes of this Act; and the Secretary of the Interior is hereby authorized, at or immediately prior to the time of beginning the surveys for any contemplated irrigation works, to withdraw from entry, except under the homestead laws, any public lands believed to be susceptible of irrigation from said works: *Provided,* That all lands entered and entries made under the homestead laws within areas so withdrawn during such withdrawal shall be subject to all provisions, limitations, charges, terms, and conditions of this Act; that said surveys shall be prosecuted diligently to completion, and upon the completion thereof, and of the necessary maps, plans, and estimates of cost, the Secretary of the Interior shall determine whether or not said project is practicable and advisable, and if determined to be impracticable or unadvisable he shall thereupon restore said lands to entry; that public lands which it is proposed to irrigate by means of any contemplated works shall be subject to entry only under the provisions of the homestead laws in tracts of not less than forty nor more than one hundred and sixty acres, and shall be subject to the limitations, charges, terms, and conditions herein provided: *Provided,* That the commutation provisions of the homestead laws shall not apply to entries made under this Act.

*Sec. 4.* That upon the determination by the Secretary of the Interior that any irrigation project is practicable, he may cause to be let contracts for the construction of the same, in such portions or sections as it may be practicable to construct and complete as parts of the whole project, providing the necessary funds for such portions or sections are available in the reclamation fund, and thereupon he shall give public notice of the lands irrigable under such project, and limit of area per entry, which limit shall represent the acreage which, in the opinion of the Secretary, may be reasonably required for the support of a family upon the lands in question; also of the charges which shall be made per acre upon the said entries, and upon lands in private ownership which may be irrigated by the waters of the said irrigation project, and the number of annual installments, not exceeding ten, in which such charges shall be paid and the time when such payments shall commence. The said charges shall be determined with a view of returning to the reclamation fund the estimated cost of construction of the project, and shall be apportioned equitably: *Provided,* That in all construction work eight hours shall constitute a day's work, and no Mongolian labor shall be employed thereon.

*Sec. 5.* That the entryman upon lands to be irrigated by such works shall, in addition to compliance with the homestead laws, reclaim at least one-half of the total irrigable area of his entry for agricultural purposes, and before receiving patent for the lands covered by his entry shall pay to the Government the charges apportioned against such tract, as provided in section four. No right to the use of water for land in private ownership shall be sold for a tract exceeding one hundred and sixty acres to any one landowner, and no such sale shall be made to any landowner unless he be an actual bona fide resident on such land, or occupant thereof residing in the neighborhood of said land, and no such right shall perma-

115

nently attach until all payments therefor are made. The annual installments shall be paid to the receiver of the local land office of the district in which the land is situated, and a failure to make any two payments when due shall render the entry subject to cancellation, with the forfeiture of all rights under this Act, as well as of any moneys already paid thereon. All moneys received from the above sources shall be paid into the reclamation fund. Registers and receivers shall be allowed the usual commissions on all moneys paid for lands entered under this Act.

*Sec. 6.* That the Secretary of the Interior is hereby authorized and directed to use the reclamation fund for the operation and maintenance of all reservoirs and irrigation works constructed under the provisions of this Act: *Provided,* That when the payments required by this Act are made for the major portion of the lands irrigated from the waters of any of the works herein provided for, then the management and operation of such irrigation works shall pass to the owners of the lands irrigated thereby, to be maintained at their expense under such form of organization and under such rules and regulations as may be acceptable to the Secretary of the Interior: *Provided,* That the title to and the management and operation of the reservoirs and the works necessary for their protection and operation shall remain in the Government until otherwise provided by Congress.

*Sec. 7.* That where in carrying out the provisions of this Act it becomes necessary to acquire any rights or property, the Secretary of the Interior is hereby authorized to acquire the same for the United States by purchase or by condemnation under judicial process, and to pay from the reclamation fund the sums which may be needed for that purpose, and it shall be the duty of the Attorney-General of the United States upon every application of the Secretary of the Interior, under this Act, to cause proceedings to be commenced for condemnation within thirty days from the receipt of the application at the Department of Justice.

*Sec. 8.* That nothing in this Act shall be construed as affecting or intended to affect or to in any way interfere with the laws of any State or Territory relating to the control, appropriation, use, or distribution of water used in irrigation, or any vested right acquired thereunder, and the Secretary of the Interior, in carrying out the provisions of this Act, shall proceed in conformity with such laws, and nothing herein shall in any way affect any right of any State or of the Federal Government or of any landowner, appropriator, or user of water in, to, or from any interstate stream or the waters thereof: *Provided,* That the right to the use of water acquired under the provisions of this Act shall be appurtenant to the land irrigated, and beneficial use shall be the basis, the measure, and the limit of the right.

*Sec. 9.* That it is hereby declared to be the duty of the Secretary of the Interior in carrying out the provisions of this Act, so far as the same may be practicable and subject to the existence of feasible irrigation projects, to expend the major portion of the funds arising from the sale of public lands within each State and Territory hereinbefore named for the benefit of arid and semiarid lands within the limits of such State or Territory: *Provided,* That the Secretary may temporarily use such portion of said funds for the benefit of arid or semiarid lands in any particular State or Territory hereinbefore named as he may deem advisable, but when so used the excess shall be restored to the fund as soon as practicable, to the end that ultimately, and in any event, within each ten-year period after the passage of this Act, the expenditures for the benefit of the said States and Territories shall be equalized according to the proportions and subject to the conditions as to practicability and feasibility aforesaid.

*Sec. 10.* That the Secretary of the Interior is hereby authorized to perform any and all acts and to make such rules and regulations as may be necessary and proper for the purpose of carrying the provisions of this Act into full force and effect.

## 24. "THE FARMING INTEREST IS NOT, AS A WHOLE, RECEIVING THE FULL REWARDS TO WHICH IT IS ENTITLED"

In August of the last year of his second term in the White House, President Theodore Roosevelt appointed a Commission on Country Life. In his letter to Professor L. H. Bailey of the New York State College of Agriculture, the President reflected the degree to which the concept of agricultural fundamentalism had been absorbed into the values of the Progressive movement. "No nation," he asserted, "has ever achieved permanent greatness unless this greatness was based on the well-being of the great farmer class, the men who live on the soil. . . ." In the same vein is a remark from his address celebrating the founding of agricultural colleges in the United States: "There is but one person whose welfare is as vital to the welfare of the whole country as is that of the wage-worker who does manual labor, and that is the tiller of the soil—the farmer." Thus the President accepted the basic premise of John Taylor's agrarianism, although his policies indicate that he developed widely differing conclusions.

Underlying both the President's letter and the Report of the Commission is the note of apprehension concerning an impending deterioration of the economic and social quality of rural life. "Broadly speaking," the Report opens, "agriculture in the United States is prosperous . . .," yet "marked inequalities have arisen" creating agricultural unrest and a movement into the cities which "tends to sterilize the open country and to lower its social status."

The Commission noted that urban-based interests, and the cities themselves, with their greater financial and market power, tended to take advantage of rural people. Moreover, the city's cultural advantages attracted young people at the same time that undesirable elements of the city population were driven into rural areas. Added to these difficulties were urban-based land speculators, monopolistic interests gaining control of streams, exploitation of forests and other natural resources, and discrimination by transportation companies and middlemen.

The Commission accepted the view, blending the older agrarianism with the spirit of the Progressives, that government should protect the most fundamental facet of national life, the mainspring of human virtue, by a rational program of public policies, aiming at redressing the balances thrown out of adjustment by a rapidly growing and industrializing nation. The Commission's recommendations are reprinted below from its report to the President.

Report of The Country Life Commission, United States Senate, 60th Congress, 2nd Session, Document 705 (Washington, D.C.: Government Printing Office, 1909), pp. 20-22, 24-25, 48-56, 60-65.

# V. The Progressives and Agriculture: 1901-1920

## I. GENERAL STATEMENT

Broadly speaking, agriculture in the United States is prosperous and the conditions in many of the great farming regions are improving. The success of the owners and cultivators of good land, in the prosperous regions, has been due partly to improved methods, largely to good prices for products, and also to the general advance in the price of farm lands in these regions. Notwithstanding the general advance in rentals and the higher prices of labor, tenants also have enjoyed a good degree of prosperity, due to fair crops, and an advance in the price of farm products approximately corresponding to the advance in the price of land. Farm labor has been fully employed and at increased wages, and many farm hands have become tenants and many tenants have become landowners.

There is marked improvement, in many of the agricultural regions, in the character of the farm home and its surroundings. There is increasing appreciation on the part of great numbers of country people of the advantage of sanitary water supplies and plumbing, of better construction in barns and all farm buildings, of good reading matter, of tasteful gardens and lawns, and the necessity of good education.

Many institutions are also serving the agricultural needs of the open country with great effectiveness, as the United States Department of Agriculture, the land-grant colleges and experiment stations, and the many kinds of extension work that directly or indirectly emanate from them. The help that these institutions render to the country-life interests is everywhere recognized. State departments of agricultural, national, state, and local organizations, many schools of secondary grade, churches, libraries, and many other agencies are also contributing actively to the betterment of agricultural conditions.

There has never been a time when the American farmer was as well off as he is today, when we consider not only his earning power, but the comforts and advantages he may secure. Yet the real efficiency in farm life, and in country life as a whole, is not to be measured by historical standards, but in terms of its possibilities. Considered from this point of view, there are very marked deficiencies. There has been a complete and fundamental change in our whole economic system within the past century. This has resulted in profound social changes and the redirection of our point of view on life. In some occupations the readjustment to the new conditions has been rapid and complete; in others it has come with difficulty. In all the great series of farm occupations the readjustment has been the most tardy, because the whole structure of a traditional and fundamental system has been involved. It is not strange, therefore, that development is still arrested in certain respects; that marked inequalities have arisen; or that positive injustice may prevail even to a very marked and wide-spread extent. All these difficulties are the results of the unequal development of our contemporary civilization. All this may come about without any intention on the part of anyone that it should be so. The problems are nevertheless just as real, and they must be studied and remedies must be found.

These deficiencies are recognized by the people. We have found, not only the testimony of the farmers themselves but of all persons in touch with farm life, more or less serious agricultural unrest in every part of the United States, even in the most prosperous regions. There is a widespread tendency for farmers to move to town. It is not advisable, of course, that all country persons remain in the country; but this general desire to move is evidence that the open country is not satisfying as a permanent abode. This tendency is not peculiar to any region. In difficult farming regions, and where the competition with other farming sections is most severe, the young people may go to town to better their condition. In the best regions the older people retire to town because it is socially more attractive and they see a prospect of living in comparative ease and comfort on the rental of their lands. Nearly everywhere there is a townward movement for the purpose of securing school advantages for the children. All this tends to sterilize the open country and to lower its social status. Often the farm is let to tenants. The farmer is likely to lose active interest in life when he retires to town, and he becomes a stationary citizen, adding a social problem to the town. He is likely to find his expenses increasing and is obliged to raise rents to his tenant, thereby making it more difficult for the man who works on the land. On his death his property enriches the town rather than the country. The withdrawal of the children from the farms detracts from the interest and efficiency of the country school and adds to the interest of the town school. Thus the country is drained of the energy of youth on the one hand and the experience and accumulation of age on the other, and three problems more or less grave are created — a problem for the town, a problem for the public school, and also a problem of tenancy in the open country.

The farming interest is not, as a whole, receiving the full rewards to which it is entitled, nor has country life attained to anywhere near its possibilities of attractiveness and comfort. The farmer is necessarily handicapped in the development of social life and in the conduct of his business because of his separateness, the small volume of his output, and the lack of capital. He often begins with practically no capital, and expects to develop his capital and relationships out of the annual business itself; and even when he has capital with which to set up a business and operate it the amount is small when compared with that required in other enterprises. He is not only handicapped in his farming but is disadvantaged when he deals with other business interests and with other social groups. It is peculiarly necessary, therefore, that Government should give him adequate consideration and protection. There are difficulties of the

separate man, living quietly on his land, that government should understand.

## II. THE PURPOSE OF THE COMMISSION

The commission is requested to report on the means that are "now available for supplying the deficiencies which exist" in the country life of the United States and "upon the best methods of organized permanent effort in investigation and actual work" along the lines of betterment of rural conditions. . . .

The means that may be suggested for amelioration of country life fall under one or more of three general classes: (a) Definite recommendations for executive or legislative action by the Federal Government; (b) suggestions for legislative enactment on the part of States; (c) suggestions or recommendations to the public at large as to what the commission thinks would be the most fruitful lines of action and policy on the part of individuals, communities, or States.

The problem before the commission is to state, with some fullness of detail, the present conditions of country life, to point out the causes that may have led to its present lack of organization, to suggest methods by which it may be redirected, the drift to the city arrested, the natural rights of the farmer maintained, and an organized rural life developed that will promote the prosperity of the whole nation. . . .

## III. THE GENERAL CORRECTIVE FORCES THAT SHOULD BE SET IN MOTION

The ultimate need of the open country is the development of community effort and of social resources. Here and there the commission has found a rural neighborhood in which the farmers and their wives come together frequently and effectively for social intercourse, but these instances seem to be infrequent exceptions. There is a general lack of wholesome societies that are organized on a social basis. In the region in which the Grange is strong this need is best supplied.

There is need of the greatest diversity in country-life affairs, but there is equal need of a social cohesion operating among all these affairs and tying them all together. This life must be developed, as we have said, directly from native or resident forces. It is neither necessary nor desirable that an exclusive hamlet system be brought about in order to secure these ends. The problem before the commission is to suggest means whereby this development may be directed and hastened directly from the land.

The social disorder is usually unrecognized. If only the farms are financially profitable, the rural condition is commonly pronounced good. Country life must be made thoroughly attractive and satisfying, as well as remunerative and able to hold the center of interest throughout one's lifetime. With most persons this can come only with the development of a strong community sense of feeling. The first condition of a good country life, of course, is good and profitable farming. The farmer must be enabled to live comfortably. Much attention has been given to better farming, and the progress of a generation has been marked. Small manufacture and better handicrafts need now to receive attention, for the open country needs new industries and new interests. The schools must help to bring these things about.

The economic and industrial questions are, of course, of prime importance, and we have dealt with them; but they must all be studied in their relations to the kind of life that should ultimately be established in rural communities. The commission will fail of its purpose if it confines itself merely to providing remedies or correctives for the present and apparent troubles of the farmer, however urgent and important these troubles may be. All these matters must be conceived of as incidents or parts in a large constructive programme. We must begin a campaign for rural progress.

To this end local government must be developed to its highest point of efficiency, and all agencies that are capable of furthering a better country life must be federated.

It will be necessary to set the resident forces in motion by means of outside agencies, or at least to direct them, if we are to secure the best results. It is specially necessary to develop the cooperative spirit, whereby all people participate and all become partakers.

The cohesion that is so marked among the different classes of farm folk in older countries can not be reasonably expected at this period in American development, nor is it desirable that a stratified society should be developed in this country. We have here no remnants of a feudal system, fortunately no system of entail, and no clearly drawn distinction between agricultural and other classes. We are as yet a new country with undeveloped resources, many faraway pastures which, as is well known, are always green and inviting. Our farmers have been moving, and numbers of them have not yet become so well settled as to speak habitually of their farm as "home." We have farmers from every European nation and with every phase of religious belief often grouped in large communities, naturally drawn together by a common language and a common faith, and yielding but slowly to the dominating and controlling forces of American farm life. Even where there was once social organization, as in the New England town (or township), the competition of the newly settled West and the wonderful development of urban civilization have disintegrated it. The middle-aged farmer of the Central States sells the old homestead without much hesitation or regret and moves westward to find a greater acreage for his sons and daughters. The farmer of the Middle West sells the old home and moves to the Mountain States, to the Pacific coast, to the South, to Mexico, or to Canada.

Even when permanently settled, the farmer does not easily combine with others for financial or social betterment. The training of generations has made him a strong individualist, and he has been obliged to rely mainly on himself. Self-reliance being the essence of his nature, he does not at once feel the need of cooperation for business purposes or of close association for social objects. In the main, he has been prosperous, and has not felt the need of cooperation. If he is a strong man, he prefers to depend on his own ability. If he is ambitious for social recognition, he usually prefers the society of the town to that of the country. If he wishes to educate his children, he avails himself of the schools of the city. He does not as a rule dream of a rural organization that can supply as completely as the city the four great requirements of man—health, education, occupation, society. While his brother in the city is striving by moving out of the business section into the suburbs to get as much as possible of the country in the city, he does not dream that it is possible to have most that is best of the city in the country.

The time has come when we must give as much attention to the constructive development of the open country as we have given to other affairs. This is necessary not only in the interest of the open country itself, but for the safety and progress of the nation.

It is impossible, of course, to suggest remedies for all the shortcomings of country life. The mere statement of the conditions, as we find them, ought of itself to challenge attention to the needs. We hope that this report of the commission will accelerate all the movements that are now in operation for the betterment of country life. Many of these movements are beyond the reach of legislation. The most important thing for the commission to do is to apprehend the problem and to state the conditions.

The philosophy of the situation requires that the disadvantages and handicaps that are not a natural part of the farmer's business shall be removed, and that such forces shall be encouraged and set in motion as will stimulate and direct local initiative and leadership. . . .

It is necessary to be careful, also, not to copy too closely the reconstructive methods that have been so successful in Europe. Our conditions and problems differ widely from theirs. We have no historical, social peasantry, a much less centralized form of government, unlike systems of land occupancy, wholly different farming schemes, and different economic and social systems. Our country necessities are peculiarly American.

The correctives for the social sterility of the open country are already in existence or under way, but these agencies all need to be strengthened and especially to be coordinated and federated; and the problem needs to be recognized by all the people. The regular agricultural departments and institutions are aiding in making farming profitable and attractive, and they are also giving attention to the social and community questions. There is a widespread awakening, as a result of this work. This awakening is greatly aided by the rural free delivery of mails, telephones, and gradual improvement of highways, farmers' institutes, cooperative creameries and similar organizations, and other agencies.

The good institutions of cities may often be applied or extended to the open country. It appears that the social evils are in many cases no greater in cities in proportion to the number of people than in country districts; and the very concentration of numbers draws attention to the evils in cities and leads to earlier application of remedies. Recently much attention has been directed, for example, to the subject of juvenile crime, and the probation system in place of jail sentences for young offenders is being put into operation in many places. Petty crime and immorality are certainly not lacking in rural districts, and it would seem that there is a place for the extension of the probation system to towns and villages.

Aside from the regular churches, schools, and agricultural societies, there are special organizations that are now extending their work to the open country, and others that could readily be adapted to country work. One of the most promising of these newer agencies is the rural library that is interested in its community. The libraries are increasing, and they are developing a greater sense of responsibility to the community, not only stimulating the reading habit and directing it, but becoming social centers for the neighborhood. A library, if provided with suitable rooms, can afford a convenient meeting place for many kinds of activities and thereby serve as a coordinating influence. Study clubs and traveling libraries may become parts of it. This may mean that the library will need itself to be redirected so that it will become an active rather than a passive agency; it must be much more than a collection of books.

Another new agency is the county work of the Young Men's Christian Association, which, by placing in each county a field secretary, is seeking to promote the solidarity and effectiveness of rural social life, and to extend the larger influence of the country church. The commission has met the representatives of this county work at the hearings, and is impressed with the purpose of the movement to act as a coordinating agency in rural life.

The organizations in cities and towns that are now beginning to agitate the development of better play, recreation, and entertainment offer a suggestion for country districts. It is important that recreation be made a feature of country life, but we consider it to be important that this recreation, games and entertainment, be developed as far as possible from native sources rather than to be transplanted as a kind of theatricals from exotic sources. . . .

The proper correctives of the underlying structural deficiencies of the open country are knowledge, education, cooperative organizations, and personal leadership. These we may now discuss in more detail.

## Need of Agricultural or Country Life Surveys

The time has now come when we should know in detail what our agricultural resources are. We have long been engaged in making geological surveys, largely with a view to locating our mineral wealth. The country has been explored and mapped. The main native resources have been located in a general way. We must now know what are the capabilities of every agricultural locality, for agriculture is the basis of our prosperity and farming is always a local

business. We can not make the best and most permanent progress in the developing of a good country life until we have completed a very careful inventory of the entire country.

This inventory or census should take into account the detailed topography and soil conditions of the localities, the local climate, the whole character of streams and forests, the agricultural products, the cropping systems now in practice, the conditions of highways, markets, facilities in the way of transportation and communication, the institutions and organizations, the adaptability of the neighborhood to the establishment of handicrafts and local industries, the general economic and social status of the people and the character of the people themselves, natural attractions and disadvantages, historical data, and a collation of community experience. This would result in the collection of local fact, on which we could proceed to build a scientifically and economically sound country life.

Beginnings have been made in several States in the collection of these geographical facts, mostly in connection with the land-grant colleges. The United States Department of Agriculture is beginning by means of soil surveys, study of farm management, and other investigations, and its demonstration work in the Southern States is in part of this character. These agencies are beginning the study of conditions in the localities themselves. It is a kind of extension work. All these agencies are doing good work; but we have not yet, as a people, come to an appreciation of the fact that we must take account of stock in detail as well as in the large. We are working mostly around the edges of the problem and feeling of it. The larger part of the responsibility of this work must lie with the different States, for they should develop their internal resources. The whole work should be coordinated, however, by federal agencies acting with the States, and some of the larger relations will need to be studied directly by the Federal Government itself. We must come to a thoroughly nationalized movement to understand what property we have and what uses may best be made of it. This in time will call for large appropriations by State and nation. . . .

## Need of a Redirected Education

The subject of paramount importance in our correspondence and in the hearings is education. In every part of the United States there seems to be one mind, on the part of those capable of judging, on the necessity of redirecting the rural schools. There is no such unanimity on any other subject. It is remarkable with what similarity of phrase the subject has been discussed in all parts of the country before the commission. Everywhere there is a demand that education have relation to living, that the schools should express the daily life, and that in the rural districts they should educate by means of agriculture and country-life subjects. It is recognized that all difficulties resolve themselves in the end into a question of education.

The schools are held to be largely responsible for ineffective farming, lack of ideals, and the drift to town. This is not because the rural schools, as a whole, are declining, but because they are in a state of arrested development and have not yet put themselves in consonance with all the recently changed conditions of life. The very forces that have built up the city and town school have caused the neglect of the country school. It is probable that the farming population will willingly support better schools as soon as it becomes convinced that the schools will really be changed in such a way as to teach persons how to live.

The country communities are in need of social centers—places where persons may naturally meet, and where a real neighborhood interest exists. There is difference of opinion as to where this center should be, some persons thinking it should be in the town or village, others the library, others the church or school or grange hall. It is probable that more than one social center should develop in large and prosperous communities. Inasmuch as the school is supported by public funds, and is therefore an institution connected with the government of the community, it should form a natural organic center. If the school develops such a center, it must concern itself directly with the interests of the people. It is difficult to make people understand what this really means, for school-teaching is burdened with tradition. The school must express the best cooperation of all social and economic forces that make for the welfare of the community. Merely to add new studies will not meet the need, although it may break the ground for new ideas. The school must be fundamentally redirected, until it becomes a new kind of institution. This will require that the teacher himself be a part of the community and not a migratory factor.

The feeling that agriculture must color the work of rural public schools is beginning to express itself in the interest in nature study, in the introduction of classes in agriculture in high schools and elsewhere, and in the establishment of separate or special schools to teach farm and home subjects. These agencies will help to bring about the complete reconstruction of which we have been speaking. It is specially important that we make the most of the existing public-school system, for it is this very system that should serve the real needs of the people. The real needs of the people are not alone the arts by which they make a living, but the whole range of their customary activities. As the home is the center of our civilization, so the home subjects should be the center of every school.

The most necessary thing now to be done for public-school education in terms of country life is to arouse all the people to the necessity of such education, to coordinate the forces that are beginning to operate, and to project the work beyond the schools for youth into continuation schools for adults. The schools must represent and express the community in which they stand, although, of course, they should not be confined to the community. They should teach health and sanitation, even if it is necessary to modify

123

the customary teaching of physiology. The teaching should be visual, direct, and applicable. Of course the whole tendency of the schools will be ethical if they teach the vital subjects truthfully; but particular care should be taken that they stand for the morals of the pupils and of the communities.

We find a general demand for federal encouragement in educational propaganda, to be in some way cooperative with the States. The people realize that the incubus of ignorance and inertia is so heavy and so widespread as to constitute a national danger, and that it should be removed as rapidly as possible. It will be increasingly necessary for the national and state governments to cooperate to bring about the results that are needed in agricultural and other industrial education.

The consideration of the educational problem raises the greatest single question that has come before the commission, and which the commission has to place before the American people. Education has now come to have vastly more significance than the mere establishing and maintaining of schools. The education motive has been taken into all kinds of work with the people directly in their homes and on their farms, and it reaches mature persons as well as youths. Beyond and behind all educational work there must be an aroused intelligent public sentiment; to make this sentiment is the most important work immediately before us. The whole country is alive with educational activity. While this activity may all be good, it nevertheless needs to be directed and correlated, all the agencies should be more or less federated.

The arousing of the people must be accomplished in terms of their daily lives or of their welfare. For the country people this means that it must be largely in terms of agriculture. Some of the colleges of agriculture are now doing this kind of work effectively although on a pitiably small scale as compared with the needs. This is extension work, by which is meant all kinds of educational effort directly with the people, both old and young, at their homes and on their

farms; it comprises all educational work that is conducted away from the institution and for those who can not go to schools and colleges. The best extension work now proceeding in this country — if measured by the effort to reach the people in their homes and on their own ground — is that coming from some of the colleges of agriculture and the United States Department of Agriculture. Within the last five or ten years the colleges of agriculture have been able to attack the problem of rural life in a new way. This extension work includes such efforts as local agricultural surveys, demonstrations on farms, nature study, and other work in schools, boys' and girls' clubs of many kinds, crop organizations, redirection of rural societies, reading clubs, library extension, lectures, traveling schools, farmers' institutes, inspections of herds, barns, crops, orchards, and farms, publications of many kinds, and similar educational effort directly in the field.

To accomplish these ends, we suggest the establishment of a nation-wide extension work. The first, or original, work of the agricultural branches of the land-grant colleges was academic in the old sense; later there was added the great field of experiment and research; there now should be added the third coordinate branch, comprising extension work, without which no college of agriculture can adequately serve its State. It is to the extension department of these colleges, if properly conducted, that we must now look for the most effective rousing of the people on the land.

In order that all public educational work in the United States may be adequately studied and guided, we also recommend that the United States Bureau of Education be enlarged and supported in such a way that it will really represent the educational activities of the nation, becoming a clearing house, and a collecting, distributing, and investigating organization. It is now wholly inadequate to accomplish these ends. In a country in which education is said to be the national religion, this condition of our one expressly federal educational agency is pathetic. The good use already made of the small appropriations provided for the bureau shows clearly that it can render a most important service if sufficient funds are made available for its use.

\* \* \*

*The Country Church*

This commission has no desire to give advice to the institutions of religion nor to attempt to dictate their policies. Yet any consideration of the problem of rural life that leaves out of account the function and the possibilities of the church, and of related institutions, would be grossly inadequate. This is not only because in the last analysis the country-life problem is a moral problem, or that in the best development of the individual the great motives and results are religious and spiritual, but because from the pure sociological point of view the church is fundamentally a necessary institution in country life. In a peculiar way the church is intimately related to the agricultural industry. The work and the life of the farm are closely bound together, and the institutions of the country react on that life and on one another more intimately than they do in the city. This gives the rural church a position of peculiar difficulty and one of unequaled opportunity. The time has arrived when the church must take a larger leadership, both as an institution and through its pastors, in the social reorganization of rural life. . . .

The country church doubtless faces special difficulties. As a rule, it is a small field. The country people are conservative. Ordinarily the financial support is inadequate. Often there are too many churches in a given community. Sectarian ideas divide unduly and unfortunately. While there are many rural churches that are effective agents in the social evolution of their communities, it is true that as a whole the country church needs new direction and to assume new responsibilities. Few of the churches in the open country are provided

with resident pastors. They are supplied mostly from the neighboring towns and by a representative of some single denomination. Sometimes the pulpit is supplied by pastors of different denominations in turn. Without a resident minister the church work is likely to be confined chiefly to services once a week. In many regions there is little personal visitation except in cases of sickness, death, marriage, christening, or other special circumstance. The Sunday school is sometimes continued only during the months of settled weather. There are young people's organizations to some extent, but they are often inactive or irregular. The social activity of the real country church is likely to be limited to the short informal meetings before and after services and to suppers that are held for the purpose of raising funds. Most of the gatherings are designed for the church people themselves rather than for the community. The range of social influence is therefore generally restricted to the families particularly related to the special church organization, and there is likely to be no sense of social responsibility for the entire community.

In the rural villages there are generally several or a number of churches of different denominations, one or more of which are likely to be weak. The salaries range from $400 to $1,000. Among Protestants there is considerable denominational competition and consequent jealousy or even conflict. United effort for cooperative activity is likely to be perfunctory rather than sympathetic and vital. The pastor is often overloaded with station work in neighboring communities.

It is not the purpose of the commission to discuss the difficulties of the rural church at this time nor to present a solution for them, but in the interests of rural betterment it seems proper to indicate a few considerations that seem to be fundamental.

1. In New England and in some other parts of the North the tremendous drawback of denominational rivalry is fairly well recognized and active measures for church federation are well under way. This does

not mean organic union. It means cooperation for the purpose of trying to reach and influence every individual in the community. It means that "some church is to be responsible for every square mile." When a community is overchurched, it means giving up the superfluous church or churches. When a church is needed, it means a friendly agreement on the particular church to be placed. This movement for federation is one of the most promising in the whole religious field, because it does not attempt to break down denominational influence or standards of thought. It puts emphasis, not on the church itself, but on the work to be done by the church for all men—churched and unchurched. It is possible that all parts of the country are not quite ready for federation, although a national church federation movement is under way. But it hardly seems necessary to urge that the spirit of cooperation among churches, the diminution of sectarian strife, the attempt to reach the entire community, must become the guiding principles everywhere if the rural church is long to retain its hold.

The rural church must be more completely than now a social center. This means not so much a place for holding social gatherings, although this is legitimate and desirable, but a place whence constantly emanates influences that go to build up the moral and spiritual tone of the whole community. The country church of the future is to be held responsible for the great ideals of community life as well as of personal character.

2. There should be a large extension of the work of the Young Men's Christian Association into the rural communities. There is apparently no other way to grip the hearts and lives of the boys and young men of the average country neighborhood. This association must regard itself as an ally of the church, with a special function and a special field.

3. We must have a complete conception of the country pastorate. The country pastor must be a community leader. He must know the rural problems. He must have sympathy with rural ideals and aspirations. He must love the country. He must know country life, the difficulties that the farmer has to face in his business, some of the great scientific revelations made in behalf of agriculture, the great industrial forces at work for the making or the unmaking of the farmer, the fundamental social problems of the life of the open country. . . .

### Personal Ideals and Local Leadership

Everything resolves itself at the end into a question of personality. Society or government can not do much for country life unless there is voluntary response in the personal ideals of those who live in the country. Inquiries by the commission, for example, find that one reason for the shift from the country to town is the lack of ideals in many country homes and even the desire of the countryman and his wife that the children do not remain home on the farm. The obligation to keep as many youths on the farms as are needed there rests on the home more than on the school or on society.

It is often said that better rural institutions and more attractive homes and yards will necessarily follow an increase in profitableness of farming; but, as a matter of fact, high ideals may be quite independent of income, although they can not be realized without sufficient income to provide good support. Many of the most thrifty farmers are the least concerned about the character of the home and school and church. One often finds the most attractive and useful farm homes in the difficult farming regions. On the other hand, some of the most prosperous agricultural regions possess most unattractive farm premises and school buildings. Many persons who complain most loudly about their incomes are the last to improve their home conditions when their incomes are increased; they are more likely to purchase additional land and thereby further emphasize the barrenness of home life. Land hunger is naturally strongest in the most prosperous regions. . . .

Teachers of agriculture have placed too much relative emphasis on the remuneration and production sides of country life. Money hunger is as strong in the open country as elsewhere, and as there are fewer opportunities and demands for the expenditure of this money for others and for society, there often develops a hoarding and a lack of public spirit that is disastrous to the general good. So completely does the money purpose often control the motive that other purposes in farming often remain dormant. The complacent contentment in many rural neighborhoods is itself the very evidence of social incapacity or decay.

It must not be assumed that these deficiencies are to be charged as a fault against the farmer as a group. They are rather to be looked on as evidence of an uncorrelated and unadjusted society. Society is itself largely to blame. The social structure has been unequally developed. The townsman is likely to assume superiority and to develop the town in disregard of the real interests of the open country or even in opposition to them. The city exploits the country; the country does not exploit the city. The press still delights in archaic cartoons of the farmer. There is as much need of a new attitude on the part of the townsman as on the part of the farmer.

This leads us to say that the country ideals, while derived largely from the country itself, should not be exclusive; and the same applies to city and village ideals. There should be more frequent social intercourse on equal terms between the people of the country and those of the city or village. This community of interests is being accomplished to a degree at present, but there is hardly yet the knowledge and sympathy and actual social life that there should be between those who live on the land and those who do not. The business men's organizations of cities could well take the lead in some of this work. The country town in particular has similar interests with the open country about it; but beyond this, all people are bettered and broadened by association with those of far different environment.

We have now discussed some of the forces and agencies that will aid in bringing about a new rural society. The development of the best country life in the United States is seen, therefore, to be largely a question of guidance. The exercise of a wise advice, stimulus, and direction from some central national agency, extending over a series of years, could accomplish untold good, not only for the open country, but for all the people and for our institutions.

In the communities themselves, the same kind of guidance is needed, operating in good farming, in schools, churches, societies, and all useful public work. The great need everywhere is new and young leadership, and the commission desires to make an appeal to all young men and women who love the open country to consider this field when determining their careers. We need young people of quality, energy, capacity, aspiration, and conviction, who will live in the open country as permanent residents on farms, or as teachers, or in other useful fields, and who, while developing their own business or affairs to the greatest perfection, will still have unselfish interest in the welfare of their communities. The farming country is by no means devoid of leaders, and is not lost or incapable of helping itself, but it has been relatively overlooked by persons who are seeking great fields of usefulness. It will be well for us as a people if we recognize the opportunity for usefulness in the open country and consider that there is a call for service.

L. H. Bailey
Henry Wallace
Kenyon L. Butterfield
Walter H. Page
Gifford Pinchot
C. S. Barrett
W. A. Beard

## 25. THE SMITH-LEVER ACT, SIGNED MAY 8, 1914

The establishment of the land-grant colleges, often as parts of the great state universities of the Middle West, gave rise to a series of federal laws which opened the way for the build-up of a quasi-public federal establishment in agriculture. The legislation utilized the principle of the grant-in-aid, a device by which the federal government appropriated funds (or public lands) for programs operated at the state or local level. This system, now widely used for a host of programs, became a pattern for the development of commercial agriculture.

The objective of this act, which provided an agricultural extension system, was to disseminate among farmers useful information resulting from research in the agricultural colleges on problems relating to crop and livestock production, soil management, marketing, rural sociology, and many other areas. The extension service at the county level was for some time sponsored and often partially supported by private organizations, first the Grange and the Alliance, later the Farm Bureau, which organized at the local level and gradually knit together a powerful national organization, the American Farm Bureau Federation, working very closely with the extension service and the land-grant colleges.

AN ACT *To provide for cooperative agricultural extension work between the agricultural colleges in the several States receiving the benefits of An Act of Congress approved July second, eighteen hundred and sixty-two, and of Acts supplementary thereto, and the United States Department of Agriculture.*

*Be it enacted by the Senate and House of Representatives of the United States of America in Congress assembled,* That in order to aid in diffusing among the people of the United States useful and practical information on subjects relating to agriculture and home economics, and to encourage the application of the same, there may be inaugurated in connection with the college or colleges in each State now receiving, or which may hereafter receive, the benefits of the Act of Congress approved July second, eighteen hundred and sixty-two, entitled "An Act donating public lands to the several States and Territories which may provide colleges for the benefit of agriculture and the mechanic arts" (12 *Statutes at Large*, 503), and of the Act of Congress approved August thirtieth, eighteen hundred and ninety (26 *Statutes at Large*, 417), agricultural extension work which shall be carried on in cooperation with the United States Department of Agriculture: *Provided,* That in any State in which two or more such colleges have been or hereafter may be established the appropriations hereinafter made to such State shall be administered by such college or colleges as the legislature of such State may direct: *Provided further,* That, pending the inauguration and development of the cooperative extension work herein authorized, nothing in this act shall be construed to discontinue either the farm management work or the farmers' cooperative demonstration work as now conducted by the Bureau of Plant Industry of the Department of Agriculture.

From 38 *Statutes-at-Large*, 1914, p. 372.

*Sec. 2.* That cooperative agricultural extension work shall consist of the giving of instruction and practical demonstrations in agriculture and home economics to persons not attending or resident in said colleges in the several communities, and imparting to such persons information on said subjects through field demonstrations, publications, and otherwise; and this work shall be carried on in such manner as may be mutually agreed upon by the Secretary of Agriculture and the State agricultural college or colleges receiving the benefits of this act.

*Sec. 3.* That for the purpose of paying the expenses of said cooperative agricultural extension work and the necessary printing and distributing of information in connection with the same, there is permanently appropriated, out of any money in the Treasury not otherwise appropriated, the sum of $480,000 for each year, $10,000 of which shall be paid annually, in the manner hereinafter provided, to each State which shall by action of its legislature assent to the provisions of this act: *Provided,* That payment of such installments of the appropriation hereinbefore made as shall become due to any State before the adjournment of the regular session of the legislature meeting next after the passage of this act may, in the absence of prior legislative assent, be made upon the assent of the governor thereof, duly certified to the Secretary of the Treasury: *Provided further,* That there is also appropriated an additional sum of $600,000 for the fiscal year following that in which the foregoing appropriation first becomes available, and for each year thereafter for seven years a sum exceeding by $500,000 the sum appropriated for each preceding year, and for each year thereafter there is permanently appropriated for each year the sum of $4,100,000 in addition to the sum of $480,000 hereinbefore provided: *Provided further,* That before the funds herein appropriated shall become available to any college for any fiscal year plans for the work to be carried on under this act shall be submitted by the proper officials of each college and approved by the Secretary of Agriculture.

Such additional sums shall be used only for the purposes hereinbefore stated, and shall be allotted annually to each State by the Secretary of Agriculture and paid in the manner hereinbefore provided, in the proportion which the rural population of each State bears to the total rural population of all the States as determined by the next preceding Federal census: *Provided further,* That no payment out of the additional appropriations herein provided shall be made in any year to any State until an equal sum has been appropriated for that year by the legislature of such State, or provided by State, county, college, local authority, or individual contributions from within the State, for the maintenance of the cooperative agricultural extension work provided for in this act.

*Sec. 4.* That the sums hereby appropriated for extension work shall be paid in equal semiannual payments on the first day of January and July of each year by the Secretary of the Treasury upon the warrant of the Secretary of Agriculture, out of the Treasury of the United States, to the Treasurer or other officer of the State duly authorized by the laws of the State to receive the same; and such officer shall be required to report to the Secretary of Agriculture, on or before the first day of September of each year, a detailed statement of the amount so received during the previous fiscal year, and of its disbursement, on forms prescribed by the Secretary of Agriculture.

*Sec. 5.* That if any portion of the moneys received by the designated officer of any State for the support and maintenance of cooperative agricultural extension work, as provided in this Act, shall by any action or contingency be diminished or lost or be misapplied, it shall be replaced by said State to which it belongs, and until so replaced no subsequent appropriation shall be apportioned or paid to said State, and no portion of said moneys shall be applied, directly or indirectly, to the purchase, erection, preservation, or repair of any building or buildings, or the purchase or rental of land, or in college-course teaching, lectures in colleges, promoting agricultural trains, or any other purpose not specified in this Act, and not more than five per centum of each annual appropriation shall be applied to the printing and distribution of publications. It shall be the duty of each of said colleges annually, on or before the first day of January, to make to the governor of the State in which it is located a full and detailed report of its operations in the direction of extension work as defined in this Act, including a detailed statement of receipts and expenditures from all sources for this purpose, a copy of which report shall be sent to the Secretary of Agriculture and to the Secretary of the Treasury of the United States.

*Sec. 6.* That on or before the first day of July in each year after the passage of this Act the Secretary of Agriculture shall ascertain and certify to the Secretary of the Treasury as to each State whether it is entitled to receive its share of the annual appropriation for cooperative agricultural extension work under this Act, and the amount which it is entitled to receive. If the Secretary of Agri-

culture shall withhold a certificate from any State of its appropriation, the facts and reasons therefor shall be reported to the President, and the amount involved shall be kept separate in the Treasury until the expiration of the Congress next succeeding a session of the legislature of any State from which a certificate has been withheld, in order that the State may, if it should so desire, appeal to Congress from the determination of the Secretary of Agriculture. If the next Congress shall not direct such sum to be paid, it shall be covered into the Treasury.

*Sec. 7.* That the Secretary of Agriculture shall make an annual report to Congress of the receipts, expenditures, and results of the cooperative agricultural extension work in all of the States receiving the benefits of this act, and also whether the appropriation of any State has been withheld, and if so, the reasons therefor.

*Sec. 8.* That Congress may at any time alter, amend, or repeal any or all of the provisions of this Act.

*Earle D. Ross*

## 26. "SELF-HELP AND INDIVIDUAL INITIATIVE REMAIN . . . TYPICAL OF LIFE IN THE COUNTRY . . ."

The spirit of Progressivism, if not always dominant between 1900 and 1920, was at least continuously in evidence. Its effect was certainly felt in many ways with respect to agriculture. The goals of bringing rural life up to economic parity with urban, of curbing the malpractices of public carriers and land speculators, and of conserving natural resources were Progressive ones.

The motivations and values of what may be termed Progressive farm policies bear only a surface similarity with those of the Populists. The latter were more direct, more radical, and more concerned with improving the position of the most disadvantaged classes, farmers as well as urbanites. In contrast, the Progressive philosophy turned invariably to the mode of vertical mobility as a solution for individual farm operators. A tendency to promote policies that were most useful to the better farmers was inevitable.

From Earle D. Ross, "Roosevelt and Agriculture," *Mississippi Valley Historical Review,* XIV (December, 1927), pp. 287-310. Reprinted by permission of the *Mississippi Valley Historical Review.*

The great early spokesman for twentieth-century Progressivism was, of course, President Theodore Roosevelt. His frequent statements on agriculture are therefore revealing.

. . . we may now consider Roosevelt's leading agricultural ideas, as he came to develop them in the course of his national observations and his formulation of national policies. Above all else, throughout his agricultural exhortations, runs the characteristic American idea of the importance of the nation's economic, political, and social welfare to the small holder, "that preeminently typical American, the farmer who owns his own farm." Like many more judicious economists, he assumed the superiority of the system of small owners over any possible system of large owners and tenants, and postulated as the alternative to ownership a condition of peasantry for the tillers of the soil.

The farm-owner, more than any other element of the population, he believed, stood for the traditional American ideals and provided an essential bulwark against dangerous social and political innovations. The "small merchants, clerks, farmers, and mechanics . . . formed the backbone of the patriot party under Washington in the Revolution; of the Republican Party under Lincoln at the time of the Civil War." In fact "in every great crisis of the past a peculiar dependence has had to be placed upon the farming population; and this dependence has hitherto been justified." And with this great heritage and tradition, the farmer still retained "because of his surroundings and the nature of his work, to a preeminent degree the qualities which we like to think of as distinctly American in considering our early history. The man who tills his own farm, whether on the prairie or in the woodland, the man who grows what we eat and the raw material which is worked up into what we wear, still exists more nearly under the conditions which obtained when the "embattled farmers" of '76 made this country a nation than is true of any others of our people." The twentieth-century leader thus shared fully the opinion of Jefferson that the "small landholders are the most precious part of the state."

It followed that in land law reform, in policies of conservation and reclamation, and in the work of the Department of Agriculture, the chief aim should be the establishment and protection of "prosperous homes." Roosevelt, as the people's tribune, stood forth as an especial champion of the small or medium-scale farmers, of the farmers who, in the words of a correspondent, which he delighted to quote, had "to plow and pitch hay themselves," the Rooseveltian equivalent of "dirt farmer." . . .

Characteristically American, too, of the frontier as of the industrial center, was his zeal for increased and extended production. Such an emphasis was but a lingering reflection of a past in which "the chief task of American manhood has been this, to go up against the land and possess it, to subdue the continent, to win for mankind its primary victory over the elemental forces of nature." To the frontier view in particular, the public domain existed mainly to be disposed of for farms, ranches, mines, or lumber-camps and the consequent development of the regions involved. In such a scheme it seemed well-nigh a sin to have resources remaining unutilized. Much of this lingering exploitative philosophy is seen in Roosevelt's reasoning, though he insisted that the benefits of all such promotions should be diffused as widely as possible by providing homes for the largest number of actual small owners; and, in marked contrast to the frontier exploiter, that thought should be taken for the future progress as well as for the present greatness of the nation.

The conservation and reclamation schemes had this ultimate productive design. He had no fears of the competition of the newly developed lands with the older regions. "The reclamation and settlement of the arid lands will enrich every portion of our country, just as the settlement of the Ohio and Mississippi Valleys brought prosperity to the Atlantic States. The increased demand for manufactured articles will stimulate industrial production, while wider home markets and the trade of Asia will consume the larger food supplies and effectually prevent Western competition with Eastern agriculture. Indeed, the products of irrigation will be consumed chiefly in upbuilding local centers of mining and other industries, which would otherwise not come into existence at all. Our people as a whole will profit, for successful home-making is but another name for the upbuilding of the Nation."

Consistent with the production ideal was the President's interest in the work of the Department of Agriculture, the experiment stations, and the agricultural colleges; and his characteristically vigorous advocacy of agricultural instruction in the schools. He was not unmindful of the business needs of agriculture, but the production side held his main interest. . . .

Latest to develop in this thinking about agriculture, as about industry as well, were considerations regarding social betterment. In the early years of his presidency, while admitting that there were many problems in connection with rural life, he felt that, all things considered, the American farmer's lines were fallen in pleasant places. "He works hard (for which no man is to be pitied), and often he lives hard (which may not be pleasant); but his life is passed in healthy surroundings, surroundings which tend to develop a fine type of citizenship. In the country, moreover, the conditions are fortunately such as to allow a closer touch between man and man, than, too often, we find to be the case in the city. Men feel more vividly the underlying sense of brotherhood, of community of interest. . . ."

Not only did the President's vision for country life, as fully expanded, include the improvement of living conditions for the farmer and his family, provision for recreation and culture for the parents and modernized education and amusement for the children, but it embraced that peculiar American character of unstable tenure, and uncertain status, the hired-man. The farm-labor problem, he was convinced, was to be met only by providing permanent employment with remuneration and conditions that made possible a satisfactory standard of living. . . .

In the attainment of this developing program of rural economic and social betterment, Roosevelt favored a moderate but gradually increasing application of governmental activity; his political philosophy, in this as in other fields, adjusted itself to his growing social convictions. In the development of this thinking regarding the relation of government to economic and social welfare, three fairly distinct stages can be noted, the pre-presidential period, the presidency, and the Progressive movement. Naturally from inheritance and environment a conservative, he departed from that position more slowly and less fully than is popularly thought. When he came to the presidency it is evident that he had no carefully thought-out social philosophy and no definite program of action. As late as 1899 he felt that the popular unrest about the trusts was "largely aimless and baseless" and wondered what, if anything, should be done about this problem, concerning which a few years later he was so confident. Even at the close of his administrations, Herbert Croly, who was later to laud him as the great champion of progressivism, found him, as regards constructive social policies, essentially a Jeffersonian individualist. Of his successor, whose not inconsistent economic policies he was to find so impossible a few months hence, Roosevelt wrote, shortly before the election, "I think it has been very rare that two public men have ever been so much at one in all the essentials of their beliefs and practices. . . ."

In part as an alternative to governmental action, he favored voluntary association of farmers. He came eventually to recognize that combination in this occupation, however difficult to achieve, was as essential under modern conditions as in any other. Governmental cooperation, he was led to see, could most effectively function through organizations, and he was especially enthusiastic over the pioneer extension work in the South — a forerunner of the county agent system. The Grange, he believed, was "good in itself" and was "capable of a well-nigh infinite further extension for good so long as it is kept to its own legitimate business."

Hesitant as he was to approve new extensions of governmental aid to private business, Roosevelt never consistently opposed the system that involved the most extreme application of such aid, and the one that had involved, in notorious instances, favoritism and special privilege to the flagrant disregard of the "square deal," the protective tariff. After being temporarily led astray, as he was convinced, by his college instruction, he became and remained a consistent champion of protection as a bulwark of national prosperity and security. For the "Iowa Idea," that notable forerunner of his own Progressive movement, he had no sympathy, but looked upon it as a "formless and vague uneasiness about the trusts in favor of tariff revision." Indignant at the attempt to associate his name with the western revisionist movement, he was convinced that, when deemed necessary, "revision must be made in accordance with the principles of the protective system, and by the friends of that system." His panegyric on the Dingley tariff in Minneapolis in the spring of 1903, reflected a full acceptance of orthodox party traditions on this issue and anticipated by some six years his successor's defense of an act of similar origin and intent in the much-denounced Winona speech: "The present phenomenal prosperity has been won under a tariff which was made in accordance with certain fixed and definite principles, the most important of which is an avowed determination to protect the interests of the American producer, business man, wage-worker, and farmer alike." The next year, in his speech of acceptance, he set forth at length the home-market argument, with all of its age-long accumulations and embellishments.

Conscientiously opposed to "tariff tinkering" either by western agricultural leaders or eastern "doctrinaires," neither of which class could be regarded as friends of the protective system, Roosevelt was even less in sympathy with western radical movements. In a notable mayoralty contest early in his career, he had represented the conservative forces aligned against the arch-agitator, Henry George. For the agrarian movements of the eighties and nineties he had the typical eastern "regular" attitude. The Alliance men he regarded as annoying obstructionists in the path of orthodox Republicanism. The reform Governor assured Senator Platt, who had questioned his economic soundness, that he was "as strongly opposed to Populism in every stage as the greatest representative of corporate wealth. . . ." Peffer was a "well-meaning, pinheaded, anarchistic crank," and Bryan himself, among numerous other undesirable attributes, was a "born demagogue," who had "every crank, fool and putative criminal in the country behind him, and a large proportion of the ignorant honest class. . . ." The campaign of 1896 he considered "the greatest crisis in our national fate, save only the Civil War. . . ." In the campaign of 1900 he looked upon himself as a sort of political missionary to the Far West, to convert the people of his adopted section from the errors into which they had been led by false guides. To his future rival in the Progressive movement, Roosevelt paid his respects in 1908 in the expression of the hope that the party platform would be "as free from the Hale type of reactionary policy as from the La Follette type of fool radicalism." . . .

The developments in the Department of Agriculture, aside from an extension of regulatory activities which applied only incidentally to agriculture, were, generally

133

speaking, those of normal growth. Marketing organizations were given a certain degree of legislative aid, but David Lubin's schemes for transplanting much-praised European cooperative systems aroused no administrative enthusiasm. Appropriations for agricultural colleges and experiment stations involved, for the most part, a normal progress along lines already marked out rather than any new or advanced tendencies. . . .

The country life movement, culminating in the work of the Country Life Commission, inspired directly by Pinchot and Horace Plunkett but appealing strongly to the President's love of the unusual, had a much less tangible basis of appeal than the more material features of the conservation program. On the contrary this movement, by reason of its unusualness and its seeming encroachment upon the affairs of private life, lent itself peculiarly to censure and ridicule. In view of subsequent developments in government by commission, such alarmist pronouncements as the following regarding this purely investigational body seem highly amusing: "The idea that a paternal Government at Washington is to concern itself with their sanitary, hygienic, business, social, and domestic interests, and help them to better their condition, involves a reversal of the theory the people govern themselves through agencies of their own and are not governed by a superior power exercising a benevolent oversight of their personal affairs." Critics of the administration's economic policies suggested, as more effective means for bettering the farmer's position than the proposed social "uplift," the removal of discriminations and corporate abuses, the establishment of a parcel post system, the lowering of telephone, telegraph, and railroad rates, the curbing of the implement trust, and, especially the revision of the tariff. One journal even questioned why agriculture should be investigated more than other interests, since for the past twenty years this occupation had enjoyed more prosperity than its rivals.

From the side of agriculture itself there was a lack of unanimous approval. The Worthy Overseer of the National Grange was highly indignant that a commission, appointed by the Chief Executive, should go "slumming" among the farmers of the country as a preliminary to the inauguration of an "uplift" program. The worthy officer's suggestion that it might be well to start an uplift movement for members of Congress doubtless would have met with the hearty agreement of the President, but he would not have agreed with the assertion that this particular order was engaged in activities for rural betterment which made the presidential commission wholly superfluous, not to say impertinent. In lighter vein, but with real pertinence, Mr. Dooley pointed out that daily life had its monotonies for the urban as for the rural dweller. Finally, Mrs. Charlotte Perkins Gilman complained of the shortsightedness that would lead to the creation of a commission of men only to investigate matters that so vitally concerned the interests of women.

It was highly characteristic of Roosevelt that to this plan of reform, in which his direct interest was aroused only at the eleventh hour of his administration, he should have held with the greatest tenacity. In the view of confidential observers, no other conflict in his stormy presidency caused him so much chagrin as the disregard and ridicule of this pet project. The refusal of Congress to make an appropriation to print the Commission's report brought to a climax the differences between executive and legislature which had featured his rule to such an unfortunate extent, and, according to one report, the failure of his successor to continue the Commission was the culminating influence in the historic break between the two leaders.

Inauspicious as was its start, and incomplete and superficial as much of its investigation was bound to be, the interest that the Commission's work and Roosevelt's discussion of it aroused served, in the opinion of competent observers, to initiate the modern country-life movement with its progressing constructive investigations and studies and its more systematic and efficient organization. Considering this far-reaching, beneficent influence, there was a better justification for placing the work of this much-ridiculed Commission upon the roll of honor of his administrations than there was for certain other policies which Roosevelt, with equal confidence, there included. . . .

# VI. *Agricultural Depression and the New Deal: 1920—1940*

## I. THE POST-WORLD WAR I DECADE

Farm mortgage indebtedness had more than doubled during the prosperous war years and continued to increase in the years immediately following. Higher freight rates, heavier local and excise taxes, and interest on larger mortgage indebtedness constituted a trinity of fixed costs that the farmer often could not meet with his shrunken income. Murray R. Benedict, a historian of United States farm policies, estimates that by 1921 American farmers were in the most unfavorable position

. . . in the memory of men then living, or possibly at any time since the nation's beginning. . . . Many farms were carrying large debts . . . costs were high; and the rural banks were heavily loaded with farmers' notes that could not be quickly liquidated.

Tales of farmers burning corn for fuel were reminiscent of the Populist years.

The long-time trend toward a commercial agriculture faced a difficult confluence of economic forces at the end of World War I. That war had resulted in an emphasis on increased agricultural production. Millions of acres of western land were developed and large power-driven farm machines were introduced. The resulting increases in production overwhelmed the market. Prices in general declined after wartime highs, but farm prices dropped further than others and failed to make any consistent recovery even in the later 1920's, when considerable activity returned to the industrial sector.

Prices were characteristically high for the farmers' purchases and comparatively very low for his sales. Coupled with the shrinking foreign demand for farm products was a noticeable decline in domestic demand due to the reduced number of draft animals on farms and the changes in dietary habits caused by increasing numbers of Americans moving into cities and into sedentary ways of life. It is a safe estimate that these changes removed the market for the crop yields of at least 100,000,000 acres of average quality cereal-producing land.

Agricultural difficulties of the 1920's resulted in organization of the county farm bureaus, created to support the agricultural agents provided under the Extension Service Act of 1916, into state and national federations. The American Farm Bureau Federation, officially organized in 1920, grew rapidly and became the Washington representative for commercial agriculture. In this capacity, the Farm Bureau was successful in articulating the needs of agriculture in terms of market prices and credit. It was also politically aggressive in bringing together other farm organizations and farm state Congressmen to form a loose legislative structure that came to be known as the "Farm Bloc." Widely representative and bipartisan, the Farm Bloc came to wield very considerable political power. Though no viable solution to the "farm problem" came forth from their councils, many efforts were made and considerable legislation enacted.

Most of the legislation enacted or attempted reflects a bias toward marketplace solutions. Middlemen were to be regulated and inspected more closely, agricultural credit was given federal support, cooperative marketing was recognized, and commodity standards were strengthened. These successes, though noteworthy, only emphasized the necessity for more effective governmental intervention in the economic activities of agriculture if improvements were to be realized. Murray R. Benedict states that ". . . disillusionment was growing. Many were aware that prosperity was not to be restored merely by controlling grain exchanges and the packing industry, or by establishing new credit agencies, or even by reduction in freight rates."

The need to develop more far-reaching regulatory measures was recognized by the leaders of the Farm Bureau and the farm bloc. Such measures were proposed in a series of attempted legislative acts known as the McNary-Haugen bills, which were based on the principle that the amount of any farm commodity that exceeded the amount that could be sold domestically at a "fair exchange value" would be taken off the domestic market and sold at the world price. The farmer producing export crops would thus receive a government-supported price for the part of his crop consumed in the domestic market. Admittedly, the administration of this plan would have been very complex, particularly in view of the great variety of crops and types of farming across the nation. This difficulty was never encountered, however, because the measure, though introduced in Congress each year from 1924 through 1928, was never successfully enacted into law.

Thus the public policies supposed to achieve "equality for agriculture" were compelled to wait until a popular revolt at the polls brought into office an administration pledged to a "New Deal." The Hoover administration of 1928-1932 witnessed the advent of the Great Depression, a period in which the industrial economy collapsed. For a time the cityward movement of the population was checked as the poor returned to seek a mythical security on the land. Temporarily, but at a disastrously low level, the long desired "equality of conditions" between rural and urban economies prevailed.

## II. TOWARD RECOVERY

By the time a new administration had been inaugurated in 1933, the farm price index had been halved—from 105 in 1929 to 48.2 in 1932—and farm income followed the price level. In a condition of such rapid deflation, credit became almost unobtainable. The shrinking of the value of capital invested in agriculture wiped out the farmers' equities in a large percentage of cases. Commercial agriculture was on the rocks when Franklin D. Roosevelt was inaugurated on March 4, 1933.

The new administration turned its attention immediately to the problems of farm policies and in a matter of weeks preparations were made for an enlarged scale of governmental intervention in the agricultural economy. The services of President Roosevelt's foremost advisers were utilized for this purpose. The primary objectives of farm policy were fairly clear: (1) surpluses in leading farm commodities must be controlled; (2) relief from mortgage foreclosures and better credit facilities must be found; and (3) a means of improving price and income relations between farms and other businesses must be provided.

The Agricultural Adjustment Act of May 12, 1933, was a broad and omnibus piece of legislation, providing in Title I for the control of acreage of basic farm crops and subsidizing farmers for acreages kept out of production. It also provided for marketing agreements for certain commodities requiring unusual marketing conditions, such as milk. The cost of these production controls was to be met by a tax paid by the first domestic processor of the commodity. Title II sought to provide means of providing emergency mortgage relief through refinancing farm mortgages, reducing interest rates on them, and extending dates of repayment. This act was followed by a number of farm credit acts adapted to the special needs of various types of agriculture. Title III of the Agricultural Act authorized the president to reduce within limits the gold content of the dollar, in order to stop the general price declines by increasing the supply of money.

Although the acreage control and price-support provisions of the law were declared unconstitutional by the Supreme Court in January, 1936, the main provisions of Title I were continued under a Soil Conservation Act passed in 1936 and then under an Agricultural Adjustment of 1938 which expanded and refined the earlier techniques. Thus an agricultural policy was established under the pressures of emergency which has continued to the present though the conditions which brought it into being have been drastically changed.

The major thrust of New Deal farm policy was directed toward recovery and improved conditions for commercial agriculture. The bigger the farm operation the greater the acreage reduction subsidies, soil conservation payments, commodity credit loans at a guaranteed percentage of parity, and so forth. After World War II it became increasingly clear that the federal farm policy was contributing to the cleavage between large-scale commercial agriculture which received substantial subsidies and small-scale farming for which no satisfactory program had been developed. In the latter sector insecurity, poverty-level income, migration, and poor public facilities for human development were characteristic. Carelessly characterized as "surplus," some of these rural families drifted into the cities where they added to the problems of slums, unemployment, and delinquency.

The existence of the rural poor was neither unknown nor totally ignored by the national policy-makers. Studies of farm tenancy and farm income distribution made during the 1920's and 1930's revealed the plight of many farmers whose operations did not fit the requirements for successful competition in the subsidized market economy as it existed. Efforts were made to help them, through a Rural Resettlement program and a Farm Security Administration. These agencies, however, could not compete for administrative emphasis with the programs designed to promote commercial agriculture. Benefits for subsistence farmers withered on the vine.

C. L. Holmes

## 27. ADJUSTING AGRICULTURE TO CHANGED CONDITIONS

Commercial agriculture, which had done relatively well during the first two decades of the twentieth century, began to falter after 1920 and was the subject of extensive study and many proposed remedies. An agricultural economist's view of this situation is reprinted below.

### THE AGRICULTURAL DEPRESSION

The immediate causes of the farmer's distress are to be found primarily in the unfavorable alignment of prices as between agricultural products and those of the other industries; and secondarily in the heavy burden of fixed charges, a large portion of which were assumed during his recent prosperous years, of which for the most part, he is unable to rid himself. The maladjustment of agricultural prices to those of other commodities may be judged from current index numbers. There is available no adequate quantitative measure of changes in fixed charges.

The most obvious effect of the war on American agriculture was to stimulate production and to expand the industry. A comparison of the census figures of 1910 with those of 1920 shows that there was an increase of 45,000,000 acres, or almost 15 per cent, in the cropped area of the country. The data of the United States Department of Agriculture indicate that the major portion of this expansion came during the war years as a direct result of the stimulus coming from war demand. While there was a vast area of new land added to the farming area of the country during the ten years, most of this was along the margins of our well-developed agricultural areas and remained raw prairie or stump land. In very large

measure this expansion in the cropped area took place in the older agricultural sections and represented the shifting of land already in farms from a less intensive use in pasture to a more intensive use in crop production. The effect of this increase in acreage was to increase the volume of production and in this the result was augmented by a succession of seasons unusually favorable to high yields which still further raised the output above the normal volume. At the same time there was a very substantial though less conspicuous increase in the production of livestock, particularly of swine and beef cattle.

It is significant at this point to contrast the nature and effects of the war stimulus on manufacturing and agriculture. During the first two years of the conflict the attention of our industrialists was being more and more turned to the profitable business of supplying munitions of war to the belligerents. With our entrance in 1917 our own government became the most active buyer of these goods, contracting for vast quantities on liberal terms, thus diverting in the largest measure possible the activities of our manufacturers from normal lines into special and temporary fields of production. This situation worked to the economic advantage of the industrialists in two respects; first, it enabled them to make the necessary expansion in full knowledge of the temporary

From C. L. Holmes, "The Economic Future of Our Agriculture," in *The Journal of Political Economy*, vol. 32 (October, 1924), pp. 506–510, 521–525. Reprinted by permission of the University of Chicago Press.

character of the production and to bargain with the government in the drafting of contracts on the basis of short-time utilization of their fixed capital. Moreover, the contracts secured from the government enabled them to gauge output exactly and to be sure of disposing of their product at a predetermined price. In the second place, this diverting of production from normal lines served to reduce the stock of goods ordinarily demanded to an extremely small volume so that with the close of the war and the relaxation of enforced economies, the consuming public was most insistently demanding goods of which the shelves and storehouses were practically empty.

In contrast to the condition in manufacturing we find that patriotism and the war demand called for substantially the same products from the farmer that he was accustomed to produce; but they were wanted in much larger volume. It was inevitable that there should be a piling up of stocks of his products when the abnormal demand should have passed. Moreover, with the exception of the guaranteed wheat price of 1919, there was nothing analogous to the government contract to take this surplus off his hands at a remunerative figure and there were no alternative lines of production to which he could turn and find for his products a crowd of eager buyers.

There is little doubt, also, that in the demoralization of the European market American agriculture is relatively a heavier loser than American industry. Historically our agriculture has been built up on the basis of the disposal of the surplus of its production over domestic needs to the industrial population of Western Europe. It is true, also, that nonagricultural products made up fully half the value of our exports at that time; but our chief market for these things was not found in the belligerent countries. Further, the war and the new tariff have combined more nearly to monopolize the home market for manufactured goods in the hands of domestic producers than to work any similar benefit for agriculture.

The question may well be asked why, in the face of falling demand and such decidedly unfavorable exchange ratios between the products of agriculture and those of other industries, does the volume of agriculture production remain so large? For it must be admitted that in the three years following the crisis of 1920 the total crop acreage showed a reduction of a bare two per cent over that of 1919 and the production of livestock actually increased. The reason is to be found in the inelastic nature of the agricultural industry. This inelasticity prevents such rapid and great expansion in times of rising price as is typical of other industries, but its more conspicuous effect is to prevent a prompt and substantial contraction of output when changing economic conditions would seem to make such contraction imperative.

There are three outstanding reasons for this inelasticity. First, a very high percentage, comparatively, of the total investment in the farm business is in land and fixed capital, making for a high proportion of fixed expenses. In businesses such as merchandising and manufacture where the major portion of the yearly outlay is for labor and raw material, a curtailment in production works something like a proportional curtailment in costs; but in farming where probably not less than 60 per cent of the annual production costs represent interest and depreciation on fixed assets, 25 per cent the imputed wages of the farmer and the members of his family, and only 15 per cent the wages of hired labor and other direct cash outlay, curtailment of production brings so little savings on variable expenses and sacrifices the use of so large an amount of undisposable resources that contraction of production is in most cases economically impossible.

The second cause of the inelasticity of agriculture is to be found in inertia of the agricultural population. It will be said that reduction in output under adverse price conditions will be brought about by a shift of a portion of the working population from farming into more profitable fields of effort sufficient to re-establish the equilibrium. There is undoubtedly a certain amount of this movement in any period of agricultural depression and in the long run it is of vital importance in economic adjustment. The trouble with its serving as a means of adjustment in an emergency such as the present is that it acts so very slowly. Farming is both an occupation and a mode of living. There is such an intimate connection between the business and the personal and family life of the farm population, the home is so integral a part of the productive plant, and the productive operations so large a part of the home environment, that a decision to abandon farming for an industrial job involves far more than purely economic considerations.

A third reason why the agriculture output is not reduced in response to a price reduction is the large measure of self-sufficiency which still characterizes farming in spite of the commercialization which our agriculture has undergone. On the great majority of American farms from one-third to two-thirds of the food supply is raised on the farm. Shelter, and frequently, fuel, is a contribution of the farm plant. In periods of depression when unemployment appears in all fields of production, farmers are loth to leave a situation which offers the certainty of even a meager satisfaction of their wants for the uncertainty of an industrial position where the loss of a job means entire cessation of income. Thus in the fall of 1922, when Iowa agriculture had just experienced its two most disastrous seasons of a generation, there was a brisk demand for farms to rent.

But little further need be said about the present state of our agriculture. Investigations show quite consistently that not only have our farmers been forced to lower standards of consumption but that there is a noticeable, and in some regions an alarming, dissipation of their business capital quite aside from whatever shrinkage there may have been in the value of farm land. This wasting of capital is manifested in failure to replace equipment and make normal repairs and replacement of buildings, fences, and other farm improvements. . . .

## OUR CHANGING AGRICULTURE

We have seen how the war has thrown out of adjustment the demand for and the supply of our agricultural products, partly by a substantial expansion in our production, and partly through an apparently permanent curtailment of foreign demand for our agricultural commodities. It has also been pointed out that the restoration of prosperity to our agricultural classes depends primarily upon an expansion of our industrial population and the growth of the home market to a degree which will re-establish an economic equilibrium between agricultural prices and those of other commodities. We have still to examine the problem of how our agriculture should be adjusted to meet this changed situation.

This problem has not only its present, but also its long-time phase. Too many of the recently proposed measures of relief have been conceived, apparently, on the assumption that we must save our agriculture as it is today or as it was at the end of 1918. The idea that a new market situation such as we have to face will necessitate a very greatly modified agriculture has not been given any very careful consideration. It would seem that our problem at the present is not to determine how we can again make our farmers prosperous while following a production program adjusted to a particular type of world-economy which no longer exists. It is rather to extend what relief is made necessary on account of the hardships inseparable from an economic change so sudden and extreme as that which we are experiencing, and to facilitate in every way possible the adjustment to the new situation. Such a problem is the more difficult because the new situation is still a changing one.

The first step in the needed adjustment to meet the present phase of the situation is obviously a substantial reduction in those lines of farm production in which the greatest surplus over home-demand now exists.

As already mentioned, cotton, wheat, and pork are the three commodities in which we have a large exportable surplus. Our production of cotton has fallen so far below prewar volume, and there is such a limited output of it from other parts of the world, that it is, for the present, in a very strong position. The products in which there is unmistakable overproduction are wheat and pork. On the basis of the present rate of domestic consumption it would require an increase in our population of fifteen million to absorb our present pork surplus and of some thirty-six million to use all of our exportable wheat. . . .

To those of us who subscribe to the necessity of a reduction in the volume of some of our more important staples, the immediate question is the method by which this reduction may best be realized. There has developed recently a considerable sentiment toward a policy of restriction in production on the part of all of the producers of a given commodity such as hogs, for example, sufficient to raise the price to a point which will give them maximum total value for the whole produced supply. The example of certain highly centralized industries such as steel is cited to show the folly of unrestricted or maximum production and the wisdom of controlled production. It seems to the writer that such a suggestion fails to take account of fundamental differences in the two fields of production. So far as he can see there are only two situations under which restriction of output can work successfully for the producer. The one is where the proportion of variable to fixed costs of production is so high that the savings from cessation of production outweigh, under certain cost and price conditions, the savings in fixed costs realized by continued operation. This exists in some freely competitive industries where the chief costs are labor and raw material. The other is where monopoly exists. In the case of most agricultural commodities neither of these conditions obtains. As already pointed out, a very high proportion of the farmer's costs are fixed rather than variable. He must, therefore, adhere strictly to the principle of maximum utilization of his resources and any effort to induce him to produce less of a given commodity whose price is sagging is futile unless there is presented to him at the same time an alternative line of production which promises a higher utilization of his cost elements.

As for monopoly, the futility of any effort to get unity of action and control with reference to a commodity so widely produced and in whose production so many individual entrepreneurs are engaged as is true of our important staples, ought to be apparent. Except in limited fields and for very short periods, the farmer has never been and cannot hope to be a monopolist.

In the light of these limitations characteristic of agriculture, it seems fairly certain that curtailment of production in the present crisis must come primarily through a process of substituting in the farmer's production program those products whose prices are higher for those whose prices are disastrously low. This is the normal process of economic adjustment and the one which, in the long run, involves the least cost to the individual and to society.

There is always the danger in this process that reactions will go too far and that the prices of one commodity after another may be depressed to a point of unprofitable production. The individual producer needs ever to be alert to avoid penalties of unwarranted and extreme changes. It is undoubtedly impossible by this or any other method in a brief period to restore to a full measure of prosperity those now engaged in farming. There must be, for some time to come, a general drawing in of the margins of production in many lines and particularly in those in which depression is now most marked. This will mean the abandonment to less intensive uses of a considerable portion of the poorest land now in use. Such abandonment is already in process. It is taking place most conspicuously in the poorer areas of the country, but even in our better farming areas an occasional farm poorly improved and of poor quality has dropped out of use. The labor thus released from agriculture is finding its way into more favorable economic opportunities in the industries.

It is by this same process of seeking the best opportunity for the utilization of resources that our agriculture will expand once more when the market broadens to require a larger and larger agricultural output. A normal growth stimulated by the demands of a growing industrial population will, it is reasonable to suppose, give us a healthier and more efficient agriculture of the future than could possibly result from an attempt to carry over intact into the new era the present system. Adjustment to a changed order of things must come sooner or later. It is probably wise not to try to impede the adjustment.

To those who would say that the present crisis is so grave as to demand something more than a passive attitude toward the normal economic processes of adjustment, it may be replied that the foregoing analysis does not point toward a policy of inactivity and indifference. The emergency truly is great enough to demand the best thought and effort of our agricultural leadership. Probably no previous period has presented so great a need as the present for the best effort of educators, legislators, and the leaders of the farmers' movement toward making general an intelligent view of the real nature of the situation, toward making as easy as possible the adjustment to the new alignment of forces, and toward developing unity of purpose and concerted action on the part of the agricultural class. There was never so great a need, and probably never so great an opportunity, for the development of a comprehensive and far-reaching agricultural policy.

*George N. Peek*

## 28. "THE ISSUE . . . IS WHETHER OUR IDEAL OF AMERICAN AGRICULTURE . . . CAN ENDURE"

In 1924, George N. Peek and Hugh S. Johnson co-authored a pamphlet entitled "Equality for Agriculture." This became a widely read document and the Moline Plow Company, their employer, aided in its distribution by publishing a second edition. Mr. Peek became a leading promoter of agricultural legislation during the 1920's and 1930's. He was a participant in planning New Deal farm legislation and became for a time the head of the Agricultural Adjustment Administration. He was a major architect of the ill-fated McNary-Haugen farm relief legislation of the 1920's. His co-author, Hugh S. Johnson, became the first director of the National Recovery Administration. The piece reprinted below presents in summary form the major arguments that were elaborated in "Equality for Agriculture."

MR. SHIPSTEAD. Mr. President, I ask unanimous consent to have printed in the REC-ORD an address by George Nelson Peek, chairman executive committee, North Central States Agricultural Conference, delivered before the Academy of Political Science in the city of New York in January, 1927, entitled "Equality for agriculture with industry."

There being no objection, the address was

From the *Congressional Record*, Vol. 68, Part 4 (1927), pp. 4403-4405.

ordered to be printed in the RECORD, as follows:

EQUALITY FOR AGRICULTURE WITH INDUSTRY

I

We are engaged to-day in the most interesting and, from the American point of view, one of the most vitally important experiments the world has ever witnessed — a test of whether an independent agriculture, enjoying the advantages and benefits of life on a level comparable with that prevailing in our cities and towns, can be established and maintained.

Excepting on the North American Continent, the labor of farm production is nearly everywhere performed by a peasant class. Farming has tended to become a peasant occupation because rewards are so uncertain and frequently so low that they permanently attract only those who are content with harder work and lower living standards than the more resourceful and aggressive demand. The uncertainty is not only one of yields but of prices; the uncontrolled risks such as weather and pests are followed by other and often equally disastrous risks in the market.

The day of the self-contained farm, existing on its own production aided by a little barter, is definitely past. So is the day when rising land values will compensate for unprofitable crop prices. The condition that has succeeded them is dangerously weakening our farm structure. The issue which the present experiment is to determine is whether our ideal of American agriculture, as distinguished from peasant agriculture, can endure.

II

The facts, figures, and causes of our post-war agricultural depressions have too long been matters for discussion. The rehabilitation of the farmer and a method of preventing a recurrence of agricultural depressions

now compel attention and immediate action.

To anyone really familiar with the present status of the farmer, certain conclusions are inevitable. He has been producing food for the Nation at prices which have been exhausting the accumulated resources of the generations which preceded him, because they have not yielded cost of production. He has been attempting to buy the actual necessities of life at prices which reduced his purchasing ability to a point which prohibited him from buying what he needed.

In the past 15 years the farm debt has trebled and actual farm-land values have declined one-fifth. During the past six years the dollar value of the farm investment has declined twenty billions, while our industrial and urban wealth has increased by that amount or more. These are evidences of a progressive draining away of wealth from the country to the city, which is inevitable as long as the products of the farm remain low in price compared with goods and services which the farmers must buy.

The purchasing power of farm products (according to the index used by the Bureau of Agricultural Economics) has ranged from a yearly average of 69 per cent of pre-war in 1922 to 89 per cent in 1925 and at the last-published calculation stood at 83 per cent in August, 1926. In the words of the National Industrial Conference Board: "It is often said if we could adjust prices to their comparative relationship to other prices which we had in the period from 1909 to 1914, everything would be all right; but, as a matter of fact, there is very little evidence that agriculture was in a sound condition in this country before the war."

The limits of this paper will not permit extended reference to evidences of the results of the disparity which have been pointed out by the National Bureau of Economic Research, the National Industrial Conference Board, the United States Department of Agriculture, and numerous other institutions and investigators. Our farm plant is contracting in comparison

144

with our population and with other industries; our agricultural exports per capita have declined 28 per cent, and our agricultural imports per capita have increased 30 per cent since 1900; there is persistent and increasing disparity between the per capita share in the national income received by farmers compared with nonfarmers; returns on capital invested in agriculture are small compared with those of other investments. Most of these are involved in the long-time trends of agriculture.

Of the recent developments the National Bureau of Economic Research says: "The great agricultural depression of 1921 and 1922 was not due to the fall in general prices, but to the fact that the prices of agricultural commodities fell more rapidly and to lower levels than did the prices of the articles the farmers bought."

Another industry finding itself unable to return production costs would restrict output and regulate its movement to market, until prices properly related themselves to costs of production. The major branches of farming, however, face this problem with the certainty that, even if the acreages of the millions of individuals could be accurately regulated no power on earth could forecast what production would be.

So the producers of our basic crops have hung on, year after year, unable to make protective devices that work for other groups operate for them. They are forced to see their total current supply equated to current demand at a disastrous price because of their inability to lengthen the equation over a number of years, through effective holding and storing against future needs.

If the wheat farmers could adjust their supply to the needs and purchasing power of their several markets they could use the tariff to protect their domestic price levels. If the cotton growers as a whole could own and carry their temporarily unneeded supplies they could stabilize their market over a period of years at the best obtainable price, instead of taking the price which the current demand affords, regardless of what the needs of to-morrow may be. The present crisis in cotton provides a case in point. Favorable crop conditions combined with a large acreage to produce a large yield. Prices collapsed upon crop forecasts to a point barely equivalent in purchasing power to 5-cent cotton before the war. Congress, a few months ago, failed to pass a measure under which the cotton growers themselves could have adjusted supply to demand. Now the Government is attempting to arrange for the withdrawal of 4,000,000 bales of cotton under conditions which may help the banker who has cotton loans, and the cotton buyers and spinners who have loaded up while prices were at the bottom, but which, under no conceivable circumstance, can be of assistance to the cotton farmer who has been forced to let his crop go.

III

This condition strongly emphasizes the need of a new agricultural policy. It must be broader than any one bill or remedy. The sound program for America must aim toward the development of a well-balanced national life—one which will not stimulate any one form of productive effort at the expense of other equally essential producers. If we pursue this it will inevitably take us into fields of taxation, of transportation, of finance, and of markets. But in the brief time allotted to me I wish to confine myself to the particular phase of the problem which organized farmers have sought to attack through legislation in the Sixty-eighth and Sixty-ninth Congresses.

When a surplus agricultural production was necessary to repay foreign investors in the United States, and to pay for our imports our national policy of expanding agriculture upon an export basis worked admirably. When our greatest national test came it was our surplus food production that fed the Allies and decided the issue of the World War. But the international balance shifted as a result of the war. We have the gold. The rest of the world owes us. These facts inevitably limit the volume of exports, both industrial and agricultural, from the United States. Our wheat, pork, cotton, and sometimes beef, can bring the farmers only the price which foreign buyers will pay for what is left after the domestic need is satisfied. This condition is crucifying agriculture. It is directly due to our past policy of agricultural expansion, and to the development of the American protective system which keeps farm costs on a high domestic plane while farm prices remain relatively low, due to the influence of world competition.

In my reference to the American protective system I include not only the tariff but such measures and devices as the Adamson law, restriction of immigration, the Esch-Cummins law, the Railroad Labor Board, and others of like purpose. These all have tended to protect, stabilize, and hold immune from world influence industry and labor, and to make effective the work of their organizations in holding up the prices of their commodities and services.

Agriculture, on the other hand, remaining unorganized is still subject to world influences on export crops, because the American price of these crops is not determined here by American conditions, but is determined in foreign markets by world conditions. We sell our surplus abroad in world competition, at a price determined by world supply and demand, and regulated by world conditions. It follows that the price of the surplus is the price of the crop. This is axiomatic.

For nearly five years this condition, as one of the principal reasons for the existing inequality, has been known by our national administrations. The agricultural conference convoked by President Harding in the early months of 1922 called, by resolution, upon the President and Congress to take such steps as were necessary immediately to restore the fair exchange value of the farmers' dollar. The chairman of that conference, who was also chairman of the Congressional Joint Commission of Agricultural Inquiry, appointed by Congress "to determine the cause of the agricultural depression," refused to permit a discussion of what is now generally recognized as the principal cause of the depression, because he said it involved the tariff. In its report, covering some four volumes of facts, figures, and diagrams, this commission failed to mention the only thing it was appointed to determine—the cause of the agricultural depression.

IV

The remedy lies in one of two directions. One, repealing all protective measures enacted for the benefit of other groups, thus enabling the farmer to buy as well as sell in a world market; the other, including the farmer in the protective system by organizing and financing agriculture so that it, too, can adjust supply to demand, and if necessary divert surplus to export, as industry does, and is encouraged to do by the Webb-Pomerene and Edge laws.

The first remedy, the repeal of all protective legislation, is legislatively impossible and certainly undesirable, since protection furnishes security for American standards of living against descent to the level of the world at large. Farmers have not advocated this policy. Even if by cheapening other goods and services their purchasing power could be restored, the low dollar price would leave them under a great disadvantage in relation to their debt. Their indebtedness has mounted from about $4,000,000,000 in 1910 to over $12,000,000,000 in 1925 . . . —a sum greater than the original foreign debt to the United States. If the farmers are ever going to pay that debt, it should be with commodities as high in dollar value as when the debt was incurred—or as near to that figure as possible. To reduce the dollar value of other goods and services might raise the exchange value of farm crops, but if the price level for all commodities, including agricultural products, were thereby lowered and held down, the debt-paying power of the farmer would be reduced.

The second remedy—to include the farmer in the protective system—is no difficult matter. It requires only a mechanism which the producers of the primary surplus crops can use to regulate the movement of their crops to market, with the cost of withholding unneeded supplies, or of diverting small surpluses to export markets, assessed against all the producers of the commodity affected. If you withhold or skim off the surplus which for natural reasons can not be controlled or prevented in the production stage, the demand can still be satisfied, but at a fair exchange value for the farmer.

This principle would work out in different ways with different crops.

The growers of cotton could secure relative price stability through balancing supply and demand over a period of years instead of currently. They could secure for themselves whatever economic advantage there may be in their position as producers and exporters of two-thirds of the world's international trade in cotton. Growers of other crops like wheat, of which the exportable surplus is relatively small compared with domestic consumption, could secure the advantage of tariffs in the domestic market.

The essential element in such a mechanism is the universal assessment or "equalization fee," which distributes the cost of caring for surpluses over all the producers of a particular crop whose excess supplies have to be dealt with to prevent price demoralization.

v

. . . Retail prices which consumers pay in many cases do not reflect the change in price levels at which farmers sell these great staple crops, which is one reason for the comparative inelasticity of demand. For example, the farm price of cotton in January, 1924, was 32.5 cents per pound; in January, 1926, it had declined to 17 cents per pound;

and today the farmer is getting 10 to 11 cents per pound on the farms of the South. There has been a drop in the farmer's price to about one-third of the price 34 months ago, yet how much has the retail price of cotton goods to the American consumer declined? The farm price of wheat dropped over a dollar a bushel in 1920, without any corresponding reduction in the price of bread, and it has had an up and down range of nearly 90 cents a bushel during the last two years, but the only way the consumer of bread learned of it was to read it in the papers.

We must recognize that increased farm prices would react on the cost of living to exactly the same degree, no matter whether the rise was due to voluntarily limited production or to control of supply by cooperative organization or to Government action.

As to stimulated production, any one of the methods suggested above would have to increase farm prices so greatly that farming would be attractive to capital in competition with other investment before production could be materially expanded. There is a long gap to be filled before that point is reached. Our per capita farm acreage and production alike are falling steadily behind our population.

The argument that increased production will follow farm legislation, advanced in a country where every public policy has been aimed at the expansion of farm production, would be absurd if it were not urged seriously by men of influence. Among them are our foremost advocates of Government help to expand farm production. Singularly enough men will condemn one method proposed to increase farm prices on the ground that its adoption would stimulate production and advocate another method to accomplish the same purpose without recognizing that the effect upon production, whatever it might be, would probably be identical in both cases. Finally, even if production should increase, the farmer alone would bear the burden of it under the plan proposed.

VI

There are many elements in the agricultural problem today that are new. They contribute to the forces that have pressed agriculture out of adjustment in our national life. It is necessary that we understand them and in the light of that understanding define a new national policy.

Foreign countries can not well pay in gold for either industrial or agricultural products, because we now have the gold; they cannot advantageously pay for our agricultural products with their industrial products because of the tariff. They can not pay for industrial exports with competing agricultural products because of the tariff, and because of our surplus production in many lines. Yet in the midst of such wealth as no other country has ever possessed, one-third of our people are witnessing the transfer of their savings and capital into the hands of other economic groups. This impoverishment of agriculture, our basic industry, must go down in American history as a dark blot upon our statesmanship.

Without further delay we should, through legislation, make it possible for agriculture to attain economic equality with industry and labor in the domestic market, and then in the future let all three groups make adjustments together to meet changing conditions whenever it seems necessary to do so, as a matter of national policy.

I repeat, the sound program for America should aim toward the development of a well-balanced national life, one which will not stimulate any one form of productive effort at the expense of other equally essential producers.

*Richard S. Kirkendall*

## 29. FARM POLITICS AND THE NEW DEAL

Many of the New Deal's most articulate members of Roosevelt's "Brain Trust" were drawn into agriculture. Under Henry Wallace, the Secretary of Agriculture, new farm programs were developed, and differing views and objectives concerning the direction of these programs quickly surfaced. There were advocates of promoting commercial agriculture who had the backing of the most powerful agricultural political forces. Others supported programs for improving the lot of the tenants and small farmers, while still others believed cooperative and communal experiments would offer the best solution to the farm problem. The extension of industrialization into rural areas was viewed by some as the most suitable alternative. Kirkendall's book, *Social Scientists and Farm Politics in the Age of Roosevelt*, presents the cross-currents and controversies that took place in this arena.

To Norman Thomas, the most striking feature of the production control program was its harmful impact upon the rural poor. This impact troubled the social scientists in farm politics, for their plans were not limited merely to efforts to improve the lot of commercial farmers and the use of the land. In accepting democratic as well as business and scientific values, the intellectuals hoped to use the land in ways that would make life

From Richard S. Kirkendall, "Planning for the Rural Poor," in *Social Scientists and Farm Politics in the Age of Roosevelt*, pp. 106-107, 109-132. Reprinted by permission of the publisher, University of Missouri Press, Columbia, Missouri. Copyright 1966 by the Curators of the University of Missouri.

better for all social groups. Even before the purge of the Frank group, efforts to tackle the problems of tenant farmers, farmers on submarginal land, and farm laborers, including Wilson's subsistence homesteads program and Gray's land purchase activities, got under way; after the purge, those efforts were expanded with the establishment of the Resettlement Administration headed by Rex Tugwell. Tugwell quickly learned, however, that great difficulties faced those who hoped to move down this path, for the most powerful pressures in farm politics favored the rural businessman.

The social scientists made some of the earliest efforts to deal directly with the problems of lower-income groups in rural America. "The simple fact that rural poverty existed in this country was never openly recognized by our government until approximately five years ago," an official noted in 1939. "Public recognition of the fact has come still more slowly. The idea of poverty has been traditionally associated with city slums. . . . "Prior to the New Deal, Wilson's experiments in tenant rehabilitation at Fairway Farms represented an interest that did not exist in many other places. The agricultural economists, agricultural colleges, and extension services paid little attention to what the 1930's found to be an extensive series of problems. As a consequence, basic research had to be done at the same time that programs were getting under way, and administration suffered from inexperience in dealing with a serious situation. Nevertheless, the planners plunged forward, moved by democratic convictions that their plans must consider all the people on the land, not just the commercial farmers and the ways to use the land itself more efficiently.

While Jerome Frank hoped to use Triple-A to improve the lot of the tenant farmers, the social scientists tended to think in terms of developing special programs for the lower ranks in agriculture. Calvin Hoover's report in the spring of 1934 had suggested that a "comprehensive policy for the economic rehabilitation of Southern agricul-

ture" was "plainly required," and Wilson's and Gray's Land Planning Committee had called later in the year for an investigation of tenancy and for legislation on the subject. In January, 1935, Hoover advised Wallace that the administration must face the fact that its farm program had "been of little net benefit to the tenants, sharecroppers, and laborers in the South" and that alternative programs must be provided for these groups. He believed that "all possible means to encourage and to require cotton producers to keep their accustomed number of tenants and sharecroppers should be made" but suggested that "extremely drastic measures to compel landowners to keep these people would be futile and ill-advised," as the market for cotton was declining and thus there was a "natural tendency . . . to dispose of surplus labor." He suggested a program to help these people "purchase small semisubsistence farms in which they can produce the greater part of their necessities." Hoover looked ultimately to industrial expansion as the solution to the ills of Southern agriculture. Through growth of this kind, he believed, the problem of agricultural surpluses would be solved by diminishing the supply of labor in agriculture on the one hand and by increasing the demand for agricultural commodities on the other.

\* \* \*

Rather than change the policies of the Department of Agriculture, Roosevelt had established a new agency to deal with the problems of the rural poor. Furthermore, he had placed a critic of Triple-A in charge of the Resettlement Administration. Tugwell hired another critic, Dr. Will W. Alexander, as his top assistant. Clergyman, educator, and expert on race relations, Alexander, working with Edwin Embree and Charles S. Johnson and financed by the Rockefeller Foundation and the Rosenwald Fund, had just published a short study, *The Collapse of Cotton Tenancy*, which criticized the crop control program for its impact on the ten-

149

ants and attempted to publicize their plight and produce action. Along with Embree, George Foster Peabody, and Frank Tannenbaum, Alexander had carried his case to the Administration, discussing it with Roosevelt, Wallace, Tugwell, Wilson, Gray, and Appleby, and had battled for the Bankhead bill. Alexander's appointment as assistant administrator was welcomed by his associates as a great and unusual opportunity to develop a program to help tenant farmers.

The new agency attempted to improve land-use practices and to elevate those who were underprivileged as a result of past mistakes in the use of the land. The people included destitute groups living in once thriving but now exhausted lumbering, mining, and oil regions, sharecroppers in the South, and farmers on poor land in the Great Lakes cut-over region, in the drought area of the Middle West, and in the Appalachians. Gray's Land Policy Section was transferred to RA, and Gray became an assistant administrator of the new organization besides being director of its Division of Land Utilization, which took charge of all land purchase and land-use planning functions. In two years, although Congress failed to provide the kind of authority that Tugwell sought for the purchase of submarginal land, Gray spent over $50,000,000 acquiring approximately 9,000,000 acres of land. "The Federal government had never before undertaken to acquire so large an area in an equally short time," Gray reported to the President. Poor farmland was converted to other uses, and conservation methods were put into practice on it. The planning staff of the Land Policy Section and the regional and state planning consultants of the Resources Board were transferred to RA, staffing the Land-Use Planning Section of Gray's division. A product of BAE's Land Economics Division, E. H. Wiecking, headed this section. It conducted a comprehensive program of national land-use planning that defined the nature of the nation's land-use problems and recommended changes in land-use practices. ". . . the major effort of our land-use planning

work at this time should center on planning for adjustments in those 'problem' areas which are characterized by critical maladjustments in the relation of people to land resources." Gray advised his subordinates.

RA provided another illustration of the way in which the New Deal built upon the work of Gray's Division of Land Economics. The research in which that agency had long been engaged supplied a foundation for this action program. Just before RA was created, the division had completed a large study of the Southern Appalachians. It concluded that the basic problems of the region grew out of maladjustments in land use and in the relation of population to land and suggested that changes could not be made unless there was "a planning agency vested with powers and resources sufficient to cope with actual problems." After the establishment of such an agency, the work of Gray's old and new divisions became so closely integrated that the chief of the BAE, Al Black, began to fear that the Division of Land Economics had become merely a service agency of the Resettlement Administration and was not giving enough attention to basic research.

Two striking features of RA were the wide variety of its activities and the broad use that it made of social scientists. In addition to land purchase and resettlement, the agency provided relief for victims of drought, guidance for migrants, loans and supervision to poor farmers to help them improve their operations, and loans to tenants to enable them to buy farms. RA also built communities and tried to develop more secure contracts for tenant farmers. Tugwell called upon a rural sociologist, Carl C. Taylor, to direct the Rural Resettlement Division, a unit that took over tasks formerly handled by the Subsistence Homesteads Division and FERA. Paul Taylor, an economist who had studied labor economics with John R. Commons and who had become a specialist on the problems of agricultural labor, supervised the early development of camps for migratory workers, a pitifully poor group of people.

These programs for the rural poor assumed that rural poverty demanded an attack upon its causes, not just relief. The situation had taken many years to develop, and only long-run programs could correct it. Nor could the solution come entirely from indirect action, such as the expansion of urban employment. Rural poverty had to be dealt with directly through specially devised programs. And these programs needed to be devised because all Americans, not just the rural poor, suffered from poverty in agriculture, for it meant inadequate purchasing power, destruction of land, disease, costly social services, and the like. In other words, the programs assumed that a planned attack needed to be made as a consequence of the interdependent nature of modern society. . . .

Tugwell emphasized resettlement, technological development, and urbanization. He looked upon subsistence homesteads as archaic and impractical, and he lacked enthusiasm for rehabilitation, believing that more fundamental changes in the use of the land were needed. He was responsible for these homestead and rehabilitation programs simply because he and Roosevelt agreed that all programs developed for the rural poor should be administered by one agency.

The family farm provided a major focal point of controversy. Tugwell did not want it to be the only goal for the programs; he believed that only the most able tenants would benefit from a program designed to convert them into owners and that it would not solve the basic problem of insecurity. He wanted the government to experiment also with long-term leases and large-scale cooperative farms as well as with various other types of cooperatives, and he was highly critical of members of Gray's unit who had strong doubts, based on the study of cooperative experiments in America, that cooperative farming would succeed. The critics of this type of farming also disagreed with one another; some, like Carl and Paul Taylor, embraced a Jeffersonian philosophy that emphasized the virtues of the small, simple family farm, while others, like Wilson's friend Elmer Starch from Montana State College and Fairway Farms, advocated large, mechanized units to be formed by reorganizing existing arrangements in areas where people were unable to make a living from the farms they operated. After Tugwell and Carl Taylor reached a parting of the ways, Tugwell substituted an advocate of cooperative farming, Walter Packard, as head of the Resettlement Division. Cooperative farming became a small but important part of RA's activities.

There were also disagreements concerning the proper organization of this agency. Hoping to avoid the difficulties he had encountered with the FERA, Gray proposed that land purchase and resettlement—both of which were to be bigger programs than they had been in 1934—should be handled by one administrative unit, but Tugwell rejected the proposal and established two divisions headed by Gray and Carl Taylor. Although the two men represented different disciplines—land economics and rural sociology—and had somewhat different points of view, cooperation was easier than it had been in 1934, for the two men were members of the same organization and were closer together intellectually than the representatives of AAA and FERA had been. Gray and Taylor worked in adjoining offices and took advantage of this opportunity to consult with one another and to coordinate their activities. Gray and his lieutenants, however, remained dissatisfied with the resettlement program.

Beyond the differences of opinion lay agreement that rural America should be approached as something more than simply the home of rural businessmen and that government should do more than increase their profits. The programs, in other words, challenged the dominant orientation of farm politics. Not surprisingly, therefore, Tugwell and the Resettlement Administration came under heavy attack. Undoubtedly, internal weaknesses in RA, Tugwell's well-established tendency to generate controversy, and nonagricultural dimensions of the

151

agency's activities contributed to the attack. Much of it, however, grew out of the challenge that Tugwell and the Resettlement Administration offered to the major powers in agriculture.

Critics were inclined to stress apparent administrative short-comings in the agency and to suggest that they resulted from the selection of impractical men to handle the programs. "Too much theory and too many professors," Congressman Clifford Hope complained. . . . "The Resettlement set-up here in Washington is so highly organized that apparently no one has jurisdiction over anything, and I have never seen a finer example of what can be done in the way of government buck-passing. . . ." . . .

Many critics opposed the fundamental assumptions of the programs. These people disliked the idea of spending money on the poor and charged that if they "had what it took" they would help themselves. "Substantial farmers, bankers and businessmen in rural areas complain bitterly against federal resettlement or rehabilitation of the needy," one commentator noted.

In their hardboiled opinion many of the Tugwell beneficiaries need a dose of energy and ambition rather than cows, ploughs and seed paid for by Uncle Sam. Local burgomasters fear that once government aid is withdrawn, the resettled and rehabilitated will become public charges which the towns and counties must support.

RA's critics included urban property owners near the community projects, businessmen who feared that resettlement would take away their customers, and financiers who preferred government credit agencies that operated according to good "business principles" and without "subsidies"; but representatives of the large commercial farmers provided the most effective opposition. Southern cotton planters opposed changes in the sharecropping system, while the corporate farmers of California and their allies in the Chambers of Commerce criticized the camps for migratory workers. As constitutional rights were respected in the camps, they provided a place where efforts could be made to organize the workers; employers could block such efforts in the camps they owned. Many commercial farmers warned that RA must not aggravate the farm surplus problem, and their spokesmen, especially in the Farm Bureau, made their reservations known, decrying aid to the "shiftless." Such powerful men as Byrd and Glass of Virginia, Bailey of North Carolina, and Harrison of Mississippi expressed these views in Congress and subjected the programs to constant pressure and criticism. They had no desire to see the government upset the class structure in agriculture. "I know what's the matter with Harry Byrd," Roosevelt told Tugwell when the Senator was objecting to a resettlement project in Virginia. "He's afraid you'll force him to pay more than ten cents an hour for his apple pickers." . . .

The major pressures of farm politics produced many difficulties for those who hoped to develop large programs for the rural poor. As a leading student of farm politics has observed, "government agricultural policy . . . is largely designed and administered for the benefit of commercial farmers." Low-income farmers lack effective pressure groups and have not been a separate force to be reckoned with in elections. "The bulk of low-income farmers are in the South, where traditional voting behavior, the one-party situation, the poll tax and the racial problem have prevented the emergence of this group as a separate force in the electorate." The realities of farm politics made life difficult even for the planners who were heavily influenced by faith in the family farm and nearly impossible for a person as unorthodox as Tugwell. Frustrated earlier than other planners, he had dreamed of major changes in the party system and had departed from Washington long before Wilson, Tolley, and other social scientists in farm politics.

Nevertheless, in contributing to the establishment of the Farm Security Administration, Tugwell, Wilson, Gray, and other social scientists had promoted significant changes in farm politics and farm policy.

For several years after the passage of the legislation of 1937, FSA played an important role in American life. Its rehabilitation program, especially, picked up new supporters and increasingly larger appropriations. The agency became an important part of the Department of Agriculture and a major participant in agricultural politics and had a significant impact upon rural life. "Between 1937 and 1942," a student of the agency has concluded, "the FSA emerged as a major challenge to the economic, social and political *status quo* in American agriculture." "Generally," Baldwin writes, "the agency was a summons to agricultural leaders, to other governmental organizations, and to private groups and individuals to match the

FSA in its fight against rural poverty and ignorance, and in its effort to convert the ideals of democracy into democratic reality." Members of the agency encountered many obstacles. In June, 1940, Tugwell's successor resigned, in part because his appearances before the Senate and House appropriations committees were being "made increasingly difficult by the opposition of certain powerful southerners and reactionary northerners who concentrated on FSA their ire against the New Deal and their fear of its threat to white supremacy." Accomplishment as well as frustration, however, characterized the experiences of those who attempted to elevate the lot of the rural poor.

*President's Committee on Farm Tenancy*

## 30. "ABUSES IN OUR SYSTEM . . . HAVE BEEN DEVELOPING FOR TWO CENTURIES . . ."

By its report in 1937, the President's Committee on Farm Tenancy made it clear that the recovery measures of the New Deal were not alleviating the economic distress of the majority of farm tenants. It was reported that "fully half of the total farm population has no adequate farm security." Tenancy since 1890 had increased from 25 percent of all farm operators to 40 percent. Owners were often that in name only, holding no more than 20 percent equity in their property.

The report identified the following insecure groups among farmers:

1. Tenants, two-thirds of whom were located in the South, while able in some cases to move up the "agricultural ladder," in all too many cases were living in great insecurity and in conditions very unsatisfactory to both them and their landlords.

2. Croppers, most of whom were in the southern states, were the most insecure of all tenants. They operated 10 percent of the farms in the United States and made up 39 percent of all tenants. Their opportunity to improve was small and frequently they became laborers, losing even the protection of their share-crop contract.

3. Farm laborers comprised 25 percent of all persons gainfully employed in agriculture in 1930. The great majority of these were employed seasonally and tended to move from place to place. Some migrated great distances, having no permanent address, and barely subsisted.

From *Farm Tenancy, Report of the President's Committee,* House Document 149, 75th Congress, First Session (Washington, D.C.: U.S. Government Printing Office, February, 1937), pp. 10–11, 21–28.

4. Farmers on submarginal land, estimated at about a half million in number, were unable to maintain an adequate standard of living under existing conditions.

5. Farmers on farms too small to provide support above the poverty level were found throughout the nation, most critically in the South and Great Plains where one-crop farming prevailed.

The committee concluded that "examination of the agricultural ladder has indicated that in recent years movement . . . has been predominantly in the direction of descent rather than ascent." While large commercial farms seemed to be forging ahead with the assistance of the government's subsidy program, a large segment of the rural population was becoming progressively more insecure.

Portions of the committee's report are reprinted below. Minority reports of W. L. Blackstone, representing the Southern Tenant Farmers' Union, and of Edward A. O'Neal, president of the American Farm Bureau Federation, are included to illustrate the divergence of views between tenant and large proprietor.

RECOMMENDATIONS FOR ACTION

*Toward Farm Security*

In preparing the recommendations on land tenure offered in the following pages the Committee has attempted to keep the entire agricultural ladder in view. The findings just outlined represent a rung-by-rung examination of groups now insecure. The suggestions based upon the findings are of two general types. The one type consists of proposals which the Committee regards as appropriate to facilitate movement upward from rung to rung by farmers who are prepared to take such steps. The other type consists of proposals which the Committee regards as appropriate to increase security on each of the ladder's various rungs. A successful general approach to the problem of insecurity as related to land use supposes action at a series of different levels.

The Committee submits recommendations for both Federal and State action, as well as for joint action under Federal-State cooperation.

*For Federal Action*

The Committee's recommendations for Federal action include measures to facilitate

farm-home ownership and to help existing owners keep their farm, measures for the rehabilitation of groups not now prepared to take over their own farms, certain suggestions for improving the condition of laborers, a program for aiding families stranded on submarginal land and taking such land out of cultivation, and proposals for the discouragement of speculation in farm lands.

All of these approaches are necessary, in the opinion of the Committee, in attacking a problem of such magnitude and difficulty. Some approaches and some measures may turn out to be more effective than others, but it would be unwise to restrict action to any one approach. Thus the Committee offers recommendations on facilitating farm-home ownership, but at the same time it is well aware of the limitations of this approach in solving the whole farm-tenancy problem. The value of the land and buildings now operated by tenants is about $11,000,000,000. The number of tenants has lately been increasing at the rate of 40,000 a year. To concentrate on facilitating ownership to the exclusion of other approaches would hardly be practical, at least until we can be reasonably sure that a good farmer on a good farm has a fair chance of holding on to his farm. In other words, while we need to create new opportunities for owner-

ship, we need even more to create conditions which will make continued ownership
possible.

\* \* \*

## Safeguards of Civil Liberties

Within the past few years tenants, croppers, and farm laborers have organized to
increase their bargaining power. Members
of these organizations assert that they have
been frequently denied the rights of peaceful assembly guaranteed them under the
Constitution. They assert further that they
have been subjected to physical violence
and that some have been forced to flee for
their lives.

We have not had opportunity to investigate these charges at first hand. But frequent press reports of violence in some
areas where croppers or migratory laborers
make up a considerable portion of the rural
population indicate that such allegations
cannot be ignored. A Federal commission,
appointed to investigate conditions among
migratory laborers in the Imperial Valley,
found substantiating evidence of such practices.

The Committee strongly recommends
that States guarantee to these groups and
enforce the rights of peaceful assembly and
of organization to achieve their legitimate
objectives.

It also recommends repeal of State laws
which make it a misdemeanor to quit a contract while in debt, since such laws abridge
civil liberties of tenants and tend to nullify
Federal antipeonage acts. . . .

## Cooperation with States in Improving Leases

The Committee recommends, therefore,
that the Farm Security Administration be
given authority and necessary funds to enable it to aid State governments in drafting
proper regulatory measures regarding tenant contracts and to stimulate and cooperate

in State research and extension work aimed
at improving lease contracts.

It is obvious that in the extension of the
new ownership and rehabilitation policies
recommended above, the Federal Government has a direct interest not only in encouraging better lease provisions and improved landlord-tenant relationships, but
also in assuring itself that the basic legislation of the States make possible the accomplishment of the objectives of its own broad
program. As recommended above, therefore, adequate funds should be appropriated by the Federal Government to the land-
grant colleges and universities to enable
them to cooperate.

It is recommended also that in selected
local areas consideration be given to trying
the experiment of including improvements
in leases among the conditions of benefit
payments under the Soil Conservation and
Domestic Allotment Act. Improvement of
existing leases is one important manner of
encouraging soil conservation. If the experiment succeeds, its extension on a broad
scale may be worthwhile.

## Need for Education and Health Services

Ignorance, no less than poverty and insta-
bility, forces many tenant and other disadvantaged families into an inferior relationship to the community. Ignorance, as well as
insecurity, is often responsible for failure to
adopt enlightened methods of farm operation, particularly of self-help to improve the
family's mode of life.

Education can go far toward enabling
these poorer farm groups to apply family
labor intelligently in improving home,
school, and community — by repairing,
cleaning, and decorating rooms and buildings; repairing and making furniture and
equipment; planting public grounds and
home dooryards; properly selecting, preparing, and serving home-produced food.

It is strongly recommended that the rural
educational systems of the various States be

more definitely aimed at providing the kind of training needed by adult members of disadvantaged farm families as well as children.

At the same time, the needs of the children should not be neglected. The elementary rural schools in many areas are such as to offer little opportunity to children of low-income families. Tax bases are inadequate; school terms are short; attendance legislation is not well enforced; teachers are poorly trained and even more poorly paid; too often methods of instruction are routine and ill-calculated to equip the children to improve their environment.

This Committee prefers to leave to educational specialists the question as to the proper contribution of the Federal Government to a better equalization of educational advantages. A number of considerations appear to justify substantial Federal aid. The classes of farm families now below the margin of security are a principal source of the Nation's population, by reason of the high birth rates prevailing among them. The congregation in given areas of large numbers of such families frequently results in a collective poverty that is a primary obstacle to the provision, from local resources alone, of adequate educational advantages.

It has been noted that large numbers of farm families are severely handicapped by debilitating diseases, malnutrition, and general morbidity. Much so-called laziness and shiftlessness trace back to a low level of vitality and the resulting mental habits and attitudes. No fundamental attack on the problem of the disadvantaged classes of farmers would be complete without inclusion of measures to improve their general level of health. To a large extent this is a matter of education in improved dietary practices and personal hygiene, supplemented by more adequate medical service and more ample provision of clinics and public-health nursing. The grouping of counties into public-health districts appears to be a promising way of improving such services. It is urged that adequate funds be made available under the Social Security

Act to take care of the health needs of rural communities, especially in areas of excessive tenancy.

### Necessity for Action

In the preceding pages the Committee has made recommendation for action both by the Federal Government and by the governments of the several States.

Sturdy rural institutions beget self-reliance and independence of judgment. Sickly rural institutions beget dependency and incapacity to bear the responsibilities of citizenship. Over wide areas the vitality of American rural life is daily being sapped by systems of land tenure that waste human and natural resources alike. Security of tenure is essential to the development of better farm homes and better rural communities.

Vigorous and sustained action is required for restoring the impaired resources on whose conservation continuance of the democratic process in this country to no small extent depends.

The final emphasis of this report is consequently on the necessity for action; action to enable increasing numbers of farm families to enter into sound relationships with the land they till and the communities in which they live.

\* \* \*

SPECIAL STATEMENTS BY INDIVIDUAL
MEMBERS OF THE SPECIAL COMMITTEE
ON FARM TENANCY

*Minority Report of W. L. Blackstone,
Representing the Southern Tenant Farmers'
Union on the President's Farm Tenancy
Committee*

As representatives of the Southern Tenant Farmers' Union on the President's Committee on Farm Tenancy I wish that I might unqualifiedly endorse the report of that Committee. I speak for our union in saying that we deeply appreciate the earnestness with which members of the Committee have approached the problem. There is much in the report with which we thoroughly concur, especially the analysis of the problem. Rather than listing our agreement in detail we confine our observations to a few major points on which we disagree with the majority of the Committee. In setting forth these observations we do not believe we can be accused of making undue claims when we state that we workers in the fields, through our unions, through our strikes, and through our willingness to stand up against beatings, espionage, and all manner of terror in our fight to improve our shamefully depressed conditions, have brought the attention of the country to our problems and led to the appointment of the President's Committee. As the specimens now under the microscope (and the presumed beneficiaries) we ought to know better than others what is wrong with us and our situation.

Our first major point of disagreement with the recommendations of the report is its proposal that the Farm Security Administration and the Farm Security Corporation be placed under the Department of Agriculture, with the Secretary and Under Secretary as two members of the proposed board of five. We note with interest and hope recent speeches of Secretary Wallace in which he states that the Department of Agriculture has heretofore throughout its history been concerned primarily with the top third of the farmers in the country and that it must turn its attention to the others from now on. But our experience has been such that we cannot believe the Department of Agriculture will be able in any near future to remove itself from domination by the rich and large landowning class of farmers and their political-pressure lobbies. The county agricultural agent, often paid in part by chambers of commerce or the Farm Bureau Federation, is a symbol of such domination. We recall vividly our inability in the days of the A.A.A. to get adequate redress of our grievances as to the disposition of benefit payments and as to dispossessing us from our

slight foothold on the land in violation of the cotton contract. Ample evidence of these violations was in the hands of the A.A.A. Very little was done about it, to say nothing of any genuine attack on the problems of agricultural labor. We consequently strongly urge that the Farm Security Administration and its operating corporation be established as an independent Federal agency and that tenants, sharecroppers, and farm workers be given representation on the central board of control.

As a direct corollary of the above suggestion we urge that a special bureau or division of the Department of Labor be established to bring to bear the investigating, reporting, and conciliating services of the Department in the field of agricultural labor, sharecropping, and tenancy where the latter falls within a degree of insecurity making the tenant virtually on a par with the wage laborer. Such services by the Department of Labor could and should be of great aid to the proposed Farm Security Administration while it is working out its program. Tenant farmers, croppers, and farm workers, shifting back and forth from one class to another —though mostly in the direction of the latter class as the report shows— are very much in the same category as industrial workers who, because they do not possess the tools and equipment essential for industrial enterprise, must work in factories owned by others. And as the Department of Labor represents the industrial worker instead of the Department of Commerce which speaks for business and industry, so the Department of Labor should represent agricultural workers rather than the Department of Agriculture which serves the landowning farmers.

We believe the report should affirmatively recommend that the Wagner Labor Relations Act be amended to include agricultural labor in its provision and likewise the Social Security Act. The report as it now stands merely says that serious consideration should be given to such proposed amendments.

Of primary importance do we consider

157

the question of local administration under the proposed Farm Security Administration. But our experience under both the Resettlement Administration and the A.A.A. has proved to us that any program will fail unless the Federal administration exercises strong enough supervision and selects local agents sympathetic enough with its policies to put them into effect. Again and again orders issued in Washington in our behalf have not been carried out. Complaints made by our people to Washington have been turned over to the officials in the field against whom the complaints were made. In numerous instances penalties have thereafter been meted out to the complainants. The county agent, as indicated before, is, generally speaking, the servant of the landowning and business interests from whom he gets a large portion of his pay, rather than the servant of the mass of the people in the farming areas.

This is particularly true in the South and in the areas where there are large bodies of agricultural labor, such as the Pacific coast with its large fruit and vegetable operations; the beet fields of Colorado, Wyoming, Nebraska, and other beet-growing States; the onion fields of Ohio and elsewhere; the citrus fields of Texas and Florida. We earnestly believe the report should include, therefore, an unequivocal assurance that strict Federal control of the proposed program will be maintained and that only local agents affirmatively sympathetic to its purposes will be appointed to the end that it may not be rendered futile through the political pressure of the landowning and business interests.

Stemming directly from the above suggestion is our recommendation that the section dealing with local boards of arbitration on tenant-landlord relationships be modified. While we welcome the proposal that tenants be represented on these boards — the first time such a proposal has even been made officially — we feel strongly that the report should specify that representation on these local boards (presumably county) should be in proportion to the number of tenants, sharecroppers, and agricultural workers involved as compared with the number of landlords or landowners. That clearly would be in keeping with true democratic processes.

Related to the foregoing recommendations is our contention that the section on civil liberties is not adequate. As those who have been beaten and terrorized (and some of us forced to flee for our lives) in our struggle to pull ourselves up out of our slough of misery, we know that a few words from responsible Federal officials on behalf of our constitutional civil rights would have helped in our past battles and will help in the ones we know are yet to come. The problem should not be passed over to the States so lightly. We believe firmly, in this connection, that the report should contain a positive statement that the program will be administered without discrimination as to race, religious or political affiliation, or organizational membership. As members of a union which has consistently been discriminated against we have reason to feel deeply the need of such a statement in the report. . . .

While approving the report's recognition of the urgent need of educational and health facilities among the tenants, croppers, and agricultural workers, we believe that more concrete proposals for immediate action in spreading these facilities could and should be made.

We are naturally strong in our conviction that the report should contain a section endorsing the unionization of these workers in the field as a means of providing an instrumentality through which all the objectives expressed in the report can best be obtained, for through unionization can and will be developed responsible leadership and the ability to pull together for common betterment.

In concluding, we cannot refrain from expressing our genuine approval of those sections of the report seeking to prevent the land of the beneficiaries getting into mortgage-holding or other speculative hands, especially the 40-year lease provision — sections which the American Farm Bureau Federation vehemently opposes. The earnestness with which the majority of the committee has approached the land speculation problem and the problem of the price of agricultural commodities is a cause for encouragement. We feel, however, that there should have been a similar amount of thought and study given to the problem of marketing and distribution because we believe the latter is quite as prime a factor in general farm conditions as commodity price and land. . . .

*February 12, 1937*

Dr. L. C. Gray,
United States Department of Agriculture,
Washington, D.C.

*My Dear Sir*: I desire to restate the objections I so frequently made during the discussion of the proposed findings and recommendations to be made by the President's Farm Tenancy Committee. The American Farm Bureau Federation, which I represent, through its executive committee, has outlined the position it desires to take in respect to the general subject of alleviating tenancy conditions prevailing in various parts of the United States. I am bound by the statement heretofore issued and I cannot, therefore, approve any recommendations or mode of procedure for administration contained in the proposed report which go beyond the limits of the announced policy of the American Farm Bureau Federation.

If my signature is to be attached to the report, I desire that it be noted in such manner as to call the attention of the reader to the limitations our organization policies and this letter require. In the event this is not deemed advisable, then I prefer not to be a signer of the report.

In addition to the limitation above described, I cannot approve the principle of withholding the transfer of title to any purchaser who is able to pay the principal indebtedness for which he obligated himself at any time that he is able to make such payment. I regard the proposed restriction on alienation of lands as contrary to sound American jurisprudence and deem it in conflict with the desired policy regarding landownership. By in large, I am of the conviction that a man who owns a proper equity in a farm or has accumulated the amount available to own such an equity is capable of the responsibilities of such ownership. Other policies related to the use of agricultural lands should be approached from the standpoint of education and demonstration rather than through limitations on the right of ownership.

That part of the report which indicates the use of credit as a basis for carrying on the program I deem of great importance. I have grave doubts that credit can carry the burden of such a program.

Without attempting further to define my attitude toward the report, I desire to state that I prefer not to be a signer of the report except on the condition stated in a foregoing paragraph.

Very truly yours,

American Farm Bureau Federation
Edw. A. O'Neal, *President*

159

*Grant McConnell*

## 31. NARROWING THE BASIS OF CONTROL

The system of agrarian democracy implicit in Jeffersonian philosophy was transformed by technological changes that were well under way by 1920. One of the main characteristics of this system, decentralization, became useful to the support of a class-oriented society and the leading farm organization on the scene at the time inherited the power that was legitimized by the value. The details of the system seemed to provide for a democracy that in fact they rendered impossible.

Agricultural policy became a product of the "superior farmers," partly by skillful application by the American Farm Bureau Federation of the principle of decentralized decision-making. The functioning of the machinery for policy-making and its effects on the resulting policies are described in the piece below. That the problems of agricultural insecurity and poverty received only minor attention by the Farm Bureau seems less strange after reading Professor McConnell's analysis.

One of the ideas most frequently encountered in agricultural politics is decentralization. This too infrequently analyzed idea is commonly used in a manner which implies that it has an intimate and self-evident relation to democracy. In one form or another, it is used as a touchstone in almost every controversy over farm organization, the administration of public policy, or the structure of power in agricultural affairs. It is important not merely because it is in high favor among farm leaders, but because it is in fact one of the keys to understanding the system of power which has been built.

Decentralization has a variety of meanings. At the most general level, it is one form of the concept of devolution. Geographical devolution, that is, decentralization, is most familiar here, but the other major form, functional devolution, has gained wide acceptance among farm spokesmen. This appears in the unstated but implicit belief that agricultural legislation and administration are the concerns of farmers only. Stated thus bluntly, the idea is absurd; anything that affects the price or supply of food and clothing is certainly a matter of general concern. In fact, however, the idea is rarely stated thus bluntly and the insistence that farmers should make decisions on farm affairs enjoys much respect. A different but related belief is that only farmers are competent to decide on agricultural matters. Congressional committees insist on hearing from real "dirt farmers" on involved economic questions, and the Department of Agriculture has a definite preference for employing people with farming backgrounds, even where the tasks require technical competence in law or statistics.

The attempt to isolate segments of public policy for decision by those most directly affected is common in American politics and is a general problem. Geographical decentralization, however, is peculiarly associated with agricultural affairs. The strength

From Grant McConnell, *The Decline of Agrarian Democracy,* pp. 166-172. Reprinted by permission of the University of California Press.

of its hold today can be explained in part historically. Many of those who give decentralization first importance as a political concept look back to the time when the nation was predominantly agricultural and most farming was of the subsistence variety. In the time of John Taylor, local problems were often the important political problems, and it was possible to envisage a society of loosely federated local communities having little need for common action. To imply today that local problems are the only important problems, however, would be absurd. Yet the idea of decentralization frequently seems to carry this implication.

The idea has a deceptively simple air. Organization of farmers and administration of government should be taken down to the grass roots, to "the real people." Perhaps there is a suggestion here of that assumption of moral superiority which Jefferson expressed: "Those who labor in the earth are the chosen people of God." Yet it is fairly evident that this is not the core of the concept. Its essential meaning seems to lie closer to the concept of direct democracy. If direct democracy in which the many make the actual decisions of government is the goal, decentralization has a certain relevance. Discussion and debate are possible only in small groups. The merits and defects of a political officer or candidate can be known better if he is a neighbor than if he is a stranger. These arguments have some value, but they are hardly central.

Several other elements are suggested in current discussions of decentralization. The most common is that administrative officers who make decisions in far-off Washington tend to lose sight of the actual conditions in which their decisions are applied. This argument probably rests on the fact that to many people national problems appear unreal. Moreover, it is true that some administrators seem to forget that they are dealing with human beings.

Closely related to this idea is the belief that anyone who exercises authority from a distance of many miles is somehow irresponsible. This is a serious charge. What is its merit? At the very outset it is necessary to ask, responsibility to whom? If it is responsibility to a particular locality, there can be little doubt that administration or governing from a distance is likely to mean a decrease in responsibility, since the distant officer will have a responsibility to other localities as well. Yet beyond this question lies another which is more important. What is the proper unit to which responsibility is to be related? The extreme position on this question would be that responsibility is exclusively to the individual. This may reach an ultimate position of anarchism. Certainly, it is not without interest that some of the outstanding statements of anarchism have had an agrarian origin. Yet if this rejection of government is ignored, what basis is there for choosing the neighborhood, the locality, the county, the state, or the nation? All are in some sense abstractions, and it becomes necessary to seek elsewhere for the basis of choice.

A geographical basis is only one of many possible bases of establishing units to which governmental responsibility is owed. Occupational, racial, and religious bases are equally conceivable. Any one of these would to some extent cut across geographical lines. Thus the problem is capable of being made almost infinitely complex. However, it happens to be true that all these possible dimensions of social difference are not equally important. It may be doubted whether the geographical dimension is intrinsically the most important. The test that seems important here is this: What are the probable effects, in terms of these other dimensions, of defining the units to which responsibility is paid on different geographical lines, local, state, regional, or national?

The classical American discussion of the problem appears in Number 10 of *The Federalist*. While this relates in its context to the large society of the nation, the principle stated applies equally here.

The smaller the society, the fewer probably will be the distinct parties and interests composing it: the fewer the distinct parties and interests, the more frequently will a majority be found of the same party; and the smaller the number of individuals composing a majority, and the smaller the compass within which they are placed, the more easily will they concert and execute their plans of oppression. Extend the sphere, and you take in a greater variety of parties and interests; you make it less probable that a majority of the whole will have a common motive to invade the rights of other citizens; or if such a common motive exists, it will be more difficult for all who feel it to discover their own strength, and to act in unison with each other.

Thus, on whatever dimension we may choose, a process of decentralization is likely to result in a narrowing of the basis of control. The particular basis may, indeed, vary from locality to locality, but within any particular unit the "distinct parties and interests" which vie for supremacy will be fewer than if decentralization had not taken place. . . .

In actual farm politics, one organization, the American Farm Bureau Federation, has succeeded in establishing itself in a position of great power. Some of the elements of its strength have little to do with its own internal organization. Its competence in securing the acquiescence and even complicity of other farm organizations is an example. Yet it is significant that the Farm Bureau has formed an independently influential organization that is somewhat narrowly based and which is, in outline, a federation of federations of small local units. In this instance, federalism has meant decentralization, and the Farm Bureau claim that its primary organization lies at the grass roots is true. The charge sometimes made that the Farm Bureau does not speak for the farmer is not wholly meaningful. "The farmer" is an abstraction. However, the question, for *what farmers* does the Farm Bureau speak, is highly meaningful. The Farm Bureau, in the words of its own publication, is an "organization of superior farmers." Moreover, the record of its actions shows that it has served as the spokesman of these "superior farmers." Thus, the narrowed basis of Farm Bureau organization approaches one of *class* within agriculture.

It should be evident that the key to Farm Bureau policy is its own organizational power. This has determined not only the policy followed in its external affairs but the form of its internal organization as well. Decentralization — building on a basis of small localized groups — has permitted a minimizing of the number of "distinct parties and interests" in its ranks. In itself, decentralization has permitted the formation of small majorities which may be pyramided into an apparently unified power easily exercised by a small group of national leaders who have arrived at their positions through the stages of state and national federations. So far as leader selection is concerned, moreover, there is even a regional stage.

Since the basis of narrowing the constituency of the Farm Bureau is one of class rather than of producer groups, it is clear that local bureaus will show considerable diversity on the latter score. A cotton group will appear as the dominant group in a cotton area, a dairy group in a dairy area, a livestock group in a livestock area. The Farm Bureau leadership has accepted the costs of this diversity. However, these costs have not been great. State farm bureaus have seldom opposed the national organization, and the conflict of interests between commodity groups has been minor and transitory. It is a type of controversy readily adapted to settlement by bargaining and logrolling among a few leaders. Thus, support for a labor policy desired by Southern or California interests can quite easily be exchanged for support of a price policy desired by Middle Western groups. The two policies do not conflict and, while the one side to the bargain may gain nothing from the other's policy which it agrees to support, neither does it suffer any loss. The result is that the national organization adopts both policies. This would appear to be the solution to the seeming paradox that, although the great center of Farm Bureau organization is in the Middle West, the Farm Bureau consistently follows a policy on matters of farm labor that benefits plantations and corporation farms in other parts of the country. Any opposition to this policy would have to come on a class basis, and the Farm Bureau organization has been formed in a way which makes this impossible.

So far as the organization of the Farm Bureau itself is concerned, then, decentralization has been the actual policy followed, and it has provided the means by which groups of farmers, diverse among themselves in some repects but similar in the important respect of class, have been unified in a national organization. Selection of the class basis of organization was somewhat of a historical accident, but, once chosen, the class basis was inevitably intensified. The effect of decentralization has been to reinforce that intensification.

Decentralization as a Farm Bureau slogan, however, has had an additional meaning, distinct from that which applies to its own organization. This is decentralization of the agencies of the federal government. From 1940 onward the Farm Bureau has sought to dismantle all "action" agencies possessing administrative structures in which there is a hierarchical flow of responsibility to the Secretary of Agriculture. This campaign culminated in a demand that the work of these agencies be placed in the hands of the state Extension services, which would be supported by a system of grants-in-aid. This is the meaning of decentralization as it is most frequently used by Farm Bureau spokesmen.

This form of decentralization is quite different from that applied by the Farm Bureau in its own organization. While the scheme of decentralization existing in the Farm Bureau permits a strong leadership at the top, the plan advocated for the governmental agencies would effectively block the national administrative direction of the agencies. The function of the Washington office would become one of passing out appropriated funds for the state organizations to spend. This function would, moreover, be substantially divorced from control of the spending. Not only would it result in forty-eight different programs, as Secretary

Wickard observed, but it would introduce a system of administrative responsibility entirely different from that which now prevails in most of the "action" programs. Administrative responsibility under such a plan of decentralization would be owed to some authority in the states and would not flow upward to Washington, except in a highly attenuated fashion.

What power, under such a plan, could be expected to exercise authority in any given state? It would be that power which is dominant in the state. We are brought back to the same set of considerations which applied to the organization of the Farm Bureau. The effect of decentralization would be to permit wide diversity among the states. It would reduce the constituency to which the political head of the programs would be answerable. Moreover, it would give additional resources to the locally dominant groups. It would be rash to assume that these groups would not use the newly delivered resources to increase their existing power. The end result would be to sharpen the lines of class differentiation within agriculture.

As long as administrative programs involve the regulation or the distribution of benefits, that is to say, the functions of government, we do not gain by drawing a rigid distinction between politics and administration. This applies to the distinction between political and administrative decentralization. The effects of administrative decentralization may arrive by a more roundabout way than those of political decentralization; they will, however, be the same.

Decentralization of political organization and government in agriculture today has two effects of great importance. The first is the narrowing of the political base. In theory this narrowing might have taken place on any of a number of different lines, but in fact it has occurred on a basis of class. The already existent lines of class have been sharpened. The second effect is the building of a structure of political power. Decentralization has been an essential condition to

163

this structure. In effect, the Farm Bureau has become an association of already existing élites in agriculture joined on a basis of class. The political power of the whole organization has, in turn, served to elevate the position of these élites, even while respecting their mutual differences.

# VII. *Farming in an Urban Society*

## I. DUALISM IN AMERICAN AGRICULTURE

Agricultural policy in the 1960's has been a product of forces differing in direction as well as intensity. One of these has been the inertia of the existing farm programs, which were built up as a part of the New Deal. The objectives of the New Deal were parity prices, control of surplus production, conservation of soil resources, and stabilization of the agricultural economy. This far-reaching public program developed institutions and organizations, both public and private, of great strength. Sectors of agriculture in which the policies paid off in terms of subsidies became quite well entrenched.

Not only did a large, powerful bureaucracy develop, but also the autonomous decision-making of private groups in league with the system tended to provide a vested interest in program perpetuation. The use of locally elected committees to make administrative decisions in Agricultural Extension and in triple A (now ASCS) are excellent examples of the Department of Agriculture's techniques. The major consequence of this type of organization has been that the public policies have favored the agricultural élite — the 10 percent of farmers that produce 50 percent of the marketed product and, to a somewhat lesser degree, the 50 percent who produce 90 percent of the marketed product. Of all farmers, the half that collectively produced only 10 percent of the total agricultural product received only minor attention in the form of public programs.

Thus by the close of the second third of the twentieth century areas of strength and of weakness in American agriculture were becoming quite visible. The tremendous productive capability of agriculture was a highly publicized characteristic but one that accurately described only a fraction of the farmers. Because one requirement of large-scale production was a decreasing ratio of people to acres, rural areas became heavily outmigrant. Yet even with outmigration, there were millions of people left behind in poverty. Thus an increase in economic class differences was partially a result of the promotional policies of the federal government.

The pattern of economic growth for agriculture required a commitment to the need for fewer and larger farms. The educational philosophy of the agricultural "establishment" sustained and justified this trend. Leon Keyserling asserts that " . . . our thinking about the farm problem is imprisoned in the myths of 'over-production' . . . and the notion that we need much fewer farmers. . . ." This apparent need for a steady liquidation of a certain part of the farm population has deepened the sense of uncertainty and insecurity in rural society. Even such a productive farm area as that surrounding Vandalia, Illinois, shares this feeling, as Joseph Lyford has observed.

## II. RURAL-URBAN INTERFACE

Beyond the justification of large-scale agriculture in production terms, another defense was necessary to provide a rationale for political support of a declining social order. Discussions of rural representation in Congress and the state legislatures brought out several aspects of the "virtues" of rural life, the need for over-representation to protect these virtues against the machine politics of cities, and the merits of rural schools, small towns, and country churches.

The insistence by the Supreme Court on equality of representation precipitated a more complete review of the relation between the country and the city. Notwithstanding considerable empirical evidence that the urban-rural classification did not provide a division into conflicting legislative groups, country voters and their representatives clung to their legislative advantage. An amendment was introduced in Congress that would give the states final authority to determine their legislative systems, but up to 1968 it had not passed with the required two-thirds majority.

The future of farming in America is obviously beset with uncertainties. The declining rural population coupled with the equal representation requirement indicates a decline in political power. Direct representation of rural areas occurs only in a shrinking minority of cases. Growing urban population and foreign demands, on the other hand, suggest a stronger market for food and fiber in the near future. Thus the economic role of agriculture is one that, combined with farm-based industries, wields great economic power which can be felt in the decisions of public policy.

In addition, the pressing social problems resulting from the influx of rural migrants into cities give national import to the conditions of American farmers. Resulting imbalances are costly in wasted human resources as well as in malfunctioning social institutions and services.

Changes in rural life and values can be expected to encompass more urban characteristics as population and population mobility increase. The use of more land for transportation, recreation, and living space rather than strictly for production is also likely. The possibilities of nonland-based food production are being explored by scientists and technologists with challenging implications for the rural social order.

*Theodore Lowi*

# 32. AGRICULTURAL SELF-GOVERNMENT

The economic welfare of agriculture has become dependent on complex policy-making machinery that combines public and private decision-making bodies. The private groups are dominated by leaders who represent the interests of important sectors of commercial agriculture and the related processing industries. The public agents are autonomous parts of the U. S. Department of Agriculture relating on one hand to the agriculture committees in Congress and on the other to farmer committees chosen at the local level. How the organization serves to insulate farm policy in autonomous public-private bodies dealing with special segments of agriculture is treated by Theodore Lowi in the selection below.

Quite early, farmers discovered the value of politics as a counter-weight to industry's growth and concentration. Land-grant and homesteading acts were followed by governmental services in research and education. Continuing distress led to bolder demands. First there were efforts to effect a redistribution of wealth in favor of agriculture. As a debtor class, farmers saw inflation as the solution, and Bryan was their spokesman for cheaper money and cheaper credit. The monopolies, the railroads, the grain merchants and other processors, the banks, and the brokers were to be deprived of power over the market by dissolution or by severe restraints. Next, farmers sought solutions by emulating the business system: the co-operative to restrain domestic trade and international dumping over high tariff walls and to restrain international trade. Yet all these mechanisms either were not enacted or did not live up to expectations.

With the coming of the New Deal and with its help, organized agriculture turned to self-regulation. The system created during the 1930's has endured to this day, and

with only a few marginal additions and alterations is accepted almost unanimously by farm leaders. Self-regulation might have taken several forms, the most likely one being a national system of farm-leader representation within a farmers' NRA. Instead, a more complicated system of highly decentralized and highly autonomous subgovernments developed, largely for Constitutional reasons. Agriculture was the most "local" of the manufacturing groups the Federal government was trying to reach. The appearance if not the reality of decentralizing Federal programs through farmer-elected local committees helped avoid strains on the interstate commerce clause of the Constitution. But this avoidance of Constitutional troubles created very special political difficulties.

### THE LOCAL COMMITTEES

The Federal Extension Service shows how the system works. It is "co-operative" in that it shares the job of farm improvement

From Theodore Lowi, "How the Farmers Get What They Want" in *The Reporter*, vol. 30 (May 21, 1964), pp. 35-36. Copyright 1964 by The Reporter Magazine Company, and reprinted with their permission.

with the states, the land-grant colleges, the county governments, and the local associations of farmers. The county agent is actually employed by the local associations. In the formative years, the aid of local chambers of commerce was enlisted, the local association being the "farm bureau" of the chamber. In order to co-ordinate local activities and to make more effective claims for additional outside assistance, these farm bureaus were organized into state farm bureau federations. The American Farm Bureau Federation, formed at the Agriculture College of Cornell University in 1919, was used as a further step toward amalgamation. To this day there is a close relationship between the farm bureaus, the land-grant colleges, and the Extension Service. This transformation of an administrative arrangement into a political system has been repeated in nearly all the agricultural programs during recent decades. The Extension Service exercises few controls from the top. There are cries of "Federal encroachment" at the mere suggestion in Washington that the Department of Agriculture should increase its supervision of the extension programs or co-ordinate them with other Federal activities.

As the financial stakes have grown larger, the pattern of local self-government remains the same. Price support — the "parity program" — is run by the thousands of farmer-elected county committees that function alongside but quite independently of the other local committees. Acreage allotments to bring supply down and prices up are apportioned among the states by the Agricultural Stabilization and Conservation Service. State committees of farmers apportion the allotment among the counties. The farmer-elected county Stabilization and Conservation Committees receive the county allotment.

These committees made the original acreage allotments among individual farmers back in the 1930's; today, they make new allotments, work out adjustments and review complaints regarding adjustments, determine whether quotas have been com-

plied with, inspect and approve storage facilities, and perform as the court of original jurisdiction on violations of price-support rules and on eligibility for parity payments. The committees are also vitally important in the campaigns for the two-thirds vote required to fix high price supports. Congress determines the general level of supports, and the Secretary of Agriculture proclaims the national acreage quotas for adjusting the supply to the guaranteed price. But the locally elected committees stand between the farmer and Washington.

Most other agricultural programs have evolved similarly. Each is independent of the others, and any conflicts or overlapping mandates have been treated as nonexistent or beyond the jurisdiction of any one agency. The Soil Conservation Service operates through its independent soil-conservation districts, of which there were 2,936 in 1963, involving ninety-six percent of the nation's farms. Each district's farmer-elected committee is considered a unit of local government. The Farmer Co-operative Service operates through member-elected boards of directors of the farm co-ops. In agricultural credit, local self-government is found in even greater complexity. The Farm Credit Administration exists outside the Department of Agriculture and is made up of not one but three separate bodies politic, a triangular system mostly farmer-owned and totally farmer-controlled.

### TEN SYSTEMS AND POLITICS

The ten principal self-governing systems in agriculture, in fiscal 1962, disposed of $5.6 billion of the total of $6.7 billion in expenditures passing through the Department of Agriculture. During the calendar year 1962, $5.8 billion in loans were handled similarly. This combined amount represents a large portion of the total of Federal activity outside national defense.

Each of the ten systems has become a powerful political instrumentality. The self-governing local units become one important force in a system that administers a program and maintains the autonomy of that program against political forces emanating from other agricultural programs, from antagonistic farm and nonfarm interests, from Congress, from the Secretary of Agriculture, and from the President. To many a farmer, the local outpost of one or another of these systems *is* the government.

The politics within each system is built upon a triangular trading pattern involving the central agency, a Congressional committee or subcommittee, and the local district farmer committees (usually federated in some national or regional organization). Each side of the triangle complements and supports the other two.

The Extension Service, for example, is one side of the triangle completed by the long-tenure "farm bureau" members of the Agricultural Committees in Congress and, at the local level, the American Farm Bureau Federation with its local committees. Further group support is provided by two intimately related groups, the Association of Land Grant Colleges and Universities and the National Association of County Agricultural Agents.

Another such triangle unites the Soil Conservation Service, the Agriculture subcommittee of the House Appropriations Committee, and the local districts organized in the energetic National Association of Soil Conservation Districts. Further support comes from the Soil Conservation Society of America (mainly professionals) and the former Friends of the Land, now the Izaak Walton League of America.

Probably the most complex of the systems embraces the parity program. It connects the Agricultural Stabilization and Conservation Service with the eight (formerly ten) commodity subcommittees of the House Agriculture Committee and the dozens of separately organized groups representing the various commodities. (Examples: National Cotton Council, American Wool Growers Association, American Cranberry Growers Association.) These groups and Congressmen draw support from the local price-support committees wherever a particular commodity is grown.

### THE FARMER HAD HIS WAY

These systems have a vigorous capacity to maintain themselves and to resist encroachment. They have such institutional legitimacy that they have become practically insulated from the three central sources of democratic political responsibility. Thus, within the Executive branch, they are autonomous. Secretaries of Agriculture have tried and failed to consolidate or even to coordinate related programs. Within Congress, they are sufficiently powerful to be able to exercise an effective veto or create a stalemate. And they are almost totally removed from the view, not to mention the control, of the general public. (Throughout the 1950's, Victor Anfuso of Brooklyn was the only member of the House Agriculture Committee from a non-farm constituency.)

Important cases illustrate their power:

In 1947, Secretary of Agriculture Clinton P. Anderson proposed a consolidation of all soil-conservation, price-support, and FHA programs into one committee system with a direct line from the committees to the Secretary. Bills were prepared providing for consolidation within the price-support committees. Contrary bills provided for consolidation under soil conservation districts. The result: stalemate. In 1948, a leading farm senator proposed consolidation of the programs under the local associations of the Extension Service. Immediately a House farm leader introduced a contrary bill. The result: continuing stalemate.

In Waco, Texas on October 14, 1952, Presidential candidate Eisenhower said: "I would like to see in every county all Federal farm agencies under the same roof." Pursuant to this promise, Secretary Ezra Taft Benson issued a series of orders during early 1953 attempting to bring about consolidation of local units as well as unification at the top. Finally, amid cries of "sneak attack" and "agricrat," Benson proclaimed that "any work on the further consolidation of county and state offices . . . shall be suspended."

From the very beginning, Secretary Benson sought to abandon rigid price supports and bring actual supports closer to market prices. In 1954, as he was beginning to succeed, Congress enacted a "commodity set-aside" by which $2.5 billion of surplus commodities already held by the government were declared to be a "frozen reserve" for national defense. Since the Secretary's power to cut price supports depends heav-ily upon the amount of government-owned surplus carried over from previous years, the commodity set-aside was a way of freezing parity as well as reserves. Benson eventually succeeded in reducing supports on the few commodities over which he had authority. But thanks to the set-aside, Congress between fiscal 1952 and 1957, helped increase the value of commodities held by the government from $1.1 billion to $5.3 billion. What appeared, therefore, to be a real Republican policy shift amounted to no more than giving back with one hand what had been taken away by the other.

*Leon H. Keyserling*

## 33. " . . . THE FARM PROBLEM . . . IS NOT INSOLUBLE"

Not all economists are in agreement that the costs, personal and social, that have accompanied the application of technology to farming, are unavoidable. As a starting point, the selection printed below analyzes these costs further and probes the causes of this "tragic uprooting of farm people."

Another approach is suggested, one that would keep people on the land, providing them with income supports through direct government action. The author believes incomes must be supported well above the poverty level both on and off the farm. If this were done, he thinks the problem of surplus production would no longer be serious. It should be noted that the position taken by this writer is not one that would be supported by a preponderance of agricultural economists; their agreement would extend to the statement of the problem but not much further.

### THE TRAGIC UPROOTING OF FARM PEOPLE

The purpose of farm life is not only to supply a great nation with foods and fibers; it is also to provide those who desire to live on and by the land the genuine opportunity to do so. Our country today has both the resources and the needs, within reasonable bounds, to afford those who want to farm a range of opportunities and rewards comparable to those who want to be merchants, professional people, or industrial workers.

Of course, in the long span of time, the progressive allocation of smaller portions of the total civilian labor force to the production of foods and fibers is the very hallmark of a rapidly advancing industrial civilization and generally rising living standards. This has conferred immense benefits upon the nonfarm population. And in those times when this process was accompanied by ample opportunity for those leaving the land of their own free will to be absorbed rewardingly in other sectors of economic

From Leon H. Keyserling, *Agriculture and the Public Interest* (Washington, D.C., February, 1965), pp. 15-17, 42-45. Reprinted by permission of The Conference on Economic Progress.

endeavor, there was no cause for rational complaint.

But the size and speed of the farm population decline since World War II has been neither voluntary nor desirable. It has contributed neither to the well-being of the farm population nor to the well-being of others. For the farmer has not been drawn off the land by opportunity; he has been forced off the land by hardship. He has not abandoned his farm; he has lost it. And he has not found a haven elsewhere; he has merely compounded the problems of unemployment, poverty, and "insoluble" municipal problems in our urban areas.

## The Forcing of Farmers Off the Land

The data which depict how many farmers have left the land have one serious shortcoming: they do not reveal that a substantial portion of the farm population has remained on the land, not because their circumstances there have been satisfactory nor even tolerable, but rather for the opposite reason that their intolerable plight has not generated either the resources or the will to try their luck elsewhere. The people who have left the land have had a hard time. But in general, they have come from less miserably depressed sectors of the farm population than those who have had squeezed out of them even that element of hope which prompts people to try to make a change.

Nonetheless, the number of farmers who *have* left the land has been appalling, all things considered. The total number of U.S. farms declined from 5.9 million in 1947 to 5.2 million in 1952, and 3.5 million in 1964. The 1964 number was almost 33 percent below 1952, and more than 40 percent below 1947. Over the same span of years, the total number of people working on farms (agricultural concept) declined from 10.4 million to 9.1 million, and then to 6.1 million. The number in 1964 was 33 percent below 1952, and 41 percent below 1947. Meanwhile, the total farm population declined from 25.8 million to 21.7 million, and then to 13.3 mil-

lion, or more than 38 percent below 1952, and more than 48 percent below 1947. Measured in ratio to the total U. S. population, the farm population fell from 17.9 percent to 13.8 percent, and then to 6.9 percent.

## Undesirable Trends in the Structure of Farming

The deflation of farm income and the forcing of farmers off the land have been both cause and effect of unfortunate changes in the business structure of agriculture. The part-time and residential noncommercial farms, which participate inconsequentially in total farm sales and are not a substantial element in the economics of the farm problem, rose from about 31 percent of total farms in 1949 to 37 percent in 1964. The substandard farms, practically all of whose occupants live in abject poverty, declined from more than 46 percent of total farms to less than 19 percent. This in itself has not been an undesirable trend; substandard farms are certainly not a consummation devoutly to be wished. But their sales in ratio to total sales of farm products declined far more rapidly, from 24 percent to 5.6 percent. And this can mean only that the relative economic position of those lowest on the farm-income ladder has worsened greatly.

The ground lost by the substandard farms would have been compensated for, at least in part, if it had represented an equivalent shift toward family-type farms. Superficially, this shift might seem indicated, for the family-type farms rose from 20.5 percent of total farms in 1949 to 40.2 percent in 1964. But a family-type farm loses a large part of its ultimate value, both in economic and human terms, if the trends in its share of total farm sales lag far behind the trends in its numerical strength relative to the total number of farms. Comparing 1964 with 1949, while the family-type farm advanced greatly by the first of these two criteria, it advanced hardly at all by the second—its share of total farm sales rose only from 47.5 percent to 51.7 percent. Moreover, from 1959

171

forward, this share hardly increased at all. What this really imports is that many farms, classified as family-type because of their volume of sales, have really become substandard in terms of income, and have borne an immense part of the burden of deficient farm income. And in absolute numbers, of course, the family-type farm has joined in the severe contraction of the total number of farms.

The net beneficiaries of the shifts in the farm structure have been the large to giant-size farms. From 1949 to 1964, these advanced from less than 2 percent to more than 4 percent of total farms, and increased their sales from 26 percent to 39 percent of total farm sales.

The shift from the family-type farm to the large and giant-size farm cannot be extenuated on grounds of relative efficiency. First of all, above the level of the substandard farms, there is no dearth of efficiency and productivity advance in American agriculture; quite the reverse is true. Second, there is no conclusive and perhaps no respectable evidence that the large to giant-size farm is more efficient than the family-type farm, when the latter receives enough income to realize its full potentials. Third, even if the shift from the family-type farm to the large and giant-size farm yielded some slight net efficiency gain within the confines of agriculture, this would be more than counterbalanced by the damaging effect to the whole national economy, resulting from the excessively rapid shrinkage of the farm population and the total number of farmers. And fourth, agriculture has now become so productive—and so has our whole economy—that we need to become more deeply concerned about the quality of farm life, and not merely about the "efficiency" of farm production.

This means that we should strive constantly for a more appropriate balance and distribution among farms of different sizes, with particular accent upon the family-type farm. While farm workers who are neither farm owners nor managers should be well paid, an independent farm family with a good income is far preferable to even a well-paid employee of factories in the field (which are not distinguished for the liberality of their wage payments). The only hope for most of the substandard farmers is that they be accorded opportunity to operate family-type farms.

Those national farm policies which have borne a real share of the responsibility for the persistent deflation of farm income must answer also for the unfortunate shifts in the structure of farming which are a by-product of this income deflation. And those undesirable policies involve not only sins of omission, but also sins of commission. For the national farm policy has done far too much for those who need help least, and far too little for those who need help most.

\* \* \*

## THE REAL REASONS FOR DEFICIENT FARM INCOME

### *The Prime Explanation: The Farmer's Relative Weakness in the Market Place*

The farm-income problem has been with us for so long because of the relative weakness of the farmer in the market place. And although this palpable truth has been the reason for almost all national farm policy, intended to compensate for this relative weakness, the results have fallen far short of this goal. Most others buy and sell in highly organized and "administered" markets, where the law of supply and demand is greatly modified, if not negated entirely by administered prices and collective bargaining. But the farmer buys in these highly organized and "administered" markets and sells in the "free" market. In consequence, even while a very small gap between what the farmer produces and what is used drives farm income sharply downward (and while this income is so far short of parity even when demand exceeds supply), industrial producers are able to take care of themselves even when there is a huge gap between their ability to produce and what is used.

The validity of this contrast is not greatly affected by the fact that others can voluntarily turn off their production, while the farmer cannot do so in meaningful concert. Besides, the power which others have applies not only to the productive process, but even more importantly to the pricing mechanism. The steel industry did not reduce its prices even during the Great Depression. Many key industrial prices rose sharply, even during some of the recessionary periods since the Korean war when the surpluses of idle industrial plants and manpower were very high and on the rise. The "paradox" of rising prices during periods of economic recession was not a paradox in the modern economy.

## The Declining Parity Ratio

To illustrate the truths set forth above: The basic foundation of national farm policy is to maintain a balance or parity between prices paid and prices received by farmers. But prices received by farmers dropped almost 8 percent from 1947 to 1953, and dropped almost 7 percent from 1953 to 1964, thus falling more than 14 percent from 1947 to 1964. Meanwhile, prices paid by farmers rose almost 16 percent from 1947 to 1953, and almost 13 percent from 1953 to 1964, thus rising more than 30 percent during the postwar period as a whole. Consequently the parity ratio, 115 in 1947, declined to 92 in 1953, and 76 in 1964—the lowest in any year under review (in the recessionary year 1953, the parity ratio was 92; in 1960, just before "the longest economic recovery on record" commenced, it was 80).

What all this means for farm income can be more fully understood, once it is recognized that even in 1947, when the parity ratio was 115, the farmer had only about 60 percent of income parity with others. This demonstrates that the parity formula is in many respects outmoded, and that a price formula is no substitute for an income objective. Farmers, like others, live by their incomes, not by their prices.

## Another Major Explanation: General Underconsumption

Applying desirable relationships between total consumer spending and its main components, the deficiency of more than 393 billion dollars in total consumer spending during 1953-1964 as a whole meant a deficiency of about 124 billion dollars in consumer expenditures for food, and about 40 billion in their expenditures for clothing. Taking into account the farm-to-market spread, these deficiencies reduced farm marketing of food about 49 billion dollars, and of products for clothing and shoes about 6 billion, totaling about 55 billion. This, in turn, reduced net farm operators' income by about 25 billion.

This 25-billion-dollar figure, contrasted with the earlier-mentioned deficit of more than 84 billion in net farm operators' income during the twelve-year period, indicates that about 30 percent of the farm income trouble has been due directly to the highly inadequate levels of general prosperity and economic activity in the U. S. About 70 percent has been due to inadequate exports, and, far more importantly, to the weakness of the farmer in the market place. These causal factors interact, because all of the deficiency in farm income affects overall economic activity.

## Effect of Inadequate Nonfarm Wages Upon Farm Income

Much propaganda has sought to place in conflict the legitimate interests of the nonfarm wage earner and the farmer. But in truth, serious deficiencies in nonfarm wages have contributed mightily to the total consumer income deficiency which has impacted so severely upon farm income. For the twelve-year period under review, and also in 1964, the deficiency in wages and salaries constituted more than three-quarters of the total consumer income deficiency. The reasons have been excessively high unemployment; abysmally low wages among millions not protected by the Fair Labor Standards Act; and the failure of wage-rate increases during recent years to keep up with productivity advances, despite much agitation that wage-rate increases have been outrunning productivity gains and contributing to inflationary pressures.

The impact of deficient nonfarm wages and salaries upon farm income is greatly aggravated because those lower down in the income scale spend relatively larger portions of their incomes for food than higher-income families. Urban consumer units with incomes of $15,000 and over spend on the average less than an eighth of their disposable income for food; those with incomes between $3,000 and $4,000, about a quarter; those in the $2,000-$3,000 income grouping, more than 27 percent; and those in the under-$1,000 income grouping, 44 percent. A rapid upward movement in the incomes of wage and salary earners in the lowest income third of the population, and particularly in the lowest income fifth, would be beneficial to the whole economy, and especially to farmers. While the spending of these people for food would fall in ratio to their total spending, it would increase greatly in absolute amounts.

## Impact of Nonfarm Poverty Upon Farm Income

In 1963, 7½ million nonfarm families with incomes under $3,000, and close to 4½ million nonfarm unrelated individuals with incomes under $1,500, lived in poverty. Drawing upon data contained in the Department of Agriculture's Moderate Cost Plan, it is estimated that these poor people suffered a deficiency of more than 7 billion dollars in their outlays for food in 1964. If their incomes had been modestly above the poverty level, the beneficial effects upon farm-product consumption measured in physical units, might well have been as follows in 1964: dairy products utilization, 7 percent higher; meat, fish, and poultry, 11 percent; fats and oils, 8 percent; vegetables and fruits, 10 percent; and all food products, 9 percent higher, or about 28 billion pounds higher. Thus, rapid progress in the war against poverty off the farm would tremendously implement the war against poverty on the farm.

## Effects of Changing Patterns of Consumer Outlays

As already indicated, per capita food outlays in ratio to total per capita consumer outlays declined from 25.4 percent in 1947 to 20.1 percent in 1964. This, and the increasing farm-to-market spread, have led to excessively pessimistic conclusions that the relative inelasticity of demand for food as consumer incomes rise augurs ill for farm income. But for reasons earlier set forth, the improved income distribution which would be so helpful to the U. S. economy and people at large, and to the war against poverty, would substantially modify the downward trend in food outlays relative to total consumer outlays. These developments would also tend to reduce the farm-to-market spread. Insofar as this spread represents processing, packaging and other distributional services, these cost elements are more prominent in food purchases of high-income families than in those of lower-income families.

More generally, as living standards rise, patterns of food consumption also change. For example, on a properly price-weighted basis, the index of per capita food consumption (1957–1959 = 100) rose from 102 in 1947 to 108 in 1964 for meat, and from 64 to 114 for poultry. Meanwhile, the index dropped from 115 to 98 for cereal products. As these trends represent substantially a shift toward more highly priced foods, their continuation would be highly beneficial to farm income, if the forces operating so severely against farm income were overcome.

*Influence of Highly Erratic Exports Upon Farm Income*

U. S. exports of wheat, measured in product amounts, dropped from 46 percent of total domestic production in 1951 to 23.3 percent in 1953, and jumped from 28.6 percent in 1958 to 40 percent in 1959. Exports of cotton fell from 25.2 percent in 1954 to 15 percent in 1955, and jumped from 22.5 percent in 1962 to 36.9 percent in 1963. Exports of tobacco, while exhibiting more stability, dropped from 29.5 percent in 1955 to 25.6 percent in 1956, and rose from 23 percent in 1962 to 26 percent in 1963. A small fraction of these ups and downs may be explained as "natural" or "to be expected." But in the main, they reflect the highly erratic and unstable characteristics of our national policies with respect to food exports, both on a commercial and a noncommercial basis.

Steve Allen

## 34. AGRIBUSINESS: THE CORPORATE FARMER

In the states of the Southwest modernized agriculture has produced tremendous wealth. Fortunes have been built upon cattle, grain, vegetables, fruit, and water rights. The *hacienda* has become a part of an industrial complex combining agricultural production with great transportation and processing firms. These interrelated enterprises are termed *agribusiness*—the interlocking farm and commercial organizations that provide much of the food and fiber for American consumers and for the export market.

The type of farming found in the Southwest requires a large proportion of seasonal labor. Although mechanization has reduced this need somewhat, the reduction in the amount of labor required has tended to increase the hardship and insecurity of those who labor on the great farms.

The author of the selection below has been concerned for a long time about the plight of the farm workers of the Southwest—most of whom are Mexican-Americans. He has joined in presenting the problems created by this form of agricultural production to Congressional committees and other policy-making bodies. He writes with a first-hand knowledge of the problem.

Thus far I have talked about the American farm worker in terms of his impoverished lot, his bleak day-by-day existence, his forlorn future. Because he is treated like the dirt in which he grovels for a living, it might seem that he is an inconsequential spare cog in a smoothly functioning machine. But in fact he is a key part of the field-to-table process, an indispensable man in an industry that rings up billions of dollars a year in re-

From *The Ground Is Our Table* by Steve Allen, pp. 43–48. Copyright © 1966 by Steve Allen. Reprinted by permission of Doubleday & Company, Inc.

ceipts. Why is he the forgotten man in the march of progress that has made American agriculture the most productive in the world? Forgotten even though it is claimed he is in short supply? The answer is bound up in the evolution of American agriculture from the individual family farm to the huge corporate land complex.

Until the era of World War I, the family farm was the stereotype of American agriculture. Its modest acreage was tended by the farmer and his sons, aided at harvest-time by a few hired hands. Symbolized by the windmill, the hand pump, the plow, and the red barn, it survives today largely in the popular imagination.

Eventually, revolutionary technical developments were introduced to farming which brought about radical change. Rapid refrigerated freight-car and truck transportation facilities, chemical preservatives, and food-freezing techniques made it possible for farmers to specialize in otherwise perishable crops and market them under more effectively controlled conditions. As growers discovered greater profits in individual, specialized crops, they switched over most of their acreage to them. This meant that the harvest season could no longer be spread over a major part of the year. There was a very busy planting season followed in time by a hectic harvest season, with periods of relative leisure in between. As agriculture moved inexorably in the direction of specialization, requiring large quotas of farm workers in certain places at certain times, the roots of the present farm labor problem took hold.

Revolutionary developments were also occurring in the factories that manufactured farm machinery. Powerful tractors pulling large plows, cultivators, and harvesters, as well as advances in methods of fertilization and irrigation, led to higher yields per acre with less physical effort and smaller labor requirements. *Fortune* magazine in June, 1955, sketched the change: "The most important development in the history of American agriculture, by all odds has been

the spectacular way its productivity has been improved in the last quarter century. Thanks to a fertile progressive technology, the average U. S. farm worker is 110 percent more productive than he was twenty-five years ago, and so 37 percent fewer farm workers, putting in fewer hours, are producing 50 percent more than U. S. agriculture produced twenty-five years ago."

One aspect of this agricultural revolution has been the accelerating trend toward the merger of small farms into larger ones. There has been an evolution toward fewer and larger farms, and a corresponding increase in the share of the total agricultural output for which the mammoth farms, ranches, and orchards are responsible. (The old image of the individual farmer endures for the simple reason that for thousands of years it was the only image. Even today, simple peasant farmers comprise more than two thirds of the population of our planet. Seventy per cent of the nearly three billion living humans are occupied in farming in one form or another. It is primarily in the United States that farming has changed so drastically.)

Agriculture has simply followed the trend of other American industries toward consolidation, bigness, and domination by the few. To identify the corporate complex, which so closely resembles the rest of U. S. industry, the descriptive term "agribusiness" has been coined. The enormous farms and ranches of agribusiness, some encompassing thousands of acres, are corporately owned, often by absentee landlords, groups of investors, or holding companies. Surprisingly, such companies as Standard Oil and the Southern Pacific Railroad are heavily involved in agribusiness through their farmland holdings. A vast amount of acreage is owned or leased by such integrated field-to-supermarket giants as the California Packing Corporation and Stokely-Van Camp.

It has been said that the strings of California's $3.6-billion-a-year agribusiness are pulled from the redwood-paneled offices on

San Francisco's Montgomery Street, the Wall Street of the West. In addition to growers, packers, processors, middlemen, and distributors, agribusiness embraces allied enterprises such as banks (the Bank of America, the world's largest, is the prime financer of California farms), shipping and transportation companies, land companies (Kern County Land Company, for all practical purposes, *is* Kern County), and utilities, plus other large corporations which have a stake in the prosperity of the field-to-table process.

The anatomy of this "giant octopus," as one packing company executive put it, can be seen by studying the interlocking directorships of the agribusiness corporations. Packing executives sit on the boards of directors of banks and land companies. Bankers who trade in farm loans proliferate on the boards of packing and land companies. Realty executives who deal in farm acreage sit on the boards of shipping and packing companies. The labyrinth goes on and on.

As a group agribusiness executives are hardheaded and dollar-oriented, which is by way of saying they are not much different from executives in other fields. The tremendous technological advances of agriculture are all to their credit, but where they differ from executives in other fields is in their archaic concept of their responsibility to human beings.

An admirable exception is Norton Simon, chief executive of Hunt Foods and Industries, the nation's largest tomato processor. A man of broad horizons who is an art connoisseur and a regent of both the huge University of California and the tiny liberal Reed College of Portland, Oregon, Simon not long ago expressed his version of the function of a modern corporation: "We are beyond the day and age of the need of capitalism for survival. We need it for only one thing—the betterment of the human being. Certainly we have a lot more than we can eat, haven't we?"

As with other industrial interests, agri-business maintains well-financed lobbies to foster public sympathy and promote favorable legislation. The late James P. Mitchell, Secretary of Labor under Eisenhower, spoke bluntly of the power of the agribusiness lobby. The effort is spearheaded by the conservative American Farm Bureau Federation, which is active on Capitol Hill. Various state and regional groups lobby within their sphere of influence. The Council of California Growers, for example, represents the large growers who supply the packers, food chains, and marketing cooperatives. The State Board of Agriculture, which has a hand in setting agricultural policy, is overwhelmingly grower-dominated. The pattern of tightly organized agribusiness lobbies is repeated in other agricultural states.

There is a mistaken impression that agri-business speaks for the American farmer, and that the farm labor problem is a burden shared by *all* U. S. farmers. Actually the problem belongs almost exclusively to agribusiness, which rules those crops requiring large quantities of seasonal labor: cotton, vegetables, and fruits. About 54 percent of all farms hire no labor whatsoever. On 41 percent of the farms the farmer and members of his family do practically all the work. *Five percent of the farms pay three quarters of the nation's farm wages and they are the huge farms of agribusiness.*

The agricultural revolution has found the small farmer sitting on the opposite side of the fence from agribusiness. In trying to get a fair price for his food and fiber, he is bucking the same powerful bloc that the farm laborer fights in trying to get a fair wage. When the small farmer goes to market, buyers do not bid for his produce. The buyer from one large packing or processing firm offers the same low price as the buyer from another—take it or leave it.

Protest against such unfree-enterprise collusion is drowned out by the clamor of such other "farmers" as the Kern County Land Company, which owns 2800 square miles of land in fourteen states, an empire *twice the size of Rhode Island*; Standard Oil, which holds more than 218,000 acres in Southern California; the Southern Pacific, which claims 201,000 acres in the same region; the Tejon Ranch in Southern California with its approximately 315 square miles, about the size of New York City's five boroughs.

John C. Van Deusen

## 35. BLACK FARMER—WHITE GOVERNMENT

Conditions among the share-croppers in the southern states reveal the seamy side of American agriculture. Among these the conditions of the black farmer have been the seamiest of all. Once entrapped by debt to his landlord, a form of peonage supported by the legal structure of the southern states has resulted. The author of the piece below cites examples of the practice of creditor landlords of selling their labor claims against their share-tenants—in essence selling the Negro—to someone in need of labor.

The New Deal offered some hope of remedying the worst features of the share-cropper system. However, too often the program was administered so as to help the landlord exclusively. White government of the black farmer has, unfortunately, not been color-blind.

The living conditions of practically all classes of agricultural Negroes are deplorable. The one-room hovel is not in evidence as often as formerly, but it is still to be seen in too many communities. The majority of their cabins are tumbledown shacks—dirty, ill-smelling and poorly ventilated. The most elementary conveniences are usually lacking. Fireplaces have generally given place to cook stoves, but otherwise there is little furniture. A circus poster may decorate the walls; possibly a fly-specked picture of Lincoln or Robert E. Lee. Ignorance and poverty make any improvement in low standards of living exceedingly slow. The almost equal backwardness of their poor white neighbors precludes their learning from this source. The food has a monotonous sameness—salt pork, bacon, corn pone and molasses. Vegetables may be added if the family have the foresight to utilize the patches of land about the cabin. Sometimes a few fruit trees are growing about and there are always wild blackberries. The more progressive Negroes will preserve a considerable amount of fruit for winter use. Others own a pig which may be fed on table refuse, and chickens often help to vary the family menu. But as a rule there is no garden, no potato patch, and little live stock. Too frequently the cow is unmilked while the family buys butter at the village store. Ill-balanced diet reflects itself in poor health. In large areas of the Southeastern United States deaths from pellagra, a diet deficiency disease, are nine times the average for the country.

The late Booker T. Washington never ceased to urge upon his people the wisdom of land ownership, and many Southern Negroes have embraced the opportunity to

From John G. Van Deusen, *The Black Man in White America,* Washington, D.C.: Associated Publishers, Inc., 1944, pp. 20-23, 27-29. Reprinted by permission of the publisher.

own farms. The census of 1940 shows 22,250 Negro farm owners in Virginia, 18,245 in North Carolina, 17,084 in South Carolina, 15,692 in Alabama, 23,427 in Mississippi, 20,115 in Texas, 10,018 in Georgia, 10,553 in Arkansas, and 11,187 in Louisiana. But this probably states the case in too favorable a light since 29.9 per cent of the land "owned" is subject to mortgage. Furthermore, the census makes no distinction between the petty producer who owns a few acres and the large land-owner. Probably at least three-fourths of the owners belong to the former class.

All things considered, the outlook of the Southern agricultural Negro is not hopeful. Both the number of owners and the acreage owned have been steadily declining since 1910. The most numerous class of Southern nonwhite farmers is the sharecropper; "other tenants" constitute the next most numerous class, followed by owners. All three classes decreased in number between 1930 and 1940. The census of 1920 showed 700,000 fewer Negroes in agriculture than in 1910, and the count of 1930 revealed a further falling off of 200,000. The enumeration of 1940 showed a further decrease of 200,000 despite the high rate of natural increase in this group. The displaced agricultural Negroes divide themselves into various classes: many become farm wage hands; others go to the towns and cities. A large number were forced onto the farm relief rolls, and other large numbers became migratory farm workers. These facts justify two conclusions: First, that the Southern rural Negro is sinking in the economic scale; and second, that he is rapidly abandoning the farm for the city. Indeed, a Bureau of the Census finds during the decade ending 1940 a decrease of 20,457 farms operated by Negroes in Alabama, 22,545 in Arkansas, 27,660 in Georgia, and 33,292 in Texas. This situation is due to maladjustment of the landlord-tenant relationship, occasionally manifesting itself in violence, but more frequently in inability to secure fair settlements, inability to make a living on worn-out soil, and mechanization. The remark is frequently made, "We couldn't do any worse off on the road, so we left."

The difficulty in securing satisfactory settlements is connected with the system of advances which keeps the tenant continually in debt. When food and clothing are bought on credit, there is every temptation to buy that which immediately costs nothing; and the end of the crop year frequently finds the tenant, after his rent is paid, unable to pay his debt to the store with the balance. Dishonesty on the part of white merchants adds to his difficulties, for the illiterate Negro keeps no books and it is easy and profitable to charge him fancy prices of supplies drawn, and just as easy and still more profitable to charge him with imaginary purchases. Usually in debt to the plantation store, Negroes find that no matter whether the crop be great or small, their debts are as big as their crops. There are exceptions, of course, but they are exceptions. Negro leaders are persistent in charging that the race is being systematically cheated, and even Southern whites admit that there has been unfair dealing.

The tenant farmer is at a further disadvantage because he cannot sell the cotton which his own hand produces. The law of most Southern states gives valid title only to the landlord. This legal advantage has been so used as to produce grave discontent among Negro tenantry. The Negro has no means of knowing the price received for his cotton. The landlord may purchase it at a low price, selling it later on his own account at a higher figure. Even if he were honest, the Negro tenant, expecting to be cheated, would hardly be convinced of that fact. Until recent years the labor supply of the South has been insufficient to meet the needs of agriculture and there was a strong temptation for landlords to use every means to retain tenants on their land. By delaying settlements until late spring, when the next crop is already in the ground, the landlord could make it impossible for the colored tenant to move elsewhere; and he then had no choice but to accept any terms which his white patron offered. Many white landowners are inclined to consider it a reflection on their character to be asked to render a statement of their tenant's account, and satisfy themselves by merely telling him that he is in debt. There is a widespread opinion among Negroes that it is useless to appeal to the courts. The landlord is the only one who keeps a record and his book would be accepted as final by any court of law. Indeed, "it is not easy to get capable lawyers to take Negroes' cases against landlords, even when it is quite apparent injustice is being done them." . . .

The county agent sometimes delivered the croppers' checks to the landlord on the theory that "it isn't customary for niggers to get checks." The result was that many a peon cropper, clad in a patchwork of rags, plowed under his cotton and got nothing for his season's labor. Query: Was the object of the A.A.A. to give the farmer more purchasing power or to help Southern landlords to collect their debts? In the meantime, the combination of N.R.A., processing taxes, and currency depreciation was boosting the price of commodities.

In the following year (1934) the government sought to avoid the "plow-under" by making contracts to reduce cotton acreage. In the furtherance of this plan it offered a subsidy of four and one-half cents a pound for the cotton which would have been produced on the acreage withdrawn from production. But again the landlord received the lion's share of the benefit, for the contract gave him four cents a pound for the cotton withdrawn from production, while the tenant received but a half cent. The A.A.A., by pegging cotton prices, was of assistance to the large landowner. But, so far as the Negro was concerned, the cotton reduction program merely resulted in a reduction of the number of tenant contracts. Any scheme to limit cotton production cannot fail to accomplish the same result. As a class, the Negro is totally ignorant of general farming, and a reduction of cotton bales must be ac-

companied by a reduction of cotton producing Negroes. Mr. Norman Thomas declared that from 15 to 20 percent of the share croppers were "sent down the road" as a result of Mr. Roosevelt's experiment in "planned economy." Those turned adrift must journey to the city in a dubious quest of employment or be thrown on doubtful charity. For those who remain on the plantation, an oversupply of labor means lower wages and more intensive exploitation.

After the Supreme Court declared the Agricultural Adjustment Act unconstitutional, the New Deal attempted to continue its objectives under the Soil Conservation Act (1936). The object of this measure was to shift 30,000,000 acres of land from soil depleting crops to soil conserving crops. The method was the payment of a subsidy of $10 an acre to farmers who would join a county producers' association and meet certain planting requirements. As in previous legislation, the major portion of the bonus was to accrue to the benefit of the owner of the land rather than the tenant. Dr. Monroe N. Work writes thus:

Many are raising the question whether under the new Soil Conservation Act, Negro farmers, particularly tenants, will fare any better than they did under the Agricultural Adjustment Act, for the old Agricultural Adjustment Administration has been designated as the agency to administer the new Soil Conservation law. The set-up per state, county and community committees are also practically the same as under the Agricultural Adjustment Act. . . .

The most helpful aspect of Southern rural life is found in the work of the farm and home demonstrators. The farm demonstrator is usually a practical farmer who has the additional advantages of special training in scientific methods. He is employed by the Federal Department of Agriculture to give demonstration work in his county or district. He gives advice on the qualities of seeds and types of fertilizers, and attempts to induce farmers to follow modern methods. The increase in the value of farm crops since 1910 testifies to the value of such work. • Unfortunately the colored farmers have not received their fair proportion of such training. Funds from the state and federal governments are available only when the county contributes its share, and lack of interest in the welfare of the colored farmer has led to neglect in the appointing of colored agents.

*Phil Santora*

## 36. **THE GREAT MIGRATION**

The retrogressive trends in southern agriculture have been hastened by increasing mechanization and the inability to make the social adaptation necessary for a progressive and achieving society. Relentless deterioration of the economy of the southern Negro farmer has caused "a vast shift of poverty-ridden Negroes" into the ghettoes of cities, for the most part in the North. This movement has created a whole new series of social problems culminating in the shattering of American urban life. Thus the failure of a sector of rural life has had unfortunate consequences throughout American society.

This is the story of the greatest migration in this nation's recent history — a vast population shift involving mostly poverty-ridden Negroes — and one whose causes and effects have become a national problem.

To get a first-hand picture of the reasons for the migration, this reporter and a *News* photographer traveled two weeks in the South. We couldn't get a complete picture — the canvas is just too huge — but we talked with enough people in Georgia, Mississippi, Alabama and Louisiana to confirm a suspicion frequently voiced.

NEEDY MILLIONS ON THE MOVE

That suspicion, baldly stated, is that Negroes, many of them made surplus by labor-saving farm machinery, are being pushed out. Some would say frozen out.

Result: The burden of caring for these people is being transferred, on a gigantic scale, to cities in the North and West.

This story, it must be stated, comes largely from people eager to complain and protest. The others wouldn't talk or weren't available.

Some idea of the proportions of the exodus is provided by U. S. Census Bureau and Department of Labor figures, which reveal that in the years 1960–65 more than two million Negroes left the South.

Of these, one million found their way to New York City. Most of the remainder, following the lead of relatives and friends in the tradition of the migrant and immigrant, went to Chicago, Detroit, Los Angeles, Washington, Philadelphia and other large cities where the opportunities for jobs — and more liberal public assistance — were more plentiful.

HANDICAPPED BY LACK OF SKILLS

Seven years ago, 60% of the country's 19 million Negroes were still living in the

Reprinted by permission of *The News, New York's Picture Newspaper*, November 20, 21, 22, 1967.

South—despite the heavy migration of the late 1930's, when Negroes left by trainloads to get lucrative jobs in war industries.

By 1965, there were 21 million American Negroes, but only 53.6% of them were still living in the South. More than half the Negroes now living in the North and West were born in the South—and the migration continues.

The main reason Negroes leave the Southern states is to seek a better life—and the reason they can't find a good life where they are is because they are pressured economically.

Some of them can never hope to make the transition, but this doesn't stop them from trying. For instance, a migrant farmer who has spent his life in cotton, tobacco and peanut fields is poorly equipped to cope with the challenges of an industrial urban area where he lacks the skills to obtain a decent job and where he often winds up on welfare.

Attorney Randolph Blackwell, director of the Southern Rural Action Project, told us in Atlanta:

"Human labor is being displaced in agriculture at the rate of 10% per year. The size of the problem, the people being hurt, the calendar of their increasing misery, and the timetable of their increasing despair have all been measured. A glimpse of the resulting consequences has been made clear in our major cities.

### THEY CHARGE A DELIBERATE SQUEEZE

Families of our Southern region are being driven from their land, homes and communities. They are simply asked to go away—any place. Get lost.

They eventually arrive in the festering center of some large city—economically and educationally naked. They are homesick. They are culturally crippled. The dream they had suddenly becomes dirty as they battle vermin and see their children using traffic-choked streets as playgrounds.

Blackwell and other leaders—both Negro and white—charge that the continuing migration of rural families is part of a deliberate squeeze by the Southern states and there is ample circumstantial evidence to support their contention.

Said a white civil rights worker:

The reasons for the squeeze are simple. The Southern states, particularly those with very large Negro populations, are afraid that the Negro will become a significant factor in politics. I've heard whites down here say, "We don't get them out, we're going to have a colored boy for governor."

The Negro here has become a victim of agricultural technology. That's true. But he is also the victim of an insidious sort of discrimination—the kind that coldly starves him off the land.

### PUTS PART OF BLAME IN WASHINGTON

A spokesman for the *National Sharecroppers Fund* said:

The Department of Agriculture is partly to blame. It seems to me that it should have foreseen agricultural mechanization years ago and that it should have taken steps to set up training programs and crop diversification to keep these people on their farms.

The department has always been under the influence of Southern congressmen—and they seek to keep their power. There are numerous instances where a Negro farmer, who has 20 acres, has only three or four in production—with a shaky market at that—while his white neighbor has 18 of his 20 acres working for him.

You hear them say that the Negro farmer hasn't the modern tools to work with and that he can't do justice to the land for that reason.

That sounds logical on the face of it. However, it is also true that the Negro farmer, applying for a loan to buy equipment, is invariably turned down.

As a result, many of these people have simply given up. They used to think they had a good year when they broke even. Now, they can't even break even. They're starving. When a man is starving he moves on—usually North.

Migration statistics show that those who do move on are in the 20 to 45 age bracket, which leaves the majority of those remaining in Mississippi, Alabama, Georgia and Louisiana in the "too young" or "too old" category.

The Charlie Miltons of the South are too old to move on—but the conditions under which they're forced to live are graphic evidence of why others migrate to the nearest cities—be they Atlanta, Birmingham or New Orleans—or farther North or West.

The thing that struck us about the shack

in which Charlie and Phoebe Milton live in Taliaferro County, Ga., is that it looks like something out of "Grapes of Wrath." The Miltons still work a "patch" of cotton—which is unusual since cotton has become a mass-produced crop and has moved out to California and Arizona.

## AN ACE-IN-THE-HOLE THAT DIDN'T PAY

Charlie Milton is 65—a slim, wiry man who has bent to toil since he was eight and who seems to straighten up with an effort. He has five grandchildren living with him and steadfastly refuses to move off his land—even to accept his son's invitation to move to Atlanta.

"Lots of people around here gave up," he told us. "They moved to the cities. Whites, too. Most of them moved to Chicago. Me? I don't know if I break even or not this year."

Charlie told us a story. "There was this farmer who turned in eight bales of cotton one season," he said. "The bossman figured and figured and finally he said, 'Frank, you don't owe me a cent. You're out of debt. You're dead even.'"

"And Frank said with a little laugh, 'Mr. Sinclair, this is one time I fooled you. I have a ninth bale over at the place.'"

Charlie laughed a dry-as-dust laugh. "So, Mr. Sinclair just told Frank he'd have to figure his bill out all over again. He did—and Frank still broke even."

Farmers in this area are not talkative. Occasionally one will stifle his distrust of strangers long enough to complain that the Department of Agriculture has told him to plow under an acre or two. They consider it odd that farmers who have been told they're unproductive still raise too much of a crop.

## THE ARGUMENT AGAINST RETRAINING

When groups argue that the farmer must be reeducated, that he should be taught new skills that will enable him to make his own way in the community, the extremist white usually points to a Charlie Milton and asks, "What can you teach him? He's been a farmer all his life."

He might be correct in assuming that Charlie can't be made into a computer programmer. However, Charlie isn't afraid of hard work and might do well in a crop diversification program.

The migration involves not only the Charlie Miltons but Negroes who have good educations—and loss of these educated people constitutes an intellectual drain on the South.

A few weeks ago, the Twentieth Century Fund published "The Advancing South; Manpower Prospects and Problems." The book contains charts showing that Negro high school and college graduates in the South leave school with their diplomas in one hand and bus tickets to the North in the other.

One of the four authors, Vivian W. Henderson, president of Clark College in Atlanta, wrote:

Discrimination against the educated Negro is as prevalent as that against the tenant farmer. A white Southerner with only a high school diploma generally makes more money than a Negro with four years of college behind him.

Let's face it. Even with the projected improvement in the Southern economy, a Negro would do better in the North or out West. That will continue unless the South makes a dramatic and immediate change in its discriminatory policies.

Since that is unlikely, the pressures will remain that are forcing Negroes to migrate to cities elsewhere, and these cities are not geared to absorb them.

## YANKEE'S VIEW OF DIXIE PREJUDICE

A transplanted Northerner from Pennsylvania, now the assistant manager of a motel in Alabama, said:

I married a Southern girl and I can see the viewpoint down here. I remember when whites in Birmingham loaded a couple of buses with Negroes, gave them each a ticket to New York and a $5 bill and laughed while the buses drove off.

Admittedly, that was an isolated instance. However, they don't want to absorb Negroes into the economy. They want them out—and whether they personally put them on buses or not, the attitude is unchanged.

They feel that there aren't enough jobs for whites, let alone Negroes. We have little trouble

183

getting help—menial help—for the motel. But there may be a shortage of manpower in the more skilled areas.

"Poor whites" have also been leaving the South, but since they are in the minority the emphasis has naturally fallen upon the migrating Negroes.

Scattered throughout the poorer sections of the South, often in the face of bitter opposition from white landowners and politicians, Negroes are banding together in cooperative marketing groups—partly to have a long-delayed voice in their own economic destinies, but mostly to cling to the land instead of fleeing to city slums as so many of their race have done over the past decade.

The "co-op" is an old device, but it is new to the Southern Negro. And while economists do not yet see it as a panacea for the ills that beset the rural South and its people, nevertheless they admit it establishes a healthy pattern of self-help.

This reporter and photographer visited some of the co-ops to see first hand some of the efforts being made to stem the tide of "The Great Migration."

### ALABAMA BLACK BELT CO-OP A SUCCESS

In race-torn Selma, Ala., more than 800 Black Belt farmers—all but one of them Negro—are making a huge success of the Southwest Alabama Farmers Co-operative Association.

In Lafayette, La., we found that a Negro Catholic priest, Father Albert J. McKnight of Brooklyn, has—after eight years—built the Southern Consumers Co-operative into a 700-member group that is branching out in several fields.

And in Crawfordville, Ga., the Citizens' Crusade Against Poverty last January started a project which members hope will grow into a significant economic factor in Taliaferro County during the coming year.

To a casual observer, it might seem that the areas in which the co-ops operate would welcome them as a means of making the poor, Negro element self-supporting and thus taking the load off the public assistance programs, meager though these may be.

However, Selma's cooperative ran into trouble early—partly because its initial promoters were civil rights workers who were active in the 1965 Selma-to-Montgomery freedom march.

Local people would not buy the co-op's major crop—cucumbers. White farmers charged unfair competition.

### CHARGE U.S. IS BEHIND MOVEMENT

When the Office of Economic Opportunity stifled its own misgivings about Selma's co-op leadership and gave the group $400,000 to continue its work, Alabama's Gov. Lurleen Wallace promptly rejected the grant. She charged Washington was financing a black power movement in Alabama; that the group was tied in with Stokely Carmichael, the black power leader.

Even when OEO Director Sargent Shriver overrode her veto, Lurleen Wallace insisted that the cooperative was merely a front for a federal plot to instill revolutionary fervor in Negroes in her state.

The cooperative has become a model for others. Farmers in the area it serves have never made more than $1,500 a year—but with better prices for their produce they are now making a decent living and are content to remain where they are. It is this last—remaining where they are—that discomfits the white politicians, say its members.

By big city standards, the members of the cooperatives would be largely classified as unskilled workers and would find it impossible to obtain any but the most menial of employment. However, they are farmers and they are happily pooling their resources—including knowledge, equipment and hard work—to become independent. . . .

Last month, Sen. Jacob K. Javits (R-N.Y.), introducing a bill calling for the organization of a Domestic Development Bank designed to assist in the development of employment and business opportunities in certain urban and rural areas, put his finger on the major portion of the problem. He said:

For several decades, the phenomenon of urbanization has been the dominant domestic trend in this country—a trend far outrunning our ability to comprehend it, and deal with it.

### GAVE BIRTH TO RIOT AND DESTRUCTION

Urbanization has proliferated the big-city slum, the slum which over the last summer repeatedly gave birth to riot and tragic destruction of life and property.

But the crisis of the core city is also a crisis for rural America, whose people are taking flight to the cities as farm manpower needs diminish. No program or effort which seeks to resolve the problems of the city slum can stand alone—rural migration needs to be halted or at least slowed and the economy of rural America brought back into equilibrium.

He touched also upon another facet of the dilemma, saying:

The second fundamental problem, one which we have tended to overlook in terms of federal programs, is the lack of involvement of the rural or urban poverty-area resident in the ownership and management of the business community which serves him.

The riots have shown us the depths of this alienation and resentment in the cities as white-owned stores were burned and looted while "soul brothers'" establishments were spared.

Though he is tragically mistaken, the slum Negro sees himself as having no stake in the economic life of his community and no realistic possibility of becoming a part of it—hence there is no community morality against destroying it.

### "ELSEWHERE" MEANS N.Y. TO MANY NEGROES

Some things were left unsaid—such as how the South is squeezing the Negro out of his home and forcing him to settle elsewhere, as was observed in some areas by a *News* team.

"Elsewhere" has meant New York City to roughly half the Negroes who have left the South during the last five years—and a great many of them have ended up on welfare.

A few weeks ago, Welfare Commissioner Mitchell L. Ginsberg said,

You have in the last five years a million people who have moved out, who were relatively middle income and who made less demands in terms of services. The influx of unskilled persons and the flight of the middle class to the suburbs is a very serious situation.

I think in the Southern states that there is a whole series of factors that operate to drive people out. It has increasingly become clear, apparently, to people down there that if they want to improve their situation they have to get out—and then, of course, the city has to pick them up.

## 37. REYNOLDS V. SIMS (377 U. S. 536)

In *Farmland*, a biweekly farm newspaper, the editor, Harold Hamil, writes of the legislative apportionment issue: ". . . this (rural opposition to equal legislative apportionment) may very well have been the last powerful assertion of traditional agrarian sentiment in national life." The move after 1962 toward equal apportionment gave great importance to the several opinions of the Supreme Court supporting the famous "one man, one vote" rule. One of the leading Supreme Court opinions in this area is excerpted below.

*Appeal from the United States District Court for the Middle District of Alabama. No. 23. Argued November 13, 1963. — Decided June 15, 1964.*

MR. CHIEF JUSTICE WARREN delivered the opinion of the Court.

Involved in these cases are an appeal and two cross-appeals from a decision of the Federal District Court for the Middle District of Alabama holding invalid, under the Equal Protection Clause of the Federal Constitution, the existing and two legislatively proposed plans for the apportionment of seats in the two houses of the Alabama Legislature, and ordering into effect a temporary reapportionment plan comprised of parts of the proposed but judicially disapproved measures. . . .

The maximum size of the Alabama House was increased from 105 to 106 with the creation of a new county in 1903, pursuant to the constitutional provision which states that, in addition to the prescribed 105 House seats, each county thereafter created shall be entitled to one representative. Article IX, § § 202 and 203, of the Alabama Constitution established precisely the boundaries of the State's senatorial and representative districts until the enactment of a new reapportionment plan by the legislature. These 1901 constitutional provisions, specifically describing the composition of the senatorial districts and detailing the number of House

seats allocated to each county, were periodically enacted as statutory measures by the Alabama Legislature, as modified only by the creation of an additional county in 1903, and provided the plan of legislative apportionment existing at the time this litigation was commenced.

Plaintiffs below alleged that the last apportionment of the Alabama Legislature was based on the 1900 federal census, despite the requirements of the State Constitution that the legislature be reapportioned decennially. They asserted that, since the population growth in the State from 1900 to 1960 had been uneven, Jefferson and other counties were now victims of serious discrimination with respect to the allocation of legislative representation. As a result of the failure of the legislature to reapportion itself, plaintiffs asserted, they were denied "equal suffrage in free and equal elections . . . and the equal protection of the laws" in violation of the Alabama Constitution and the Fourteenth Amendment to the Federal Constitution. The complaint asserted that plaintiffs had no other adequate remedy, and that they had exhausted all forms of relief other than that available through the federal courts. They alleged that the Alabama Legislature had established a pattern of prolonged inaction from 1911 to the present which "clearly demonstrates that no reapportionment . . . shall be effected"; that representation at any future constitutional convention would be established by the legislature, making it unlikely that the membership of any such convention would be fairly representative; and that, while the Alabama Supreme Court had found that the legislature had not complied with the State Constitution in failing to reapportion according to population decennially, that court had nevertheless indicated that it would not interfere with matters of legislative reapportionment. . . .

On July 12, 1962, an extraordinary session of the Alabama Legislature adopted two reapportionment plans to take effect for the 1966 elections. One was a proposed constitutional amendment, referred to as the "67-Senator Amendment." It provided for a House of Representatives consisting of 106 members, apportioned by giving one seat to each of Alabama's 67 counties and distributing the others according to population by the "equal proportions" method. Using this formula, the constitutional amendment specified the number of representatives allotted to each county until a new apportionment could be made on the basis of the 1960 census. The Senate was to be composed of 67 members, one from each county. The legislation provided that the proposed amendment should be submitted to the voters for ratification at the November 1962 general election.

The other reapportionment plan was embodied in a statutory measure adopted by the legislature and signed into law by the Alabama Governor, and was referred to as the "Crawford-Webb Act." It was enacted as standby legislation to take effect in 1966 if the proposed constitutional amendment should fail of passage by the majority of the State's voters, or should the federal courts refuse to accept the proposed amendment (though not rejected by the voters) as effective action in compliance with the requirements of the Fourteenth Amendment. The act provided for a Senate consisting of 35 members, representing 35 senatorial districts established along county lines, and altered only a few of the former districts. In apportioning the 106 seats in the Alabama

House of Representatives, the statutory measure gave each county one seat, and apportioned the remaining 39 on a rough population basis, under a formula requiring increasingly more population for a county to be accorded additional seats. The Crawford-Webb Act also provided that it would be effective "until the legislature is reapportioned according to law," but provided no standards for such a reapportionment. Future apportionments would presumably be based on the existing provisions of the Alabama Constitution which the statute, unlike the proposed constitutional amendment, would not affect.

The evidence adduced at trial before the three-judge panel consisted primarily of figures showing the population of each Alabama county and senatorial district according to the 1960 census, and the number of representatives allocated to each county under each of the three plans at issue in the litigation — the existing apportionment (under the 1901 constitutional provisions and the current statutory measures substantially reenacting the same plan), the proposed 67-Senator constitutional amendment, and the Crawford-Webb Act. Under all three plans, each senatorial district would be represented by only one senator.

On July 21, 1962, the District Court held that the inequality of the existing representation in the Alabama Legislature violated the Equal Protection Clause of the Fourteenth Amendment, a finding which the Court noted had been "generally conceded" by the parties to the litigation, since population growth and shifts had converted the 1901 scheme, as perpetuated some 60 years later, into an invidiously discriminatory plan completely lacking in rationality. 208 F. Supp. 431. Under the existing provisions, applying 1960 census figures, only 25.1% of the State's total population resided in districts represented by a majority of the members of the Senate, and only 25.7% lived in counties which could elect a majority of the members of the House of Representatives. Population-variance ratios of up to about 41-to-1 existed in the Senate, and up to about 16-to-1 in the House. Bullock County, with a population of only 13,462, and Henry County, with a population of only 15,286, each were allocated two seats in the Alabama House, whereas Mobile County, with a population of 314,301, was given only three seats, and Jefferson County, with 634,864 people, had only seven representatives. With respect to senatorial apportionment, since the pertinent Alabama constitutional provisions had been consistently construed as prohibiting the giving of more than one Senate seat to any one county, Jefferson County, with over 600,000 people, was given only one senator, as was Lowndes County, with a 1960 population of only 15,417, and Wilcox County, with only 18,739 people.

The Court then considered both the proposed constitutional amendment and the Crawford–Webb Act to ascertain whether the legislature had taken effective action to remedy the unconstitutional aspects of the existing apportionment. In initially summarizing the result which it had reached, the Court stated:

> This Court has reached the conclusion that neither the "67-Senator Amendment," nor the "Crawford–Webb Act" meets the necessary constitutional requirements. We find that each of the legislative acts, when considered as a whole, is so obviously discriminatory, arbitrary and irrational that it becomes unnecessary to pursue a detailed development of each of the relevant factors of the [federal constitutional] test.

The Court stated that the apportionment of one senator to each county, under the proposed constitutional amendment, would "make the discrimination in the Senate even more invidious than at present." Under the 67-Senator Amendment, as pointed out by the court below, "[t]he present control of the Senate by members representing 25.1% of the people of Alabama would be reduced to control by members representing 19.4% of the people of the State," the 34 smallest counties, with a total population of less than that of Jefferson County, would have a majority of the senatorial seats, and

senators elected by only about 14% of the State's population could prevent the submission to the electorate of any future proposals to amend the State Constitution (since a vote of two-fifths of the members of one house can defeat a proposal to amend the Alabama Constitution). Noting that the "only conceivable rationalization" of the senatorial apportionment scheme is that it was based on equal representation of political subdivisions within the State and is thus analogous to the Federal Senate, the District Court rejected the analogy on the ground that Alabama counties are merely involuntary political units of the State created by statute to aid in the administration of state government. In finding the so-called federal analogy irrelevant, the District Court stated:

> The analogy cannot survive the most superficial examination into the history of the requirement of the Federal Constitution and the diametrically opposing history of the requirement of the Alabama Constitution that representation shall be based on population. Nor can it survive a comparison of the different political natures of states and counties.

The Court also noted that the senatorial apportionment proposal "may not have complied with the State Constitution," since not only is it explicitly provided that the population basis of legislative representation "shall not be changed by constitutional amendments," but the Alabama Supreme Court had previously indicated that that requirement could probably be altered only by constitutional convention. The Court concluded, however, that the apportionment of seats in the Alabama House, under the proposed constitutional amendment, was "based upon reason, with a rational regard for known and accepted standards of apportionment." Under the proposed apportionment of representatives, each of the 67 counties was given one seat and the remaining 39 allocated on a population basis. About 43% of the State's total population would live in counties which could elect a majority in that body. And, under the provisions of the 67-Senator Amendment, while the maximum population-variance ratio was increased to about 59-to-1 in the Senate, it was significantly reduced to about 4.7-to-1 in the House of Representatives. Jefferson County was given 17 House seats, an addition of 10, and Mobile County was allotted eight, an increase of five. The increased representation of the urban counties was achieved primarily by limiting the State's 55 least populous counties to one House seat each, and the net effect was to take 19 seats away from rural counties and allocate them to the more populous counties. Even so, serious disparities from a population-based standard remained. Montgomery County, with 169,210 people, was given only four seats, while Coosa County, with a population of only 10,726, and Cleburne County, with only 10,911, were each allocated one representative.

Turning next to the provisions of the Crawford-Webb Act, the District Court found that its apportionment of the 106 seats in the Alabama House of Representatives, by allocating one seat to each county and distributing the remaining 39 to the more populous counties in diminishing ratio to their populations, was "totally unacceptable." Under this plan, about 37% of the State's total population would reside in counties electing a majority of the members of the Alabama House, with a maximum population-variance ratio of about 5-to-1. Each representative from Jefferson and Mobile Counties would represent over 52,000 persons while representatives from eight rural counties would each represent less than 20,000 people. The Court regarded the senatorial apportionment provided in the Crawford-Webb Act as "a step in the right direction, but an extremely short step," and but a "slight improvement over the present system of representation." The net effect of combining a few of the less populous counties into two-county districts and splitting up several of the larger districts into smaller ones would be merely to increase the minority which would be represented by a majority of the members of the Senate from 25.1% to only 27.6% of the State's population. The Court pointed out that, under the Crawford-Webb Act, the vote of a person in the senatorial district consisting of Bibb and Perry Counties would be worth 20 times that of a citizen in Jefferson County, and that the vote of a citizen in the six smallest districts would be worth 15 or more times that of a Jefferson County voter. The Court concluded that the Crawford-Webb Act was "totally unacceptable" as a "piece of permanent legislation" which, under the Alabama Constitution, would have remained in effect without alteration at least until after the next decennial census. . . .

II

Undeniably the Constitution of the United States protects the rights of all qualified citizens to vote, in state as well as in federal elections. . . .

In *Baker v. Carr*, 396 U.S. 186, we held that a claim asserted under the Equal Protection Clause challenging the constitutionality of a State's apportionment of seats in its legislature, on the ground that the right to vote of certain citizens was effectively impaired since debased and diluted, in effect presented a justiciable controversy subject to adjudication by federal courts. The spate of similar cases filed and decided by lower courts since our decision in *Baker* amply shows that the problem of state legislative malapportionment is one that is perceived to exist in a large number of the States. In *Baker*, a suit involving an attack on the apportionment of seats in the Tennessee Legislature, we remanded to the District Court, which had dismissed the action, for consideration on the merits. We intimated no view as to the proper constitutional standards for evaluating the validity of a state legislative apportionment scheme. Nor did we give any consideration to the question of appropriate remedies. Rather, we simply stated:

Beyond noting that we have no cause at this stage to doubt the District Court will be able to fashion relief if violations of constitutional rights are found, it is improper now to consider what remedy would be most appropriate if appellants prevail at the trial.

We indicated in *Baker*, however, that the Equal Protection Clause provides discoverable and manageable standards for use by lower courts in determining the constitutionality of a state legislative apportionment scheme, and we stated:

Nor need the appellants, in order to succeed in this action, ask the Court to enter upon policy determinations for which judicially manageable standards are lacking. Judicial standards under the Equal Protection Clause are well developed and familiar, and it has been open to courts since the enactment of the Fourteenth Amendment to determine, if on the particular facts they must, that a discrimination reflects *no* policy, but simply arbitrary and capricious action.

Subsequent to *Baker*, we remanded several cases to the courts below for reconsideration in light of that decision.

\* \* \*

III

A predominant consideration in determining whether a State's legislative apportionment scheme constitutes an invidious discrimination violative of rights asserted under the Equal Protection Clause is that the rights allegedly impaired are individual and personal in nature. As stated by the Court in *United States v. Bathgate*, 246 U.S. 220, 227, "[t]he right to vote is personal. . . ." While the result of a court decision in a state legislative apportionment controversy may be to require the restructuring of the geographical distribution of seats in a state legislature, the judicial focus must be concentrated upon ascertaining whether there has been any discrimination against certain of the State's citizens which constitutes an impermissible impairment of their constitutionally protected right to vote. Like *Skinner v. Oklahoma*, 316 U.S. 535, such a case "touches a sensitive and important area of human rights," and "involves one of the basic civil rights of man," presenting questions of alleged "invidious discriminations . . . against groups or types of individuals in violation of the constitutional guaranty of just and equal laws." 316 U.S., at 536, 541. Undoubtedly, the right of suffrage is a fundamental matter in a free and democratic society. Especially since the right to exercise the franchise in a free and unimpaired manner is preservative of other basic civil and political rights, any alleged infringement of the right of citizens to vote must be carefully and meticulously scrutinized. Almost a century ago, in *Yick Wo v. Hopkins*, 118 U.S. 356, the Court referred to "the political franchise of voting" as "a fundamental political right, because preservative of all rights." 118 U.S., at 370.

Legislators represent people, not trees or acres. Legislators are elected by voters, not farms or cities or economic interests. As long as ours is a representative form of government, and our legislatures are those instruments of government elected directly by and directly representative of the people, the right to elect legislators in a free and unimpaired fashion is a bedrock of our political system. It could hardly be gainsaid that a constitutional claim had been asserted by an allegation that certain otherwise qualified voters had been entirely prohibited from voting for members of their state legislature. And, if a State should provide that the votes of citizens in one part of the State should be given two times, or five times, or 10 times the weight of votes of citizens in another part of the State, it could hardly be contended that the right to vote of those residing in the disfavored areas had not been effectively diluted. It would appear extraordinary to suggest that a State could be constitutionally permitted to enact a law providing that certain of the State's voters could vote two, five, or 10 times for their legislative representatives, while voters living elsewhere could vote only once. And it is inconceivable that a state law to the effect that, in counting votes for legislators, the votes of citizens in one part of the State would be multiplied by two, five, or 10, while the votes of persons in another area would be counted only at face value, could be constitutionally sustainable. Of course, the effect of state legislative districting schemes which give the same number of representatives to unequal number of constituents is identical. Overweighting and overvaluation of the votes of those living here has the certain effect of dilution and undervaluation of the votes of those living there. The resulting discrimination against those individual voters living in disfavored areas is easily demonstrable mathematically. Their right to vote is simply not the same right to vote as that of those living in a favored part of the State. Two, five, or 10 of them must vote before the effect of their voting is equivalent to that of their favored neighbor. Weighting the votes of citizens differently, by any method or means, merely because of where they happen to reside, hardly seems justifiable. One must be ever aware that the Constitution forbids "sophisticated as well as simple-minded modes of discrimination." *Lane v. Wilson*, 307, U.S. 268, 275; *Gomillion v. Lightfoot*, 364 U.S. 339, 342. As we stated in *Wesberry v. Sanders, supra*:

We do not believe that the Framers of the Constitution intended to permit the same vote-diluting discrimination to be accomplished through the device of districts containing widely varied numbers of inhabitants. To say that a vote is worth more in one district than in another would

. . . run counter to our fundamental ideas of democratic government . . . .

State legislatures are, historically, the fountainhead of representative government in this country. A number of them have their roots in colonial times, and substantially antedate the creation of our Nation and our Federal Government. In fact, the first formal stirrings of American political independence are to be found, in large part, in the views and actions of several of the colonial legislative bodies. With the birth of our National Government, and the adoption and ratification of the Federal Constitution, state legislatures retained a most important place in our Nation's governmental structure. But representative government is in essence self-government through the medium of elected representatives of the people, and each and every citizen has an inalienable right to full and effective participation in the political processes of his State's legislative bodies. Most citizens can achieve this participation only as qualified voters through the election of legislators to represent them. Full and effective participation by all citizens in state government requires, therefore, that each citizen have an equally effective voice in the election of members of his state legislature. Modern and viable state government needs, and the Constitution demands, no less.

\* \* \*

A nation once primarily rural in character becomes predominantly urban. Representation schemes once fair and equitable become archaic and outdated. But the basic principle of representative government remains, and must remain, unchanged — the weight of a citizen's vote cannot be made to depend on where he lives. Population is, of necessity, the starting point for consideration and the controlling criterion for judgment in legislative apportionment controversies. A citizen, a qualified voter, is no more nor no less so because he lives in the city or on the farm. This is the clear and strong command of our Constitution's Equal Protection Clause. This is an essential part of the concept of a government of laws and not men. This is at the heart of Lincoln's vision of "government of the people, by the people, [and] for the people." The Equal Protection Clause demands no less than substantially equal state legislative representation for all citizens, of all places as well as of all races. . . .

*Joseph P. Lyford*

## 38. THE TALK IN VANDALIA

The changes in rural communities over the past two decades have made a deep impression on the attitudes of the people. These changes seem to have contributed to the proverbial conservatism and pessimism of the American farmer, to whom they spell a steady decline of status in the community. The feeling of impending disaster, reflected in the comments of residents of Vandalia, indicates the extent to which a sense of insecurity has accompanied the "commercialization" of agriculture.

The selection printed below conveys vividly the growing sense of disadvantage of the rural condition. It is from a report by the Center for the Study of Democratic Institutions, which is devoted to "clarifying questions of freedom and justice, especially those raised by the emerging power of twentieth-century institutions."

Judged by the map, the city of Vandalia (population 5,500) has a fine location. It lies across a junction of the Pennsylvania and the Illinois Central Railroads, appears to be the center of a criss-cross of highways, and is on the edge of the Kaskaskia River, which winds its way diagonally downstate to the Mississippi. But the map reader will be deceived. The Kaskaskia, swollen and icy in winter, subsides by summertime into a winding trail of mud and snags; the new superhighways—Routes 40 and 70—pass by to the north, and the only concession by the Pennsylvania's "spirit of St. Louis" is a raucous bellow as it hurtles through a cut in the center of town an hour before noon. The Illinois Central is more considerate. Occasionally a freight train shunts back and forth a few blocks outside of town to pick up some crates from one of the small factories along the tracks. "No trains stop here," the stationmaster says. The indifference of the railroads to Vandalia is paid back in full by the town's oldest practicing Democrat, eighty-eight-year-old Judge James G. Burnside. "We don't pay any attention to the railroads any more," he remarks. "They're just passing acquaintances." . . .

When he is not in the front parlor of his home, which he uses as his office, Mr. Evans is in the lobby of the Evans Hotel. He built the hotel in 1924 and, along with a hardware business and various real estate dealings, it made him probably the richest man in Vandalia. Last year, his eighty-first, the $106,000 library he gave to the town

From Joseph P. Lyford, *The Talk in Vandalia*, pp. 1, 4–10, 13. Reprinted by permission of The Fund for The Republic, Inc. and Harper & Row, Inc., Publishers.

opened its doors. "We were a money-saving family, all of us," he says. "We're Welsh by descent. I was never a man to sell, I always bought and added to it. When I sold the hotel I'd been saving all the time. I guess I'd saved too much. I didn't have any use for the money, so I built the library. When I built it, I didn't try to cut corners. I didn't try to save as if I was building for myself."

Mr. Evans leans back, and crosses his arms when he talks about his town.

This is a historic city. When they moved the capital from here to Springfield in 1839, our population was only 400. We've gained a little bit all the time. Population-wise we've never had a setback. We've never had a boom. We held our ground. A big percentage of people own their homes, including a lot who work at the factory. This makes us a good town for a factory. The companies know our workers are not fly-by-nighters. Their employees are here to stay. They have money invested in our town. Homes today build from $12,000 to $18,000, and we have a good building and loan program. Banks will lend money to anybody here who wants to build a building. We have good, sound, sincere bankers. Back in the late 20's, when people were trying to buy more and more land for their farms, the bankers warned them against it. When the crash came, we weren't so badly off as some. We had hard times in 1932, oh mercy.

I think the town is going to develop pretty well. Rental housing is pretty scarce. The homes here are good ones, and people have made substantial payments on them. I don't know what we're going to have to do to keep our young people here, though. When they go to the city, they don't come back. They want new people to get acquainted with. Industry might be the answer. We should have more opportunities for skilled workers. The Crane Packing Company has been very good. They have a training program for employees and they are expanding. The shoe factory is a shoe factory. Their idea is how much work you can get out of your help. It's as good a shoe factory as there is. It's a good town, but we have one bad problem. It's the farmers. The farmers are in trouble.

Evans is not the only person who worries about the Fayette County farmers. The townspeople think and talk a great deal about them these days. They have always depended on them in the past, and they are no longer sure of them. The uncertainty may explain why the business of farming, tradi-

tionally honored in the State of Illinois as an independent way of life, is undergoing rapid sanctification. Probably more speeches are delivered at Kiwanis and Rotary clubs on the virtues and contributions of the tillers of the soil than on any other single subject; it is also the favorite topic of the country's political circuit riders during campaign season. The community's businessmen prepare banquets in honor of local agriculture; the Junior Chamber of Commerce's first big dinner of 1962 was held to proclaim Siebert Hoover the "Outstanding Young Farmer of the Year" and present him with tickets to a Miami or New York vacation. Agricultural experts from the University of Illinois and the Department of Agriculture, armed with pamphlets on fowl disease and hog pest, criss-cross the territory with advice on all phases of scientific farming. Secretary of Agriculture Freeman's emissaries from Washington are available to discuss the farm program at the smallest gatherings. The Farm Bureau offices have special classrooms where experts lecture local farmers and their wives on the economics of farm management. And, in contrast to the days of the Great Depression in other parts of the nation, the banker and the farmer maintain friendly, interdependent relations throughout Southern Illinois. The two bank presidents in Vandalia talk about farmers as if they were business partners and mutual allies under attack by the rest of the nation's economic interests.

The popularity of the farmer in the abstract has not always thawed out farmers in particular, some of whom still harbor ancient resentments against the town. . . . But many of the farmers seem to feel closer to the town than before the war, partly because of the knowledge that a lot of other people besides farmers are involved in their economic troubles, and partly because the farmers' own social life has become more and more interlaced with the life of the town. As the one-room rural schoolhouses have dwindled, over the farmers' opposition, from three dozen in the school district to a half dozen, farm mothers have become members of the PTA's of the Washington, Lincoln, and Central elementary schools. There is more talk in the homes of educational problems jointly shared with the townspeople.

Those farmers who work in the factories —"Saturday farmers," J. B. Turner, the county farm agent, calls them—have a growing association with non-farmers, and some even join labor union locals in the shoe and heel factories. Also, the growing cost of running a farm because of the new machinery required and the rising prices of land have increased the extent of the farmer's dependence on local financial institutions. The farmers buy more and more of their food locally—most of them have disposed of their dairy cows and buy their milk at the Tri-City Supermarket and the A & P. The farmers' machinery is repaired by local mechanics. Feed dealer Norman Michel, who carries as many as 21,000 people on his credit rolls, is a farmers' banker in his own way. Vandalia shapes its commercial activities to suit the farmers' tastes, and the farmer, his wife and children, and his trucks are a regular part of the scenery on Gallatin Street. This is not to say that the town has been taken over by the farmers: in one sense it is the farmers who have changed their habits and tastes even in dress—to fit the town.

The farmer has responded in other ways to the town. He participates more in local events. He comes more to the city's churches. One outstanding farmer is chairman of the school district's Board of Education. Many of the more prosperous farm families contribute their women's time to fund drives. The high school's football and basketball teams are getting a little more help from the farm youngsters who used to shy away from extra-curricular activities after the last bell. One still hears complaints from the townspeople that the farmer is hard to reach, but he is less and less remote.

Partly as a result of his accumulating difficulties, the political attitudes of the farmer seem to have become less distinct from those of his fellow-citizens in town. If any-

thing, his views on such matters as health insurance, social security, the United Nations, even labor unions, have often become more tentative than those of some of his city brethren. The realization that government may be the only power capable of restraining the technological and political forces gnawing at his economic position has affected the farmer's outlook considerably, and more than he will admit.

In matters of local politics, the farmer rarely finds himself at odds with the town, probably because politics in Vandalia is not a serious matter. The last great political controversy in the memory of the dean of Vandalia's lawyers, ninety-year-old Will Welker, was over temperance. Only on the school issue, not one that divides on party lines, does the farmer sometimes dig in his heels and refuse to budge. His stubborn desire to hold on to the one-room country schools defeated two attempts to float bond issues for elementary schools construction in Vandalia. Even in this case, he was finally won over to support of the bond-issue program once he had the assurance that the rural schools would be allowed to continue. On those rare instances when a farmer talks world politics, his views are unexceptionably moderate on one side or other of the center: the voice of the John Birch Society is hardly audible in Southern Illinois. President Kennedy, feared by many tight-jawed Lutherans and Baptists during the campaign as a possible threat to ancient Protestant values, is now spoken of mildly enough, and more often with praise than not.

The growth of the farmer's ties to his community, and the pleasant folklore of which he is in the center, are not especially helpful to him in his present extremities, and this is true of farmers all over Southern Illinois. Businessmen's eulogies of the farmer's "way of life" seem to have become louder and more frequent in direct proportion to the approach of his economic doom. No amount of talk about how the farmer is the backbone of the nation alters the fact, as farmer Phil Gehle points out, that a tractor that cost him $1,600 in 1946 has a price tag now of $2,400, and that a bushel of corn 1946 brought $2.25 as compared to $1.00 or less in 1962. The praise that rings in the farmer's ears has a little too much nostalgia in it to be entirely reassuring. It is almost as if he were hearing distant relatives discussing his virtues while he was being lowered into his grave. The farmers, least of all, have any illusion about the future. Those who remain on the soil around Vandalia live among ruins of abandoned farmhouses which are visible in almost any direction. The sturdy, independent way of life that makes Senator Dirksen's heart beat faster is rapidly becoming an anachronism in Fayette County.

The farmer's decline casts a cold shadow. Vandalia would suffer without its factories — their loss would be a fearful blow to the town's hopes for the future — but it could not survive without its farmers. As Dr. Josh Weiner puts it, "the job of the people in town is to supply the farmer all the services he needs." Even the factories, with the possible exception of the Crane Company, depend heavily on the farmers and their families for their labor supply. Saddled with a heavy investment in farm machinery, the farmer must cultivate at least 250 acres or seek extra employment. Any less will usually not be enough to bring him the income he must have to pay his debts, maintain a household, and handle his interest payments to the farm-equipment dealer or the bank. So the small farmer turns to heel and shoe factories for additional income, and often his wife and daughter work in the shoe factory or the dress factory. Without the "Saturday farmers" and their families, it is doubtful whether the plants could get their employees from any other large source at the $1.15 per hour that is the starting pay at all but Crane.

J. B. Turner, the county farm agent, a heavy man in his sixties who looks like an unfrocked Southern Senator, says that while Fayette County has 1,467 commercial farms, averaging 231 acres and bringing in a total income of over $13,000,000, nearly 500 people who live on these farms have other jobs as well. Almost half of them work 100 days or more a year in the factories, in the oil fields as servicing and maintenance personnel, and at the Norge plant in Effingham and the Caterpillar Tractor Company in Decatur, thirty miles away. The farmer is able to handle both a farm and a job because he is mechanized. Most of the farms have electrical equipment and modern conveniences; out of 2,100 county farmers who answered a poll by the University of Illinois, 1,400 had telephones and a slightly smaller number had freezers or refrigerators. Farmers own an average of two tractors apiece.

With all this capital equipment, the farmers are not getting any richer. It is estimated that the average net income of a Fayette County farmer is somewhere around $3,400 as compared to a state average of $4,500. But the fact that he has had to become more and more of a capitalist has certainly made his life more complicated. To stay afloat, he has to become a mechanic, an expert on governmental policies, a soil scientist, and a bookkeeper. For some, the economics and the competition have been too much. For others, farming has become distasteful because it has turned in a very few years into a totally different way of life.

In this new era a Vandalian who has become more and more important to the farmers is Harry Rogier, president of the First National Bank. His institution, and its competitor across the street, the Farmer and Merchants Bank, have never inherited the traditional rural dislike of the moneylender. This is partly because there happen to be some farmers in Rogier's own family tree — Rogier himself grew up on a farm and still puts in many hours a week of hard physical labor on his acreage before and after banking hours — and also because the financial decisions of his bank have provided the underpinnings of a great many of the surrounding farms. Rogier's bank, which has a "friendship room" in the basement, complete with piano, for community use, is not cast in the cold, impersonal mold of lending institution which earned so much bitterness in other parts of the country during the depression. The same applies to the bank's officers. One vice-president, Dale Tedrick, is a leading county Democrat. He says that President Kennedy's feed-grain bill is "the best thing that ever happened to the American farmer," and he often wears a Franklin D. Roosevelt campaign button to banking conventions.

As a matter of fact, most of Vandalia's bankers and those in other rural Southern Illinois communities speak about the economic policies of both Republican and Democratic administrations in the past fifteen years with an impartial bitterness and vehemence that has much of the flavor of the old Populists. The recognized spokesman for bankers like Rogier is the *Independent Banker*, which holds that the farmer has been the victim of a conspiracy by every organized economic pressure group in the society, and that the farmer has "suffered the worst economic depression in the his-

tory of the United States since the turn of the century." The alliance of rural banks like Rogier's with the farmers, who in Fayette County are largely a debtor class, gives them a character quite unlike most banking enterprises in the East.

*   *   *

The almost automatic dig at the federal government that one hears from many farmers and businessmen like Rogier seems to have little relation to their economic behavior. The farmer who speaks sourly, if without any real passion, about "government hand-outs" is almost invariably willing to go along with the soil bank and feed-grain programs and to avail himself of the technical and advisory services of the Department of Agriculture and the University of Illinois's extension program. . . .

*John F. Kennedy*

## 39. AMERICAN AGRICULTURE—MESSAGE FROM THE PRESIDENT

President Kennedy's statement on national agricultural policy reveals the breadth and also the continuity of the federal government's involvement in agriculture. It is quite natural that this urban President should view agriculture as a part of the national whole, whose improvement was interdependent with the national welfare. In his view a suitable objective is to bring the farmer even with the "city dweller in the march toward economic health." The compatibility of this outlook with that of rural leaders at the turn of the century is striking.

*To the Congress of the United States*

In recent times, it has become customary to speak of American agriculture in terms of distress and failure, as a burden on the taxpayers and a depressant on the economy. But this is only one part of the picture. As the provider of our food and fiber, American agriculture is a highly successful and

highly efficient industry. In no other country, and at no other time in the history of our own farm economy have so many people been so well provided with such abundance and variety at such low real cost.

Nor is this bounty confined to our own people. We are today the world's largest exporter of food and fiber. Seventy percent of these exports are sales for dollars, one of

From the *Congressional Record*, Vol. 104, Part 4, 87th Congress, 1st Session (March 16, 1961), pp. 4095–4098.

the principal bulwarks of our export trade. The other 30 percent is made available under special programs to promote economic development abroad and to relieve hunger and suffering—efforts that are fundamental to our world leadership and security.

In short, our farmers deserve praise, not condemnation; and their efficiency should be a cause for gratitude, not something for which they are penalized. For their very efficiency and productivity lies at the heart of the distress in American agriculture which —while it represents only a part of the picture—constitutes that part to which our efforts must be devoted. The steady and continuing decline in income has been most serious for the 7 million people engaged in farming operations, and substandard conditions on the farms—which are so important to our economy—lead directly to substandard conditions in all segments of the national economy. Farming remains our largest industry—it employs 12 times as many people as work in steel and 9 times as many as in the automobile industry. It employs, in fact, more people than steel, automobiles, public utilities, and the transportation industry combined. The farmer is a consumer as well as a producer, and other economic groups are affected by the continued drop in farm purchasing power. Some $40 billion is spent each year for production goods and services needed on our farms and for the consumer goods used by farm families. Six million people are employed in the manufacture and distribution of the supplies that farmers use. Each year farm families spend from $2.5 to $3.0 billion for new automobiles, trucks, tractors, and other farm machinery; and $3.5 billion for fuel, lubricants, and maintenance of motor vehicles and machinery. It is deeply in the interest of all Americans that our agriculture be not only progressive but prosperous.

Yet as our farm families enter the 1960's their incomes are lower relative to the rest of our population than at any time since the 1930's. Although there has been a continuous rise in consumer prices during the past 10 years, farm income has steadily declined.

Abundant production has filled our bins and warehouses, but 1 out of 10 American households have diets so inadequate that they fall below two-thirds of the standard nutrition requirements.

These paradoxes are of concern to all of us —the farmer, the taxpayer, and the consumer. They affect the vitality of our Nation, the strength of our most basic industry, agriculture, and the economic health of every community in the land.

Much of the current problem results from four factors:

*First.* The inability of millions of separate producers to control either output or price of their products. Acting individually the farmer can neither plan his production to meet modern requirements, and shift away from commodities for which there is limited demand, nor bargain effectively for a fair return.

*Second.* A technological revolution in agricultural production, which is still underway, that has resulted in generally increased yield from a reduced input of acreage and manpower—so that today each farmer produces the food and fiber necessary for 25 pople, while at the turn of the century each farmer produced the food and fiber for only 7 people.

*Third.* A faulty system of distribution, which allows one-half of the people of the free world to suffer from malnutrition at the very same time our surpluses have reached a point where the availability of adequate storage facilities has become a real problem.

*Fourth.* The steady and continued increase in farm costs. The average farm requires an investment of $36,000. The farmer's interest costs have increased over 300 percent in the past decade. His equipment costs have increased 75 percent.

The solution lies not so much in severe restrictions upon our talent to produce as upon proper channeling of our abundance into more effective and expanded uses. American agricultural abundance can be forged into both a significant instrument of foreign policy and a weapon against domestic hardship and hunger. It is no less our

197

purpose to insure that the farm family that produced this wealth will have a parity in income and equality in opportunity with urban families—for the family farm should be protected and preserved as a basic American institution.

Our intention is to accomplish these goals while eventually reducing the cost of our programs to the taxpayer. This can be accomplished in part because it is cheaper to use our agricultural products than to store them. Present storage costs total over $500 million a year or $1.4 million every day.

But it must also be our purpose to see that farm products return a fair income because they are fairly priced. No farm program should exploit the consumer. But neither can it subsidize the consumer at the cost of subnormal incomes to the farmer. We cannot tolerate substandard conditions on the farm any more than we can in industry. A fair return is a necessity for labor, capital and management in industry. It is equally necessary for those who produce our food and fiber.

It must be our purpose to provide an agricultural program that will eventually eliminate the vast farm surpluses that overhang the market and overburden the economy; that will permit effective economies of administration; that will recognize the right of the consumer to fair prices; and that will permit the farmer to receive a fair return for his labor. This will be neither simple nor easy. It will require the cooperation and effort of the farmer, government, and the urban dweller. But the alternative is not alone a substandard rural economy—it is a weakened nation.

A WIDER RANGE OF TOOLS TO BOOST FARM INCOME

This administration's studies to date on how to meet our responsibilities in agriculture have led us to the following conclusions:

There is no single farm problem, and no single solution. Each commodity requires a somewhat different approach.

Swift and frequent changes in weather, acreage, yield, and international market conditions require Federal programs alert and sensitive to change.

The Secretary of Agriculture is now equipped with broad responsibilities for the maintenance of farm income. In order to fully and effectively meet these responsibilities he has had authority to set and adjust the level of support prices, set the level and terms of loans, prescribe acreage allotments, specify conservation payments, establish marketing agreements and orders, and take other steps to adjust supplies and protect the prices and incomes of farmers. But these powers have not been fully employed in recent years; and neither are they sufficiently flexible for all contingencies.

I am deeply concerned—and I believe the Congress shares that concern, along with most of our consumers, taxpayers, and the farmers themselves—that our farm program is drifting into a chaotic state, piling up surpluses, penalizing efficiency, rewarding inertia and noncompliance, and constantly being torn and weakened by disputes and conflicting pressures. This is not a situation that can be ended by any one sweeping act of magic. It will require diligent study, hard work, imaginative initiative, and sound, constructive leadership. But I believe that the decline in farm income and the drift in farm policy can both be gradually reversed by the program I recommend.

This will require that the Secretary of Agriculture make full and effective use of all the responsibilities now reposed in him; and that the Congress establish guidelines to enable the administration to exercise responsible leadership in consultation with those farmers most concerned in establishing sound programs for each commodity for which they are needed.

\* \* \*

Agricultural programs must always involve an effort to take the best of the available alternatives. Our task, building on past experience and present authority, is to find a simple and rapid accommodation to changing circumstances which is both effective and consistent with our democratic traditions. I believe that the present proposals will go a long way toward achieving these goals. . . .

## ENCOURAGEMENT OF COOPERATIVES

One of the methods by which farmers can increase their bargaining power and thus remedy to some extent their weakness in the marketplace is through the effective operation of their own cooperatives.

To this end I recommend legislation to reaffirm and protect the right of farmers to act together through their cooperatives in the processing and marketing of their products, the purchasing of supplies, and the furnishing of necessary services. This legislation should specifically permit farmers' cooperatives to purchase, acquire, and build processing plants and related facilities and to merge with other cooperatives so long as such activities do not tend to create a monopoly or substantially lessen competition.

## LOW-INCOME FARMS

In those areas where farms are predominantly in the lowest income group, entire rural communities have suffered severe economic damage. The small businesses are liquidating, the community facilities are deteriorating, and community institutions are weakened. These present a special problem.

The area redevelopment bill now under consideration by the Congress is needed by farmers as urgently as it is needed in cities and towns. I reiterate my urgent recommendation for the speedy enactment of this bill, and thus enhance the resources available to the Secretary of Agriculture as he mobilizes all the services available to him, such as FHA, REA, Forest and Extension Services, to assist in the development of better levels of living, better income opportunities, and

better communities in our rural depressed areas.

## FARM CREDIT AND REA

One of the features of modern agriculture that poses an increasing problem to farmers, especially during periods of low income, is the need for increased capital investment, accompanied by the high cost of credit.

I am directing the Secretary of Agriculture to liberalize and extend the lending operations of the Farm Home Administration so that any needy farmer can obtain loans for operating capital and for farm home improvements at low cost, and I recommend that the present legislation be amended to permit farm improvement loans to be secured either by mortgages or by other acceptable forms of security.

I have further directed the Secretary of Agriculture to initiate two measures that will encourage the storage of grain on the farm and strengthen economic activity in farming areas:

(a) Modifying present farm credit regulations to permit farmers to borrow up to 95 percent (instead of the present 80 percent limit) of the cost of materials for building farm storage facilities and equipment; and

(b) Guaranteeing that farmers will be able to earn 2 full years' storage payments for continuing to store 1960 crop wheat, corn and grain sorghum, and at least 1 year's storage payments for continuing to store other 1960 crops.

The loans are for 5 years at an interest rate of 4 percent. The effect of this directive will be to increase the demand for steel, wood, and other building materials, to procure the additional farm storage needed for 1960 crops, and to place an estimated $40 million in credit funds in the rural economy in the months ahead.

I have also directed that the Rural Electrification Act be administered in accordance with the original intent and purpose of that program, which has done so much to advance agriculture throughout the Nation.

199

Over 95 percent of our farms now have electricity. But much remains to be done. There are constantly increasing demands for additional power. Only one-third of our farms have modern telephone installations. The cooperatives which so successfully brought light and power to the farm can make an enormous contribution to the continued development of our rural communities. . . .

### SOIL AND WATER CONSERVATION

We have so taken soil conservation for granted in this generation that we forget it is a task which is barely underway. By June 30, 1960, the Soil Conservation Service had helped 1,301,450 farmers and ranchers to complete basic conservation plans and an additional 500,000 were being assisted. But this represents only 27 percent of all farms and ranches in soil conservation districts. Nearly three-fourths of this important job remains to be done.

I am requesting the Congress to provide the funds necessary to accelerate this program for permanent soil conservation practices and to increase our efforts for small watersheds as well. These smaller projects, now being planned and developed, may well hold the key to our future water and soil requirements at a time of rapidly growing population.

### CONCLUSION

The measures I have recommended are not directed solely to the purpose of aiding the farmer. Nor are they simple prescriptions for Federal assistance to a harried segment of our population. Rather they are directed toward broad goals of achieving agricultural production geared to meet needs for food and fiber at home and in the free world under programs that will enable the farmers of this nation to earn a fair income.

We cannot expect to solve the farm problem in a day or in a year, or perhaps even in this administration. But we can and must adopt a new approach based on a clear recognition of the goals we seek, a realistic appraisal of the problems involved, and a firm determination to solve these problems and attain these goals.

The bills I have suggested will be debated and discussed in terms of general administration policies and powers. Various portions will undoubtedly be challenged as restrictive upon the farmer or inconsistent with complete freedom in the market. But I am convinced that the objectives of these programs will, when accomplished, provide for a reasonable balance between supply and demand. They will eliminate the hardship and suffering which inadequate returns force upon so many of our farm families; they will reduce our surpluses to manageable proportions; they will relieve the taxpayer of the unnecessary drain upon the Federal budget; they will spur our national economy, and they will assure the consumer of stable price levels.

Responsibility must be accompanied by the authority to accomplish these goals. If we move forward along the lines I have recommended, the entire Nation will benefit. The farmer can join the city dweller in the march toward economic health.

*Barrow Lyons*

## 40. UNENDING VISTAS

A dominant theme in the history of American agriculture is the application of science to natural resources for the satisfaction of basic needs. This application has widened in every direction—using arid lands, transforming nonarable into arable land, utilizing acreages for optimum benefits—with, during the twentieth century at least, some concept of conservation in mind. In all, the soil has been the essential resource.

The point in time when agricultural production will move to a nonland-based technology will mark one of the great evolutionary changes in human history. The toll exacted by the expanding industrial system upon land-use suggests that land-based farming may be supplemented by utilization of other sources of food and fiber.

Two problems are suggested. One is the continuing place of traditional farming and the relationship of the farmer to the national interest economically and, as well, politically and socially. The other is the feasibility of "farming" in ways not yet widely recognized among the leaders of our agricultural policy. This latter problem is explored by Barrow Lyons in a chapter, "Revolution in Agriculture," in his book on America's natural resources and their use.

Science applied intensively to the improvement of modern farming, including great advances in farm machinery, has effected in recent years an enormous change in American rural life. The pressure of these improvements has been felt sharply by some in the necessity for an increasing application of capital per acre to make farm management successful. Marginal farming has become less and less profitable. The "poor" farmer is finding it progressively harder to retain tenure of land. But the farmer who keeps abreast of change prospers vastly.

The emigration of the "Okies" from the cotton-growing areas of the Mid-South was a spectacular illustration of what is happening; but the same sort of thing has been occurring to some degree all along the line. The man who cannot command sufficient capital for efficient modern farming is being forced into other occupations.

At the same time the business of farming has become more technical. That has required greater education. The farmer is becoming both a highly skilled technician and a better informed citizen. He is acquiring deeper insight into human psychology and becoming more aware of social and economic problems. Politically he is better oriented than formerly.

In some areas, where large accumulations of wealth have gone into scientific farming, as in the rich Central Valley of California and the region of the lower Rio Grande, a type of landed gentry not so different from

From Barrow Lyons, *Tomorrow's Birthright: A Political and Economic Interpretation of Our Natural Resources* (New York: Funk & Wagnalls Co., 1955), pp. 82–83, 89–97, 99–101. Reprinted by permission of the publisher.

the former Junkers of Prussia is developing. This is being partly offset by organization of the farmhands who work on the great estates. The National Agricultural Workers Union, affiliated with the American Federation of Labor, has been organizing in this field, but its progress has been slow.

The hope of many who have observed these changes in the social structure of rural America is that the family-type farm will remain the general pattern in this country, but that it will enjoy an ever-increasing prosperity in proportion to its increasing efficiency. This would mean the stabilization of a large group of well-educated, independent and thoughtful citizens as one of our chief bulwarks against monopoly and other forms of exploitation. The organized farmer, although sometimes reactionary, has been a check upon predatory wealth and often a balance to labor leaders who have acquired great political power.

The release of people from the soil because of technical improvements in farming has made possible their absorption in an expanding industrial society. But, because new industrial processes which substitute organic raw materials for inorganic products are being introduced, a new kind of farming now in the making may give agricultural production an augmented function in our future economy.

\* \* \*

#### THE TESTED APPROACH

We have seen great results from the research work. There is no reason why research should not continue to produce results for a long while to come, by increasing our understanding of the processes of plant and animal growth, improving seed and livestock strains through breeding, and the introduction of new varieties.

Improvement in plant varieties comes through development of strains superior in size, disease resistance, strength and length of fiber, drought tolerance, improved flavor, earliness, hardiness, vigor in growth, or combinations of these qualities. Everyone knows of the yield increases due to hybrid corns. The success of cotton growers in California has depended upon the introduction of an improved strain; and now we hear of another improvement in cotton that, unlike the long-staple variety of California, will not be confined to a relatively few favored farmers.

Just as the varieties of plants have been improved through breeding, so have superior strains of farm animals been produced. Yields per animal have increased steadily in the last fifteen years, just as have yields per crop acre. In cattle production there has been a consistently larger calf crop and a reduction in death loss. Better feeding and prevention of disease tends to produce more meat and milk per cow. Yet, although the milk produced per cow has increased surprisingly, the average unquestionably will rise higher. The average milk production per cow, for animals on which full-year records were kept by dairy herd improvement associations in 1951, was 9,195 pounds compared with a national average of 5,313 pounds that year—73 percent higher for the carefully selected herds. More feed per cow and better balanced rations would bring results.

The Department of Agriculture also reports information obtained from the Corn Belt over a period of years which indicates that there was a reduction of 10 to 15 percent in the quantity of feed consumed by hogs to produce each 100 pounds of pork from the decade of the 1920's to the decade of the 1930's.

A startling disclosure was made in the agricultural journals four years ago when it was found that a commercial product called APF (animal protein factor) added to the feed of hogs, tremendously increased their capacity to absorb food and grow. Even runt pigs and chicks were enabled to grow as fast as normal animals. APF is obtained from dried cereal residue in the production of antibiotics, such as aureomycin and streptomycin used in the treatment of a number of virus diseases.

The *Farm Journal* reported in June, 1950, that one farmer discovered that pigs fed on corn-peanut meal plus a small amount of APF gained more than 1⅓ pounds a day, as compared with a gain of ¾ pound a day on the same ration without APF. Moreover, the APF-added meal produced a gain of 100 pounds on 386 pounds of feed, as compared with 410 pounds of the usual mixture. . . .

### FISH FOR THE MILLIONS

. . . Most people do not realize how important a source of food the sea has become because of improved methods of fishing. In value the catch of the United States and Alaska fishermen now amounts to around a billion dollars a year; and the fishing industry is growing. Before the last World War the fisheries catch of the world was estimated at 39 billion pounds a year. About 98 percent was in the Northern Hemisphere. Asians caught almost half of the seafood, Europeans almost one third, North Americans about one eighth, and all others about 3 percent. The Japanese were the world's greatest fishermen, accounting for 22 percent of the world's catch. United States and Alaska fishermen ranked second with 11 percent, those of the U.S.S.R. third with 9.3 percent, and the Chinese fourth with 7.9 percent.

Great gains have been made by the Government in restoring depleted fisheries for certain species through protection of the reproductive cycle. This has been especially true of the shad run on the eastern coast of the United States. Most fisheries are on shallow continental shelves. What the deeper waters of the sea may yield is unknown.

That the consumption of seafood in the United States could be increased is certain; and, probably, it should be increased. Science long has known that fish is as nutritious as meat, but only in recent years has it been discovered that seafood has some virtues not always possessed by meat. Cattle fed on grass and grain from worn-out soils, or soils naturally deficient in critical minerals, sometimes fail to relay to the human system all of the nutrients required for the best of health. Seawater, on the other hand, contains all of the vital minerals required by the human body; and fish, crustaceans, and mollusks provide them.

About two thirds of the world's catch of seafood is now used for human food, the other third to make fish meals and oil. In 1948 about a billion pounds of menhaden caught off the Atlantic and Gulf Coasts were reduced to feed for livestock and poultry, or to feeding oils, paint oils, soap, and oils for technical processing. This was a substantial addition to land-produced foods. It could be expanded considerably. . . .

The volume of fish eaten also could be increased through construction of fishponds on farms almost everywhere. With a few waterfowl to fertilize a pond, the growth of vegetable and minute animal life upon which fish feed can be stimulated. Many varieties of panfish are raised in such ponds. The Chinese for centuries have supplemented their diet in this way. American farmers are catching on.

### VAST NEW HORIZONS

While improvements in agriculture have steadily increased the yield per acre of cropland and reduced the amount of human labor required to produce a given quantity of food, an attack on the problem of feeding men and animals has been commenced from an entirely different direction. Some very disturbing questions are raised by this innovation.

Essentially, agriculture is the means by which man adapts to his own uses the ability of plants to produce basic carbohydrates, fats and proteins. The products produced in greatest volume by plants are carbohydrates, compounds analyzing for carbon plus hydrogen and oxygen, the elements of water. The simplest forms of water-soluble carbohydrates are the sugars, resulting from the photosynthetic action of chlorophyll upon carbon dioxide absorbed by the plants through openings on the underside of their leaves and water absorbed chiefly through the roots. These soluble carbohydrates undergo in the plant a gentle dehydration and polymerization to yield such insoluble carbohydrates as starch, insulin, and cellulose.

A second important type of substance evolved through plant synthesis comprises the carbohydrate degradation products, which include vegetable oils, rubber, and resins. They are produced when carbohydrates are subjected to reducing and oxidizing agents.

The third group of plant chemicals comprises amino acids and proteins, which result from the interaction of the degradation products of the first two types with ammonia or amines likewise present within the cells of growing plants. The presence also of phosphoric acid and its derivatives makes possible the incorporation of this acid in any of the three types.

Now it has been known for a long time by biologists that these products of plant life are evolved in some of the simple plant forms as well as in the more complicated. For instance, algae, single-cell plant forms, produce all of the basic human nutrients. Under favorable conditions algae and yeasts multiply much faster than any of the higher plant forms.

So, during World War I, when Germany was hard pressed for enough food, her scientists sought whether algae and yeasts might not produce food more quickly and cheaply than the usual food plants. The important factor was the nutrient content of what was produced. Today most foods are measured scientifically by their nutrient content.

THE FERTILE ALGAE

The possibilities of this field are most easily understood by taking an example. Green algae of various sorts are found in almost every stagnant freshwater pond, but there are varieties which also grow in seawater. Everyone is familiar with this plant, whether he knows it by name or not.

It has been found that the variety of green algae called *Chlorella vulgaris* can be cultivated in shallow tanks or ponds with great ease, especially in climates where there is an abundance of sunlight. Cultured in a dilute solution of the proper chemicals and exposed to sunlight, or even high-actinic artificial light, while a stream of air containing 5 percent carbon dioxide is bubbled through the medium to supply raw material and agitation, the most surprising harvest is obtained. In four days the algae multiply by about 200 times. An acre of algae so cultivated will yield about four tons of dry substance, one-half of which is carbohydrate in composition.

Compare this yield of carbohydrates—two tons in four days—with that of corn. The average yield of an acre in corn is one to one-and-a-half tons of carbohydrates in 90 days. The algae in the same period produces 22 to 33 times the yield of corn. But only one corn crop a year can be produced from an acre, whereas the production of algae can be a very nearly continuous process. Indications are that something like 100 times the carbohydrate yield of an acre in corn can be obtained from an acre of *Chlorella vulgaris.*

The reasons for this are simple. The green algae reproduces rapidly by cell division. Virtually its entire body is photosynthetic. Almost its entire mass, therefore, is used in manufacturing carbohydrates from carbon dioxide and water in the presence of strong light. It does not reconvert the carbohydrates it manufactures into other products to form root and stems, essential to the corn plant, so that all of the carbohydrate produced is recoverable.

There are many varieties of algae which are able to synthesize protein as well as carbohydrates. Recent experiments conducted by Arthur D. Little, Inc., for the Carnegie Institution of Washington, have shown that dried algal cells grown under favorable conditions contain over 50 percent protein, or more than is found in the edible parts of any of the higher plants. Primarily seeking a means of producing food economically and quickly for the peoples of underdeveloped countries, the Carnegie Institution embarked upon this series of experiments in 1951. They followed previous laboratory work done at Stanford Research Institute in 1948-50 where basic research in the propagation of the algae, *Chlorella pyrenoidosa*, has shown much promise. The Carnegie Institution project was for the purpose of developing plans for large-scale culture of algae, which involved not only biological research but engineering problems.

In reporting this work the Carnegie Institution asserts that the first attempt in this country to translate the biological requirements of algal culture into engineering specifications for a large-scale culture plant has resulted in demonstration that such a plant is "technically feasible." As yet, the costs per pound of food produced does not compare favorably with conventional methods.

Nevertheless, evaluation of the experiment has stimulated the belief by those responsible for it that improvement in methods and selection of more productive strains of algae will result soon in lower costs. Even now, the report on this study points out, methods of culture which have been worked out might have survival value for a nation whose food supplies were cut off by war.

The Carnegie Institution's report also points out that, while the large-scale algal culture consumes energy in pumping, centrifuging and drying, a positive energy balance is achieved. In other words more energy is captured by the algae from the rays of the sun through photosynthesis than is required to grow and process them.

"Therefore," the report concludes, "an algal culture unit when combined with a steam generating plant in which the algae were burned would become an energy converter, capable of converting solar energy into high-temperature heat, which in turn could be converted into electric power. In this case the source of carbon dioxide would not be a problem, since the combined plant would be a closed system for carbon, except for some losses in operation." In short, man in time may learn how to do for himself what the coal forests did for him eons ago. And, if one wishes to follow the staid and sober Carnegie Institution scientists into what today seems a fantastic flight of imagination, one can foresee an algae food unit making food out of sunlight and organic waste on a space station hovering far above the earth's atmosphere. . . .

## THE VERSATILE YEASTS

Yeast, like algae, is a micro-organism which multiplies rapidly by cell division. It does not possess chlorophyll, however, and therefore is not capable of building carbohydrates. But it can use them as building blocks to make proteins and fats; and it can also break them down into carbohydrate decomposition products, such as the alcohols. The latter process is fermentation.

Yeast proved to be the most practical of the micro-organisms to which the Germans turned in World War I to help them get enough of the bulkier proteins and fats. One of the reasons for experimentation with micro-organisms in wartime was that it was believed they could be grown in factories without interfering with other crops; and they could utilize waste products.

The idea was sound. In World War I the Germans developed a strain of protein yeast which supplemented a deficient diet during the blockade. Although this was produced on a commercial scale and was nourishing, it did not taste good either to cattle or to people. During World War II, both the Germans and British did better.

In England, a strain of bakers' yeast, *Torulopsis utilis*, was said to have a meat-like taste and was rich in vitamin B complex. It contained about twice as much protein as fresh beef or dried milk per pound, and was approximately equal in protein content to soybeans. It had all of the essential amino acids in good balance, was rich in lysine, which generally is deficient in plant proteins.

This yeast multiplied ten times in weight in ten hours, and could be cultivated in a continuous manner by withdrawing yeast cells and adding nutrients. Sugar or molasses was fed the yeast cells to provide carbohydrates and nitrogen, and phosphorus was supplied as ammonium sulfate and superphosphate. The transformation of nitrogen into proteins was said to be almost 100 percent, while the transformation of the carbohydrates was more than 50 percent, most of the remainder being formed into other cell substances.

Interestingly, the pig as a converter of feeds into meats and fats is from 20 to 40 percent efficient, whereas yeasts have been found to be from 50 to 60 percent efficient in converting raw nutrient materials into food. But the yeasts will convert a good many materials upon which pigs would not thrive so well—sawdust, for example. *Torulopsis lipofera* and *Rhodotorula gracilis*, says Dr. Hale, are both capable of building up a content of 60 percent in fat under proper nitrogen nutriment and aeration.

\* \* \*

### THE WORLD OF CHEMURGY

Dr. Hale had coined a word to denote the processes of producing slow chemical changes, chiefly in organic compounds, through the operation of sunlight and the life processes of algae, molds, yeasts, bacteria and other living organisms. He calls this *chemurgy*, from the two Greek words: *chemeia*, chemistry and *ergon*, work.

Chemurgy uses for the production of both edible and non-edible products materials taken from air and water by the inexhaustible energy of the sun. Thus, this field has opened opportunities for man's creative genius which present unending vistas for activity and the development of new satisfactions. Manufacturing activity can carry the cost of food production, and food can be supplied to workers much more cheaply than at present, and perhaps without any cost, Dr. Hale declared.

The profitable market for all that the farmer can produce, whether it be from growing the higher plants upon the soil, or the simpler plant forms in tanks and ponds, will be industry, if Dr. Hale's view is valid. The farmer will be linked to industry by yearly contracts to produce what is required.

If there were such a close linking of virtually all farm production to industrial production through yearly production contracts, a struggle between agricultural and industrial interests to dominate the pattern of relationships would seem inevitable. We have seen such a struggle between the growers of cotton in the South and the cotton processors of the North. The conflict over slavery which led to the War Between the States was aggravated by this economic conflict. We have seen farmers organize politically to protect their interests in virtually every important type of crop. We have also seen the meat packer, millers, sugar refiners, dairy companies and other agricultural processing industries in conflict with growers, and exerting political pressures.

These are developments which are occurring now, but which may not have disturbing effects for many years, unless accelerated by hot atomic warfare. Then, nothing else would matter.

### SURPLUSES AND CONTROLS

Never before was it so important to the smooth functioning of society that a balance be maintained between production and consumption—and never before was this so difficult. Technical advancement in every field has made it possible to produce the basic requirements—food, clothing, and shelter—with a constantly smaller proportion of the population actively engaged. Conversely, never before did we enjoy so many things that we could get along without when we have to do so. One result is revealed when inflationary prices threaten purchasing power, or when technological unemployment becomes a menace. Under those circumstances a complex of deflationary forces can be set off that react one upon another to diminish employment, which diminishes purchasing power, which diminishes employment, up to the point where the government has to exercise powerful controls to restore production and purchasing power. . . .

Price supports and production controls seem to many an inescapable accompaniment of the growing capacity of the farmer to produce abundantly—a power that will increase as agricultural science progresses. These controls are likely to continue until profitable markets are discovered for all that American agriculture can produce under the most advanced methods, including chemurgical processes in food producing factories. And the volume of such production is not yet in sight.

Probably crop shortages are not as yet a thing of the past. There will be times when weather conditions, or wars, reduce the year's new food supply below normal. Storage for surpluses will provide for such emergencies, and also for the flexibility to maintain prices at reasonable levels.

And, as we make progress in the solution of these economic contradictions arising from more abundant output we shall better understand what constitutes a proper relation between organized society as represented by democratic government, and private business as represented by producers, processors, dealers and consumers—all with vital interests in producing and distributing food.

Increasingly government will be called upon to bring the leaders in conflicting segments of society face to face. It will confront them with scientific and economic facts. It will ask them to suggest solutions for problems. That administration which uses this technique most astutely, and interferes least by arbitrary executive order or legislation, will be most acceptable to the American people. Economic activities based upon agriculture offer great promise as the field in which this method of resolving economic problems in a democracy can be most profitably developed.

# Suggestions for Reading

The standard bibliography of agricultural history and development in the United States is Everett E. Edwards, *A Bibliography of The History of Agriculture in the United States*, published in 1930 as a government document. Though by no means up-to-date, this document should be consulted by anyone interested in the principal nineteenth and early twentieth century works on this subject. The Department of Agriculture publishes, on an irregular basis, bibliographies of the works added to the Department Library, now said to be, next to the Library of Congress, the largest Government library in existence. The Department also publishes a *List of Available Publications of the U.S. Department of Agriculture*. For a bibliography that includes both significant twentieth century secondary works and recent public documents, Senator George McGovern's excellent collection of readings, *Agricultural Thought in the Twentieth Century*, The American Heritage Series (N.Y.: Bobbs-Merrill Company, Inc., 1967), should be consulted. The literature cited in *Century of Service: The First Hundred Years of the United States Department of Agriculture* (Washington, D.C.: U.S. Department of Agriculture, 1963) is listed, pages 419–44, and constitutes a comprehensive bibliography of public documents, journal articles, monographs, and books. *Century of Service* was prepared by the Committee on Agricultural History, appointed by the Secretary of Agriculture in 1962," . . . to give direction and leadership to a study necessary to the preparation of a history commemorating the centennial of the United States Department of Agriculture . . ."

The standard pre-Civil War history of agriculture is presented in two companion volumes, Lewis C. Gray, *History of Agriculture in the Southern United States to 1860* (Washington, D.C.: The Carnegie Institute, 1933) and Percy W. Bidwell and John I. Falconer, *History of Agriculture in the Northern United States, 1620–1860* (Washington, D.C.: The Carnegie Institute, 1925). Volume I of the two-volume work edited by Thomas C. Cochran and Thomas B. Brewer contains a number of excellent articles, several of which suggest interrelationships between agriculture and the larger economy. Volume I is titled *Views of American Economic Growth: The Agricultural Era* (N.Y.: McGraw-Hill, Inc., 1966). Volume II carries the subtitle *The Industrial Era*; it, too, is worth consulting for articles related to agricultural development. The importance of agriculture in the early economic development of the nation is stressed in Paul Gates, *The Farmer's Age, 1815-1860* (N.Y.: Holt, Rinehart, and Winston, Inc., 1960).

Land settlement is one of the most significant aspects of agricultural development in the United States. The leading references on this subject are cited in the introductory section of Chapter II of this work. In addition, a useful edited work is V. R. Carstenson, *The Public Lands; Studies in the History of the Public Domain* (Madison: University of Wisconsin Press, 1963). A work more oriented toward economics and sociology than history is Howard Ottoson, ed., *Land Use Policy and Problems* (Lincoln: University of Nebraska Press, 1963). Finally, the complexities of disposing of western lands, both arid and semi-arid, is exhaustively treated in E. Louise Peffer, *The Closing of the Public Domain: Disposal and Reservation Policies, 1900-1950* (Stanford: Stanford University Press, 1951).

In general, treatments of agriculture in the pre-Civil War period tend to be characterized by a humanistic approach — the influence of Jefferson was immediate and obvious. Even though he pursues a negative thesis in this respect, A. Whitney Griswold makes clear the strength of the Jeffersonian agrarian myth in *Farming and Democracy* (N.Y.: Harcourt Brace and Co., 1948). All works on American political thought of the period from 1790 to 1840 must include reference to the "agrarian utopia" of Thomas Jefferson. An excellent essay on this subject is Benjamin F. Wright, "The Philosophy of Jeffersonian Democracy," *American Political Science Review*, vol. 22 (Nov. 1928), pp. 870-892. Indispensable material is also found in Vernon L. Parrington, *Main Currents in American Thought*, vol. I (N.Y.: Harcourt, Brace, 1958).

One of the most comprehensive treatments of agricultural history is Murray R. Benedict, *Farm Policies of the United States, 1790-1950: A Study of Their Origins and Development* (N.Y.: Twentieth Century Fund, 1953). Less detailed, but valuable for their treatment of government policy toward agriculture, particularly recent policy, are Dale E. Hathaway, *Government and Agriculture: Public Policy in a Democratic Society* (N.Y.: Macmillan, 1963) and Harold Halcrow, *Agricultural Policy of the United States* (Englewood Cliffs: Prentice-Hall, 1953).

A valuable history of agriculture in the second half of the nineteenth century is Fred A. Shannon, *The Farmer's Last Frontier, 1860-1897* (N.Y.: Farrar & Rinehart, Inc. 1945), a book that skillfully combines the carryover of the agrarian myth with the rising commercialism of the farming enterprise. Another worthwhile account focusing on the problems of land settlement in the trans-Missouri West is Gilbert Fite, *The Farmer's Frontier, 1865-1900* (N.Y.: Holt, Rinehart and Winston, 1966).

The agrarian protest movements that characterized the 1870's through the 1890's have been the subjects of many important books, among which may be noted Jonathan Periam, *The Groundswell: A History of the Origin, Aims, and Progress of the Farmer's Movement* (Cincinnati: E. Hanneford, 1874); Solon J. Buck, *The Agrarian Crusade* (New Haven: Yale University Press, 1921); John D. Hicks, *The Populist Revolt* (Minneapolis: University of Minnesota Press, 1931); and, with a broadened historical perspective, Carl C. Taylor, *The Farmers' Movement: 1620-1920* (N.Y.: The American Book Co., 1953).

Moving into the twentieth century, agriculture participated in the "knowledge explosion" with one result — the vastly increased and more specialized outpouring of books and other written materials on various aspects of agriculture. The literature tends to become technically oriented, with a large input of agricultural economics. The contributions in this field of John D. Black of Harvard should be noted, such as the collection by James P. Cavin, ed., *Economics for Agriculture: The Selected Writings of John D. Black* (Cambridge: Harvard University Press, 1959). Other worthwhile studies are D. Paarlberg, *American Farm Policy: A Case Study of Centralized Decision-Making* (N.Y.: Wiley, 1961); Edwin G. Nourse, Joseph S. Davis, and John D. Black, *Three Years of the Agricultural Adjustment Administration* (Washington, D.C.: The Brookings Institution, 1937); Rexford G. Tugwell, "Problem of Agriculture," *Political Science Quarterly*, vol. 39 (Dec. 1924), pp. 549–91; and Rainer Schickele, *Agricultural Policy* (N.Y.: McGraw-Hill, 1954).

A number of works, usually less technical in nature than those indicated in the paragraph above, give voice to the thread of discontent and uncertainty that runs through rural life in the twentieth century and is expressed by organizations aimed at remedying the grievances or disparities perceived by farmers. For this *genre*, the reader should consult the following: Theodore Saloutos and John D. Hicks, *Agriculture Discontent in the Middle West, 1900-1932* (Madison: University of Wisconsin Press, 1951); James Shideler, *Farm Crisis, 1919-1923* (Berkeley: University of California Press, 1957); Loren Soth, *Farm Trouble* (Princeton: Princeton University Press, 1957); Donald R. McCoy, *Angry Voices: Left-of-Center Politics in the New Deal Era* (Lawrence: University of Kansas Press, 1958); Wesley McCune, *Who's Behind Our Farm Policy?* (N.Y.: Praeger, 1956); and Don F. Hadwiger and Ross B. Talbot, *Pressures and Protests: The Kennedy Farm Program and the Wheat Referendum of 1963* (San Francisco: Chandler Publishing Company, 1965).

Although it is sometimes hard to identify the source of pressure activating some of the farm organizations, the legitimacy of concern is well documented in the Report of the President's National Advisory Commission on Rural Poverty, *The People Left Behind* (Washington, D.C.: U.S. Government Printing Office, 1967). The reader interested in pursuing this topic should also see C. E. Bishop, ed., *Farm Labor in the United States* (N.Y.: Columbia University Press, 1967) and *Hungry Children* (Atlanta: Southern Regional Council, 1967). A good analysis of farm income distribution is presented in Edward C. Higbee, *Farms and Farmers in an Urban Age* (N.Y.: Twentieth Century Fund, 1963) and an excellent study of sociological factors can be found in Arthur J. Vidich and Joseph Bensman, *Small Town in Mass Society: Class, Power, and Religion in a Rural Community* (Princeton: Princeton University Press, 1958). These factors are related to the ideology of agrarianism in Wayne C. Rohrer and Louis H. Douglas, *The Agrarian Tradition in America: Dualism and Change* (N.Y.: Bobbs-Merrill Company, Inc., 1969).

In Grant McConnell, *The Decline of Agrarian Democracy* (Berkeley: University of California Press, 1953), the author shows how the myth of agrarian utopia was displaced by the economic power and technology of modern farming. Charles Hardin pursues a specialized aspect of this subject in *The Politics of Agriculture: Soil Conservation and the Struggle for Power in Rural America* (Glencoe: The Free Press, 1952).

1 2 3 4 5 6 7 8 9 10